THANK YOU,
HERMANN GOERING
The Life of a Sports Writer

About the Author

Born in 1935 on the Isle of Wight, Brian Scovell was one of the *Daily Mail*'s longest-serving and best-loved sportswriters. His books about Jim Laker and the England managers were nominated for the 2007 British Sports Awards and he has also written books about Dickie Bird, Brian Lara, Ken Barrington, Bobby Robson, and Trevor Brooking. His last book was about Bill Nicholson. *Thank You, Hermann Goering*, his autobiography, is his twenty-fifth book.

THANK YOU,
HERMANN GOERING
The Life of a Sports Writer

BRIAN SCOVELL

AMBERLEY

To Audrey (she never liked the name!) Esther Scovell (née O'Sullivan),

known to her intimates as 'Dollies',

for her eternal love, inspiration, laughter, and beauty.

Front cover: On the Nursery at Lord's, 2009; with Diana at Gloucestershire CCC, 1986; listening to Bobby Robson at Wembley, 1989. *Back cover*: With Michael Slater in 2005; Audrey Scovell, modelling at the age of nineteen.

This edition first published 2012

Amberley Publishing
The Hill, Stroud
Gloucestershire, GL5 4EP

www.amberley-books.com

British Library Cataloguing in Publication Data.
A catalogue record for this book is available from the British Library.

ISBN 978-1-4456-0895-2

Typesetting and Origination by Amberley Publishing.
Printed in the UK.

Contents

CHAPTER ONE

Love Is All You Need

This is a love story about a young man of humble background from the Isle of Wight. Until he was nearly eight he had no interest in sport and rarely read serious books, but after an accident late in 1943, indirectly caused by a German bombing raid, he spent two years in hospitals and was left with a stiff right knee. Lying in bed, he read the *Daily Herald* each day and followed the writings of the chief sports writer Tom Phillips. He also listened to the football and cricket commentaries on the ward's only portable radio. Soon he became a passionate lover of both sports, and vowed he would become the Tom Phillips of one of the national newspapers in Fleet Street.

Fifteen years later, he reached his goal. He was appointed as a cricket and football reporter for the *Daily Sketch*, which was owned by Associated Newspapers, also owners of the *Daily Mail*, which he joined later, in 1971. He stayed on for forty blissfully happy years before retiring to write books. But his real love was not for cricket or football, or writing – it was for a stunningly beautiful girl named Audrey (she hated that name!) Esther O'Sullivan, of Addiscombe in Croydon.

I was living in the YMCA nearby, and in my 1963 diary I had the telephone numbers of fifty-seven girls. No, I wasn't a Casanova or a Warren Beatty. But I'd met plenty of women in the Bromley Young Conservatives, and working in Fleet Street and travelling around the country on reporting jobs it was easy to meet young ladies. If they knew you were working for a national newspaper, with your photograph on the sports pages most days, a surprisingly large number of them were keen to go out with you.

Before Audrey came along, there was only one girl I was keen on, and she was engaged to be married to a banker, who was working in Nigeria and was soon to return to London for the impending marriage. She worked at the BOAC's building in Victoria and she was very attractive and very personable. Several nights a week, I picked her up after her second job – she was raising cash for the wedding – and took her home. She worked in an upmarket coffee house. There was little time for anything other than an animated chat and a quick kiss. A fortnight before the wedding, she told me she was having second thoughts. Not wanting to gazump the prospective groom, I had to make my excuses. Afterwards she sent me a silver pen and a wonderful farewell letter. The wedding duly went ahead and as far as I know it was a success.

On 16 March 1963, still without a regular girlfriend, I decided to go to a dance at

Addiscombe CC, although I was not a dancer of any ability. With a leg that didn't bend, I could only gyrate to the twist-and-shout music. I was unshaven and wore a thick blue sweater knitted by another girlfriend. It was normally used to clean the car. Just before the last dance was about to be announced, I noticed two girls on the other side of the room, one tall and beautiful, another smaller and almost as gorgeous. I went straight up to the taller one. Before I could ask for a dance, she smiled and said, 'Do you have a car? It's been sheeting it down and we need a lift!'

She wasn't being bossy. She was just practical. Not many young men owned cars in those days and the twins – yes, they were, although they weren't identical – were unwilling to walk the mile home without an umbrella. I was relieved; we only had one 'dance' as I stumbled around the dance floor. 'Let's go,' I said.

So off we went. Audrey, the tall one, asked me what I did and was suitably impressed. I asked her what she did. 'I work at ITN as a production assistant,' she said.

'That's a coincidence,' I said, 'our office is just round the corner in Fleet Street.' The ITN building, which employed people like Andrew Gardner, Peter Snow, Alastair Burnet, and Reginald Bosanquet, the son of Bernard Bosanquet (the genius who pioneered cricket's mystery ball, the googly) was situated a few yards up Southampton Row, opposite Bush House, the home of the BBC World Service. 'Do you know Reggie?' I said.

'Yes,' she said, 'I usually powder his nose before he goes on. Half the time he's plastered. Can't face the camera with a red nose!' Bosanquet's father was fifty-five when Reggie was born in 1932, which might have explained a few things. The TV presenter was married three times and died at the age of fifty-one. 'Bosey' senior also died young, at the age of fifty-nine. She also told me she had powdered the faces of, among others, Harold Wilson, Sir Alec Douglas-Home, George Brown, Earl Attlee, and James Mason. I asked her which one she liked most. 'I don't know about that,' she said. 'George Brown asked me, out but he was a bit tipsy!'

We were getting along well, and when the car arrived outside the twins' end-of-row house she said 'Do you fancy coming in for a coffee?'

Amazing, I thought. She ushered me into the front room. Everyone had gone to bed. She told me she came from a family of nine and nearly all of them, including the twins, were born in Patna in India. One, Maurice, died at a very young age, and the eldest was a boy named Pat who wrote sexy Henry Miller-style novels about his experiences in the Indian Navy and the Royal Navy and had eventually become a naval architect. Apparently, he was a ladies' man (he went on to have three marriages) and lived in California. There were seven daughters; two lived in California, one in Vancouver. The twins, now coming up to twenty-one, were the youngest. Wow! What a family! Their Irish-born father, Eric William O'Sullivan (1897-1978) was a manager on the Indian Railway and was famous for ejecting Mahatma Gandhi off a train for not having a ticket. Naturally, the post-colonial authorities didn't support his action and in 1948, after the Partition, the family went home by ship, a six-week trip via the Suez Canal. Their mother, Lucy Regina Roberts (1908-97), was Welsh; she had married at the age of eighteen. The family lived in a large, sprawling house full of servants and Lucy had hardly cooked before she arrived back to England. It was a culture shock for the whole family. They had to do all the work themselves and with Willie (we called him Willie, not Eric) announcing his retirement (to concentrate on his inventions, which never worked) the older girls had to share the load, financially and in every other way. Lucy senior, a wonderful lady who was always laughing, had to go out to work as a secretary.

Audrey was named after St Audrey, who was born in 699 and is the patron saint of throat complaints. St Audrey died from a tumour of the neck. My Audrey had thyroid problems as well; she needed surgery and for the rest of her life she had to take tablets. This connection was the first of many I discovered in our life together. Lucy, who had similar thyroid problems, worked in films, including the James Bond series, and both of the twins were extremely bright and vivacious.

Audrey brought in the coffee and said, 'Well, I'm off to bed now. Got to get to the office early next morning. Nice to see you!' I was left to chat with Lucy, not a hard task. By now it was 1.30 a.m. and she wanted to go to bed as well.

The next morning, I wrote in my diary, 'Met a 20 year old, beautiful girl 5-8 and 36-25-37, giggly and intelligent.' I then rang her and suggested we might go to the Academy Cinema in Oxford Street to see Antonioni's film *L'Eclisse.*

'That should be fine,' she said, 'but Lucy would like to come as well.' That wasn't quite what I had planned. At lunch I met one of my best friends, Gerry Williams, a football reporter on the *Mail* who later became the tennis correspondent. Latterly in his distinguished career he worked as Sky's tennis expert. He was a brilliant interviewer and a thoroughly good guy. At first, Gerry was keen to go on a double date, but he backed out and I had to take both of the girls for dinner and to the film myself. I wasn't in the same class as the senior members of the *Sketch* staff, who collected weighty expenses each week. It turned out to be a costly evening, but it was worth it.

Two nights later, I finished covering a game at Highbury after having rung Audrey earlier to say I was going to pick her up at ITN and take her home. That was a good ruse. Most Tuesdays and Wednesdays, I went to football matches and could pass by and act as her personal driver – the ITN cars were manned by tiresome young men who kept pestering Audrey for her number. It became a regular event, with me waiting outside until she came out. It could be 11 p.m. or even midnight, and love was blossoming. Suddenly, I realised that I was a very lucky young man. Andrew Gardner called her 'the Sophia Loren of the studio' and he was right. She was a real beauty and she was invited to have pictures taken of her at the Lucie Clayton Model Agency. But she only did that as a joke. 'I'd never be a model,' she said. 'It's too boring.' The O'Sullivans were Catholics and after several months of intense courting I asked Audrey if she fancied going on a holiday to Majorca. To my surprise, she agreed, and her parents showed no opposition to this impertinent idea. We had an idyllic fortnight in old Palma, not along the crazed south-west coast.

She'd left her Catholic school in Sanderstead with only three O-levels, but her intelligence and knowledge of so many things, including opera, classical music, theatre, and films, were astonishing. She would walk into any room and light it up with her smile and conversation, whatever the company. She always showed interest in the other person. I took her to Lord's and many other famous grounds. She didn't really like cricket but she was very willing to share my interests. She was subtly helping to change me, to make me a better and less selfish individual. Many years later, when she staged a surprise sixtieth birthday party for me at the Long Room at the Oval, I said in my speech, 'She taught me how to love.' Not really the physical side of it, but the world around us, other people, even trees. Until then I was too busy to look at trees.

We went everywhere together. I was the only sports writer who took his wife. We went on a two-week trip to Belgium and Germany to cover the Little World Football Tournament in my battered red Fiat 500, but most of the time we went sightseeing in Amsterdam, Brussels, Cologne, Baden-Baden, and San Sebastian. It was so exciting that we didn't think about marriage. We were too busy. Eighteen months into the affair, Audrey suddenly said she was thinking about working in New York.

'What on earth for?' I said.

'Half of our family lived or worked in the USA and I'd like to do the same,' she said.

I think she was giving me a nudge, so I wrote a 1,200 word proposal of marriage on four pages, headed 'The Hotel Duisburger Hof, Duisburg', which I nicked from our bedroom, and it arrived on her twenty-third birthday. She laughed, but never said 'yes'. We took it as granted. The next day, I took a press team to Beddington CC and we beat a Millwall FC team by two runs. I had to reprimand Harry Cripps, the famed left back, for wearing black plimsolls. So he went out and painted them with white marking used for the creases. From there, we went to a party in the evening to celebrate.

'Where's the ring?' she said the next day. I hadn't given any thought to it, and on the Saturday we went to Richard Ogden's shop in the Burlington Arcade in Piccadilly and paid £55 for a sparkling engagement ring of zircon, a green-blue stone, with a diamond on either side set in platinum and gold. She loved it. 'It suits my large fingers,' she said.

I spent the rest of the day playing in the third team at Beddington CC while she washed her hair at home and tidied up. Years later, I found a letter from her to her brother Pat, which said, 'Thank goodness we don't have to get a mortgage. Brian's house is completely furnished with all fittings and furnishings from Heal's. It is only a year old and the cat, as yet unnamed, has been installed so it is all set up. I only have to move my clothes from across the park.'

She always had style. For a while, she lived with two of her sisters in a luxurious flat in Huntingdon House on Cromwell Road. She thought it would be a good idea if we were married at Brompton Oratory, to qualify her as a local resident. We went to see Father Williams at the Church of the Immaculate Heart of Mary, which is the right title for the second-largest Roman Catholic Church in London, after Westminster Cathedral. He accepted us. He told me that he had been a priest in Niton, a mile or two away from where I grew up. Designed by Herbert Gribble and consecrated in 1884, the Oratory stands 200 feet tall and has more metal frames for candles than in any other church I have visited. Since 25 December 2000 – the day she died – I've lit hundreds.

It was where Alfred Hitchcock wed Alma Reville in 1926 and where Edward Elgar, the 'Pomp and Circumstance' man, married Alice Roberts in 1889. We celebrated the news by taking Graham 'Garth' McKenzie, the barrel-chested Australian Test fast bowler, and his girlfriend from *Vogue* to Talk of the Town to see Shirley Bassey. I had got to know Graham when I interviewed him after he struck a six over the Tavern in the Lord's Test – the ball had landed on the foot of an old lady walking the pavement outside. I went outside to speak to her for a feature about the incident and she was delighted to be presented with the ball as a souvenir. Garth was one of the nicest, calmest Test players I'd encountered, and the four of us had a great night.

Audrey found a marvellous place for the reception, the fifteenth-century Crosby Hall on the north side of Battersea Bridge, where Richard III, Henry VIII, Sir Thomas More, Queen Elizabeth I, Sir Francis Drake, Sir Walter Raleigh, and William Shakespeare had dined at various times. It was first built in 1466 off Bishopsgate in the City of London. After a fire in 1675, it was rebuilt. It was scheduled to be demolished in 1908, but heritage devotees intervened. The Great Hall was dismantled and rebuilt, brick by brick, at Cheyne Walk, Chelsea, the site of Sir Thomas More's country garden. It was leased to the British Federation of University Women, and early in the 1970s a tycoon named Christopher Moran, learning that the GLC had been disbanded by Margaret Thatcher, bought the freehold and spent over £25 million renovating it. Audrey inquired about Crosby Hall in the midsummer of 1965 and asked how much it would cost to hire and was told £10! Both sets of families were prepared to settle on a cheap wedding, because none of them were tycoons, but now we were having a grand marriage of almost royal proportions. I celebrated by ordering 100 bottles of champagne; it worked out at £1.50 a bottle.

I have to say that the bride wasn't perfect. She had a habit of being a little late, and as the clock passed 2.15 p.m. the 130 of us assembled in the cavernous Brompton Oratory were becoming anxious. My groomsman, Bryon Butler, the longtime football correspondent for the BBC, said, 'Don't worry. The most beautiful of brides are always a bit late.'

It was 2.22 p.m. when the procession entered. It was a long walk. I turned to see her and she was in the process of lifting her veil to tickle an itch under the eye. A tear fell down my cheek. 'My God,' I thought, 'I never realised how beautiful you are!' Her long, white, simple dress was ravishing. What a star! That was the only time I have shed a tear at the Oratory.

At her memorial service there on 22 January 2001, my children Gavin and Louise and I vowed that we would celebrate an extraordinary and almost saintly life without tears. Gavin stuck a notice on the bathroom mirror that said, 'Daddy, Be strong today, Mummy would want you being happy and jolly.' The simplest words are the best and some years later I found a card that Audrey – who became a self-taught artist after our children were born – had designed. On the front it said, 'I Love You.' Inside, 'Forever and Forever.' I had forgotten about it, but in the opening line of my address, I wrote, 'It started with a glance across a dance floor on 16 March 1963, which launched a love affair that will never end.' We both thought that. It was a beautiful sunny day for the memorial service, just as it was at our wedding on 1 October 1965.

There was a funny incident at the wedding. Father McKenzie, the O'Sullivan family priest in Addiscombe who conducted the service, was halfway through the ritual of asking if there was any impediment that might prevent the wedding taking place when a voice shouted from the rear, 'Yes, I object!' We all spun round and an old man with a white beard, looking like a vagrant, was on his feet waving his arms. Everyone laughed and the service continued. We had booked a room at the London Hilton Hotel in Park Lane for our first night and requested a front room facing Hyde Park and as close to the top of the building as possible. When we arrived, we discovered our room was on the fifth floor overlooking a building site. We decided not to make a fuss, but later on I wrote to Nicky Hilton, the son of Conrad Hilton (1887-1979), the founder of the hotel chain. His full name was Conrad Nicholson Hilton Jr, but he was known as 'Nicky'. His granddaughter is Paris Hilton, famous for not much except her name. He married Elizabeth Taylor in 1950 and the marriage lasted only a few months before he married Trish McClintock, an oil heiress. Several weeks later, Nicky replied with a sympathetic letter but offered no redress. He was divorcing Trish in 1965 and he probably had other things of his mind. I've since been to many dinners at the Hilton; I don't hold it against the family.

On 19 July 2008, I was invited to the sixtieth birthday party of our friend John Shepherd, the eminent gynaecologist and international yachtsman, at the Royal Corinthian Yacht Club in Cowes. Sitting next to me was Michael Shepherd, John's younger brother, who is now manager of the London Hilton. I told him about our experience on the fifth floor and he said, 'I'll put that right immediately. Let me know when you are available.' Two months later, my friend Gill and I stayed on the twenty-third floor, facing Hyde Park, and we had a wonderful night. Forty-three years later, fair play and sportsmanship had returned to Park Lane. On the same day, I read that Pope Benedict XVI had apologised to the Aboriginals on behalf of the Catholic Church in Sydney and called on Australians to forsake greed and go back to the right values. It made me think. I courted Audrey for twenty months before we were married. We didn't live together before marriage and we didn't jump into bed on the first date or even the 100th. Anticipation is the most exciting part; eventually you fall in love and hope that it will last forever. I am not a married counsellor, but I think courting should be reinvented. It is almost extinct.

Our honeymoon was exceptional. No jaunt to Majorca or Benidorm for us. No, we booked an air cruise organised by the Lord brothers. Was that a connection? Perhaps not. But they may have been descendants of Thomas Lord, who founded the first and second Lord's cricket grounds. We travelled with forty-five other passengers in a propeller-driven Triumph Herald aircraft, firstly to Athens, and then to Rhodes and finally to Crete, then largely unnoticed by the big hotel chains. On our first day in Athens, Audrey wanted to see the Acropolis and I had to tell her I had a press ticket for the Greece *v.* Russia match. So she went alone.

I was sitting in a high chair at the rear of the press box when a Greek reporter, upset by one of the referee's decisions, barged into me and I fell backwards to the ground. Fortunately I wasn't injured, otherwise the honeymoon would have been ruined. We were so delighted with our three-stop expedition to Greece, the home of the Corinthian spirit, that I booked another one the following year. This time we started in Lanzarote, stayed in Agadir (which had just been half-demolished by an earthquake), found ourselves bounced across the Atlas Mountains to Marrakech for a few days, passed through Tangiers, then ended up in Tunis. I avoided watching football, but I did play some fifty-a-side games on the vast beaches of Tangiers.

Audrey and I usually knew what the other was about to say. Sometimes she waited outside Ravensbourne Station to pick me up when I had some luggage or parcels and we'd been discussing earlier in the day whether to go to the cinema or wherever. I was thinking about dropping the idea on the way home and when I got into her relic of a car, a Vanden Plas that had 'Historic Car' stamped on its road fund licence, she would say, 'It's been a tiring day, why don't we stay in tonight?'

The distinctive blue car kept breaking down, but she insisted it should be repaired. 'It's ideal for carrying my art work,' she would say. She had a freelance mechanic nearby who loved tinkering with it, and he always got it going again.

Audrey died on Christmas Day 2000 – you can never forget a date like that. I was sleeping at the Derby Hotel opposite Cromwell Hospital, where she was lying in a private room, no. 147 on the first floor. We could look at it from the top floor of the hotel. We had hired a suite and Gavin, Louise, and I did four-hour vigils at her bedside. When it was my turn on Christmas Eve, I crossed the empty road and I saw a car approaching from the direction of Brompton Oratory, which is only a few hundred yards away. It was a Vanden Plas, blue but with a different registration number. How many historic Vanden Plas cars are driving along the Cromwell Road on Christmas Eve? I was shaken, but smiled. Her car was coming to say goodbye, I thought. The car signalled to turn right into the car park at the hospital. When I reached Audrey's room, I told Gavin about this almost mystical happening. I said, 'That's great, Mummy's just arranged that.' He agreed. We were both more contented, ready for the end, which we knew would come within hours.

This was the first of many coincidences that followed her death, and they still happen. I would be concerned about something, perhaps thinking about her, and a car with a registration number containing 'AES', her initials, would come towards me. Recently, it happened when I was about to go into St Joseph's Church, where her funeral took place, to light a candle. A fire engine sailed past. Its registration contained the same initials. When this happens, which is often outside that particular church, I feel so elated – as though she has cuddled and kissed me. 'AS' was appearing everywhere. I discovered the other fire engine stationed at the main Bromley Fire Station had a registration with 'AES' in it. Both Gavin and Louise have 'AS' in their postcodes and there is one on the metal tab on my set of keys, offering £10 as a reward if they are found. I didn't put it on; it was just there. One day I had to collect a massive pile of Sunday newspapers because I was leaving home before the usual delivery. The postlady's car registration contained the letters 'AES'. In the weeks when I was reassembling my life, I had a number of recurring abscesses in my mouth and had several teeth taken out. Not wanting to wear a denture, I decided to have some expensive implants and spent many hours in dentists' rooms. Right at the start, I was flat out on the dentist's chair, staring up into the bright lights of a rectangular Daray light case, and suddenly saw 'AS' in the bottom right corner. That was all; just that. I realised that her spirit was still with me. I joked that I had cancelled my email and that instead I had my personal 'amail'. Most people doubt that there are 'messages' from beyond, but I have the evidence.

After I wrote a book about the Cobbold brothers, John and Patrick, the nephews of Harold Macmillan who were the chairmen of Ipswich Town FC, my good friend Gill and I were in a posh bookshop in Aldeburgh and I was sitting at a desk signing copies. It is one of the best independent bookshops in the country and it had won an award in the previous year. It is a distinctive shop. That day the owner had a large vase of oriental lilies on show. Oriental lilies were Audrey's favourite flowers. The shop was busy and a florid-faced man shouldered his way through the browsers and came up to me. He said in an angry voice, 'You've written a load of lies about my family!' He mentioned one of his relatives, Ivan Cobbold, who tried to take over the football club and died soon after.

'If you are talking about Ivan,' I said, 'I knew him and he used to ring me. What I have written about him is true and anyway, you can't libel someone who is dead.'

The man kept wittering away, asking for a retraction. I tried to be polite, but the atmosphere suddenly changed when a smartly dressed man at the rear shouted out, 'Mr Scovell, I am a lawyer and I am willing to act for you on this case!' Everyone burst out laughing, and the irate man walked out.

As we left, Gill said, 'I've just bought a book for you, it's about Audrey Hepburn. With the lilies appearing as well we'll probably run into an 'AUD' now!' We drove the short distance to our hotel and an estate car was parked in front of the rear door and a light above was reflecting on its registration. Yes, it was an 'AUD'. We took pictures of it to prove it. Do people have similar experiences? I am sure they do. Animals can receive 'messages' and react to them. For example, before the tsunami in 2004, many of the animals in Indonesia, India, and Sri Lanka retreated to higher ground because they sensed danger. If animals respond that way, why not humans?

Since 1958, when I worked at Norwich for a brief time, I have had a great affinity with Norwich Cathedral. In 2008, I visited it to say some prayers of thanks after hearing some good news about my children. As I came out, I thought about Audrey. She would be delighted. As I walked across a nearby lawn, I saw the ultimate 'AUD' car registration – AU02 AEO. At a distance, it looked like 'AUD', but never mind. Two mentions of her on one number plate was marvellous.

Some months later, I celebrated my fiftieth year of driving without losing my no claims. But backing out into my road on Palm Sunday, the rear of my car clipped the offside wing of a parked MG across the road. 'Oh St Christopher, there goes my no claim!' I thought.

As I stepped out to speak to the lady who was approaching the MG to lambast my carelessness, an 'AES' cruised by, reassuring me, rather hopefully, that it wouldn't be a disaster. I apologised to the woman and she said, 'Don't worry, that's why insurances were invented!' We exchanged details in a relaxed manner. I drove off and I went to light some candles at St Joseph's Church. As I crossed the road, an 'AUD' drove up and it was as though she was giving me the thumbs up.

I think my story is an inspiring one, not just for me, but for others who love the departed dearly and still remain in contact and believe they will meet again in another place. A few weeks after Audrey died, I was half awake in bed when my mobile phone rang. It was lying on a small table. I reached out in the dark and thought I had pressed the 'on' button. I wasn't sure about that, but I held the phone to my ear and I heard her distinctive laughter. 'Where are you?' I said.

She was giggling. 'I'm in a wonderful place,' she said. 'You ought to come. Tell Mary [her best friend, another artist]. Tell Deanne...' The line faded and I couldn't hear her anymore. Even now, I am not sure whether she spoke to me or whether I dreamt it. But I thought it was a very heartening sign.

I have written about Audrey because she has been an integral part of my life since 1963 and I wouldn't have been a successful journalist without her love and support. When a top businessman, or a man from any field, is about to retire, he takes the plaudits and in his speech he might just squeeze out a cliché, maybe that most popular one – 'Behind all successful men there is a great lady not far behind.' I think too many men undervalue their wives. If they were more appreciative of them, it would raise the self-esteem of women generally. In America, the feminist movement has improved the status of women, mainly by confrontation. I believe the better way is by exchanging mutual love. As I completed this chapter, I saw David Cameron invite his wife Samantha to come on to the podium at the Conservative conference in Birmingham; he was one of the first politicians to thank his wife in public. Gordon Brown soon followed, and his wife Sarah said a few words about him at the Labour conference. It is love that brings children into the world and it is love that maintains proper families. Cameron is right. Broken families are the cause of most of our problems.

Politicians often show their wives off for photo shoots – the Blairs, the Obamas, the Browns, the Camerons, the Sarkozys, others – and they hope to convince the public they are true family men and that we ought to vote for them. It doesn't need big hugs and lingering kisses. A look can be enough.

CHAPTER TWO

Accident Starts Play

In the high summer of 1943, I had an accident that changed the course of my life. I was seven, had hardly read a serious book, had no interest in sport, and enjoyed taking the dog for walks. My mother wanted me to work in a bank; she once said to me, 'Bank clerks earn a good salary and they are not likely to be sacked.' Our family was always short of money and rarely paid up when the tally men called (tally men collected cash from families contracted to pay each month for goods and rent because they couldn't pay the whole lot at once). Sometimes we had to hide behind the door to avoid facing them with another excuse. When my father's jobs ended, which was often, he would be back on the dole. He rarely had a full-time job.

I hadn't thought of a job at that age, but banking seemed tedious. More exciting was the discovery of a large, round mirror, two feet in diameter, that my brother and some of his friends had brought home one day. When it was sunny we took it to the top of our sloping garden, which overlooked the English Channel, and tried to reflect the rays of the sun onto the sea below. Often it worked. My mother once said, 'One day these Germans planes will see your mirror sending messages and will drop bombs on us. You wait and see!' From our home on the Isle of Wight, we had a grandstand view of the ships out in the Channel and of the dog fights between the RAF's Spitfires and Hurricanes and the Luftwaffe's Messerschmitts Bf 109s, Heinkels He 111, Junkers Ju 87s and 88s, and Dornier Do 217s. A number of these aircraft would burst into flames and disappear below the waves. Two Spitfires were shot down within walking distance of our house at Ocean View Road, in Ventnor, and three German aircraft, two Ju 88s and one Do 217, were downed on the Bonchurch side of Ventnor. Once, a pilot manning a Ju 88, badly holed and flying very slowly, fired off his final shots and a man standing in a telephone box opposite my house was killed by a bullet through the temple. We only found out about it the next day when a neighbour told us. When the sirens sounded – and they were sounded 1,603 times throughout the Second World War on the normally peaceful Isle of Wight – the Air Raid Precaution officers ordered householders to go to their air raid shelters, or, if they didn't have one, to retreat to a cellar. As we didn't have either, we crouched under the stairs. My father was an occasional APR watcher, climbing up to high roofs armed with a pair of binoculars to spot German planes. That time, he had taken a day off.

Our part of Ventnor was under the path of the incoming Luftwaffe aircraft. Their target was the RAF radar station, which was built in 1939 at the highest point of the Isle of Wight, the 800-foot-high St Boniface Down. Charles Dickens and some of his friends loved staying at Bonchurch and climbed it every day before breakfast in the mid-1850s. Perhaps that was the reason why he died at the age of fifty-eight. My father spent more than a year working on building the four 240-foot wooden towers carrying the radio receivers and the four 350-foot steel masts used as transmitter aerials, as well as the buildings that accommodated the staff, including Army officers, low-ranking men and a large number of the Women's Auxiliary Air Force. He was sworn to secrecy, and except for saying 'they're building these pylons up there' he didn't tell us the real reason until after D-Day when the German Army was in terminal retreat. Originally there were sixteen radar stations, hastily built in 1939 around the south coast, and they were able to warn against any potential air attacks; they saved Britain from occupation.

Winston Churchill and his experts thought that Goering made a calamitous mistake at the height of the Battle of Britain in August 1940 when he decided to curtail the bombing of the radar stations and concentrate on bombing the RAF airfields and, later, London. German spies told him that radar hadn't been perfected, which wasn't strictly true. It gave the British pilots just enough time to get into the air and take on the Luftwaffe. Heavily outnumbered, the 'Few' suffered crippling losses. In the words once used by the Duke of Wellington, 'It was a damned close run thing.' Each day newspapers reported the facts of planes being shot down, but said that the British losses were far fewer than the German losses in order to keep up morale. In one of his orders, Adolf Hitler mentioned Sandown Bay on the Isle of Wight as a place for invasion before moving to the mainland. Fortunately, his Operation Sea Lion was aborted. Otherwise, my family could have been killed or taken off to a concentration camp in Eastern Europe.

Adrian Searle's highly informative work *Isle of Wight at War 1939-1945* reports that 1,748 bombs were dropped on the Garden Isle, including six V-1 rockets. I saw three of them, and one landed close to the Ventnor Golf Club, less than a mile away. The number of buildings damaged totalled 10,873. Part of the High Street was demolished, including several shops and part of the police station. Seven people died. Seventy years later, the space is occupied by a car park, a permanent remainder of the German bombing raids. Around that time, I attended the Saturday children's film shows at the Rex Cinema, but I was not present when it was bombed. There were no casualties. The *Isle of Wight Mercury* reported, 'An elderly lady who was rescued was cheerful, despite losing her false teeth. They were found later and returned to her.'

The raids were called 'tip and run raids' and later in the war, faster German fighter planes caused even more damage. The Focke-Wulf Fw 190s flew no more than fifty feet above the waves to avoid detection by radar. During the late 1930s, German Luftwaffe pilots had probably stayed in the Hermitage, a large house on Whitwell Road used as a youth hostel. Those very pilots were now responsible for the damage.

One of the last air raids was partly responsible for the accident that left me with a permanent limp. We were under the stairs that day when we heard a loud bang as an Fw 190 strafed the area, but when we emerged after the all-clear there was surprisingly little sign of serious damage. The next day I was playing with the mirror at our usual spot at the garden when my mother shouted, 'Lunch time is ready. Come in!' I started running down the steep path, tripped, and suddenly tumbling over. I felt no pain, so I got up and carried on down the path. As I arrived at the stone floor kitchen my mother pointed to my right leg. 'What is that sticking out of your knee?' she said.

I looked down and saw a pale blue bone between two slithers of blood-soaked skin, like a scene in a butcher's shop. I burst into tears; it didn't hurt, but the shock was too much. 'Sit down and put your leg up on the pooffee,' she said. There was no telephone in the house or, indeed, in any of the cottages on our road. There were no toilets inside the houses either. We had to use outhouses in the garden.

She applied some handkerchiefs soaked in water to stem the flow of blood around my knee. 'You know what's happened,' she said. 'That glass greenhouse next door was probably blown out by the raid. A piece of glass must have taken the top of your knee.' The family doctor who looked after us when we moved from St Lawrence to Ventnor in 1939, a German, had been interned under the Defence Regulations. A number of other Germans were taken away from their families. A forty-two-year-old woman, Dorothy Pamela O'Grady from The Broadway, Sandown, was charged with nine counts of committing acts under the Treachery Act – impeding the operations of the British Forces by approaching foreshores (while walking her dog), cutting a military telephone line, and possessing a document with information of defence measures. After a two-day trial, conducted in camera, she was found guilty. Mr Justice MacNaughten proceeded to don the black cap and sentenced her to be hanged. She declined to speak. She would have been the first and only woman to be so treated in Britain, but at the Old Bailey in February 1941, her appeal was upheld and she was sentenced to fourteen years in prison. With remission, she returned to the Isle of Wight in 1955 and Ted Findon, the eighty-six-year-old editor of the former *Isle of Wight Chronicle* with whom I would later work, interviewed her. He wrote, 'I don't think she really wanted to come back. She had such a good time in Holloway! She was looked on as a Mother Superior there and was probably regarded as more important than the Governor.'

My mother asked a neighbour to run to the corner shop 200 yards away to ring our doctor, J. Bruce Williamson, a very tall and imposing Scot who smoked incessantly and drank heavily. He lived near the Rex Cinema, overlooking the Esplanade. On the map it wasn't far, no more than a mile, but without any transport we usually had to go down several hundred steps to visit his surgery. On the way back it was much more taxing. It was almost half an hour before his large, high-powered car parked outside 5 Kimber Cottages. 'What's happening ya' bonny lad?' he said, holding a cigarette in his hand. My father smoked, but only in moderation, and my mother, who didn't, offered him an ashtray. I was sitting in a chair in the front room and he picked me up and put me on the kitchen table, which was covered by a white tablecloth. He pulled a bottle of iodine out of his brown leather doctor's bag, poured some on to a piece of lint and applied it to my knee. 'That's not painful is it?' he asked.

'A bit,' I said. It was really painful, awful. Iodine is still being used today.

'Bring some boiling water and put it into a clean basin,' he told my mother. I noticed he was pulling out some catgut and a needle, to be sterilised in the hot water. With no anaesthetic, he stitched the wound up. Well, I suppose that happened on battlefields, but looking back I am still surprised that he did it, even in wartime. He inserted seven stitches with a slightly shaking hand, wiped up the last vestige of blood, and said, 'Just you take it easy and you'll be as fit as rain within a week or so. I'll call in over the weekend and see how it goes.'

Alas, he was totally wrong. Within two days, my temperature had jumped to 105°F. My mother went to the shop and rang Dr Williamson. 'Brian has a very high fever,' she said. 'You must come.' He did, and he summoned an ambulance. I was taken to Ryde Hospital and put into the children's ward. For the first week I was in intensive care and there were fears that I might not survive. By the second week I had started to come around. It was a near miss. If you are given another chance it is up to you to use all your efforts and energy to make sure it succeeds. I soon learned that lesson; my mother drummed it into me. And I was never resentful about the way Dr Williamson treated me. In wartime, anything goes. If there was anyone to blame, it was Reichsmarschall Hermann Goering, the Oberbefehlshaber der Luftwaffe, who ordered these aircraft to attack the Isle of Wight, the headquarters of the British Navy at Portsmouth, the strategic docks of Southampton, and the aircraft building factories around the county of Hampshire. In the latter months of the war, my father worked for the renowned, hard-drinking, hard-swearing yachtsman Uffa Fox, the drinking friend of the Duke of Edinburgh. There has only been one Uffa – he invented the airborne lifeboat that saved the lives of many brave pilots who were shot down over the sea.

Sixty-five years later, there was an extraordinary sequel when I met Rob Thornton, a fellow pupil of my old school Ventnor College. I told him that I was thinking of a cheeky title for this book, using Hermann Goering as a part of it, and he said, 'Do you know Goering and some of the other Nazi leaders had a meeting with Earl Jellicoe at his house in St Lawrence, close to where you were born in 1935? They wanted to talk about the possibility of England and Germany coming to an agreement. Some people living in the area knew about it. Goering gave the order to take one of his cars to the Island from Germany and he used to drive around in it. He rented a house in Chale but I don't know which one.'

Two days later, I visited Bonchurch Church to see the plaque, prominently positioned before the altar, commemorating the death of Earl Jellicoe late in 1935. A cheery old lady was spraying polish on the wooden pews and cleaning them with a duster and when I mentioned Jellicoe, she said, 'I used to sit across the aisle to him, in the pews for the poor. He was a lovely man. His wife was named Gwendoline Cayzer and she was our cub mistress.' Mrs Newnham, also a Gwendoline, was eighty-six. She told me that she lived in a house named Ailsa Craig in Ocean View Road, 300 metres from Kimber Cottages. 'I knew your mother very well,' she said. 'She had a limp, I remember. Yes, it's true about Goering. I spoke to a number of people who saw him. Of course we were at peace in 1935. There was no reason for Germans being prevented from visiting this country. Jellicoe lived in St Lawrence Hall, which was destroyed by fire in 1951. In those days there were many famous people visiting the Island, including King Edward VIII, the former Prince of Wales, who used to meet the Nazis with the Duchess of Windsor, and Haile Selassie I, the Emperor of Ethiopia, who sometimes stayed at the Beach Hotel in Ventnor during the Second World War. And of course there was Queen Victoria, who spent a lot of her life at Osborne House in East Cowes.'

Goering was Hitler's second-in-command by 1935. German historians say he encouraged the Fuehrer to annex Austria, but he opposed the seizure of the Sudetenland and Czechoslovakia because he thought that would lead to a world war, with Great Britain in conflict with Germany. He warned Hitler that Germany would lose. Hitler overruled him and for a spell Goering was sent on gardening leave to San Remo in Italy. In that period, it is perfectly feasible that Goering put out feelers to the British Government, via Jellicoe, with a view to signing a non-aggression pact between Germany and Britain. Instead, Hitler's Foreign Minister Ribbentrop signed a non-aggression pact with Russia, leaving the way clear for a war against Britain. Realising that he would be isolated, Goering accepted Hitler's plans and resumed his various roles. But Hitler's later decision later to attack Russia sealed his fate. Nazi Germany couldn't fight on two fronts.

Jellicoe was Britain's nearly man. He could have been a national hero, like Lord Nelson; both are buried in St Paul's Cathedral. John Jellicoe was born in Southampton on 5 December 1859, and through hard work and diligence he rose to become Commander-in-Chief of the Home Fleets in 1914. He led the Grand Fleet in the Battle of Jutland in 1916, the mightiest clash of big-gun armoured warships that has ever been. The verdict was a 'winning draw' for him, not an outright victory. He was criticised for not chasing the remaining vessels of the German High Seas Fleet when they turned back to their bases, fearing that their faster destroyers might exact heavy damage. In the Battle of Copenhagen in 1801, Nelson was ordered to withdraw by his commander Sir Hyde Parker. Looking through his telescope, he was asked if he had seen Sir Hyde Parker's signal and he said, 'Now damn me if I do.' He turned to Captain Foley and said, 'You know Foley, I have only one eye – I have a right to be blind sometimes. I really do not see the signal.' If Jellicoe had followed his bold example, he might have finished up as another Nelson. Lloyd George, the British Prime Minister, soon lost confidence in Jellicoe and in 1917 he was sacked from the position of First Sea Lord.

Goering had a much more chequered history. Born in Rosenheim, Upper Bavaria, on 12 January 1893, he was abandoned by his mother and left with a surrogate family. In 1914 he became a flying observer in the First World War and was awarded the Iron Cross before becoming a pilot. Shot in the thigh, he recovered and became commander of Jagdstaffel 27, the unit that was commanded by one of Germany's greatest flying heroes, Freiherr von Richtofen, the 'Red Baron'. Goering was recognised as a hero and was awarded the Order of Merit, the Blue Max. He claimed twenty-two kills, but his fellow pilots thought that was an exaggeration. After the war, he became a stunt pilot in Sweden and on his return his life changed when he heard a speech delivered by

Adolf Hitler in 1922. A year later, he took part in the bloody Munich Beer Hall Putsch and he was injured in the groin. He fled to Austria. In 1925 he spent several months in the Långbro Asylum in Sweden and was hooked on morphine. He continued taking it for the rest of his life. Back in Germany after an amnesty, he signed up with Hitler and his Nazi party and within three years he was elected to the Reichstag. Astonishingly, he was soon elected President. From being incarcerated in a mental hospital, he became the second most powerful man in Germany in just six years.

The author Joachim Fest said of him, 'Pompous and on the verge of ridiculous, he was a mixture of condottierre and sybarite. He was as vain, cunning and yet he was more popular than any of them and for a time was more popular than Hitler himself.' Goering was arrested by US troops in May 1945 and was convicted on four counts in the Nuremberg Trials and sentenced to death. On October 15 1946, two hours before he was about to be hanged, he swallowed cyanide passed to him by a guard. One of the best quotes attributed to him was, 'Guns will make us powerful: butter will only make us fat.' He was very, very fat, but by the end of his life, he had lost a lot of weight. Perhaps I should write to Angela Merkel, the German leader, and ask for an apology for the way Goering and his men left me with a limp. Perhaps not.

Joachim von Ribbentrop, the German ambassador to the Court of St James in the late 1930s, was supposed to have attended the St Lawrence meeting with Jellicoe. According to American sources, he had an affair with Wallis Simpson, the US-born double divorcee who later became Duchess of Windsor. She was the mistress of Edward, Prince of Wales and when King George VI died in January 1936, Edward became King Edward VIII. Delivering a highly emotional message to the nation on BBC radio, he announced he couldn't stay as King 'without being with the woman I love', and he abdicated. Eleven months later, the under-sexed Edward married the highly-sexed Mrs Simpson and they were exiled to Bahamas. Later, in peacetime, they lived in Paris.

One of von Ribbentrop's missions was to organise parties with aristocrats and people who were close to Stanley Baldwin's Conservative Government to elicit information about British intentions over appeasement – allowing Hitler to reoccupy land that was taken away from Germany by the Treaty of Versailles at the end of the First World War – or whether they were serious about rearming and standing up to Germany's bullying tactics. Declassified US Government files, released seventy years later under the Freedom of Information Act, showed that the Duchess of Windsor was a regular attendee of these gatherings at the German Embassy. There was a suggestion that she was paid by the Germans for handing over information. Ribbentrop, who spoke good English, had a number of meetings with Edward and fixed up the Windsors' tour of Nazi Germany in 1937. There was a photograph published in most English newspapers, denounced by Winston Churchill as 'treacherous', of the smiling Duchess shaking the hand of a bowing, smiling Adolf Hitler, with Edward standing next to the Duchess looking very happy. The King was holding his homburg, a hat first used in Prussia.

Historian David Starkey called the allegations about the Windsors being Nazi sympathisers 'preposterous' but John Julius Cooper, gossip writer and son of the

Conservative minister Duff Cooper, knew the Duchess when he was a teenager. He said, 'King Edward was pro-Nazi and if the Nazis invaded England he would have been put on the throne as a Quisling king. We would have lost the war.' A spokesman for English Heritage told a *Sunday Telegraph* correspondent, 'These allegations have not been refuted and relevant British archives remain closed for the time being.' Under the thirty-year rule, the British Government normally release sensitive documents; the fact that nothing has emerged about the Windsors' involvement with the Nazis suggests that the Americans were right. President Franklin Roosevelt once said to a friend, 'Mrs Simpson played around ... with the Ribbentrop set.'

Von Ribbentrop was awarded the Iron Cross in the First World War. His wife Annelies, a mother of five, was a controlling, scheming woman who drove him away, pushing him into extramarital affairs. When he greeted King George VI in May 1937, he raised his right arm and said 'Heil Hitler', an awful gaffe. *Punch* called him 'Van Brickendrop'. He was charged with war crimes and on 16 October 1946, he was the first politician to be hanged during the Nuremberg Trials. He took seventeen minutes to die and his last words were, 'I wish peace to the world.'

Rob Thornton told me of another amazing story in Whitwell. It concerned the first and only successful German raid on English soil in the Second World War, when a detachment of German commandos based in Alderney landed at Woody Bay, a nice, secluded beach where my parents took my brother and me most Sundays in the late 1930s. The commandos attacked the radar station close to Rob's hotel.

The *Ventnor Independent* reported in March 2008, 'It has always been claimed that no German landing party ever set foot on British soil. Nevertheless speculation of a German raid at St Lawrence has been circulating among a few interested parties for some time. The incident is said to have come to light some years ago when an Islander visiting Germany was confronted with a German war veteran who claimed to have taken part in the landing. He said it was a commando raid intended to capture equipment at an Island radar station, thought to be the low level unit at St Lawrence. The small party arrived by gunboat and scaled the cliff.

'They had anticipated little more than Home Guard resistance but were in fact confronted by regular soldiers. A fire fight ensued with the Germans eventually retreating without losses. Some doubted the validity of the story on the grounds the raid would have surely become local knowledge and thus revealed long ago. Others feel this type of incident would have been hushed up at the time for reasons of morale and the demand for secrecy may have lingered on. Aldrian Searle, the Isle of Wight author, has now revealed he has been researching the event for some time and confirms the raid certainly took place. Even more surprising is the revelation that the operation was a partial success in that some equipment was taken and one or two British personnel were captured, presumably for interrogation. This would have been of considerable embarrassment to the authorities and explains why news of the event never leaked out. Indeed there is a suggestion that reference to the raid has been permanently removed from military archives.'

Rob told me that the German raid was in retaliation for a British raid on a German radar installation in France. At the time, the British were well ahead of the Germans in radar and in decoding secret messages. Rob said, 'The St Lawrence station had a lot of well-educated young women in the Women's Auxiliary Air Force who worked on the project and one very bright one insisted that the German battle cruiser *Scharnhorst* had been detected passing through the English Channel. At that time, you could only see blips on the screen, and it was very hard to show which vessel was which, but she insisted it was the *Scharnhorst*. Later it was discovered that she was right. She was promoted and worked on the Enigma project at Bletchley. Within months, *Scharnhorst* was sunk by a British squadron headed by HMS *Belfast* (the ship now moored next to Tower Bridge) on Boxing Day 1943 in the Battle of the North Cape. The St Lawrence station was used as a backup for the one on St Boniface Down and the Ventnor one was bombed twice in August 1940 and was put out of action for a short time.'

In 2008, I visited the concrete bunker that housed the St Lawrence station and it was still in good shape, partially hidden by trees. Next to it were two battered concrete huts for the WAAF and Other Ranks. The station would have been hard to detect from the air. Apparently there are plans to turn the bunker into housing – affordable housing, one hopes.

Dr Williamson, our errant doctor, must have had a few drams of whisky before he stitched my right knee after my accident. Now, more than sixty years later, I still have an ugly scar measuring seven centimetres long and a centimetre wide. That wonky knee has done remarkable service and at the age of seventy I was still playing cricket. If I hadn't had my accident, I would never have taken up cricket and sport and may well have finished up in a soul-searching job on the Isle of Wight. My 'good' knee was the first to go but it had a good innings. On a Forty Club cricket tour to Italy in September 2007, I felt more pain than usual and it restricted my usual lope down the pitch. Dr Richard Willatt, my doctor in Bromley, thought it was osteoarthritis, the dreaded 'Arthur' that has affected so many sportsmen, young and old. His diagnosis was correct. On the early evening of 3 March 2008 I had arthroscopy of the knee, colloquially known as a clean-up, and was discharged a few hours later. A nurse armed me with painkillers, which I detest, but because the pain was sharp after the effects of the anaesthetic had worn off, I took some. The next day I had hiccoughs for almost ten hours. Normally the longest time for having hiccoughs is half an hour. I spoke to the consultant, Dr Fares Haddad, about it. 'That must be a record,' he said. (Later I learned that someone else held the record, after hiccoughing for more than a week.) He showed me the MRI pictures of the knee and I marvel that I played so much cricket without having had this type of surgery many years earlier.

A few days later I was travelling in a no. 73 bendy bus back to Victoria when I noticed a blue sign on the Bonham Carter House in Gower Street, which said, 'This was the first time an anaesthetic was performed in this country, in 1846.' It made me smile. If Dr Williamson had performed his job properly, I would have walked normally for the rest of my life. I would never have had the chance to become a broadcaster and a sports writer for the national newspapers.

While reporting a football match at The Dell, Southampton, in 1969, I was introduced to the club's honorary consultant, who worked part-time and had treated my right knee as a boy. He was very apologetic. 'If it had happened after the war, you wouldn't have had any problems,' he said. Eight months after the arthroscopy, which failed, I had a half-knee replacement. Replacement knees are almost as common as hip replacements, but they can be trickier. I hope this one works. More and more sportsmen are now having replacement surgery but most of them cannot afford to pay for it and sometimes they have to endure extreme pain for months, even years, before the NHS can intervene. One of the luckiest is Brian Close, with whom I worked and played on many enjoyable occasions. Brian is ambidextrous and still plays golf regularly, despite having an artificial hip and a dodgy knee. He captained the Yorkshire Colts until he was in his early seventies, and exercises in a pool each day. He played football for Leeds United, Arsenal, and Bradford City, and his cricket career lasted a phenomenal twenty-eight years. In his time a lot of cricketers aged over forty played professionally. In 2009 there was not a single one.

In 1943/44 I spent six months in the Ryde Hospital. I remember being in a bed near a roaring open fire. Bits of ash often fell on the uncovered arms and chest of a boy of similar age who had been badly burnt. He died a few days later. A boy named David Prior, from Freshwater, was admitted at the same time as I and he was my best friend of that period. We were told that we were the first patients to be given penicillin in the Isle of Wight. It was invented by Sir Alexander Fleming, who had a home in Shanklin, four miles from my home. In my case it didn't work: it was too early in the development of the drug. But for a while my body was covered with hair and the nurses stared at me in surprise: a boy with the hair of a grown man. I have always been hirsute.

While at Ryde Hospital, I developed an infection that led to septic arthritis, one of the most difficult diseases to cure. The knee joint is the most complex joint in the body and it is extremely difficult to put right any defects. Today's powerful drugs ensure survival, but in 1944 the odds were against it and I was very thankful to the doctors and nurses at the hospital for saving me. After six months, I was transferred to another hospital, the Lord Mayor Treloar Orthopaedic Hospital in Alton, Hampshire. It was built for Canadian soldiers in the First World War and they were housed in five long wooden buildings. After the Great War ended, it was turned into a hospital similar to the Royal National Hospital for Tuberculosis next to the cricket ground in Ventnor, a hospital that has since been demolished and replaced with a beautiful park. The people in charge of hospitals in those days believed in fresh air as a cure for consumption (i.e. tuberculosis). The windows were nearly always left open and there was no proper heating, so hundreds of patients died at the National Hospital from pneumonia after catching colds. I was in Block Five of the Treloar Hospital and for most of the year, our beds were wheeled out to the balcony so that we could sunbathe for hour after hour. I have a picture of me sitting up in the open air with a broad smile; my mother dated it 'November 1945'. We had great suntans.

I spent a further eighteen months in that hospital and I enjoyed it, which sounds odd but is true. The boys wore smocks and no underpants, and an Irish matron in her forties loved pulling up the sheets to see your private parts. I had to hold on to the sheet to protect my privacy. No one complained and she was never punished. In the winter there were no visits for three months, in order to avoid the spread of germs. It was very different to today's hospitals. There was no prospect of taking a telephone call from home, except in emergencies, and the only way to communicate was to write a letter. I started writing to my mother and I wrote to her every week until she died in 1978. She loved writing letters.

When I was transported in an ambulance from Ryde to Alton via the old-fashioned steam-driven ferry across the Solent, it was my first visit to the mainland. People born on the Island – we call the Isle of Wight '*the* Island' because the inhabitants think it is finest isle in the world and the only one worth bothering about – are better known as Caulkheads. The word comes from ships. 'To caulk' is 'to stop up seams of ships with oakum and melted pitch'. Mainlanders who visit the Island are known as Overners. In normal circumstances, I would have been discharged after a few weeks at the Ryde Hospital, but another complication set in: the adhesions around the knee seized up through lack of exercise, leaving my right leg unable to bend more than five degrees. The hospital at Alton was the nearest orthopaedic hospital. They specialised in long-term remedial treatment, which usually meant prolonged rest. I had three manipulations on my knee. The first time, I was taken to an operating theatre and put on a bench. A doctor and a couple of nurses assured me that it wouldn't hurt. 'We'll give you a whiff of chloroform,' a nurse said. It brought back memories of my first instance of being administered chloroform, at Ryde Hospital. A nurse held a pad of cotton wool with chloroform poured on to it and suddenly thrust it into my face. I panicked and started to struggle. Soon I was on the floor fighting to get away from these people, who seemed to be set to finish me off. I lost my senses and when I woke – I had no idea of how long I was out – a nurse said, 'That wasn't too bad.' I had to disagree. The prospect of further assaults was daunting, but at Alton they were more careful. The doctor tried to manhandle my leg and start bending it again, but each time he jumped on it, I felt acute pain. After three visits to the operating theatre, the doctors finally admitted failure.

Another doctor ordered that my leg should be put back into a plaster from thigh to ankle, much bigger than the one I had at Ryde. I had difficulty getting up. The weight of the plaster was a handicap, but the worst part of it was the continual itching. The nurses gave me powder to ease the irritation, but it never worked. After three months I was wheeled into a small room and the matron and a nurse started to cut the plaster off with huge scissors. About to reach a premature state of puberty, I was wearing my underpants, so the matron was disappointed on that occasion. Removing the plaster took a long time, and when the virgin leg, red and sore, was finally exposed to the air, they realised that the condition of my knee hadn't improved at all. A consultant was summoned and his verdict was that the stubborn knee joint had to be put in an extension – a wooden contraption strapped to the end of my bed with a lead weight on a piece of rope attached to my right foot. It was designed to straighten my leg.

Not being able to get out of for several weeks, I often contented myself during the summer by catching the dragonflies that abounded in the hospital. I wrote to my mother, 'Please can you send me some reels of cotton. Urgent.' The next time she visited she asked why. 'I'm training dragonflies,' I said. When I caught one, I tied cotton around one of its leg. With some of the other boys doing the same, it was like a Battle of Britain dogfight between Spitfires and Fw 190s. Most of the boys were in there for years; I was hoping I would have more luck. Each morning a young lady came and taught drawing, reading, writing, and mathematics. But the chief attraction was a copy of the *Daily Herald*, which was delivered every weekday, and a small portable radio. I was the only customer for the newspaper and I would turn to the back page to read the articles of my new hero Tom Phillips. He was famous for 'putting his shirt' on his favoured boxer. When Bruce Woodcock, the British heavyweight boxer, was about to fight Lee Oma, the America heavyweight, Phillips assured his readers that Bruce would flatten him. 'I'm putting my shirt on him,' he said. It was one of the few occasions when Phillips was right. Lee Oma was duly flattened after a few minutes and the headline, which I liked immensely, was 'Lee Ar..Oma!' because it looked as though the American had taken a dive.

When anyone asked me what I would like to do when I grew up, I always said 'Be a sports writer working for a Fleet Street newspaper.' I was then eight. Sixteen years later I achieved it, with the *Daily Sketch*. In the mid-1970s, when I was working for the *Daily Mail*, I was queuing up for my expenses one day and the person in front was a rather frail, old man reeking of cigarette smoke. 'Name?' said the clerk, rather rudely.

'Phillips,' said the man. 'Tom Phillips.' I was shocked. This man had fired my ambition many years earlier. He was a star. When he collected his cash and turned away I should have introduced myself but I didn't. I regret that very much. I may have lifted his spirits. A few weeks later he died and I regretted it even more.

Lying in bed gave me plenty of time to read not just a newspaper but quality books brought in from the local library. I always had the work of Dickens, Kipling, and Twain held up in front of my face. There was little demand for the portable radio, which had crackly reception. When there was a big football match, or a Test match, or a fight, I would ask the teacher to borrow it. Football matches and Test matches were always played in the day, but at night it was difficult to listen to Raymond Glendenning's commentaries and the summaries from Barrington Dalby at big fights because the ward lights were always turned out at 6.30 p.m. I had to hide the radio and listen to it with the sound turned down, under a sheet. One day a night nurse came in and said 'Who's that talking over there?'

I said, 'It's him,' pointing to a boy who was asleep, 'he's been talking in his sleep.'

The next day I would get out my notebook and start writing my report of the event. I listened to the commentaries of Howard Marshall at Test matches and took in every word. Sixty years later, I listen to today's commentators in my car and most of them are shouting and screaming. It is difficult to know who did what. Do today's youngsters understand sport in the way I did? And what about the ghastly music that is played over commentaries? We need a Mary Whitehouse to campaign against these excesses. In my hospital bed, I lapped up the magic words enunciated in good English and imagined myself as another Marshall or Glendenning. I was mad about sport and reading books and it was one of the most pleasurable times of my life. I had a goal and I was going to do all I could to reach it.

Three months went by, and the decision was made to release me from my extension. Two nurses helped me up and as I stood on my feet and tried to take a step, I fell headlong into the arms of the prettier of the two nurses. 'You will have to learn to walk again,' she told me. They brought me a set of crutches and it didn't take too long to master them. I could dash down the corridors almost as fast as the fitter boys in Block Five. One day the teacher brought along a small cricket bat, a cricket ball, and a set of stumps, presented by a parent. We were always receiving parcels. It must have been organised by charitable organisations or churches. Every month I would receive a parcel of sweets, fruits, books, and other goodies from a lady in Cape Town who signed herself 'Miss E. Dawson'. I never knew her Christian name, but she wrote memorable letters, full of good advice. She lived in the Ladies' Christian Home in Vrede Street and fifty years later I walked up the hill to the home, a smart, Victorian building under Table Mountain, and asked the receptionist about Miss E. Dawson.

She checked the records. 'Her name was Ethel and she came from Sussex in England and died twenty-five years ago,' she said. 'She was a very generous lady and much liked.'

I learned a lot about the history of South Africa from Miss Dawson and I always wrote back. She was probably a lonely lady, without family. Living in a home, one of her pleasures in life was to help others. I told the receptionist, 'She taught me a lot, particularly about the cruelty of apartheid. She must have been a wonderful lady and I'll never forget her.'

My first experience with cricket was disastrous. The teacher invited me to bat at the field nearby and I had to put down my crutches and take hold of the small cricket bat. By the time I had hit the ball – not too far – and bent to pick up my crutches, there was hardly time to go more than a few yards down the pitch before being run out. After a lot of practice, I managed to steal a few singles, but never a two. By now I was following the exploits of my latest heroes, like Denis Compton, the Brylcreem publicist, Len Hutton, the first professional captain of England, and Jim Laker, the record-breaking off spin bowler about whom I wrote a book in 2006. In the early 1960s, I wrote Jim's articles in the *Sketch*. On one occasion, he asked me, 'Can I write it myself?'

I said, 'Sure, but I'll have to look at it first.' His first offering was written in copperplate writing and except for a few clichés, it was very serviceable.

'You will have to phone it over,' I said. He always did. He loved chatting up the copytakers, particularly the ladies. Can you imagine one of today's stars being asked to phone copy to a newspaper?

Before the winter set in, I disposed of my crutches and was able to go on long walks around the hospital grounds, even to Alton town centre. There was a small exercise pool and I spent hours in it, building up the muscles in my legs. Unfortunately the muscles around my right knee had packed up, like the adhesions. The knee could still only bend five degrees. I was delighted. Those five degrees enabled me to run. If the knee was fully straightened, I wouldn't have been able to run as fast.

When I reached Fleet Street, one of the leading football writers was Sydney Spicer, who worked for the *Sunday Express*. He was more than six feet in height and he too had a rigidly stiff leg. It was almost impossible for him to sit in press boxes of that time, particularly the one at White Hart Lane. We called it 'the sardine tin'. Years later, when I was advising a lot of clubs about their press facilities and urging them to build more spacious ones, Tottenham was one of the last of the top echelon still holding on to the old arrangements. The old box was taken over as a corporate box and another one was built behind the dugout on the halfway line. When Vinnie Jones ended the career of Gary Stevens with a brutal tackle on the far side of the raised pitch, hardly anyone in the press box saw it properly. The seating is exactly the same today: there is no space for anyone to pass by. The Football Writers' Association officials, including me, had countless meetings with the successive chairmen of Tottenham and they promised they would build a proper press box. But now a new ground is in the offing and in 2009 I had a number of meetings with the officials and architects.

I have helped twenty-seven clubs since 1980, when I drew the outline plans for the press rooms at Highbury. I asked Jeremy Wilson, the architect working on the new White Hart Lane, 'Which are the best facilities you have encountered?'

'Arsenal's, because they were ahead of their time,' he said.

I don't want to write much more about a knee that doesn't bend, about operations and replacements, but but there *was* a very funny sequel to my last series of surgeries. My artificial right hip, which was supposed to have passed its sell-by date, one day started sending ugly signals – *ouch* and more *ouch*. After several months of failing to cure it with exercises, I turned to the NHS and arrived at the Princess Royal University in Bromley for an appointment with a consultant. I sat there for almost two hours without seeing anyone. There had been a mix-up and I ended up becoming the final patient of the day. Rather irate, I tried to complain, but a stout middle-aged lady with a slight accent began pummelling the outside of my hip. When she found the exact place – with me shouting out in pain – she explained, 'You have the greater trochanteric pain syndrome, also known as trochanteric bursitis. We can cure it with one injection, or if it doesn't work first time, we can have three more. There is a good chance it will be cured.'

Highly relieved, I said, 'Well, thanks very much. It's worth waiting for. By the way, where do you come from?'

She laughed. 'I am a German,' she said.

I told her that I wouldn't be asking Angela Merkel for that apology after all.

CHAPTER THREE

Houses that Fell in the Night

I was born in the Toll House, otherwise known as Woody Bank Cottage, in St Lawrence. The Toll House is on a sharp corner of the scenic Undercliff Road, which has always been prone to subsidence. A few years ago, the EU contributed towards the £20 million cost of filling in a massive hole that had completely blocked the road. Most of the area is built on 'blue slipper' clay, which is constantly on the move. However, the Toll House, built in 1830 in a similar style to those Martello Towers in Spithead outside Portsmouth Harbour, stands firm. But a number of the other houses our family has lived in have collapsed or subsided. It seems as though a curse has followed us around.

The birth took place upstairs on 21 November 1935. Voltaire (1694-1778), the French philosopher, was born on that day; he was reckoned to be the Swift of France. His most famous work was the satirical *Candide*. Brigitte Bardot and the Dalai Lama also share the birthday, and it was the date Donald Duck first emerged. And the German Navy surrendered on 21 November 1918. Otherwise, it isn't a memorable date. Charabancs (long vehicles with seats facing forward, the predecessors of today's coaches) rattled by during the summer weeks, interrupting my midday naps. The Toll House's front door was six feet high and anyone taller would hurt themselves. If he or she took a couple of steps out, they would be on the road, risking death. It was an odd place to choose, but my parents had little option. Neither of them were going to be rich and it was difficult to meet the weekly rent. Most of our food was grown in a nearby allotment and my mother had to take me and my brother Allan Bertram, born on 5 January 1930, and push my handsome pram two miles into Ventnor, to the only street with shops, and then back. It was a hazardous business.

My father, Percy Henry John Scovell, a carpenter, was born in 1902. He came from farming stock, a family of thirteen. Several of them died before the age of five. He had a cheeky smile and although he wasn't too literate, he had a good sense of humour and entertained my mother with his geniality. He was in and out of jobs and although he had plenty of relatives, none of them had any money either. Somehow they gained pleasure from living close to the land, rearing their own chickens and even picking fruit from other gardens – 'scrumping', as it was known. There were a few rowdy young people who misbehaved, and I can remember my father cuffing some of them on the ear. He was only five-foot-three. The sole policeman along that part of the Undercliff encouraged it, and as for bingeing, hardly anyone could afford to buy more than the odd pint of beer. Were people happier in those days? Looking back at the faded, black-and-white pictures of my parents and their relatives, I would say they were. They were uncomplicated people, enjoying simple pleasures. The postman, Bonas Sprake, used to knock at the door and hold a letter against the light and say, "ere's a letter for you and it looks as though it's from your brother Fred.' Or whoever.

Fred was never a candidate for quizzes. On one occasion he chased my father round the garden of the family house in Niton, brandishing a pitchfork in his hands. Two of his sisters, Ivy and Doll, were lovely Christian spinsters who looked after the rest of the family. They helped bring up Violet Barber, who was illegitimate and didn't know her parents. She was known as my 'aunt' even though she wasn't related to us. With no social services to help out, people had to do that – bring up children without financial help. Vi was a very kind and loving lady and when I first moved to London, she and her husband Ken, a skilled craftsman who had worked in New Zealand for some winters, took me in as a paying guest for a while. Ken had a reputation as a womaniser and we suspected he had some lady friends. I fear he bullied Vi over the years.

The name 'Scovell' comes from a small village near Caen in Normandy called Escoville. Jack Scovell, who was a secretary with the Queen for some years before he was knocked down by a car and killed, contacted me and showed me the history of the family. Jack was a wonderfully contented and happy man and it was very sad that we lost such a very decent member of the Scovells at such a comparatively young age, sixty-four. He wrote a letter to me in 1984, saying, 'One of our relatives, Kenneth Scovell, has traced our background and says he has many valuable documents including one which proves that we are of Norman aristocracy through the Compte d'Escoville. He traces the Island Scovells to an Andrew Scovell, who came here in 1545 (my grandfather was an Andrew, and the previous two generations also had Andrews). The name is in the *Domesday Book*. I have been to the village of Escoville and I knew a Lieutenant of the Paras who was in charge of the platoon that took and held the Chateaux until forced out by German artillery, when the building was destroyed the day after D-Day. A major named John Harris won a Military Cross in the three-day battle and I met his daughter Bridget after he died in 2009 at the age of ninety-five. He was awarded a second MC for his bravery in General Montgomery's campaign into Germany in 1944-45. "I have a picture of my father with Monty pinning his medal on his chest at Escoville and it's my most treasured possession," she said. It is believed that Spain was the original country from where the Scovells came from and it is a fact that my great-grandfather, who was a well known Island smuggler, was also called 'the Spaniard' and wore an ear ring. From photographs it appears that all the males had that piratical look.'

From the Norman 'Escoville' comes the clue that the correct way to pronounce our name is 'sco-vell' (rhyming with 'hotel') but I was told by an expert on surnames that it should be 'scove-ll' the pronunciation which is used by Islanders (rhyming with 'shovel'). I had to put up with 'Shovel' at school and at work. A cutting from *The*

Times' diary in 2004 provides further evidence that we are descended from the French aristocracy. It said, 'Another reader, Marion Scofield Quinn, makes issue with Iain Finlayson's (and Mark Urban's) claim that Major General George Scovell ("The Man Who Broke Napoleon's Codes") was "of no great family". Quinn tells us that all Scovells and Schofields descend from the Escovilles of Escoville in France, and that the first one came over with William the Conqueror. In the 1100s, this man's descendant was a Sir Ralph de Scoville, who was a bit of a murderous Norman baron to all accounts but very fascinating.' Now we know. Sir Ralph helped build Norwich Castle. Sometime later, I was walking around the ramparts and the guide, who was conducting a group of Americans around, started talking about our distinguished relative.

In Easter 2009, Gavin and I did a whirlwind tour of the battlefields of the First World War in the Somme region and the Second World War battles around Caen and Omaha Beach. Even with the aid of Gavin's sat nav it was difficult to find Escoville, a hidden hamlet of 736 inhabitants six miles east of Caen. Rain was teeming down and there was little sign of life. There were no shops, no bars or cafés, and no supermarket. The churchyard was filled with elegant gravestones and only one Scoville was mentioned. We saw the mayor's secretary in the her office and she explained: 'They all left, they are everywhere around the world.' There was a six-foot-tall granite monument next to the church, bearing the words 'To Our British Liberators in Gratitude, July 1944'. Half a dozen hoodies were larking around in a small shelter. They were rather incongruous.

On another occasion, I was being shown round a winery near Stellenbosch in South Africa when a member of our Forty Club group – veteran cricketers who specialise in sampling the best wines around the world – shouted, 'I've just spotted a notice about one of your family.' He pointed to a poster depicting 'The Flight of the Huguenots' from Northern France in 1685, after Louis XIV revoked the Edict of Nantes and hundreds were expelled. The Dutch East Indian Company offered them free voyages to the Cape and most took up the offer. One of the names was 'Scoble'.

Having an unusual name is a big bonus in life. Most people say to you, 'How do you pronounce it?' So I usually repeat my line about the murderous Sir Ralph and how we use different pronunciations, from the common version 'Scuvvle' to the more posh 'Sco-vell.'

My mother, christened Maude Janet Scovell, was born in 1907 and was abandoned at the age of four when her mother, a beautiful lady who had Spanish blood, left her husband Andrew Souter. Despite years of placing advertisements in newspapers trying to trace her, my mother never met her again. She disliked the name Maude, and with different parts of the family calling her Kitty or Poppy, strangers were confused by her nomenclature. Her father, born in 1875 in Lossiemouth, came from a long line of fishermen. He had many good qualities but he also had a fierce temper and I suspect that was the reason why his wife left. Andrew's father was also named Andrew Souter and his father lost his life along with his crew in a storm at sea in 1885 at the age of forty-two. His grandfather, again named Andrew, also lost his life at sea by drowning. My grandfather refused to go into the fishing industry, and when his brother died and left him two boats he still, unsurprisingly, refused to go to sea.

My grandfather's mother, Janet Garden, died in 1895 in a Glasgow mental asylum and in her death certificate she was described as 'an imbecile'. In those days, anyone with psychological problems were thought mad.

My grandfather had two children: my mother and a son named George, who was born in 1905 and died four years later. On George's gravestone, my grandfather wrote, 'In Living Memory of our son "Ackie", his memory ever cherished.' Losing his father at the age of ten, his mother at the age of forty-nine to a mental home, seeing his only son die so young, and then discovering that his wife had gone forever two years later, must have had a profound effect on him. I could understand how he turned out to be an angry man with a grudge against the world. But he also had a sense of humour, because when I asked him once why he had called my mother Poppy, he said, 'When she was a baby she kept pop, pop, popping all the time... from her back passage.'

My mother was brought up by aunts in Lossiemouth, Morayshire, and she must have had a disturbing upbringing. Her father was an itinerant carpenter and cabinet maker working all over the country, and his brother, a rather austere and unsmiling man, stood in as a reluctant surrogate father. At a young age she contracted poliomyelitis, a viral infection that attacks the nervous system, causing muscle paralysis. She walked with a limp for the rest of her life and never complained. She was the most stoical person anyone could meet. Later in life she started taking driving lessons and it took five tests before she eventually passed. Her father worked for a Canadian ship company in Amherst, Nova Scotia, doing war work, and she was proud of her academic achievements at the Amherst High School. 'I always had good marks,' she said, proudly showing her term reports. Her marks rarely dropped below seventy-five per cent and if she had a better start to life, she might well have succeeded in a professional job. When the First World War ended, she returned to Lossiemouth with her father and left school at the age of fourteen to work as an assistant cook at the posh mansion where Ramsay MacDonald, the first Labour Prime Minister, lived. He headed the Government in three terms, 1923-4, 1929-31 and 1931-35, beating the other Scots premier, Gordon Brown, by eighty-four years. James Ramsay MacDonald was a remarkable man. Born out of wedlock – as they used to say in those days – in a tiny fishermen's cottage, he was elected to Parliament at a young age. Lacking charisma and with no one backing him, except a trade union, he eventually became the leader of the Labour Party and, soon after, Prime Minister. He had five children and was left a widower. He was the first Prime Minister to fly in an aeroplane, which took him from London to Inverness and back. He took his retinue of housekeepers, but not my mother. For some years he was a pacifist and his policies held back the nation's rearmament until the Conservative leader Stanley Baldwin, who succeeded him in 1935, ordered a rapid expansion of the military, which included the new Spitfire aircraft, the radar system, and everything else that was needed to catch up with Germany.

Winston Churchill didn't like him or his policies and ridiculed him, saying, 'When I was a child I was taken to the celebrated Barnum's Circus which contained an exhibition of freaks and monstrosities but the exhibit I must desired to see was the one described as "the Boneless Wonder". My parents judged that the spectacle would be too revolting and demoralising for my youthful eyes. I have waited fifty years to see "The Boneless Wonder" and there he is sitting on the Treasury bench.' Churchill spent several holidays in the Isle of Wight from 1878 to the mid-1890s and claimed that he saw the sinking of the sailing vessel *Eurydice*, when 300 people drowned off the south of the Island. But one of his relatives said, 'He was only four. He merely heard about it and described it as one of the worst tragedies of English shipping.' On the Scovell-seeking trip to Normany in 2009 I saw a reference in an exhibition about the Battle of Delville Wood to another sea disaster, on 21 February 1917, when the SS *Darro* ran into a troopship SS *Mendi* at 4.55 a.m. The *Mendi* sank in fog off the Isle of Wight and 616 mainly black South African troops drowned.

One of MacDonald's friends was Alexander Souter, my great uncle, who later became Provost of Lossiemouth and owner of the main clothier in the main street, the Polytechnic. Another friend of MacDonald owned a large house near Niton on the Island and invited the Prime Minister to spend summer holidays there in the 1920s. That was why my mother went to Niton, two miles from St Lawrence, and how she met my father. They were married two years later. We spent happy hours on the secluded beaches along that coast, particularly the one that was featured in one of the biggest drug hauls sixty years later, when customs officers seized several million pounds worth of drugs. The consignment had been brought by a yacht from South America, and customs, acting on a tip, were waiting offshore to intercept it. In the half-light, some members of the gang struggled to the beach, spilling some of the sacks, before being apprehended. They were later charged and sentenced for long periods of imprisonment. My children and I were there the next day and a customs officer told us, 'One man is still at large. Have a go for the reward.' We trudged around the fields but nothing was found.

There has been smuggling since the early history of the Island. Some of our ancestors were smugglers who migrated from northern France to Shalfleet, a small village that had plenty of Scovells and Skovells. As the Second World War approached, my father started working on the building of the radar station at St Boniface Down in Ventnor, and he found it difficult to cycle the four miles up and down each way without having many days off. He believed in discipline, and if my brother and I behaved badly he would say, 'Any more of that, you'll get a clip on the ear!' Another restraint, the ultimate, was the threat of 'the strap', a piece of leather that I never saw used. My mother taught us proper values and she stuck to them, often telling us off with stern words if we tried to rebel. Today we see mothers asking small children in supermarkets, 'Would you like that?' Inevitably, the child will pick something that may not be good. In our childhood we weren't given an option. There were a few overweight children around, but the vast majority were lithe and fit, like the children you see today in the Far East and Africa. They walked almost everywhere, or rode a bike. Boys often had knives because they were Cubs or Scouts and they needed to cut things up as part as their training. We never heard of anyone being stabbed or threatened.

Our local prison, Parkhurst Prison, imprisoned the really evil men of Britain – murderers and hard criminals. Around that time, there was on average 11,000 prisoners in the United Kingdom from a population of 45 million. The Government closed prisons because they weren't needed. Today, with 82,000 imprisoned from a population of 60 million, there is an acute need for new prisons. The total is expected to rise to 100,000 within the next decade. So many prisoners are being let out because there are not enough cells, reinflating the crime figures. Where has it all gone wrong? Like many people of my generation, I think it goes back to lack of discipline – right back to the cot. Most parents of that era were united in marriage and were in charge; they didn't abdicate their responsibilities to little children, who are incapable of making the right decisions. If someone stole, or was rude to a policeman, or vandalised anyone's possessions, everyone in the town knew about it and older people would reprimand them. The populace was almost self-regulated. They saw the local bobby on a bike all the time and the police were friends, not young, faceless men racing up and down in speeding patrol cars and jumping out to confront people and fill in forms, as they do today. My parents weren't regular churchgoers, but they believed in God and followed the creed 'love thy neighbour'. The majority of Britons seem to have forsaken these beliefs. They think this wonderful world came about by natural means, like a flick of a switch, not thinking that someone, or a Force of Good that most people cannot comprehend, initiated the idea and made it all happen.

I often wonder if my father could behave today as he did then, when he would go up to naughty young men and tell them off. Would he be stabbed? Three years ago a group of idle youths congregated at a beautiful small space near my house in Bromley and caused an immense amount of trouble, smoking pot and keeping the neighbours awake into the early hours.

I went out to see them and said, 'Why are you causing all this strife? Some people live nearby who served in the war and saved this country from being occupied by Hitler and his mob. You would probably be in concentration camps or in the SS without them. Show some respect and grow up!'

One aged around seventeen said, 'We're bored.'

'Bored?' I said. 'You've got so many things laid on for you now. Get out there and take advantage of them! You're very lucky to live in a rich, prosperous country!'

I realised they might attack me so I left. I went straight to the new £20 million police station, half a mile from my house, and found I couldn't get in. I had to ring from outside and was told to leave a message. I scribbled out a note about this threat to public safety and heard no more.

A few days later, I spotted two community officers and told them there was another disturbance caused by these nasty young men and asked them to investigate. The tallest one looked startled. 'I can't do that,' he said.

'Why not?' I said.

'Well, we'd be outside of our limit,' he said.

'Come off,' I said, 'it's just a quarter of a mile.'

He wouldn't help. But more householders joined in over the weeks and after countless messages from all quarters, the local constabulary finally took an interest and finally cleared the nest of hooligans. They haven't reappeared. I recommend this course of action to all disaffected ratepayers throughout the country.

My latest house, in Widmore Road, Bromley, has been burgled twice. On a couple of later occasions, two potential burglars climbed over the seven-foot-high fences, but were scared off. Audrey's artistic skills helped to recover the most expensive piece of her jewellery in the first burglary, when her car and various other items were stolen. The thief left his bicycle behind, with his fingerprints on it, and that led to his conviction some months later. He was a drug addict from nearby Greenwich and he asked for 285 other offences to be taken into account. Audrey had drawn the antique necklace and went back to Bromley Market, where she had bought it, and met the lady who had sold it to her.

'Is there any chance of getting it back?' she asked.

The stallholder looked closely at it and said, 'I'm pretty certain it came from Camden Town Market.' So Audrey went there, met another lady who knew about the piece, and retrieved it. The thief had sold it back to her!

My second experience of an intended robbery took place recently when someone daubed white paint on one of my fences and tried to break the stout glass in my integral garage. It happened at 8 p.m. in January. Hearing a peculiar noise outside, I switched some lights on and the person made off. I was advised to ring the police and this time a lady police officer arrived the next morning to take fingerprints, followed later by two community officers who took details. The next day, Bromley Council's Victim Support called in to give advice about improving the already-impressive security arrangements. If this procedure is now general throughout the country, it restores my confidence in the police.

In 1939 my parents had to leave the Toll House and looked for an affordable rented house in Upper Ventnor. They settled on a bungalow close to the golf course on Rew Down, overlooking the English Channel. The view was stunning, but from the first day we arrived, big cracks began appearing in most of the walls. Within a year, we could see out through the cracks. That helped the ventilation on a hot day, but in the winter it was purgatory. The row of properties was built on vents and if the council hadn't acted as it did, some householders and the remains of their properties might well have disappeared down gaping holes.

They warned us to move as soon as possible and we did – to Kimber Cottages on Ocean View Road, 400 yards southward. That terraced house had an outdoor toilet and no bathroom (we had a tin bath hanging from the back of the kitchen door, which was brought down every Saturday night and filled with hot water from the stove). It, too, was on a vent, except the cracks here opened more slowly.

We stayed there until the start of 1947, and when I returned in 2004 I was surprised to see it was still in place. A ginger-haired young man was sitting on the step smoking a hand-rolled cigarette and I introduced myself and asked if I could have a look around, especially in the garden at the rear where I had hurt my leg. He was keen and showed me in. I noticed the stone floor appeared to be sloping towards the road. 'That's right,' he said. 'That's why the owners paid just £15,000 for the house!'

He took me to the top of the garden. It was a beautiful, sunny day and looking towards the sea I could see what appeared to be half of the British Navy steaming past Ventnor. I told him, 'That reminds me of the day when I fell over in 1943. There was a big dogfight between British and German fighter aircraft going on. A convoy of ships from America was attacked by the German planes and the RAF pilots were trying to take them out. We could see some of them being hit and going down into the sea.'

'I didn't know about that,' he said. 'Seems quite exciting!'

Fay Brown, Ventnor's part-time historian, recently told me that thirty-five houses had been demolished in a small area in Lowtherville, victims of the vents. The post office and the general food store, from which we had our weekly supplies delivered by bicycle, have also disappeared. Fay lives 150 metres away from the epicentre of the underground disturbance and so far her house has not been affected. My brother Allan lived just across the road from her for many years. As a builder, he knows intimately the nature of the land – which houses are safe and which are on the risk list.

The start of 1947 brought the coldest weather ever registered in the British Isles. The land was covered in frozen snow for the first three months. Football was cancelled until Easter. That was the time our family decided to move to Lossiemouth, 600 miles north. The decision was forced on us because Alexander Souter, my mother's uncle, was eighty-one and seriously ill. As a bachelor, there was no one to look after him. My grandfather wrote to my mother and asked for help. She was reluctant, but as Alexander was a comparatively rich man and we could be beneficiaries, she decided to move to the north of Scotland. We packed as much as we could of our possessions and even took the cat, Tiddles, in a catbox. We made the journey on the record-breaking steam train the *Flying Scotsman*, which took us from King's Cross to Aberdeen, travelling almost as fast as today's high-speed trains. The historic engine is now in a rail shed in York, awaiting restoration funds.

We were mystified when the cat didn't pee all over the place. We took another train from Aberdeen to Elgin, and then a bus to Lossiemouth, and the total travelling time amounted to almost twenty-four hours. On arrival in the gaunt-looking, windswept town we struggled up the hill with our bags to the flat over the Polytechnic clothing shop where we would live. The highly agitated Tiddles started mewling and my father opened its box and the cat jumped out and went straight to the fireplace and began relieving himself. It was several minutes before he finished and soon there was a huge pool of piss soaking into the carpet. 'He's been well trained!' said my mother.

The weather was so bad that it was difficult to get out of the house. I often missed school days at Elgin Academy, six miles away by bus. The family living next door owned a bicycle business and they were extremely friendly, lending us items that we lacked after our sudden flight from Ventnor. Their vivacious daughter was one of the first from their circle to attend a university – the University of Aberdeen. When she was in her late twenties, she was found dead from hyperthermia while on a climbing expedition to the Cairngorms. It devastated the family and they never recovered.

Living in such close proximity to the sometimes-volatile Andrew Souter brought on many rows and several times my mother threatened to take us back to the Isle of Wight. My grandfather would come home drunk and start shouting at her. His favourite exclamation was 'Geewhizz', so that is what we called him. It was not a happy time. Fortunately, Alexander died on 3 March 1948, and after the funeral, we packed up and returned south. Most of his assets went to his brother, but at least we had our expenses paid from the estate, and my mother received a reasonable sum to buy a house of her own. And, yes, Tiddles came home with us. Lossiemouth's economy rested on seine net fishing and Alexander owned two fishing boats, which in some weeks brought in large sums. On other trips, they came back with nothing and the crewmen faced starvation. It was like Sebastian Yunger's *The Perfect Storm*. Most weeks my grandfather and I braved the cold weather to stand on the harbour wall, waiting for the boats to return from their fraught trips. We got to know the skippers of the Souter boats and they would throw herrings and other fish at our feet, saying, 'Take a fry home for ya' supper.' 'Fry' meant a supply of fish. We had to attach a line through the lower jaws of the fish, tie them up, and carry them home. It was heavy to carry, but we did it. We virtually lived on fish.

I returned to Lossiemouth in 2005 and discovered that the fishing fleet was no more. The harbour was only occupied by a few yachts. I asked an old, grizzled fisherman why. 'Aye, laddie,' he said, 'it's died and the RAF has taken over.' He pointed towards the west, at the RAF station just a mile from the centre of the town. Every few minutes, fighter aircraft were taking off, deafening the residents as they flew over the town for training exercises in the Moray Firth. Part of the training was low-level flying, and it was a miracle that none of the aircraft crashed into the houses. 'We've just got to live with it,' the man said. 'The place would die if the RAF moved out.'

Back in the town of vents, the search was on for a bigger house. We didn't go far – my parents chose a detached, five-room house at St Albans View, just 200 yards from Kimber Cottages. The only advantage was that it was close to the two shops, a bus stop, and the church. But the major disadvantage was that the row of houses was down thirty-two unlit steps from Ocean View Road, i.e. the bus route. With two members of our family, my mother and me, having dodgy legs, it wasn't a clever decision. It was also precariously close to the vent line. We were surrounded by steps: front, back, and on one side. I started going to watch cricket at the ground overlooking Steephill Cove and there were more than 250 steps down to the next road below my house. But it was good exercise, especially carrying all my cricket gear. The traffic noise was a distraction and after a couple of years we were on the move again. My mother, the main decision-maker of the family, decided to buy a stone-faced house in East Street, named 'Tilehurst'. It was just round the corner from the library I frequented every week. It was much quieter and had two extra rooms, which enabled her to take in summer visitors to help meet the bills. Up to ten people stayed with us and I often helped with serving breakfasts and early dinners, and also with the washing up.

The day we were scheduled to move out of St Albans View, I had just returned from exercising a neighbour's two dogs. I did this twice a day. Our crossbreed terrier, Winston, named after the former Prime Minister, had already been taken out. One of the neighbour's dogs had a habit of attacking people, including me. An old lady living close by paid me 7s 6d a week for doing it. It was danger money. Once the nasty one jumped up at me and dug his teeth into my left hand and refused to let go. It took some calming words to persuade him to unbite me. I still have the scar. It was March and everywhere was covered in snow, including the roof of our house. I was reading the *Daily Express* before leaving for school when I heard a loud whooshing noise from above. 'The snow must have melted and fallen,' I said to my mother. I looked out of the window and suddenly realised that our front garden had disappeared. I rushed out of the side door and saw the fallen gardens of most of the houses, including ours, piled up against the side of St Alban's Church, some thirty feet below. The curse had struck again.

The buyer of the house blamed us. 'Your Dad was banging in some posts into the ground last week and it destablilised the gardens,' he said. The last time I visited the site, many years later, the mound was still there. It is one of the few churches where you can climb up to the roof without using a ladder. The preacher was named Andrew Rumball and when we first moved in, he talked me into joining the choir. After a few frustrating attempts at singing, I handed in my resignation, which was rather fortuitous because Rev. Rumball was later charged with committing offences to young boys. He was found guilty and sentenced to eleven years in prison. We never saw him again.

The curse of the vents caught up with the family in the 1970s, when the three-storey house we bought for £8,000 at The Upper Heights in Foxgrove Road, Beckenham, in Kent, started breaking up. John Major lived less than half a mile away, at West Oak, in The Avenue, and he had a similar problem, only not quite as bad. At the time, he was moving into politics after beginning his working life in banking. His father, who started out as a circus performer, was sixty-three when John was born. He had led an unusual life, particularly in America, where he worked with Harry Houdini and other vaudeville stars. The Majors struggled to survive financially and John had to complete his O-levels by post, like me. He had the same feeling for cricket as me, having lived in Brixton within walking distance of his beloved Brit Oval, watching Laker and Lock, the Bedsers, and his other heroes. The Majors' house in Beckenham was actually smaller than ours, but both were built on clay. In his autobiography, he wrote, 'Elizabeth [his daughter] was growing and we needed more space and we bought a modern end-of-terrace house, West Oak in Beckenham. It was a small estate in lovely wooded grounds, full of mostly young married couples and we were very happy there. When I was adopted for the Huntingdonshire constituency, Norma and I immediately decided to move there and put West Oak on the market. Unfortunately for us, subsidence of a neighbouring house in our terrace reduced its value and made it more difficult to sell. It took months, and throughout that time I commuted from my home in Beckenham to my job in the City and to Huntingdon. We found a lovely house in St Neots and to my fury, we were gazumped by a partner in one of the local estate agents. Eventually we found a conventional four-bedroomed detached house in the beautiful village of Hemingford Grey, and moved in just before Christmas 1977.'

I didn't know him in Beckenham but got to know him after he left 10 Downing Street, in his sideline activity of being President of Surrey CCC. I persuaded him to speak at the annual dinner of the Cricket Writers' Club and I was surprised there was so little security on his arrival at the InterContinental Hotel in Park Lane. There was just one policeman on a motorcycle.

Sir John asked me, 'What sort of speech I should make?'

I said, 'It's a balance between a few light-hearted remarks and some serious thoughts about the state of the game. But it is up to you.'

He spoke for just over half an hour and his speech went down extremely well – some jokes, some anecdotes, and a few comments about cricket and sport generally. He said he regretted not sticking to his plan to invest £30 million into sport in his final year as Prime Minister and giving way to his Cabinet colleagues. He was given a rapturous round of applause and I went to him and congratulated him.

He was sitting signing some autographs when a sports editor who appeared to have drunk too much, leaned over his shoulder and said, 'Your speech was a disgrace. You should have kept that £30 million subsidy.'

Sir John turned round and he was shocked and upset. The man withdrew and several of our CWC colleagues apologised. Two days later, the newspaper concerned carried a single-page interview with Sir John – a favourable article to repair the damage.

He is passionate about cricket and in the summer of 2007, his book *More than a Game* was vying with my book about Brian Lara in the Lord's shop. Alan Prior, the manager, said, 'Yours is just ahead.' That didn't last – Sir John's sold 60,000 in hardback and I believe mine failed to reach what was then Brian Lara's world tally of Test runs, 11,912.

Our house in The Upper Heights, no. 82, was third from the end on the left going up the cul-de-sac. It backed on to Beckenham Place Park. I became chairman of the Estates Committee and persuaded the local council to fit a gate to the fence, enabling the residents to have a key to let themselves out and in. I encouraged the local boys to play football, and gave them some coaching (Bobby Robson was one of my coaches when I took my FA Preliminary Coaching Badge in 1969). One of those boys was Matt Lawton, now the chief football correspondent of the *Daily Mail*.

Another boy, Chris McGrath, lived three doors up, and when he was six he called at our house and said, 'Can I come and read your sports books?' So most Saturdays he would sit in our front room and read. 'I want to be a cricket writer,' he told me.

The family moved to Ipswich and we kept in contact. Many years later, Karen, his mother, rang to say he had gained a degree at Oxford University and was studying law but now wanted to be a racing correspondent. I put him in touch with Tony Garnett, the sports editor of the *Ipswich Evening Star*, and Tony hired him as a casual. Within two years, Chris joined *The Independent* and in 2007 he was voted Racing Correspondent of the Year. He is a very fine writer.

The gate to the park proved to be a controversial move, and the police had several complaints about flashers. Audrey saw one while taking the children on a walk. 'Nothing to fear from him,' she said. 'Very small!' Anyway, the gate was sealed up. Thirty years later, councils are now trying to get children back out to parks to exercise themselves and take up sport. It may be too late, with less than sixty Premiership footballers now available for the England team. All the other places have been taken by foreigners earning obscenely high salaries, plus fees for image rights, otherwise known as legalised bungs.

Our misfortune at the Heights was that we were at the wrong end of the row. Six houses were moving down the hill and our house was one of the worst. It brought back memories of the property in Upper Ventnor, which was demolished in 1939.

We should have checked the foundations more thoroughly. As the cracks opened, we contacted our insurance company and were told that it wasn't their responsibility. The National House Builders' Council (NHBC) has a ten-year guarantee that covers new houses, allocating compensation up to £5,000 in the first two years, and then dropping down to £2,500. I first wrote to them in September 1970, but they kept stalling and I took the matter up on behalf of the other residents. We sent a petition to the council, and they were unhelpful. My solicitor told us our only chance was to keep pressuring the NHBC. Four agitated years later, the NHBC agreed to pay for the repairs, and Rock & Alluvium Ltd moved in with drills. 'We're going down to pin the house down to twenty-six feet,' said the foreman. It was like living in a coal mine – dust everywhere, and indescribable noise. Four months later, water started pouring through the ceilings of the top bedrooms, ruining Audrey's extensive wardrobe.

In December, the man from the Rock said, 'It's now stabilised. No sign of movement.'

'And no sign of movement from the NHBC,' I replied.

In the spring of 1975, the work still hadn't been finished. I wrote an amusing feature in the *Daily Sketch*, published on 6 March, about the affair. At 9.30 a.m. the day it appeared, the man from the NHBC rang, offering a meeting. Within a fortnight, they agreed to pay the £26,000 needed to restore the properties, and the work was finally completed at the end of March. The residents congratulated the *Sketch* writer but failed to take the Scovells out for dinner at the Savoy or a similar eatery. It was a classic case of the power of the press triumphing, and I should have done it years earlier.

Except for the building faults, it was a splendid place to bring up children. There were no worries about babysitters and the only crisis we experienced was when my daughter Louise locked herself in the toilet of our great friends Dr David Davies, a pathologist, and his wife Susan. Their house was opposite. No one could break the toilet door open and firemen had to come and break it down.

In 1978 we sold no. 82 to a couple of Czechs for £21,500, after reducing the price and disclosing the fact that the house had been underpinned. We checked with solicitors about good places to avoid clay undersoil and were told that Widmore Road in the centre of Bromley was a possibility. We drove along Widmore Road and saw a 'For Sale' sign – this was before strange people took to ripping these signs down in this part of town – and we liked the look of the attractive art deco house, with its white walls and green-tiled roof. It was almost Mediterranean in appearance. I had often walked past a similar-looking house in Shanklin when I worked for the *Isle of Wight Guardian*, and I had longed to own it. We were advised that the price of £40,000 was excessive and we went to see another ninety-nine houses. 'That's my first hundred for several seasons,' I said to Audrey. 'I think that's a good time to quit. Let's go back and see the art deco place.'

The 'For Sale' sign had gone but luckily it was back up again on that same day. We had another look inside and measured the width of the walls. Some were more than a foot wide. 'I can't see this place cracking up,' I said, and we clinched the deal at £37,500.

One of the most admired houses in the borough, it was designed by an architect called Robert Adlard, who won an award for it. It is Grade II listed, so none of the developers who smash down 1930s housing and replace them with tiny-roomed flats can make a fortune from the destruction of my house. It could be the last 'proper' house standing in the road. One of the nearby houses was bombed in the Second World War and was rebuilt. Now I discover that a house next door has had subsidence problems, apparently caused by three of my small trees, whose roots damaged their drains. So I had them cut down. How can I shake off this curse? Not by moving back to Ventnor. No, I will be sticking it out in Bromley to the end, I think.

CHAPTER FOUR

Hopalong!

Having missed almost two years' schooling, I had some catching up to do and my mother was thinking about putting me into a private school. She worked as a cook at Steephill Castle – now demolished and replaced by houses – and at the end of the Second World War that job ended. My father's intermittent pay packets were sometimes replaced by the dole and the family couldn't really afford to pay for education. So I went back to the junior school at Lowtherville, which I had attended previously. One day my mother turned up at the school and, looking over the fence, she saw some rowdy boys jostling me. One knocked me over and she rushed into the playground and told them to behave themselves. It was rather embarrassing, because since my accident, I was invariably being called various insulting names – 'Peg leg', 'Hopalong', 'Hoppity'. My mother told me, 'Just tell them sticks and stones can break your bones but words can't.' I tended to ignore them, but now they were calling me 'Mummy's pet' and other derogatory things.

These days anyone cruelly 'sledging' others (a cricketing word that originally meant 'wielding a sledgehammer') could lead to a disciplinary case and even punishment. Insulting a disabled person is just as bad as racist abuse, or should be. My reaction then was to carry on and show that I could do the same things as normal boys. The abuse spurred me on. I could run just as fast as most of them, and in the playground I could kick the ball just as hard and head it further, and when it came to tackles, I could win a few using my 'good' leg.

I think I earned the respect of most of the boys and soon I was recruiting the best ones to play in a team I organised, the Lower Ventnor team, which would take on the Upper Ventnor team at Steephilldown at holiday times. We put down coats to mark the goals and we played proper games. I sent in reports to the *Isle of Wight Mercury* about these matches and they duly appeared at the bottom of the sports page. In one report, I modestly reported, 'During the first half, the two defences were on top and good goalkeeping, particularly from Wheeler (Upper Ventnor) kept the scoresheet blank.' I was the other goalkeeper. Among our team were Rob Mew, who later became the chairman of the council, Don Badman, whom I beat in a three-round boxing contest at school, Derek Newnham, whose family owned the dairy that supplied our milk, and Jim Daly, who played for England at junior-level table tennis. A number of the boys went on to play for the Ventnor teams. No one coached them. They were self-taught, self-motivated. This was before the days of television. The closest I came to an injury came when my brother was experimenting with his new bow, which he used to propel darts. I was standing idly around on the other side of the garden, not noticing what was happening, when a dart crashed into my left cheek, just under my eye. He rushed up to me and pulled it out, saying, 'I didn't see you over there. Don't tell Mum or I'll whack you!' I never told her or anyone else until years later.

I also arranged cricket matches between the Lower and Upper part of Ventnor, on the same ghastly multi-purpose 'pitch'. I told the *Mercury* readers, 'The lack of a playing field in the Ventnor district was sadly stressed when the irregularities of the pitch marred what promised to be an interesting game.' There were sixty-six byes and each team scored eighty-nine, with the result being a tie. The readers must have wondered what the boys had to do to stage an 'exciting' match.

I started a campaign, calling for the creation of a sports ground in the town. As the place was full of hills and vents, the councillors obviously thought it would be too costly; any prospective piece of land would need to be flattened. Under a headline in the *Mercury*, an anonymous writer (me!) wrote, 'How can a town of 7,000 inhabitants be without playing fields? Ventnor advertises itself every year as a holiday resort. In response, thousands come to this English Riviera. They bring children who naturally want to play games. But there are no playing fields for them. A few putting greens and the beach make poor stand-ins. If the introduction of a sports ground means a slight increase in rates, I should support it notwithstanding. The hundreds of children who are at present forced to play in the streets, on the downs, or not at all, would benefit immensely. In time the lack of a field must have a detrimental effect on the status of sport in Ventnor. Already the complete absence of young talent in all field sports has become noticeable. The cricket teams are composed of mainly players of the old school. What will happen when they finally retire? The football club is more advantageously placed but the players, however promising, cannot improve without practice. Everyone should make this his duty to obtain a playing field for Ventnor's youth.'

No one took much notice but twenty-odd years later Ventnor FC took over a strip of land not too far from the top of Steeplehilldown where we played our little matches. In 2008 Hugh Hornby wrote a book called *Uppies and Downies: The Extraordinary Football Games of Britain*, and Matt Dickinson of *The Times* wrote, 'Long before we won a reputation for physical football, we were booting each other about for fun.' Hugh must have overlooked the matches between the boys of Upper Ventnor, more than 500 feet above sea level, and the lads of Lower Ventnor, just above sea level. Our matches were played without a referee or assistants, and the strongest and loudest won every argument, every game. And no one was really hurt.

In the winter of the early years of the 1950s, I watched Ventnor FC's first team matches at the top part of the ground used by Ventnor CC. The ground, aptly named Steephill, had a bizarre look. At the north side there was a steep slope down to the cricket square. It was too costly to flatten it and when Ventnor CC won promotion to the Hampshire League, they were barred because of that slope. The football pitch looked like a tin roof ripped off by a typhoon – twisted and misshapen. There was hardly a level square yard on it, and I used to tell the others, 'It's ideally made for someone with one leg shorter than the other.' My right leg was an inch shorter than my left, and I had to wear a made-up shoe. Now the club has a £300,000 cricket academy. Brian Gardener, a cricket lover, spent £1.6 million on a unique new ground six miles away: it is totally flat. I am very proud indeed that the club that made me a cricketer has one of the best academies in the land and a ground that can accommodate first-class cricket.

As a boy, we played football on a cramped, sloping field next to the Flowers Brook putting green and one of our players, John Wheeler, was so keen to stop the ball going over a sixty-foot-high cliff, he slid over the edge and landed on rocks below. He had a fractured head, arm, and various other bones, but survived. An old lady named Olivia Parkes, nicknamed 'Britannia', lived in a dilapidated wooden house on stilts, once known as The Old Boathouse. It was on Myrtle Beach, not far away, and she was renowned as the most eccentric woman on the Island. The roof of her odd abode was frequently bombarded by thoughtless boys who threw stones at it. Even with holes appearing, she stayed there for thirty-eight years. In the Second World War the Army took away the steps leading down from the cliff and put barbed wire everywhere, to deter German invaders. But this didn't stop Britannia. She clambered along the rocks to the nearby Flowers Brook and crawled under the barbed wire and walked into the town to shop every day. With no electricity and no heating, and no water except rainwater, she survived there before the police arrived in 1958 and persuaded her to move into a council flat. She said, 'I missed the sea air but I had no love of it. Now I have water laid on, that's a big improvement because I had a long way to fetch water.' She died four years later, at the age of eighty-one.

When we moved to East Street, we played football most evenings on a bombsite in North Street, often breaking windows with stray kicks. The surface was bumpy and to fall was to risk having your knee skinned, which I studiously avoided.

On 2 September 1942, two Fw 190 tip-and-run raiders strafed the Esplanade and town centre with their cannons. One bomb – each plane carried one bomb – landed on North Street, destroying a row of eight houses. Although several people were injured, not one died. Adrian Searle reported, 'There were some miraculous escapes, perhaps the most remarkable being that of Percy Boxall, manager of the local building firm, who was buried up to his neck by a mass of bricks and debris in a passageway, but emerged with relatively minor wounds to his head and ankle.' My father worked with Percy for a brief spell.

For some reason, men who work on building sites are the worst for abusing people, particularly disabled people. Even in my sixties, I was still being shouted at. One day I was walking up Kensington High Street, close to the *Daily Mail* offices, and a man in a lorry, sitting with another man, started chanting, 'Hopalong, hopalong!' and pointing at me and laughing. He thought it was funny. I ignored him. The same sort of people shout comments at women, which usually embarrasses them. One of the reasons why my mother sent me to a private school, Ventnor College, was to have a disciplined and responsible environment where I had the chance to have one-on-one tutoring. She had to take a job as a waitress at The Copper Kettle in the High Street to pay the school fees. With her intelligence and personality, it was demeaning. But when young people say, 'Which is the best present you can give?' I always say, 'A good education.' I was always grateful to her for enabling me to pursue my ambition to be a writer. She wanted to write herself, but she was denied the opportunity.

Between the ages of nine to twelve I spent a lot of time having physiotherapy at various hospitals, in Ryde, Newport, Southampton General, and Elgin, Morayshire. The purpose was to restore some movement to my right knee. These young ladies would attach metals pads around my knee and strap them up. When they switched the power on, I could feel brief tugs at the skin, which was supposed to reactivate the muscles. Every technique failed.

Once I was travelling alone in a separate compartment on the Isle of Wight railway from Sandown to Newport on my way to St Mary's Hospital when a middle-aged man, the only other person in the compartment, asked me about my stiff leg. He seemed friendly. I rolled up my long trouser leg and showed him the scar. He put his hand on it and started rubbing. Soon his hand was slowly moving up my leg. This was my first experience of homosexuality. I screamed loudly, but there was nothing I could do but move to the far side and wait for the next station and get out. The man stayed where he was, which was reassuring. There was no one in sight. It was an unmanned station. I moved up the platform and got into another carriage.

In my brief time at Lossiemouth, I had to attend a hospital in Elgin for regular sessions. My mother and I arrived at 10 a.m. one day and it was 6 p.m. when I was treated – eight hours of waiting. With so much time spent on physiotherapy, taking dogs out, and playing sport, there was little time for girls. I had a female penfriend in Portsmouth, and one in New York, and I never met either. Once at the Rex Cinema I was sitting next to a pert little girl when she started nudging me and putting her hand on my dodgy knee. I discouraged her. I had had enough massages on my knee, I thought.

Charles Green was the headmaster at Ventnor College, an unusual, fee-paying school that he ran with his wife Victoria. He told us he ran in trials for Britain in the 1924 Olympics. He was rotund and it was hard to believe that he was an athlete. He was a kindly, caring man who looked like a character in Dickens. I kept in touch with him until he died in 1969, when I was established as a Fleet Street sports writer. His upright wife trained as a ballerina and maintained good order, despite the shambolic state of some of the properties that housed the school. One building was in Ocean View Road, 100 metres down the hill from Kimber Cottages, and after a few years the vents caught up with it. It was demolished, otherwise the number of pupils might have been cut down drastically overnight. Another one was close to the War Memorial and it started to slide backwards, into a stream. Along with a large house in an unmade road next to St Alban's Church, it had to be abandoned by the school. In my five years at Ventnor College, four different properties were used, and three of them were affected by subsidence.

The headmaster was so busy finding new properties that he didn't have enough time to sign up highly paid teachers, but I was lucky to come under the influence of one of his outstanding signees, Charles Salisbury, then a well-known cartoonist. Charles worked for *Punch, Answers, Everybody's*, and various other magazines. His life changed when he met a young lady in Ventnor, the daughter of a coach and garage owner. They married and settled down in the non-vent part of Ventnor. Unfortunately, Charles' career as a cartoonist was stymied by a long strike by magazine owners. With three children, he found himself desperately short of money. Charles Green persuaded him to take a teaching post at the college and luckily my life was again transformed. Charles Salisbury was like the Robin Williams character in the film *Dead Poets Society*, who inspires his pupils to take up poetry. Charles loved books and he took me to the Seely Library in Ventnor every Saturday morning to introduce me to the great writers, writers like Charles Dickens, George Orwell, Thomas Hardy, Guy de Maupassant, Leo Tolstoy, O. Henry, F. Scott Fitzgerald, Graham Greene, Ernest Hemingway, Barbara Tuchman, and A. J. Liebling. J. P. Priestley, who spent his final years on the Isle of Wight, might not be 'great' but he was a good storyteller and a wonderful broadcaster. I read several of his works. Soon I was reading up to six books a week, many of them 500 or more pages. Until then, my writing was abysmal. Under his direction, I gained a better understanding of good writing. Style comes from reading and when I first met Ian Wooldridge in 1960 – when I first joined the *Daily Sketch* and he moved from the *News Chronicle* to the *Daily Mail* – I learned that he had done exactly the same in New Milton. He, too, read prodigiously, but the difference was that he became the most outstanding sports writer of his time and I was a willing also-ran. Well, maybe it was not quite as bad as that. Ian left school with three O-levels at the age of sixteen; I left at fifteen with seven. He was four years older than me and he was one of my mentors. He devoured all the books written by Hemingway and he loved the way of life of debonair characters like Denis Compton, Keith Miller, Douglas Jardine, and Muhammad Ali. He believed in the Corinthian spirit. I tried to follow his example, with one difference – I was a lifetime teetotaller and he loved a drink.

The Seely Library is still there, 200 metres from one of our old houses in East Street. The name comes from the one of the finest Isle of Wight philanthropists, Colonel Charles Seely. The Colonel often entertained General Giuseppe Garibaldi, the man who unified Italy, at his home at Brook House in West Wight. The main attraction for Garibaldi was the Colonel's wife, Mary. The three-times married Garibaldi had an affair with her over several years.

A relative of the Colonel's was General Jack Seely, a friend of Winston Churchill. He was Secretary of State for War in 1914 and was forced to resign over the Curragh crisis, when English Black and Tans, soldiers based in Kildare, refused to take on the Ulster Unionists. The General had a meritorious First World War, but the real hero was his horse, Warrior, who survived half a dozen of the bloodiest battles in France. Warrior had short legs and was a regular winner of point-to-point races in the Isle of Wight. Being shorter than the other horses, he seemed to miss all the fire. The General recommended him for the Victoria Cross, saying, rather immodestly, 'He went everywhere I went.' The War Minister thought it was inappropriate for a horse to be given a VC. Warrior was still going strong at the age of thirty-three, when General Seely felt that the extra corn rations needed to keep the hero alive couldn't be justified. The heroic horse went to heaven, according to the racing writer Brough Scott, who is related to the Seelys.

Charles Salisbury was also supposed to be the sports master at the college but although he was keen on sport, he wasn't good at either cricket or football. Snooker was his game. Some of the parents failed to pay up the half-crown voluntary subscription to cover the cost of sports equipment, so we had to manage with a battered old cricket bat, one pair of pads, and two pairs of gloves for cricket practice, plus one sad-looking leather football. I started to watch well-attended games – up to 500 people would turn up on a Sunday – at the Ventnor CC. At the tea interval, my best friend Jed Steele and I took turns to bat and bowl on the outfield, close to the pavilion. We borrowed a wooden chair as the wicket. Some of the watching players were impressed with our ability and invited us to come along to the nets. I remember bowling to the first team opener Frank Cowley, who urged us on by putting a sixpence on the stumps. If we managed to bowl him out, we would collect the sixpences. We did, on a regular basis, so he soon stopped that practice.

Jed developed into an exceptionally good left-handed batsman. His father was an expert on building television sets in the early 1950s, when sets were not on ready sale. We watched the 1953 FA Cup Final on Mr Steele's small, homemade set – the Stanley Matthews final, which should have been known as the Stan Mortensen final, because Mortensen scored three goals in Blackpool's 4-3 victory. The screen was fuzzy, and it was hard to see what was going on.

By the time I was fourteen, I was playing for the second team, bowling slow left arm Chinamen and batting number eleven. No one asked about my awkward gait and the captain, 'Brisher' White, usually put me where the most chasing was done in the outfield. He bowled slow, high-flighted leg breaks pitched well outside the leg stump, with eight fielders on the leg side. He took wickets regularly, mainly from catches, and it seemed odd that no one else copied this unusual strategy. Would Monty Panesar take more wickets if he followed the Brisher method? I started off with five successive ducks, but at a game on a small, sloping ground right next to Parkhurst Prison, Brisher told me he wanted me to open the batting. He must have recognised the quality of my forward defensive shots. 'Get your head down and I want to see you still batting up to tea,' he said. The grass was long and the pitch sluggish in pace, and after an hour I managed just a single. In my second hour at the crease, I scored another single. A run per hour! That must be a record! After ten minutes more in the middle, with tea about to be called, I snicked a full toss to the third man and with no fielder nearby, we ran three, more than doubling my total. The innings closed at 69-9 with our new opening batsman on five not out. At tea there was a raffle and I drew the winning prize, a box of chocolates. I went on to take three cheap wickets and we won by ten runs.

The deputy governor congratulated me. 'Well done my boy,' he said. 'Next time we'll lock you up – you've driven away all the spectators.' Parkhurst was one of my favourite pocket-sized grounds; now it is an empty space.

Fifty-eight years later it was like rerunning an old film. With my left knee still causing problems, I wasn't intending to play at Frant on 15 September 2008, but the Woodpeckers were one short. Frant is one of the oddest long-established village grounds in the country and the drop from the east side to the west is at least sixty feet, six times more than at Lord's. It is sometimes difficult to stay upright, especially when both legs are wobbly like mine. Frant's pitch is always helpful to the bowlers and on this day the ball seamed around, shot along the ground, and bounced higher than usual. I opened and as our attacking batsmen started to topple from catches, treading on their stumps and running themselves out, I decided to repeat my Parkhurst episode. I batted through the forty-six overs with a succession of runners in two and a half hours and the Woodpeckers made just sixty-five. I thought I might have scraped into double figures, but the scorer said, 'You only got seven and there were no fours or sixes. But six watchers fell asleep.' Frant were on 38-7 at one stage but with the help of twenty-one extras, they scraped through to victory.

Chris Tooley, the former Oxford University captain who kept wicket, said, 'You might have set a world record: the first batsman with eight runners to bat through the whole of the innings.'

The next day I checked with Bill Frindall. 'It might well have been, scoring just seven, one short of your runners, but Lancashire's Graeme Fowler batted through the innings twice in the same county match against Warwickshire at Southport in 1982,' he said. 'He pulled a muscle in the field and David Lloyd ran for his unbeaten 100. And in the second innings, he scored 128 not out.' Ah, but he didn't have eight runners.

Most cricketers believe that a batsman cannot call for a runner unless he is taken ill or injured during a game. But a player named Ian Harris, who had an artificial leg after a farming accident, was banned by a league in Cornwall in 1993, and he appealed. The matter was referred to Marylebone CC, the game's lawmakers, and John Stephenson – the late secretary, not the present John Stephenson, MCC's Director of Cricket – ruled that a permanently disabled cricketer should be allowed to have a runner. 'Otherwise, no disabled player could play the game,' he said.

I never looked on myself as being disabled, and I could bowl long spells without much bother. I had figures of 7-5-7-7 while bowling out the 70th Heavy Ack-Ack Royal Artillery for thirty-one at Ventnor when I was sixteen. My skipper, Syd Coleman, obviously thought seven overs was too few and on the next day he had me bowling twenty-one overs in succession to take 6-52. I never felt tired and my leg stood up to the pounding of my right boot on the bowling crease. Unlike the other, faster, bowlers, I came off an eleven-yard run up at Shanklin and one of the reasons for that was the dip at the top end, a relic of the ground-staged tennis tournaments before the Second World War. I didn't want to trip over it, so I started my run from that point. Most of our opponents were villages, and played out in the country. We travelled by bus because most of us didn't have cars, and those who did loved having a few drinks in a pub after the end of play. In one game at Westover, I was in my usual place in the field, on the leg side, when a batsman pioneered a kind of reverse sweep, sending one of Brisher's deliveries high towards extra cover. The ball landed in a cow pat with a loud splosh.

'Brian!' he shouted.

I looked round and saw at least half a dozen fielders closer to the ball than me.

'Come on,' he shouted. 'It's yours.'

I ran towards the heap of brown excrement and gingerly extracted the brownish coloured ball. There was no running water and I tried to clean my hands by rubbing them into the grass. The smell lingered for some time, and some of the others complained about the aroma when tea was taken.

Ventnor's Wednesday side wanted an opening bowler, so I opened the bowling with medium-fast deliveries, with the idea of swinging it both ways. It didn't always work, but on two occasions I bowled through the innings. I still remember the figures: 25-5-17-5 in one game, and 25-7-25-5 in the other.

Today any sixteen-year-old would only be allowed to bowl seven overs before he came off. The England and Wales Cricket Board still sticks to that outdated edict and most experts, chiefly Bob Willis and Sir Alec Bedser, say it is ludicrous. 'The way to build up your body is to bowl,' said Sir Alec. 'It never harmed me.'

Sir Alec was one of my best contacts over the years and when his twin, Eric, died in May 2006, Sir Alec's friends feared he wouldn't pass the age of ninety; the pair had been inseparable. They used to dress the same way and Eric had once said, 'Our lives have been so close that we are, for all purposes, one. We share everything and have never fallen out.'

The Surrey committee gave them £20 worth of premium bonds when they retired in 1961 and they stuck their envelopes in a drawer at their home in Woking and forgot about them. On the same date in January, thirty-one years later, they each opened their separate envelopes and found £500 prizes. Said Alec: 'We asked an expert to calculate the odds against that and he said, "Start at 20 billion to one."' After Eric died, Alec rekindled a long-term friendship with a lady named Christine. She spent a lot of time with him until she too died, in 2008. Alec finally passed away in 2010, but right up to the end, he was talking good cricket sense.

The Isle of Wight has never produced an international footballer or cricketer. There have been a number of League footballers and county cricketers, but no real stars. At 147 square miles, it is roughly the same size as Barbados, yet Barbados has supplied seventy-two Test players out of the overall total of 269 West Indian Test players. It must be the weather. Barbados has never had a full day rained off in Test matches.

At the end of the 1952 season, Terence Dudley, the director at the repertory company and one of the batsmen, came up to me and said, 'What's happened to your leg? Have you hurt it?'

'I've had that since I was seven,' I told him.

'Oh,' he said.

Well, he *was* rather short-sighted. By this time, I was fifteen and in the first team. One of the most amusing incidents came when the Botham of the team, Peter Mabey, who ran a post office (this was before post offices were closed around the country by Adam Crozier, the former chief executive of the Football Association). Peter pulled a short ball straight towards our veteran umpire, Johnny Douglas, who was sitting on his shooting stick. The projectile was coming straight at Johnny's private parts. Horrified, Johnny threw himself backwards, his legs sticking into the air... and the ball smacked into his backside. He was very relieved.

Playing so much sport – I played tennis and table tennis as well as cricket and football, and occasionally boxed – didn't stop me carrying on with my part-time writing. After homework most days, I wrote my reports on the home football games at Ventnor and hid them away in a cupboard. They weren't that good. I also wrote a weekly sports article in a large book, as though I was the next Desmond Hackett – the *Daily Express* sports writer who was known as 'the man with the brown bowler'. One piece was about Randolph Turpin beating Sugar Ray Robinson on points and then being knocked out by Robinson in the return fight in the Madison Square Garden ring, sixty-four days later. Twelve years on, when I was working for the *Daily Sketch*, I was sent to cover a fight at Earls Court, and sitting behind me was Randolph Turpin. He kept jumping up and shouting advice, but it was impossible to catch what he was saying. It was obvious that he was suffering from brain damage. It had a profound effect on me. Up to then I was keen on boxing but seeing the state of Turpin, and the way some ill-mannered people were behaving, almost like savages, soon ended my love affair with the 'sweet science'. Within a few years, Turpin had committed suicide by shooting himself in the head.

When I was fourteen, I had written to Desmond Hackett asking for advice on becoming a national sports writer. He wrote, 'Dear Mr Scovell. The advice I have for you is to leave the Isle of Wight immediately.' He was right – but it took me eight years to depart. When I achieved my objective, I became a good friend of Des. He had a cheeky approach to life and he didn't take himself seriously. Before the days of television, he was able to get away with writing some outrageous articles, many of which were made up. Once, after an England game in Rio de Janeiro, he wrote, 'Bonfires were being lit all over the Maracana Stadium in celebration of Brazil's historic win.'

A *Daily Express* sub editor cabled him, saying ,'It's been pissing down with rain out in Rio. There weren't any bonfires mate!'

Today sports writing is virtually dictated by editors and inside men, who watch the events on televisions in their offices. They have a better view of what is happening than the writers who are actually present at these events. They also give orders about how stories are handled. If the writer is strongly opinionated and insists on doing it his way, he could find himself out of a job. A Des Hackett wouldn't survive today.

The first piece I ever wrote in the *Isle of Wight Mercury* was a letter under the heading 'Correspondence'. It was published on 9 March 1951. I was fourteen. It said, 'Sir. May I point out that a very high proportion of the fouling of pavements by dogs is caused by unaccompanied dogs. It is to be deplored that people in possession of dogs should not devote time to their exercise. Signed B. D. Scovell.' Rather pompous, I feel. Having taken three dogs out twice a day, and often let them off their leads, I was one of the prime causes of this outbreak of pooing and peeing in the streets of Lower Ventnor. The next edition carried several letters supporting me. If the National Statistics people had counts of dog fouling, Ventnor would be close to the top of the league. Now it is an offence, yet you still don't see many people picking up the mess and putting it into a plastic bag.

Charles Salisbury directed me to *The Willings Press Guide*. He said, 'This has all the details of the newspapers and magazines and this may be useful to you.'

I took it out from the library and renewed it so many times that the man in charge told me, 'This time will be the final one, someone else might want it!'

I looked up the address of the *Daily Mail* and wrote to the editor, asking if I could visit its offices, 'because I want to be a sports writer'. He passed it to someone else and after a short time a letter had arrived from the personnel officer explaining that the *Mail* arranged occasional tours of Northcliffe House, where the newspaper is produced. It finished, 'If you wanted to come along, let me know.' This was like bowling out Denis Compton with one of my Chinamen. What joy! Just like me, Denis used to bowl that unusual left-handed delivery, the wrist spinner that turned into the right-hand batman. Amazingly, in 1961, I played in Brian Statham's benefit match at Didsbury CC and I had him caught for seventy-five off one. There was a crowd of around 3,000 and they were hoping he would reach a century. The pitch was damp and as the ball slipped out of my hand, his attempted drive went straight up into the air and I hoped that someone else would try to catch it, not me. But I hardly had to move, and with a feeling of guilt, I caught the ball. As Denis walked off, smiling, he patted me on the back. He was a true sportsman and a hero.

I wrote to the personnel manager at the *Mail* and he wrote back, asking me to report at Northcliffe House, at the bottom of Carmelite Street, at 11 p.m. on a certain day. I thought it must have been a mistake – 11 p.m.? I rang him and he said, 'Oh no, the print doesn't get started close to midnight.'

I was fourteen, a school boy, yet to visit London. My mother knew an obscure aunt living on Prince of Wales Road in Kentish Town and wrote to her, asking if she could help. She wrote back, saying she would pick me up at Waterloo and take me by bus to her home, have tea, and then tell me how to get to Fleet Street. She wasn't willing to go with me for some reason, but would give me a bed in her second bedroom. So I went on my own and returned on a night bus, arriving at around 2 a.m. My first impression inside the attractive stone building – which was named after Alfred Harmsworth, later Lord Northcliffe, who founded the *Mail* in 1896 – was the noise. Inside the editorial floor, there was a gabble of noise, people shouting and cursing, typewriters crackling away, bits of news being rushed from one point to another by an overhead carriage system... Cigarette and cigar butts and paper of all kinds littered the place. Telephones were constantly ringing and reporters were scribbling down details about the next day's stories. They would tap out their piece, rip the paper out of the typewriter, and shout, 'Copy!' Young boys would arrive, take the copy, and take it to the sub editors' room for editing.

Today it is the opposite. Mainly stern young men sit at their computers, hardly speaking for hour after hour. What was the worst damage to health, the smoke and dirtiness of the 1950s, or the sore eyes and dull minds of the 2000s? I would say neither – I would prefer to be out watching sport and writing about it, not sitting in offices.

A dozen or so other people were on the conducted tour, and I was by far the youngest. One or two reporters with ties and smoothed-down hair came up and welcomed me, but it was difficult to have a proper conversation. We were ushered to the basement, where the newspaper was to be printed, and after a man explained what was happening, the switch was turned on and with a mighty roar, the machines sprang to life and a huge roll of newsprint unrolled on the presses. The words of the journalists were printed and the paper was transformed into copies of a newspaper, which were automatically made up into parcels. The smell was awful, choking. Men were waiting outside the open sections to pick up the parcels and throw them into the vans, which filled the streets, blocking the traffic. When a van was filled, the driver sped off to one of the mainline railways stations and disgorged the parcels, ready for the night trains. It was very exciting.

Just under ten years later, I started working in Fleet Street and eventually became a *Daily Mail* man. In my youth, I had never read the *Mail*. My mother preferred the *Daily Express*, which sold more copies than any other newspaper of the day. Today, national newspapers are printed with the push of a button in various parts of the country. It may be more effective and easy, but it doesn't capture the excitement I experienced so many years ago.

Before the introduction of technology, far behind almost every other industry, the newspaper trade was virtually run by Luddites, stubborn trade unionists who refused to move with the times. More than 100 years ago, copy was transferred to hot metal by the fingertips of expert linotype machine operators; this printing process was used until the early 1970s. Phantom 'employees', with names like Mickey Mouse and Donald Duck, were drawing casual wages, and it took some time before the new bosses, headed by Rupert Murdoch, ended the corruption and moved to new quarters. Fleet Street and its environs were full of public houses, built hundreds of years previously, which had late closing times to accommodate the newspaper workers, including the journalists. Most of the writers were excessive drinkers, and some became alcholics.

One day I was looking through a list of books written by journalists in the Ventnor Library when I noticed the name of an author, John Macadam. I had read his work in the *Daily Express* and I ordered a copy. Entitled *The Macadam Road*, it cost 75d and I finished it inside a day. Macadam came from the Scots school of writing, where they love frothy descriptions of people and events. The chapter that affected me more than any other was about Benny Lynch, the Scottish boxer, who died at an early age because of his alcoholism. Macadam, born in Glasgow, went into journalism after working in a shipyard, and was employed by half of the leading newspapers in Scotland before going to Fleet Street, where he worked for the *Sunday Dispatch*, the *News Chronicle*, the *Daily Express*, and the *Daily Sketch*. His face was dominated by a huge handlebar moustache. Fellow Scotsman Ken Montgomery, the chief executive of the Football Writers' Association, who knew him well, said, 'He was a bit of a cranky man but what a writer!'

Macadam rose to become a squadron leader in the RAF and claimed to have taken part in the D-Day invasion and the battle of Arnhem. He was treated with derision when he tipped Tommy Farr to beat Joe Louis in 1938, and the fight went the distance. In his book he claimed, 'I nearly interviewed Hitler.' Like Lynch, Macadam was a heavy drinker himself, and when I met him in 1961 I soon realised that he had a serious drinking problem. Sadly, he died at the age of sixty-three. He should have heeded the words he had written almost thirty years previously about the tragic Benny Lynch.

When I joined the *Sketch* in 1960, it was common to see the best of the journalists staggering out of pubs and hailing taxis at all times of day and night. Hardly any of them were able to drive themselves home. Their wives must have had lonely lives.

The sight of seeing my Scots grandfather behaving in a similar fashion had already convinced me that being a teetotaller was the right course to follow.

Except for an experience when I was about to rise to speak at the annual dinner of the Podington CC in Northamptonshire, many years later, I have never touched alcohol. On that occasion, I had been drinking Coca-Cola, and my glass was almost empty as I got up. The chairman said, 'Do you want a refill?'

Without seeing that he had a bottle of wine in his hand and not a bottle of coke, I said, 'Yes please.' I picked up the full glass, took a gulp and swallowed it straight down before I realised it was wine. It wasn't one of my better speeches.

These days journalists are so busy thumping away on their laptops that they have very little time to drink. The proprietors moved the newspapers to places like Wapping, Canary Wharf, the old Barkers Building in Kensington, and other distant places, far away from Fleet Street. Some sports writers still like a drinking session, but it is nothing compared to the days of Macadam and his drinking friends. The bankers are now the big drinkers in the City of London, not the journalists. I think I made the right choice of profession.

I read heavyweight books written by politicians in my youth, including all six volumes of Harold Macmillan's memoirs. He was one of my heroes. I liked his style and he was known as being unflappable. I also read many volumes written by and about Winston Churchill. After he died, his body was laid in state in Westminster in 1965 and Audrey and I queued up half the night to file past his coffin. I was sixteen when I first covered a political meeting, at Ryde Town Hall. The speaker was Aneurin Bevan, the Labour Health Minister who brought in the National Health Service in 1950 and threatened to resign if the Government charged for spectacles. The charge was dropped and Bevan stayed in office. He had a mop of white hair and spoke like a charged-up evangelist. I wrote in my piece in the *Mercury*, 'Mr Bevan stated that he was thirteen when he went to work down the pits in South Wales, like his father and brothers before him. He did not want to go but had to because he was on a social escalator and landed there. He found in 1921 that the nation did not want miners or steel workers and families were on the verge of starvation. In his spare time he read history books and come across great names like the Cecils, the Stanleys, and the Churchills. Some had been there since the sixteenth century, and when he entered Parliament they were still there, opposite him. From 1924, there were 2 million people unemployed. The Tories in the Isle of Wight slept, woke up to place a cross opposite St Peter's name, and they went to sleep again.' He was a rousing speaker and preached hate as well as good sense. His phrase about the Tories – 'lower than vermin' – stuck with him. He could have been another Lloyd George, but I felt he alienated too many people with his inner rage.

The best political speaker I ever heard was Oswald Mosley, the leader of the Blackshirts, who supported Nazism. One weekend, I went to see him speak in Trafalgar Square and his voice and delivery swayed thousands. What he said was vile; he spouted hate through a microphone. Immature people were taken in by it and up until the Second World War, he attracted thousands of members to the British Union of Fascists.

In another meeting in Newport, I heard Quintin Hogg, a Conservative minister who specialised in ringing a bell to attract interest. He, too, was an impassioned speaker, and he came up with a marvellous retort to a heckler who kept interrupting his speech. 'Listen to me, young man,' he said, 'when you have a double first at Oxford, as I have, you can speak. If not, sit down and be quiet!' The audience roared with laughter. This part of electioneering has died out, sadly.

Late in 1953, I received a letter from the Portsmouth Ministry of Labour and National Service saying that I had to attend a medical for the purposes of signing up. Every male over eighteen who was fit was conscripted into the services for a period of two years. The pay was minimal, but there were opportunities to travel around the British Empire. It sounded enticing. When I arrived at the board – all expenses paid – I said to the senior officer, 'I have a stiff right leg, so do I need to be examined?' I pulled up my trouser to show my scar and I flexed the knee a few degrees.

'Oh,' he said. 'But you'll have to be examined.'

One part of the test was to cough as the doctor held your testicles. He told me, 'Other than your right knee, everything is working very well indeed.'

An hour later I was called in to see an RAF officer and he said, 'Bad news my boy. You've failed. I would be happy to take you into the RAF – you're officer material, no doubt about that.'

I had been asked which branch of the services I preferred and I nominated the RAF despite not having flown. The officer gave me a green card, 'VNT 1283', saying, 'B. D. Scovell was examined at Portsmouth on 14 December 1953 and was placed in Grade Four.' There was no Grade Five. My registration expired six years later and by then National Service had ended. Nowadays there is a call for it to be restarted to curb the stabbings, shootings, and general lawlessness that includes young people brutally beating older people to death in the streets.

I would oppose that. We should not give guns to young men and train them with a view of killing anyone, even in war. They should play more sport and be inspired by heroes. But we don't have any British-born heroes in this country and haven't had any for some time. The globalisation of sport needs to be reversed in this country, to allow more places for our own performers – the successors to Denis Compton, Sir Stanley Matthews, George Best, and others. Free kit should be supplied by the Government to those who want to join the Scouts, or any other organisations that take young people away from their computers and Playstations and also keep them off of the streets late at night, forsaking binge drinking and drugs. Grants for university students could be rearranged so that part of the money goes to paying for graduates to help in developing countries in their gap years. Instead of moaning – 'There is nothing to do!' 'I don't know what I am going to do!' – they should learn compassion for people who haven't had the same opportunities. They should respect others, and it would be to their own benefit. Be ambitious, determined and love what you are doing. Here endeth the sermon!

CHAPTER FIVE

'My Son Is a Better Football Reporter than Your Football Correspondent!'

One day my mother was rummaging around in a drawer, and she found one of my football reports of a Ventnor FC match. She read it and came into my bedroom, waving it. 'That's a well-written article, you ought to get it published in the *Mercury*,' she said.

She knew Roy Wearing, the editor of the *Isle of Wight Mercury* and the son of the chief executive of the local council. When I took the dogs out, I often walked along to the end of the Esplanade, where the rollerskating rink was situated, and watched him playing hockey in matches. He also played cricket for Ventnor. I didn't really know him, but my mother insisted that we should come together to see him and tell him that I should be hired immediately. The next day, we turned up at his little office and she asked him, 'What do you think of Brian's little article?'

Roy, who was a nice and friendly man, read it and said, 'Yes, he's got a bit of talent.'

My mother wasn't satisfied with that faint praise. 'He's a better football reporter than your football correspondent,' she told him.

Roy was rather startled. I was still at school, fourteen years old, and with no O-levels to my name. Fred Hunt wrote the reports of the first team matches, and he worked in the printing department. He wasn't a proper journalist. 'Well, I think I can get Brian to come along and write a short piece about the second team matches,' he said. 'We'll see how it goes. If it is printed, I'll pay him seven and six [roughly 37p].'

My first match was at home against Parkhurst Reserves (there were no prisoners among their players). My article, about 650 words in length, filled two-thirds of a column. It featured the ringing phrase, 'Kicking towards the Hospital End of the field in the first half, the home side were the first to threaten danger when a shot from Godsell went inches wide of the goal.'

It was ghastly, but looking through my cuttings years later, I noticed a scribbled line, saying, 'Written in collaboration with F. Hunt.' So blame Fred! Roy was happy with his recruit and when Fred was ill (he never took a holiday), I filled in for him.

I travelled with the team bus and had to be careful about what I wrote. My introduction in the report of the 2-2 draw at Apse Heath started, 'The standard of play in this match was very poor. Some of the Ventnor players didn't try hard enough.'

At the next match I was standing on the halfway line when a middle aged Irish woman rushed towards me brandishing a rolled-up umbrella. 'You silly, stupid boy,' she screamed. 'How dare you criticise my boys! Get out of it, go!' She started hitting me around the back of my head with her brolly. Several men roared with laughter and one held her back and that ended the bombardment. I learned that she was employed as the cleaner at the public toilets and was known as 'Miss Flush'. She was a regular watcher of the matches and after the next game, when I praised Ventnor's performance, she went up to me and apologised. 'You were quite right,' she said.

The following season, the club secretary wrote to the *Mercury*, saying that 'unfair things had been written about the team and some players had the left the club because of it. This has to stop.' I defended myself in another article and a letter appeared as well, written by the same lady who had attacked me. This time she supported me.

With all this writing, I had to buy a typewriter, but with little money spare from the family's weekly income, I had pay for it myself from the money I earned from the old lady who owned the two dogs I took out daily. I had to sign up a hire purchase agreement, paying 30s a month for eighteen months, which was a total outlay of £30, including interest. The machine was supposed to be a portable one, but it was in a heavy wooden box and it wasn't easy to carry it around to places like Lord's and Wembley Stadium when I eventually joined the *Daily Sketch*. I used that Remington Rand typewriter for almost fifty years, churning out millions of words, and I still have it, although it lies idle after a succession of Microsoft laptops, which seem to last no more than two years apiece.

I enlisted with a secretarial school to learn typing, and found myself the only male. The stern-looking lady in charge handed me a type of bib that I had to attach to the typewriter, making it impossible to see the keyboard. She also presented me with a card that carried the letters and notations of the keys. 'You've got to do it by typing by touch,' she said. 'Otherwise, you will finish up using only two fingers.' Soon I was working at sixty words a minute, than eighty, using all the fingers. I also signed up to learn Pitman shorthand. Again, I was the only male. It was hard going, trying to scribble down these odd hieroglyphics while she dictated boring bank reports. Nowadays, most journalists use a more modern way of fast writing. Nearly all use tape recorders. Late in my career, I bought a tape recorder and soon lost it. I never bought another. During the World Cup in Mexico in 1986, one of my best friends, Harry Miller of the *Daily Mirror* (who sadly died of cancer at a relatively young age), recorded an interview with a senior FIFA officer about security, and when we left the room, he said, 'That should give us a back-page lead.' Back at the hotel, he turned on his recorder and all he could hear was the background noise, which drowned the words of the FIFA man. It taught me a lesson: you can't rely on a tape recorder every time. Your memory is the best aid for a journalist. You need to remember key phrases and fortunately I have a good memory. A shorthand note, of course, is still very useful... *if* you are successful in transcribing it into English, which sometimes doesn't happen.

Another good lesson is: don't trust quotes passed on by other journalists, unless it is played back from a tape recorder or vouched by people you can rely on. In the final minute of a match between West Ham and West Bromwich Albion at Upton Park in 1982, West Ham captain Billy Bonds, one of the game's most renowned tacklers, slid into one of the Albion midfielders right in front of the dugout, under the overlooking press box, and was sent high into the air. Ronnie Allen, the Albion manager, and his staff all jumped, shouting, 'Get him off, ref!' The referee disagreed, awarded a free kick against West Ham. The game resumed.

Before press interview rooms were introduced, the football writers at Upton Park stood in the corridor outside the dressing rooms to interview the manager and players – those who wanted to speak. Those who didn't want to walked past. Ronnie Allen, whom I knew well from his days at Crystal Palace and who played in a number of cricket matches I organised, came out and a man from *The Sun* asked him, 'What about that tackle by Billy Bonds?'

Allen didn't want to be too critical, and said, 'Well, it wasn't nice, but I don't want to stoke it up.' Allen left and walked through to the hall and out to the car park to go to his car. The *Sun* man followed him and continued talking to him. The rest of us were still in the corridor, waiting for the West Ham players.

Ten minutes later, the *Sun* reporter returned and said, 'Allen has called Bonds a gorilla. That will make a good headline!'

I said, 'Are you sure?'

He said, 'Yes, I've got it written down.'

We took his word for it and the headline in *The Sun* was 'Bonzo the Gorilla'. The headline of my piece was more restrained: 'Allen doesn't bother Bonds.' Allen was quoted: 'I couldn't see how Bonds was allowed to stay on the field. He was running about like a gorilla.'

A month later, I was in the corridor outside the dressing rooms at the Dell when Allen came out, saw me, and started screaming abuse. 'You ****, I never used that word gorilla,' he said. 'It made me look like a fool.' The door of the Southampton dressing room opened and several of Lawrie McMenemy's staff popped out to see what was happening. The referee and his assistants all came out of their room as well.

That was the last time I saw Allen that day, but at the end of the season I was queuing up at Heathrow to check my passport and ticket for the trip to Bilbao at the start of the 1982 World Cup when I turned around to see Allen approaching. He had been appointed by the FA as an adviser to Ron Greenwood's squad. I expected another outburst. Instead, he came up and shook hands. We had many laughs about that.

Billy Bonds lives in Bromley near me, and we still talk about his King Kong exploits. Bill is a thoroughly genuine man who loves playing cricket. He was one of the most admired and loved players at Upton Park and was very upset when he was sacked as manager ten days before the season started in 1994. He had been at the club for twenty-seven years and found himself replaced by his assistant, Harry Redknapp, whom he once described as 'a bit of a monkey'. His abrupt dismissal ended their friendship. Today he laments the fact that tackling has almost disappeared from the English game. 'It's a great art and the fans love it,' he recently told me.

The gorilla affair brings back memories of another of England's most feared tacklers, Peter Storey of Arsenal. I always had a good relationship with Bertie Mee, who managed Arsenal between 1966 and 1976. He was very keen to give me his ex-directory telephone number. Over the years, he was extremely helpful – a real gentleman. He was the club's physiotherapist until he was appointed manager, and this calm and stately man built up a team and a spirit that took Arsenal to the heights; they won the Double in 1970-71.

One day in 1962 I went to see him at Highbury and he invited me into his office. I always asked managers, 'Any young talent coming through?'

He said, 'Yes, Peter Storey, who has just signed on his seventeenth birthday. I think he will play for England. Come and meet him.' We went downstairs to the marble-floored dressing room, much more spacious and stylish than the Wembley dressing rooms, and sitting alone was this tall, dark-haired young man. He was very shy and it was difficult to get much out of him. He came from Farnham, the Surrey town that later produced England cricketer Graham Thorpe, whom I know well. Both men were single-minded, tough and unrelenting. But, in the main, decent men. Storey played for England on nineteen occasions yet few of the critics gave him much credit. Bertie Mee and Alf Ramsey had a different opinion: they both recognised his worth.

In 1976, Storey had some personal problems and Mee, who was also on his way out of Highbury, was willing to let him go. Vic Railton, the Cockney football writer of the *Evening News*, carried a story about his problems and I was asked to follow it up. Vic was one of the outstanding news gatherers of the day, sitting at his office ringing up contacts all day long and into the night. He rarely went to a live game. These days, a Vic Railton wouldn't exist, because today's footballing personalities are shielded by agents and few give out their telephone numbers. Railton was relentless, and he never gave up. One day he wanted to know the verdict at an FA disciplinary hearing concerning corruption at a certain club. He rang the press officer. 'I've got to get the verdict in time for the second edition,' he said.

'It will be put on the PA agency when the decision is reached,' replied the press officer.

'You stupid prat,' said Vic, as he slammed down the phone.

He swore in almost every sentence. Often he rang the wives of footballers, saying, 'Where's that **** of a husband? I need to speak to him!'

I was sitting in the FA hall, close to the room where the case was being heard, and after the announcement was made, too late for Vic's edition, the press officer confided that the hearing was just finishing and the phone was ringing on the table. Sir Matt Busby was on the panel and he answered it.

'Matt,' said Railton, 'I've got to get the story in by twelve. What happened?'

Matt was so surprised that he let slip the official decision. That's called persistence. Vic ran up a record number of scoops before he collapsed and died from a heart attack, and he was still on the job in his final days.

The day after Railton's piece about Peter Storey, I wrote a few paragraphs about the footballer's problems. After the next conference, the sports editor asked me to go to see Storey for an interview. I knew Storey would be at his pub, the Jolly Farmers in Islington, and I was rather hesitant about going without any protection. 'He won't welcome me,' I said.

The boss smiled. 'Don't worry,' he said, 'we've got a French photographer on trial and he can come along to sort Storey out.' He introduced the Frenchman... who was shorter than Nicolas Sarkozy! I drove my Rover 2000 – I have never had a company car in the forty years that I worked with Associated Newspapers – and parked right outside the pub, ready for a quick getaway if things went wrong. The pub had swing doors, like the set of a western, and as I went into the main bar, Storey, dressed in a black leather jacket, and two of his friends, similarly dressed like mafia men, saw me, screamed, and charged towards me. I turned swiftly around and went out, leaving the swing doors to crash into Storey. That gave me a half a second's advantage as I ran around my car, jumped in, and turned on the ignition. The Frenchman was about to step out of the vehicle but with a look of fear, he got back and slammed the door, just in time, because an over-the-ball tackle from Storey's right boot thundered into it, leaving a slight dent. I shot off, leaving Storey shouting expletives.

Later in the season, he was playing for Fulham and I was reporting a match at Carrow Road. I was standing in the corridor waiting for interviews when the away dressing room opened and Storey, who hadn't played, emerged pushing the skip down the corridor. It was like a clash of the gunslingers, me against Pete. I couldn't run off this time. As the skip approached me, Pete looked up and smiled, holding out a hand. 'How are you?' he said.

Despite the pub incident and some of the other things he got up to, I have always found him a good companion, with a sense of humour. It was sad to see him end up the way he did. In 1979 he was fined for running a brothel and later served time in prison for a variety of crimes, including counterfeiting and importing pornography videos. Early in 2008 he sold his nine-carat-gold FA Cup winner's medal and Football League winner's plaque from the 1970/71 Double. They made him £28,000. In today's climate, he would have earned more than that in a week. Like many outstanding footballers of his generation, he was born too soon. He mixed with the wrong people. Now he living in France, happily married to a French lady.

In my shorthand days at Newport in the early 1950s, the prettiest girl in the room was the daughter of one of the directors of the company that owned the *Isle of Wight County Press*. I had several chats with her and she gave me the address of the editor so that I could write and apply for a job as a trainee journalist. Knowing a relative of one of the bosses proved to be a disadvantage. I soon had a brief letter of rejection from the editor and the director and his family moved house before I had the chance to make the proposition I had rehearsed: 'Let's go and see the latest Ealing Studios comedy starring Alastair Sim.'

I asked Roy Wearing if he could offer me a job at the *Mercury*, but he was apologetic. 'We haven't got any money,' he said. The other small newspapers at Shanklin, Sandown, and Ryde also had no vacancies. The multi-talented Roy was appointed editor at the age of twenty and when he retired through illness at the age of fifty-four he had brought out 2,000 weekly editions and written almost 45 million words. The majority of the papers were hand-set and folded by hand.

There was no chance of me going on to further education, and I had to leave school at the end of the year – after my fifteenth birthday – without any prospect of a job. For a while I was on the dole, which was demeaning. The spare time gave me the opportunity to study at home for my final three O-level examinations, which I passed. Later I took the four A-levels I needed to enter the National Council for the Training of Journalists' course, with a view to gaining the Certificate of Training and then the National Diploma, the equivalent of a university degree. I passed the four A-level subjects in British Constitution, Economics, English, and English Literature – all softies – by taking postal courses and working at home. The postal costs were enormous. It kept me busy and it took several years before I was presented with my Certificate in 1957 and my National Diploma two years later.

In the summer of 1951, I was playing three cricket matches a week, chiefly because I was unable to get a job. The Ministry of Labour staff were becoming fed up with my failure to find one and by October they offered me a post as junior clerk in the finance department of the Isle of Wight County Council. I had to take it at a miserly salary of £150 a year, but it left me time to read books on the hour-long bus journey into Newport and back home in the evening, in time for cricket practice. Dealing with the public cured my shyness and taking the refreshment tray around twice a day helped my relations with the young girls on the staff. We all had tedious jobs and needed a few laughs.

I was still writing my football pieces in the *Isle of Wight Mercury*, so when the first county championship cricket match took place between Hampshire and Worcestershire at J. S. White's ground in Cowes, I turned up with a letter from Roy Wearing saying that I was the cricket correspondent. I was let in and sat in the tented press box alongside some of the leading national newspaper writers. Rather boldly, I volunteered to phone their copy and I still have their reports handwritten in pencil. There was no available telephone at the ground, and I had to go to the nearest houses, knock on doors, and ask permission to make a reverse-charge call. Harry Ditton of the *News of the World* and Barry O'Brien of the *Sunday Dispatch* gave me 5s between them to be telephonist. I named the wrong newspaper when I approached the first householder. When mentioned the *News of the World*, the man shouted, 'I'm not going to talk to them, get out!' I knew Harry Ditton later in life and he was a lovely man. You couldn't imagine the sports editor of a newspaper owned by Rupert Murdoch hiring someone like him; he was too nice!

My two years as a civil servant was acutely frustrating, but at least I had time to pass a few more examinations and improve my education. When I was interviewed by Leslie Baines, the Clerk of the County Council, I had to produce my National Registration Identity Card, which was first given to me at the age of five. My mother had signed it on my behalf. It was a simple card, 'EPHB 145 4', stamped with my address. I still have it. ID cards were phased out, but a similar document, if issued today, wouldn't cause a run on the pound and might help catch the criminals and terrorists who are harming this country. So many young people today claim they are bored and use that as an excuse for bad behaviour, but I tried to fill every waking day by studying, reading, exercising the dog, helping with the washing up in the summer when my mother ran her B&B, playing cricket, football, table tennis, and tennis, going to the cinema twice or three times a week, writing letters, ogling girls, and helping with the shopping. It was all very enjoyable, but I knew I had to get a full-time job as a sports writer.

Twenty20 cricket was said to be invented in this country in 2003, but it wasn't. After the Second World War, a number of 'limited over' leagues were formed around the country. Most of them were twenty-over-a-side matches, played from 6 p.m. onwards to get the games finished before dark. Those were the days of the six-day week, and these evening matches gave young people the opportunity to play some cricket. I played for NALGO, the local government union, and my opening partner Ed Satherley and I relished the conditions. Matting was unrolled onto a concrete pitch and it was ideal for quicker bowlers. Ed was a great character and still is. Dark and swarthy, he tore up to the wicket like Ian Wooldridge's character 'Terror Tomkins' (invented for a *Mail* column), and he probably hit more unprotected batsmen than anyone in the Isle of Wight. We had some good cricketers in that league and some of them tried to play the game the right way – *The MCC Cricket Coaching Book* way. But most of them were cross bat sloggers and easy to dismiss. Big money has now taken Twenty20 around the world and there is a danger that Test match cricket could suffer. There has to be a good balance between the two, as with pop music and classical music, and the authorities need to maintain it, otherwise the bad – too much ugly slogging or over-experimental bowling – will drive out the good.

CHAPTER SIX

Working in a Journalistic Sweatshop ... And It Was Great Fun!

On 3 December 1953 I was interviewed by George Gordon Saunders, known as 'GG', in the pokey, dirty office at the third floor of the *Isle of Wight Guardian* building, opposite the Shanklin Conservative Club. He didn't inspire me with much hope. I had sent him some of my cuttings from the *Mercury* and I was hoping to be appointed as the junior reporter with responsibility for sport. Excessively thin, even emaciated, he spoke about the difficulties of running a small local newspaper when most of the population hardly earned a penny outside the summer season, which was contracting every year. Obviously he wasn't going to offer a large salary, but £3.50 a week was barely more than my wage at the County Hall. Bill Miller was the junior at the *Guardian* and when he started in 1950 he was paid £1 a week. When he left, he was on £4. He was tied to a four-year apprenticeship and when his time was up, he went to New York, looking for a job. He turned up at *The New York Times* and they told him, 'Go and learn the job at a smaller outfit.' So he went to Virginia and was appointed general assignment reporter for the *Newport News Daily Press*. He worked for thirty-three years in the US for various publications, including *The Boston Globe*, before returning to the Isle of Wight, where he lives in a delightful stone-walled house that was once owned by Earl Jellicoe. The original part of the house had a sloping ceiling in the toilet and at six-foot-two, Bill kept whacking his head into it. 'It left a bloody, stained area and we had to do something about it,' he said. He now manages to duck his head when going through some of the older door frames. GG signed me up on a similar contract to Bill's and it was like a form of slavery.

The person who ran the *Guardian* was not GG, the owner, but his daughter, Joan, who turned out to be a thoroughly nice lady, quite different from her father. She had a positive approach to life and always had a welcoming smile. She suggested things I should cover and I carried them out with speed. The *Guardian* usually had just four pages – it went up to six at busy times – and I filled most of the columns. I did practically everything: all the sport, most of the births, deaths, and marriages, the news stories, the meetings of the hoteliers, the suicides, the seaside shows, the theatre, and anything that made news. When we were short of copy, I would write anonymous letters, signing with appendages like 'Anxious Parent' or 'Long-Suffering Bus Traveller'. I also wrote three first-person columns, one as 'Junius', who was politically to the right, one as 'Lysias', who commented on civil matters like dog mess and the possible closure of the Isle of Wight railways, and one as 'Phil Par', the Nigel Dempster of the *Guardian*.

GG explained the linage deal that he promised would enhance my earnings. 'We send copy to the Portsmouth and Southampton evening newspapers and they pay us a penny and a half per line,' he said. 'Anything really newsy is also sent to the national newspapers and the money goes into the pot. I take half, Joan has a quarter and the other quarter will go to you.'

I soon discovered that although I wrote most of the copy, my quarter share of the income brought in a pittance. One of GG's family stood up for him years later, saying, 'Did you know he served through the First World War as a private? He survived the Battle of the Somme. I think that affected him a bit.' If I had known that at the time, I might have been more sympathetic towards him.

In charge of the printing department was Ernest Bull, or 'EB', a humourless man of the same ilk. Ernest lived several hundred yards from the office and went home for lunch while Les Wheeler, the assistant printer, and I had reserved seats at the Copper Kettle thirty yards from the office, where the engaging Kath was our regular waitress and confidante. There was always a queue of holidaymakers outside, because the food was freshly prepared and cheap, and most of them complained about us being let in first. In and out in twenty minutes, we walked swiftly to our regular seat on Keats Green, named after the poet. Keats stayed at Eglantine Cottage in 1817 and 1819, when he wrote some of his most famous works. I once reported a ceremony when a plaque was unveiled, and I used a quote from one of Keats' descendants: 'Few places can boast of greater happiness than Shanklin. Its inhabitants are like one large family. Ill nature is not known among them.'

When, in 1821, he died from consumption in Rome at the age of twenty-five, Keats' sales amounted to perhaps 200 copies. Fanny Brawne, his lover, wrote, 'I fear the kindest act would be to let him rest forever in the obscurity to which unhappy circumstances have condemned him.' But his peers, among them Percy Shelley and Leigh Hunt, recognised his talent, and within a generation he was championed by Tennyson and entered the English canon.

A sign on Keats Green quotes the first line from *Endymion*, a long poem that is thought to have been started in Shanklin: 'A thing of beauty is a joy forever.' The green overlooks Sandown Bay, and there was no better place to have a moan about the meanness of GG and EB. Mr Bull allowed us an hour for lunch and if we were late he always complained. He should have seen the typewriter I used – it was almost on fire. We used to moan, but it was wonderful experience for a young man with ambition.

The papers were printed on Thursdays, ready for deliver the next day. I had to fold them as they came off the printing machine – up to 3,000 copies. I put up with it, but Bill Miller once told me: 'After a while I said I was a journalist, not a folder of newspapers and I wasn't going to do it again. GG said, "This skill will come in useful later in your career." What a laugh!'

If the printing machine broke down, which it did on occasion, there was sudden alarm, with GG cursing and blaming Les and the other members of staff. Most of them printed other things, and the *Guardian* was a sideline to the main business.

Peter Saunders, GG's son, was in charge of the printing. He, like his sister, was a nice person. I worked most evenings – overtime was never paid – and as the last bus from Shanklin in the winter was at five minutes to ten, I often had to leave meetings before the end. The next day, I had to contact my friend at the *Chronicle*, Lew Grant, to see if I had missed anything. Lew came from Aberdeen and his first job had been as a postman. When he moved to the Isle of Wight, he took a job at the *Chronicle* and he was the most diligent journalist I have ever worked with. He was a voracious reader, like me, and he had a slight hearing problem, which meant he had to ask people to repeat things. He checked everything doubly, even trebly.

Lew's hearing did let him down in 1976, though. I brought a celebrity cricket team to Shanklin CC to commemorate the twenty-fifth anniversary of the opening of the pavilion. Southampton's Bobby Stokes, who scored the winning goal in that year's FA Cup Final, played; few of us knew that he had a serious drinking problem. A few years later he died from it. Bobby was a bubbly little man and it was a sad end for him. Ron Tindall, the former Chelsea footballer and Surrey cricketer who is still coaching in Perth, was another star, along with Nigel Cowley, the Hampshire off spinner, now a first-class umpire. Also named in the side, according to Lew's piece, was 'Tony Grazier, a West Indian radio cricket commentator'. Lew got that one wrong: Tony *Cozier* is *the best* radio commentator on cricket around, not just in the West Indies. Right at the end of Lew's report, he wrote, 'Former *IW Guardian* reporter Brian Scovell, now a *Daily Mail* sports writer, who brought the eleven to the Island, topped their score with fifty-two.'

It was a proud day for my mother. She had never seen me play cricket until that day and she thoroughly enjoyed the day. 'I didn't know you were a batsman,' she said. Within two years, she had died of cancer of the pancreas. Her final years were spent bracing against awful pain and she never complained.

Another journalist who played for us that day was Alastair Ross of *The Sun*. He helped run the Fleet Street press team for a few years and led two tours to the West Indies. One of the players, a sub named Charlie Brookes, went out drinking until 4 a.m. He walked into the sea and was drowned. That put a damper on the tour to St Kitts and Nevis. Alastair died at a young age as well – he went the same way as Bobby Stokes. His Scots father John, also a Fleet Street football writer, was a talkative character who drank excessively. Alastair boasted that his father's coffin went to the wrong town for his funeral in the Highlands. 'He missed his own funeral,' he said.

Alastair never drove a car and once, during a rail strike, the sports news editor rang him on a Sunday and said 'We need you in the office. Get down here.'

Alastair, who was living in Cambridge, said, 'I can't, I don't drive.'

'You've been claiming car mileage for years, you so-and-so,' said the sports editor 'You'll have to return the money!'

When Lew Grant died late in 2007, his great friend Joan Smith spoke the address. She said, 'In one period he worked eleven nights in a fortnight and Betty, his wife, hardly saw him.' Lew and Betty took in displaced people from Eastern Europe after the Second World War and took no payment. They literally gave away holidays. He was a big-hearted little man.

Lew was working as a football reporter two weeks before he died at the age of eighty-five. The man who gave him a lift to his last game, at Brading FC, told me, 'A goal went in and for the first time he didn't see who scored it. He was a bit upset but I grabbed hold of one of the players on the touchline and asked him who put it in. Lew was so relieved.' Lew never drove a car. He went everywhere on a bicycle.

In my early days with the *Guardian* I upset the Isle of Wight Schools Amateur Boxing Association Committee with my report of the championship finals at Sandown. The joint manager, Mr E. F. Abell, had a 700-word letter published, saying, 'Your reporter has deliberately set out a cheap sensational story by gross exaggeration instead of keeping to a factual report as a true sports writer should. "Anything for a story" seems to be your reporter's slogan, no matter how much exaggeration, misrepresentation, and abuse is used. To speak of a schoolboy as "the sixteen-year-old assassin" and the "Wild Bull of the Pampas" is totally unworthy of your sporting columns and ought not to have been printed.' Mr Abell concluded, 'The Association has decided to invite Mr Scovell to our next committee meeting on Friday 17 at 6 p.m. so that he can substantiate the assertions he has made and if he has the courage of his convictions, he will accept the invitation. There he will have the pleasure, or otherwise, of facing the trainer of the so-called Ventnor Assassin.'

True, my report was overdramatic, but boxing has always been like that: it's part of the razzmatazz. The theme of the article was that the current batch of pugilists in the Isle of Wight were fighters, like Rocky Marciano, rather than boxers, like Nel Tarleton. Joan Dodds (who had married Peter Dodds, a vintage car owner and estate agent) gave me the same space for my reply. I chided the ABA people, writing, 'My present weight is eleven stone eight pounds but I could make the middleweight limit with a little talking to. However, I must insist on a fifty feet ring to meet a whole committee. In a sixteen feet ring it would be inviting disaster. As for appearing in front of the committee, like a naughty schoolboy appearing before the Head, I can only say what point would there be? I have no evidence, no proof to submit. Anyway, it reeks of the Star Chamber court system which, fortunately, was erased from our Constitution some centuries ago. If the committee want to waste their time further, I suggest a friendly discussion, in a public hall, might suit the case. I don't mind being put on trial.'

I wrote to Robert Findlay, the sports editor of the *Daily Express*, and enclosed the relevant cuttings. He wrote back: 'Most readers will agree with you.' His letter started 'Dear Scovell' and I didn't take offence. In those days, professional people addressed younger people by their surnames until they got to know them. Fabio Capello introduced the custom to the England football squad. Obviously he thought England's players needed more discipline. The downward trend went into a skid in 1973, when Professor Sir Harold Thompson, then chairman of the FA, called Don Revie 'Revie' when the Leeds manager took over from Alf Ramsey. Revie was very upset and told Thompson, 'When I get to know you better, I will call you "Thompson".' Nicknamed 'Don Readies' for his habit of giving brown envelopes to those he thought needed some assistance, he introduced bad habits into the game and gave too much power to the players. This is still happening, despite the Italian influence.

Bob Findlay of the *Express* had some faults too – like gambling and drinking too much – but at work he was a hard taskmaster and later he played a big part in my life. I also wrote to my friend Des Hackett, who wrote back saying, 'I am rather surprised at the attitude of the Schools' ABA. You gave them good coverage and if they had any sense they would realise that a little colour adds interest to a report. At least you had the satisfaction that your reports are being closely read and they are carrying a considerable interest. Keep on with the good work.' The boxing officials failed to respond to my suggestion about a public discussion.

Upsetting readers is part of being a journalist and a story that caused ructions in Shanklin at the time was over a wedding between a twenty-two-year-old local girl and a South African soldier serving in the Royal Artillery in England. One of my tasks was to ring the local vicars and priests and ask them if there were any weddings in the offing. The vicar at St Saviour's Church gave me the address of the girl and I went to see her. Her father opened the door of the family house and showed me into a rear lounge and invited me to have tea. His daughter Patricia and her boyfriend joined us and both looked overjoyed. I asked them, 'How did you meet?'

She said, 'I answered a marriage advertisement.' She was happy to give the background and all three of them showed no concern about how it happened.

'It all worked out so amazingly well,' said Jack, the father. 'I just can't believe it.'

My story was headlined 'Story with a Happy Ending'. The next Friday morning, when the newspapers arrived, Pat's mother was first to read my report. She exploded. 'That's ruined your marriage!' she said to Pat. 'Everyone thinks that you had to advertise for a husband! It will bring shame to the whole family.'

She rang the *Guardian* and asked for me. 'That story about Pat meeting the bridegroom is completely untrue,' she said. 'I demand an apology.'

I tried to explain. 'I didn't make it up,' I said. 'Pat and her father told me how it happened. It is true.'

She insisted on a retraction so I passed her on to Joan. Eventually, Joan agreed to write another version for the next week's edition without actually retracting anything, so honour was upheld.

My best moments came when I interviewed the showbiz stars at the Shanklin Theatre. The leading stars at the weekly repertory show in my first season were Alec Ross and Sheila Hancock, who were married. Alec was the male lead and Sheila, who was born on the Isle of Wight, headed the female cast. As I so often wrote, both were brilliant. It was obvious that both of them would be West End stars. It turned out to be true in the case of Sheila – she is still working in her seventies. But Alec died of cancer at a young age and when her second husband John Thaw died of the same illness years later, I wrote to her offering my condolences. I reminded her that I interviewed her at the Shanklin Theatre several times and she said she remembered the tall young man with the limp. The character actor Anthony Bate was another member of the troupe and he is still working. Two other performers I met were Tommy Trinder and Arthur Askey. I first met Tommy when he opened a fête at the Old Church in Shanklin. 'I love Shanklin,' he said. 'I was at the Shanklin Pier in 1937 and 1938 and Arthur and I had a wonderful time – the income tax people hadn't heard of us!'

I met Tommy a few years later when he was chairman of Fulham Football Club. He always invited the press into the boardroom and handed out the drinks. His loud voice dominated the proceedings – until Jimmy Hill arrived, and turned up the volume. Fulham was rated by the journalists as the happiest club in the country. The directors and the players didn't take themselves seriously and no one else did either, except maybe Johnny Haynes, who was Britain's first £100-a-week footballer in 1963. Tommy was always ribbing him about his salary and Johnny always came up with a tart reply. No player in the history of the game has struck a more accurate, more telling, cross-field pass than Johnny. 'He made me,' said Tosh Chamberlain, the left-winger. 'And I ruined it with the next pass!'

Tosh was loved by everyone. In one game against Preston he found himself unable to take the ball past Willie Cunningham, the Preston full-back. Totally exasperated, he shot straight at Cunningham's private parts, laying him out in the mud. 'I had to do it, that was the only way to get round him,' he told me. I often rang Tommy at his home and it was difficult to get off the line. He loved talking about football and its personalities.

An habitué at one of Trinder's after-match sessions at the Cottage was Stanley Halsey of the Sunday Pictorial. Brian Glanville, who often came up with unusual words, wrote of him in his book *Football Memories*. 'I spent much of my time in Fleet Street, frequently with Stanley Hasley, to whom I became a kind of amanuensis. Stanley was a rare, slightly exotic bird among the sports writers of the time. Middle-aged, of ruddy countenance and well spoken, he had been a naval officer in the war, and was said to have spent at least one term at Eton. He was gloriously vague, perpetually troubled and a notable drinker with a penchant for puns. He was famous for drinking binges.'

'Amanuensis' means 'one who writes from dictation or copies manuscript', but Stanley's main job was to come up with snippets about football transfers. Several times on England trips abroad, he was so drunk he was close to missing the return flight to London and had to be rescued by his colleagues. 'Some years later,' wrote Glanville, 'he disappeared. The word went round that he had died in hospital. Many of us mourned. There was always something deeply endearing about him, a curious dichotomy between what he was and what he did. There was, I believe, even a memorial service for him, to which George Casey [his sports editor] sent a wreath. Years passed. Then a journalist who had left his car in the Scotland Yard car park was driving it out when he recognised, with a shock and a start, the car park attendant. It was Stanley. "And I spent all that money sending flowers for the bastard," said Casey.'

I was there when Stanley Halsey probably asked a question that has only ever been asked once at a footballing press conference. It happened at Craven Cottage. Bedford Jezzard, the Fulham centre-forward and manager, was being interviewed, and Stanley said, 'Beddy, can I ask you something?'

'What is it?' said the popular Jezzard.

Stanley took off his glasses, looked at him, and said, 'What was the score?'

Jezzard was taken aback. 'Was there something which I don't know?' he said. 'I thought it was 2-1 to us.' The other journalists burst into raucous laughter.

'Oh,' said Stanley as he swilled his whisky in his hand, 'I just wanted to check.'

Other notable figures I interviewed in Shanklin and Sandown included Jimmy Tarbuck, David Nixon, Dick Emery, Lonnie Donegan, Cyril Fletcher, Bernard Braden, Barbara Kelly, and the *Daily Mail* war correspondent Noel Monks. They all told good stories. I spent many enjoyable hours on Shanklin Pier, which has since been destroyed. Ventnor Pier has gone too, but Sandown's still remains. The small concert theatre on Shanklin Pier was filled with laughter from the jokes and antics of some of the finest comedians in Britain. It was full almost every night throughout the summer. Some of the jokes were smutty, but unlike today's comedians, the material wasn't offensive.

The owners of this goldmine, for a while, were H. Terry Wood and his wife Sadie, a compulsive smoker who was a wonderful character. The Woods lived in a fantastic white art deco house with a green-tiled roof. It had an unequalled view of Sandown Bay from the top of the cliff between Shanklin and Lake; perhaps my admiration for the place was one of the reasons I bought my own green-tiled art deco house in Bromley. The Woods' place was called 'Villa Judapa' and it was rumoured that a former film star had lived there in the 1920s. After Terry Woods died, the name was changed and new owners took it over. Later, when I thought I might be rich enough to buy a house of such opulence, I asked my friend, the estate agent Peter Dodd, what the chances of making a bid were. 'Don't touch it,' he said. 'The sandstone cliff has been slipping for years. There are often falls and every time it happens, they move the path further back. By the time you're about to retire the garden may well have slipped down on to the beach.' Oh well! The house was sold recently and the price was not far short of £1 million. It is still standing, dominating the coastline.

The first piece I wrote for the *Daily Mail* appeared on 11 September 1956, and its readers must have needed a magnifying glass. It said, in small type, 'Beach Cleared – Shanklin, Isle of Wight, beach was cleared yesterday after a mine was found under a cliff. It was exploded by Portsmouth Bomb Disposal Unit.' A sub editor must have tampered with it. I never started with 'Shanklin...' And as for the final clause in the first sentence – 'after a mine was found under a cliff' – I ask you! This editorial sabotage plagued my work throughout my career and I am not the only one to suffer: few journalists see their work untouched. Jim Swanton, the great man of English cricket reporting, always rang up *The Daily Telegraph*'s sports editor if someone missed out a comma in his column. He was such an imposing man that few editors, sub editors, or even newspaper proprietors dared to alter his copy – even if he had written a defective sentence, which he did occasionally. Ian Wooldridge's prose appeared as he wrote it, but he was an exception. Good sub editors are key men on sports desks; they correct mistakes. Without them, the standard of journalism would suffer. I had good relations with nearly all of them, but a few always wanted to change things. If a writer has a good reputation for accuracy, it can't be right that someone sitting in an office, not watching the event himself, can alter the author's views, but it still happens. Nick Davies wrote in his book *Flat Earth News*: 'Costs are being cut and standards eroded by greedy proprietors.' He is right. Most of them are asking their readers to go online. It would save billions of trees and the 136-page newspapers, some even bigger, would be phased out. But I prefer reading a newspaper to looking at a computer screen. Even sub editors are being phased out.

Although Parkhurst Prison houses hundreds of the most dangerous criminals in Britain, no one escapes these days. Like Alcatraz, the island prison off San Francisco that has long since been shut, the Island's geography is the perfect way of deterring prisoners. On most days at the *Guardian*, I rang the duty sergeants at the two local police stations. One day the Shanklin officer tipped me off that a prisoner, thirty-nine-year-old Herbert Walton, had escaped. To my shame, I came up with this hoary cliché in my report: 'He led the police a merry chase before surrendering to three police officers near Shanklin Cricket Ground five hours later.' Walton had only six more months to serve, but he was sentenced to seven years for attempting to break into a sports pavilion. Silly man! For a while, I had a friendly warder who could supply information, a man who played against me on the Parkhurst Prison cricket ground. Once, he told me there was an attempted breakout, with some prisoners getting onto the roof. He told me that I couldn't report it, and nothing appeared.

In my youth I never saw a black man on the Isle of Wight until a GI from Carolina, a soldier in the US Army who took part in D-Day, turned up in Ventnor and married a young girl. He was the first, and he didn't stay after the end of the war. His wife went with him to America. Now more than half of the prisoners in Albany Prison are non-white.

The saddest story I covered in my four years working for the *Guardian* was the case of the husband who walked into the sea at Sandown and drowned because he couldn't face having sex with his newly married wife. Sometime later, the partly decomposed body of a man was washed up at Welcome Beach, in Shanklin. He was identified as thirty-five-year-old Len Paine of North Finchley, London. The couple had just started their honeymoon at Grange Hall Hotel, Sandown, and later in the evening he had an altercation with his wife, Grace. He struck her in the face and rushed out of the bedroom. He was never seen alive again. In her evidence at the inquest, Grace said, 'He was very upset about not being a proper husband.'

Mr J. V. Bullin, the coroner, said it had been a very distressing case and that Mrs Paine had borne it bravely. He recorded a verdict of suicide and added that he had worried about his own approaching marriage, but evidence showed that his fears had been groundless. I put the story over to six national newspapers and they all used it. My twenty-five per cent of the linage proceeds was a meagre amount, but it put my name around the news desks of Fleet Street. I felt I was on the way there. In those exciting days, I rarely took a holiday. Doing that job was exhilarating, joyous. My holiday usually consisted of a cricket week, playing every day for Shanklin.

A major perk was interviewing the carnival queens in both towns, Shanklin and Sandown. One, Maureen McDougall, was keen on publicity. We had several dates, but I was getting behind with my studies and I had to call a halt. She now lives in Australia. Another carnival queen was the nineteen-year-old wife of a vicar; her crowning made a good feature in one of the Sunday newspapers. She was very good-looking and had a stunning figure. She told me, 'I never intended to enter. It was all a joke. Some friends persuaded me to do it.'

The happy couple were on their honeymoon in Shanklin and her husband, Rev. Albert Kay of Beddington (whose cricket club I played for in the 1960s) had been sent to the Isle of Man for his next post. Albert was twenty-six and Pamela was nineteen. He said, 'I feel sure the young men at my new church will be highly delighted.'

Sir Joseph Qualtrough – the speaker at the Isle of Man's House of Keys, the chairman of the IOM Tourist Board, and a leading figure in Manx Methodism – said, 'We Methodists are very broad-minded and we shall take Mrs Kay on her merits. If she is friendly and interested in us, we will respond.' Three Methodist ministers refused to comment.

There was a number of girls I was keen on, but at this time I wondered whether going on dates was worthwhile. I preferred playing cricket. Having appalling figures of fifteen overs, two maidens, 132 runs and three wickets in one game failed to curb my love for it. When Shanklin played against a Hampshire county eleven at Westhill, the *Guardian* correspondent (me) wrote, 'Phew! What a game! That was the dazed reaction of some 1,200 cricket watchers on Sunday after seeing four and a half hours of the most craziest and most exciting cricket they will probably see in a lifetime. They saw 533 runs, sixty-five fours, and seventeen sixes hit out of the ground.' I was too dazed to remember how many sixes came from my bowling. It must have been seven at least.

Denis Cuthill, the man in charge of the IW Water Works, was captain of the Shanklin side and he brought me on as second change. He asked me, 'Which pace, slow or quick?' I opted to bowl my seamers.

My second ball swung in, pitched, and moved away, beating the bat of Roy Marshall, a West Indian-born Hampshire opener who was one of the finest batsmen of his generation. 'Well bowled son,' he said.

The next ball screamed past cover point. The next went straight to the far long off boundary. I felt like asking to be taken off. Denis said, 'I think you would be better off bowling your spinners.' I should have stood up for myself and put on my sweater. But he asked me to bowl my Chinamen and ordered the fielders to scatter along the boundaries.

Alan Rayment, not one of Hampshire's best batsmen but still a good one, started peppering the allotments alongside the leg side boundary. Twenty runs came off that over and the crowd started chanting, 'Take him off. Off, off off!'

Denis said, 'Don't take any notice, they're idiots.'

Des Eagar, the former Hampshire captain and secretary, was umpiring at my end and he offered some advice. 'Don't bowl every ball with spin, and change the pace a bit,' he said. He told me he used to bowl Chinamen, too. 'What about slipping in a googly?' he said.

'That will go even further,' I said.

Hampshire's number seven batsman was Henry Horton, the man John Arlott described as 'the straightest bat in England'. When he reached eight, the straightest bat went off the straight and narrow and my slow non-turning Chinaman finished in the hands of Mr Cuthill at deep midwicket. Rayment passed his century in fifty-four minutes and he, too, was caught off my bowling, this time by David Hayles, our fast bowler, at long on. Derek Shackleton came in. He was one of my heroes, the medium-pace bowler who never bowled a bad ball. He hit a six off me before he was dismissed for thirty-five. Mr Cuthill reasoned that I should stay on and take my punishment. I demurred. Just as he was about to tell me to take my sweater two overs later, the number ten batsman, P. Bailey, took a swing and missed a Chinaman; it removed the bails. Gerry Hill, the skipper, declared on 353-9 to prevent me taking a four-wicket haul – the old meanie. Shackleton was second in the national bowling averages that summer and he only took one wicket in his six overs as Shanklin were bowled out for 180. Rayment, who was rated the number one outfielder of the day, showed us how to bowl leggers and googlies and took 3-50. He failed to dislodge our number eleven (i.e. the ubiquitous *Guardian* correspondent), who was nought not out.

John Macadam may have said he had a near-miss interview with Adolf Hitler, but I managed a great interviewing coup at the age of twenty. A cricketing friend tipped me off that Jim Laker and his wife Lilly were going to stay at one of the best hotels in Shanklin after his record-breaking – and never to be beaten – 19-90 for England against Australia in July 1956. Jim was one of the sporting heroes of the decade and everyone wanted to talk to him. I didn't ring him up at their room but just turned up after breakfast unannounced.

He was surprised. 'How did you find out?' he said.

'A cricketer I know who knows some of the staff,' I said. 'I won't keep you long.'

He wasn't the usual Yorkshireman. I played with Len Rodwell, the Yorkshire Colt, who had been in the RAF at Ventnor four years earlier. He was a brash young man with plenty to say. Jim was the reverse: quiet and taciturn. Maybe that was because his father, Charles Laker, was a stonemason from Breeding, Sussex, a very different part of the world. Charles was a serial womaniser and a conman. The boys where he grew up thought he looked like Tom Mix, the Hollywood cowboy. Charles would sign autographs, 'Tom Mix, the man on the range'.

Jim didn't really want to say much about his nineteen wickets except that the pitch helped his style of bowling. Lilly, his Vienna-born wife, was more friendly. 'I don't follow cricket,' she said, 'but I go with my friends to the game sometimes without knowing what is happening.'

In 1938 she and her family fled Vienna when the Nazis began murdering Austrian Jews. She joined the Auxiliary Territorial Service in the British Army in Egypt and met Jim in Cairo in 1943. Their first date was at a cricket match. After a while, she said, 'I thought English people were supposed to be fair. How is it proper for eleven men to play against two?'

The couple met again in London in 1950 and Jim invited her out to dinner. 'I prefer lunch,' she said. A year later they married. She hadn't heard from her parents for twelve years and believed that they were victims of the Nazis. Suddenly, the Red Cross told her that they were living in a farm in the south of France. She contacted her father and with Jim's financial help, they were settled in London for the remainder of their lives.

There was no best man when the Lakers married and only a handful of people were invited. One was Michael Barton, the former Surrey captain. I wrote the book

19-90 Jim Laker in 2005 and just before Michael died, he told me, 'Jim made a very fine speech that day and I wasn't surprised by his later success as a TV commentator. At first meeting Jim gave the impression of being a blunt Yorkshireman. But this was misleading He was in fact a very sensitive man. The sensitivity was perhaps magnified by certain difficulties in life about which we know nothing. He was extremely intelligent, both as a person and as a bowler.' The 'certain difficulties' were to do with his youth. Jim was illegitimate and his father left the family when he was two, never to be seen again.

CHAPTER SEVEN

Migrating to the Mainland

Anyone wanting to become a sports writer has to persevere. And to never give up. In the final year of my apprenticeship at the *Guardian*, I wrote to nearly all the 150 sports editors of the evening and morning newspapers in England at that time and six offered the chance of an interview. Only two, the *Burton Daily Mail* and the *Loughborough Monitor*, wanted my services. Many of the sports editors sent frosty, deterring letters, some praised my determination to pass my examinations by post, and hardly any of them encouraged me to go on until I had more experience. That was what I needed: experience of working on daily newspapers.

I wrote again to Robert Findlay on 4 February 1958 and he wrote back, 'Dear Scovell. I am afraid my answer to your application is exactly as forecast in the last paragraph of your letter. There are few openings for sports reporters in Fleet Street. It is rather easier to become a sub editor but you don't indicate that you have any experience or aptitude in this department. We don't as a rule take people on national papers until they are well established elsewhere for the simple reason that we have no time to train them. Why not lower your sights a little and try for the Manchester office of one of the nationals? Henry Rose is the sports editor of the *Manchester Express* there but I doubt if he has anything at the moment.'

Four days later Henry Rose was one of twenty-three casualties of the Munich air disaster. Eight Manchester United footballers and fifteen others – including crew members and journalists – died in the disaster. My letter to Henry never reached him.

In 1962, during my time at the *Sketch*, Bob was appointed to the sports staff. 'You're the whippersnapper who kept pestering me from the Isle of Wight!' he said. He was an very ebullient and enthusiastic man from Glasgow who rarely stopped talking. He had a similar start to life as John Macadam. He was born in 1910, the son of a labourer who died when he was only three. He left school at fourteen and started out as a hotel pageboy before taking a part-time job, phoning sports results to Glasgow newspapers. In 1928 he joined the *Scottish Daily Express* and eventually worked in the main office in Fleet Street as sports editor under that great editor Arthur Christiansen, who was renowned for daily bulletins that blamed and praised the staff. The *Express* was the top-selling newspaper, selling 4.6 million copies a day. Today it is kept alive by profits from Richard Desmond's murkier publications, including pornography.

Bob loved writing bulletins, too, and he often wrote to me. I asked for a day off once and he wrote, 'You certainly cannot have a Sunday off. I am extremely disappointed at the lack of worthwhile stories emanating from you and I must confess that sometimes it appears that reporting is secondary to organising football matches.'

Actually, he was right. I ran the *Sketch* football team and later the *Mail* one for more than thirty years and they took time to assemble. Bob's personality changed almost every hour. He was a rabid gambler, ringing his bookie through the day with his bets. After the race, he would ring back and if it was bad news, he would slam the phone down and would turn on someone. If it was a winner, he was a different man.

That year another memo reached me, saying, 'Yes, you can have Friday off and while I am about it, you are doing a very fine job.'

He worked for both the *Sketch* and the *Mail* from 1962 to 1975 and was English sport's hat trick king – he was the only person to be the sports editor of the *Express*, the *Sketch*, and the *Mail* in succession. He was a big drinker but he lived to the age of ninety-four. In his last year, he said to his long-time friend Steve Richards, formerly of the *Daily Herald* and the broadsheet *Sun*, 'That's it, I want to go.' For the last time, he packed away the kilt he wore at every Burns Night and died peacefully.

I was very proud to be asked to speak the address at his funeral. 'He attributed his fitness to walking from Waterloo Station to Fleet Street at a very fast rate,' I said. 'Whether he could walk back late at night was debatable. Bob loved a wee dram, or sometimes a wee litre. He was made a freeman of the City of London and had a distinguished record in the Second World War in Salerno, Arakan, and Rangoon. He helped raise the Union Jack over Government House when Rangoon was recaptured from the Japanese.'

Bob wrote memos to most of the staff, mainly about their expenses. One I liked was sent to Laurie Pignon, the tennis and football writer who is now heading for ninety, and may beat Bob's great age. He wrote, 'You claimed £46.11 last week whereas Brian James claimed £26.46. How can the tennis writer, working out of season, claim more than the football writer? This must stop. It will have to come from your own money.'

I liked another one, when he wrote, 'I know you are a great reporter but don't worry about the writing. I've got someone else to do it.'

Bob became a good friend of Keith Miller, the Australian Test all-rounder who shared his love of betting. Bob signed Miller up as a cricket writer with the *Express* and from the first time I met 'Nugget', I liked him; we became good mates. He loved the ladies. Audrey and I were staying at a hotel in Birmingham once when I was reporting on a Test and I introduced them. Within a few minutes, Audrey was enraptured by his style and wit. He was renowned for his sexual conquests, including a society lady and her daughter, who entertained him on a regular basis. I always had my cricket bag in the boot of my car and in 1964 I was doing net practice at Old Trafford after close of play in a Test when I heard Keith shouting, 'Get a crash helmet, I'll bowl a couple to you!'

I didn't have a helmet: I've never worn one. He picked up a ball, walked back three or four paces, and suddenly turned and ran in and bowled a terrifying bouncer straight at me. Fortunately I was able to lean back and avoid being hit. He laughed. 'Not bad,' he said as he walked off to his car.

In his heyday he could bowl just as fast off a brief run-up as he could off his normal run. He invariably turned up late at county matches, phoned over his racing selections, cribbed a few facts about the scores, and scribbled a couple of hundred words about the play before phoning his piece over by a telephone borrowed from another journalist. Then he went off for an assignation in Mayfair or whatever. He and Denis Compton were both debonair, handsome characters who inspired millions to follow cricket. The latest home-produced candidate to be tried by England for that role was Andrew Flintoff, and for all his niceness and naivety, he isn't in the same class.

Before quitting the Isle of Wight and embarking on my great adventure, I concentrated on contacting the bigger evening newspapers, the ones in the cities. I wrote again and again to Brian Whiteaker, the editor of the *Express & Star* in Wolverhampton, still one of the bestselling evening newspapers in the country. It was once described as 'the best weekly newspaper which comes out nightly'. Brian offered me £11.18s a week as a general reporter. Typically bolshy, I wrote back saying I would prefer to work on the sports desk.

He responded, saying, 'We might be able to use you on sport but it will be mainly on general news.' Not having had any more offers, I had to accept.

I travelled by train from the Garden Isle to the heart of the Black Country and looking out the window I felt despair seeing so many blackened factories and squalid back-to-back houses. Smog hung over the this dreary, cough-laden, choking part of the Midlands. Should I turn around, I thought, and go home? Don't be a coward, man! The editor's secretary had fixed up a room for me with a middle-aged woman who took in lodgers along Tettenhall Road and my depression deepened. There was no heating in the bedroom, no washing facilities, and the furniture was distinctly Victorian.

The next day I walked to the Queen Street building, where the *Star* was printed, and got a warm, uplifting welcome from Malcolm Graham, the managing director, and from everyone else, including the young man who brought the tea round. Tony Cox, the chief sports writer, was particularly helpful. The sports editor, George Gillott, said, 'If you want to see a Wolves game at Molineux I'll fix a press ticket for you.'

I jumped at that and the next night I saw my first floodlit game. Wolves were about to win the League Championship in two successive seasons under the strict management of Stan Cullis, and it was great time to be there. Wolves were playing these pulsating friendlies against the best club sides in Europe and the excitement was stifling. The banks of standing supporters were swaying like corn in the wind and the noise was almost overwhelming. The diminutive Johnny Hancock was slinging the ball over from the right and Jimmy Mullen did the same from the left. Advised by an eccentric football nut named Commander Reep, Cullis always took the short route to goal, which meant a long passing game, and it worked for a while. Billy Wright, the captain, who also captained England, was an intelligent footballer, but he had no objections about the way Wolves performed. He was a gentleman without an ego. If anyone deserved a statue outside his beloved ground, it was him. Later, when I reported Arsenal matches and he was manager from 1962-66, he was one of the best managers to deal with, but his failing was his niceness. Occasionally a manager has to get nasty. Billy couldn't do it. He was the first English international to gain 100 caps, and his eventual total was 105.

Once Malcolm Graham said to me, 'Is that right, you are a useful all-rounder?'

Modestly, I said, 'Well, I usually open the bowling and recently I've opened the batting as well.' He put me straight in the *Star* side as opening bowler and opening batsman. Don Howe, who was born in Wolverhampton a month earlier than me, started out with the Wolverhampton youth side but after a trial at Molineux, he joined West Bromwich Albion as an amateur, and went professional in 1952. He also played for the *Star* cricket team and we often opened both batting and bowling together. It started a friendship that still lasts. He personifies the honesty that still lingers in professional football in this country, although I have to say that too many of the other kind are now taking over – the money launderers, the dodgy dealers, the cheats. Don would have added more international caps to his total of twenty-three but for breaking his leg at Highbury at the age of thirty-one. His right leg crashed into the head of goalkeeper Tony Waiters and the surgeon bolted a foot-long metal splint to the bone of his lower leg, which is still there. 'The doctor told me that if it wasn't doing harm, keep it,' he said.

I went to see him at the Royal Northern Hospital next day. 'It's taken the place of the old-fashioned plaster,' he said. 'I'm the first person to undergo it and I don't feel a thing. I won't have to go through all that bother of building up wasted muscles as you do after being in plaster. I'm having a great time. It's like being in a luxury hotel.'

Unfortunately, he never played again and went into coaching. He is still coaching occasionally and his record is unmatched. He was the longest-serving England coach – 120 matches under Ron Greenwood and Bobby Robson. I ghostwrote his book, *Handbook of Soccer*, which was published in 1987. Pelham, the publishers, reported, 'It's selling well in Italy.' So Fabio Capello, the present England manager, may well have been a reader!

My dream of being the next football correspondent of the *Star*, writing on the Wolves' games, soon ended. Clem Jones, the news editor, told me I was being transferred to the Halesowen beat, also covering Old Hill, Brierley Hill, and Stourbridge. No more football for me. I was rather dented to leave my new lodgings for another part of Tettenhall. Enoch Powell lived nearby, but the only time I met him was in 1981 when I went into a first-class compartment returning from Ipswich to Liverpool Street, and he was sitting opposite. We started talking and it was one of the most entertaining ninety minutes of conversation I have ever had. His gift for words was incredible. He could have led the Conservative Party but was too outspoken. He will always be remembered for his 'rivers of blood' speech – delivered in the Birmingham Town Hall in 1968 about the peril, as he thought, of the country being flooded by migrants. Most of what he said turned out to be true, but his words were intemperate and he lost the support of the middle ground. No one could argue that this country is not overpopulated; the effects of being too generous and throwing open the door are now being felt. Powell was a close friend of Clem Jones and he showed Clem a copy of his speech before releasing it to ITV the following day. Clem gave the copy to his wife to look at and she was horrified. She thought the speech was so inflammatory that 'it will be the end of our friendship'. Powell had quoted a letter received from a lady who was a Tory constituent. It talked about black people putting excreta in her letterbox and young blacks taunting her in the street. It might have been written by my landlady – she had racist views. Powell was an intellectual who towered over the rest of the Shadow Cabinet and he used his speech in his bid to become Tory leader. What he lacked was the common approach, and despite being giving a rousing reception at the next Tory Conference, Ted Heath was voted leader and one of his first decisions was to remove Powell from the Shadow Cabinet. Powell's career went in reverse. The Tories took the whip from him and he stood for the Ulster Unionists and was grouped among the political oddbods. His career never recovered, and he died in 1998.

Without a car, I had to look at advertisements for likely lodgings in Halesowen – not the liveliest town in the Midlands – and I found one that looked suitable. It was a sprawling house in a smallholding off the main Stourbridge Road. The ample car parking space was filled with cars, jeeps, vans, and caravans, and the couple who owned it, Frank and Eth Hands, proved to be ideal hosts and friends. Frank worked nights at Longbridge, building Leyland cars. During the day he had a business transporting caravans to buyers all over Britain. Somehow he managed to squeeze in a few hours of sleep. His wife was very gregarious, full of fun, and never short of a few words. Inside the house everything was strewn around and there were four or five other lodgers, all men of mature years. The kitchen was the control centre, with Eth doing all the cooking, waiting, and clearing up. We spent hours most nights discussing politics, art, history, football... almost everything. I learned a tremendous amount from them. Being a lodger in that sort of environment helped me to become a more rounded person and it is sad today that an increasing number of young people live alone in one-room flats.

I was still working on my diploma for the National Council for the Training of Journalists. Buddy, one of our debaters, suggested I should write my thesis on the Clean Air Act, which was passed in 1956 after 4,000 people had died from smog two years earlier. In the Isle of Wight I never saw smog. 'You can't beat the Black Country for smog,' he said.

The next day, in my usual 9 a.m. call to Clem Jones, I said, 'I've decided to do my thesis on the Clean Air Act and can you let me write some features about it in the paper? I could be the unofficial smog correspondent.'

Clem, who was later to the editor, and a very fine one as well, said, 'Great idea. Get started immediately.'

I went to see Mick Archer, the chief executive of Halesown Council, who was an expert in the field. He proved a great friend and put me in touch with the right people. He was a prominent official of the Halesowen CC and was able to get me into the second team on Saturdays. After I passed my diploma and was working for the *Mail*, I was asked to speak at the cricket club dinner. The main course was 'pork chops with roast and new potatoes and vegetables'. There was no swank about the Black Country. Whatever deficiencies it had, they were made up for by the quality of its people.

I spent less than a year working for the *Star*, and although it wasn't what I really wanted to do, it suited my purposes. I wrote a couple of brief stories each day and the rest of the time I was able to continue my final studies. I completed my 11,000-word thesis and passed the written examination for my diploma. In the summer I played cricket three times a week, for Halesowen, the *Star*, and Lye CC's Thursday side. Mobile phones were some years ahead and it wasn't easy to reach me. By 3 p.m. the news desk wasn't interested in taking any more copy. The final edition had already gone. In March 1959, I passed my driving test on the second attempt with my light blue Morris Mini, which cost me £500, the money left to me in my grandfather's will. Three days later I drove to Norwich and back, 370 miles, to attend an interview with Ted Bell, the sports editor of the *Norwich Evening News*. His offer of £825 a year, much higher than my previous salary, was quickly accepted.

There is no better place in Britain to work than Norwich. I spent an idyllic three months working for the *Evening News* and the morning paper, the *Eastern Daily Press*. I was appointed the speedway correspondent, following the triumphs of Ove Fundin, the Swedish world champion. I knew little about speedway, but Ove was a good talker. I wasn't keen on the sport, especially the smell belching from the machines.

I stayed at the YMCA, only 400 metres from the office, and at the back of the building there was an outdoor cricket net. My batting improved with so much practice, and I was chosen for several leading clubs, including Norwich Natives, the Barleycorns, and the YMCA. I was playing alongside some of the minor county players and in several matches I opened with Clive Radley, the former England and Middlesex batsman, and the recently retired coach of the MCC groundstaff. He was fourteen and not many batsmen got him out. Radders has given a lot back to the game he loves and I look on him as a good friend. Not long after I arrived, a nationwide strike by evening newspapers began and it lasted several weeks. What a life! Cricket three or four times a week, tennis in the evenings, and jaunts to seaside resorts with various young ladies. One of them, a nurse named Elaine Handford, introduced me to golf at Earlham Golf Club. She beat me first time out, but my first ever round of 111 was considered a worthy beginning. Alas, I never beat that 111 and decided to retire, although later I played abroad occasionally.

This life of luxury did not last long. I saw an advertisement saying, 'Young journalist required by the Cricket Reporting Agency in Fleet Street.' I applied and went for an interview. There were three people in charge of the agency: Norman Preston, the short, stubby, Pickwickian figure who was editor of *Wisden*, Ebenezer Eden, in charge of rugby, and Harry Gee, who headed the football section. Their offices were on the fifth floor of the Press Association and they supplied news and reports about all three sports. The PA still provides the same service. Now it is based in Victoria. I think Norman liked me because he wrote, 'Following our interview today, we have decided to engage you at the Senior Minimum Rate of £18-15s-0, rising to £19-7s-0 after six months and to £20 after twelve months' service. We should like to begin as soon as your present employers will release you and we trust that you will find our office congenial and that you will soon settle down.'

The first figure was £16 15s but he had altered it to £18 15s. Good man. Working for an agency is ideal training. I was being accredited to games at Highbury, White

Hart Lane, Stamford Bridge, and the other London football grounds. I had to pick up a telephone and dictate 'snaps' to copytakers at 85 Fleet Street. It would be flashed over to the sub editors, who checked the copy and put it on the wire. Within minutes the news was arriving at offices all over the country. It put a lot of onus on the reporter. Any mistake could prove disastrous. It was also pressurised and I relished that. It taught me to compose from my head, without writing anything down on paper. I learned how to put my right hand on the speaking end of the phone to keep out the crowd noise while dictating copy – otherwise the man or lady on the other end had difficulty hearing what was said. Some of the copytakers were brilliant and some even corrected my grammar.

Once, one voice sounded bored and after I was halfway through dictating a football report from Highbury he interrupted and said, 'Any more of this?'

'Well, the Gunners are a bit boring,' I said.

Norman took a special interest in cricket and I found myself covering county matches. He had a sharp temper if he thought something had gone wrong. Often he was the man responsible for these slip ups, as we discovered.

I stayed with Ken and Vi Barber in Yew Tree Way in Addington – their house has since been demolished to make way for a housing estate – before moving into the Croydon YMCA. It didn't have a cricket net but it had a wonderful indoor gym that could stage indoor football matches. When I was off work, I joined in the sessions and it improved my passing skills. I stayed in room B6 and one night I heard a loud bang as someone slammed the door. I thought it had been locked. I got up to check and found my wallet had disappeared. Robberies were almost commonplace. My empty wallet was found a few days later, stuffed at the back of a toilet. Sleep wasn't easy in that part of the building. My neighbour was a Buddy Holly fan; he dressed like Buddy and wore the same glasses. He played music throughout the night. 'Buddy' and my new friends had strong views about everything, which was good for my development. Most of them came from abroad and were students. We had many exciting arguments about the state of the world. I was one of the few residents who owned a car and one day at breakfast, the son of a Kenyan lawyer got up on a chair and said, 'Gentleman, my dear friend Brian Scovell is offering us lifts to Trafalgar Square this afternoon to attend a political rally for the Communist Party. Hold your hands up if you are interested.' Dozens of hands shot up.

I said, 'That's fine but I've only got four seats available. Ladies only as well!'

In my third year at the YMCA, the man in charge, Lloyd Wheelhouse, called me in and said, 'People keep ringing up on the only public phone in the building asking for you and saying they are from the *Daily Sketch*. You don't work for them?'

I had to admit I did.

'I can't have a famous journalist living here,' he said. 'That's not fair to the others. You will have to go.'

So I was slung out. My mother knew a lady from Auchtermuchty, the small Scottish town that Sir John Junor, the peppery editor of the *Sunday Express*, often wrote about in his column. She and her husband lived in Royston Road in Beckenham and had a spare bedroom. I didn't have time to look for something better and it was close to

Kent House station, where I could go straight to Blackfriars, 300 metres from Fleet Street. They were in their sixties and totally humourless. There was no central heating upstairs, so I said, 'Is it possible to bring my old electric fire?' She was reluctant but finally agreed.

A week later I heard her husband on the telephone in the hall talking about me, describing me as 'Mr Kilowatt'. As Scots, they believed in saving their money and not wasting their electricity. I suggested I should add something to my rent and they agreed on an extra 50p a week.

People used to save up in those days and I had enough money to put down a deposit on a house. I'd seen an advertisement for a housing development half a mile from Selhurst Park, the ground of Crystal Palace. It was served by three railways stations, all within walking distance. When I saw the development, just recently finished, I decided to buy one for £4,400 and soon evacuated from suburban Royston Road. I saw it in the daytime, but after moving in I realised the house was next to the railway. Trains shunted through the night, most nights.

Charles Salisbury was on his own after his divorce and I invited him to be my first lodger. There was no sign of subsidence, only incessant clanking. D. H. Lawrence had lived a quarter of a mile up the road in the 1920s when he was a teacher. Charles was the man who got me into Lawrence's work, and that of many more great writers. It was like having your own university lecturer in the house.

Norman Preston, who only read cricket books, wanted me as a long-term appointment, but when I heard that the *Daily Sketch* wanted a young sports writer, I told him, 'Sorry Norman, but my ambition from the age of eight has always been to work for a Fleet Street newspaper.' He grunted and moaned but he couldn't do anything about it.

Above: 1. Desolate Escoville (pop. 700) near Caen, Normandy, where the Scovells started out *c.* 1066.

Below left: 2. My grandfather Andrew 'Geewhizz' Souter at seventy-five in Ventnor, July 1953.

Below right: 3. My maternal grandmother, who abandoned my mother at the age of four. (*A. Brooks*)

Above: 4. My parents and my grandfather 'Geewhizz' on Ventnor Pier, June 1955.

Left: 5. My mother at fifty.

Below: 6. Catching the sun at the Lord Mayor Treloar Hospital, Alton, on 4 November 1945.

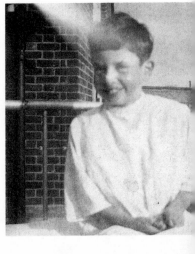

Right: 7. The 1830 toll house in St Lawrence where I was born.

Below: 8. The camouflaged radar station at St Lawrence, which was attacked by German troops in the Second World War.

Above left: 9. Aged three months, with my brother Allan and my mother, in 1936.

Above centre: 10. Orthopaedic patients in Alton. I am on the left.

Above right: 11. Dressed as a Scout patrol leader with Winston in front of the part of the garden that would later collapse into the churchyard, 1950.

Left: 12. Celebrating my 21st birthday.

Right: 13. My portrait, courtesy of the *Daily Sketch*, in the days of 'Rex Brian'.

Below: 14. With my mentor, Charles Salisbury, in 1964. Imitating Henry Cooper.

Left: 15. The O'Sullivan twins: Audrey (front row, second from left) and Lucy (far right).

Below: 16. Audrey (left) is voted 'Miss Boots' in 1960.

Above: 17. The wedding at Brompton Oratory, 1 October 1965. Left to right: Kate Walmsley (née O'Sullivan), Lucy Teodorczuk (née O'Sullivan), me, Audrey, Eric William O'Sullivan, Maude Janet Scovell, Maureen Wesson (née O'Sullivan), Percy Henry Scovell.

Right: 18. One of the wedding invitations sent out by Audrey's parents.

Mr. & Mrs. E. W. O'Sullivan
request the pleasure of the company of

Mr and Mrs W.P. O'Sullivan

at the marriage of their daughter

Audrey Esther

with

Mr. Brian Souter Scovell

at Brompton Oratory, Brompton Road, S.W.7
on Friday, 1st October, 1965, at 2-15 p.m.
and afterwards at
Crosby Hall, Cheyne Walk, Chelsea, S.W.3.

165, Lower Addiscombe Road,
Addiscombe,
Surrey.   R.S.V.P.

Opposite: 19. The Scovells on our big day.

Above: 20. Learie and Norma Constantine become the godparents of our daughter Louise.

Right: 21. Santa meets the Scovells in Trafalgar Square, 23 December 1972.

Above: 22. With Trevor Brooking, Gavin, and Louise at 84 Widmore Road, Bromley.

Below: 23. With Louise, Gavin, and Audrey.

Above: 24. Audrey and Louise at Yale University on graduation day.

Below: 25. Cake time, with Gavin.

Above: 26. With Percy Henry Scovell and Audrey in Bradford on Avon.

Below: 27. An audience with Pope John Paul II at the Vatican, 1990.

Right: 28. Audrey at a Royal College of Art life-drawing class.

Below: 29. Taking tea at Mumbai's Brabourne Stadium.

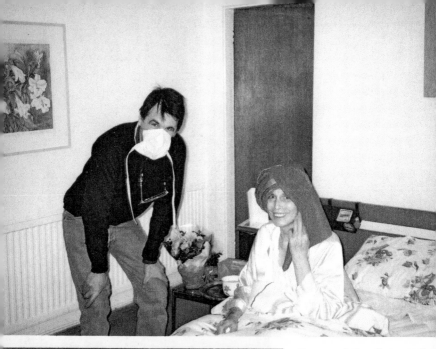

Above: 30. Audrey plays a practical joke on her artist friend Tony Farrell. Three weeks later she died, on Christmas Day 2000.

Left: 31. Evidence that 'Auds' still appears in my life! This sighting took place outside the Wentworth Hotel in Aldeburgh – I'd just been signing my book *Football Gentry* in an independent bookshop.

right: 32. Bill Nicholson – Mr Tottenham with Audrey.

below: 33. Bowled comprehensively! Must have been a no ball!

Above: 34. Audrey at twenty.

Below: 35. With our great friends, the Owen-Browne cricketing family, at Tilford CC – Jane, Melanie, Patrick, Dickie, Neil Runkel, me, Barbara, Gill, and Louise.

CHAPTER EIGHT

Signing Up for the *Sketch* under Pseudonyms

It was good fun working for the PA but I knew I had to join a national newspaper as soon as possible. You need luck in any sphere of life and late in March 1960 I was standing in the press tea room at White Hart Lane, packed in like one of Boris Johnson's commuters, when I heard Laurie Pignon saying, 'I'm getting a bit fed up with this football business. The *Sketch* needs a young whippersnapper to help me out.'

Laurie was the tennis writer. I didn't know him at the time but I knew he wasn't keen on reporting football throughout the year. Without speaking to him, I dashed out to the telephone room at the rear and dialled the number of Associated Newspapers. I asked for the name of the sports editor at the *Sketch* and was told 'Solly Chandler'. I recognised the name, because he had been high up on the news side of the *Express* for some years and had made his name by breaking the 1955 story about the British diplomats Guy Burgess and Donald Maclean – two of the notorious 'Cambridge Five' – fleeing to Moscow.

I asked to be put through to him and he said, 'Hello, this is Sol, Sol Chandler.'

I introduced myself and asked if I could come round to see him.

'When are you available?' he said.

'Tomorrow morning.'

The *Sketch* building was 300 yards from the PA and next day I was being ushered into his office. Solomon (that was his full name) was short in stature, with heavy glasses and smoothed-back grey hair. I guessed he was in his late fifties. He was very friendly and seemed to like my pushy way of applying for a job. I had all my certificates with me but he ignored them. Instead, he asked the key question. 'Who do you know?' At that time I didn't know too many, but in the more than fifty years in journalism since I must have met over 10,000 people. I've been fortunate to visit eighty-eight countries, more than Hillary Clinton, and not many people go to half of the countries of the world. But at that time, I didn't know many first-class footballers or cricketers.

When Solly asked me that question, I was taken by surprise. Working with an agency, you see plenty of people at a distance without getting to know them as well as the staff men of national newspapers. 'Oh,' I said, 'well, Walter Winterbottom, Alf Ramsey, Sir Stanley Rous, Jim Laker, Denis Compton...'

He interrupted me. 'Wow!' he said. 'You seem to be the right young man for us. I'll offer you £1,000 a year to start and we'll see how it goes.'

Rather stunned by the rapidity of the operation, I said, 'That's the same I get at the PA.'

'All right, about an extra £5 a week?' he asked.

Here's a good lesson for any young journalist: don't rush into accepting the first offer. 'I will have to think about that,' I said.

It was his turn to be surprised. He must have thought I was cheeky. 'Give me a ring tomorrow morning,' he said.

For the rest of the day, and half the night, I wondered whether I'd made a mistake. Perhaps I was too bold? But when I rang the next day, he started by saying, 'I've been thinking about your salary. I've decided to up it by £150 a year. Is that all right?'

Relieved, I said, 'Fine, thanks very much Sol.'

We were mates from the start. He wanted me to start work on the opening day of the cricket season. 'I'll put you down to cover the champions' game against MCC at Lord's. You've been there I suppose.'

'Oh yes,' I said. Actually, I hadn't, but I had passed by the ground once while on the top deck of a bus.

The *Sketch* was a breezy, well-laid-out newspaper with its title in red. It cost tuppence and the editor, Colin Valdar, walked with a slight limp, like me. On 27 April, he wrote to me. 'Dear Brian Scovell. This is to confirm your appointment to the sports-writing staff as arranged with Mr Chandler, beginning on May 1, 1960. Your salary will be £26 10s a week and the engagement will be subject to three months' notice on either side. I look forward to welcoming you here and I hope that you will have a successful career.' Valdar never spoke about his leg problem and he never asked about mine. But he was a great walker and he must have saved thousands of pounds in taxis.

I stayed on the payroll for forty years and when I 'retired' and went freelance I met someone at the pensions department and asked, 'How many employees with Associated Newspapers lasted forty years?'

He came back and said, 'I've checked with the computer and it's thirteen out of 30,000 and most of them weren't frontline journalists.'

Sol never mentioned my byline. The first piece I wrote, on page seventeen, was bylined 'By Sketch Cricket Reporter.' The headline was 'Listen to the Old Vic' – a typical Chandler headline. The intro was, 'Effort, chaps! If new Yorkshire skipper, 39 year old Vic Wilson, were an amateur that's what he would be telling his players today. But as a professional he probably had something more to the point to say at chilly Lord's yesterday after his team's pathetic performance against MCC.'

It was Sol's own work, not mine, but I learned a quick lesson: start with a lively paragraph that will grab the interest of the reader. Sol loved an exclamation mark. He drank a lot and after long lunches he would return at around five and scan the pages. Most days he didn't like what had been designed and started again. Within a few minutes, he produced a much more lively make-up. That was a regular occasion.

Early on, Sol called me in and said, 'We've got to have a name on the cricket pieces, what about "Rex Brian"?'

I wasn't in a position to argue. All the papers would give out pseudonyms to young writers in case the new recruits weren't very good. Junior staff could then be sacked and replaced without the readers noticing the turnover of staff. Sol gave me 'Rex' because he was an admirer of Rex Harrison, the Liverpool-born actor who played Professor Henry Higgins in *My Fair Lady*. But 'Rex' wasn't his real name. He was christened Reginald, a name that wouldn't have stirred the libido of many female filmgoers. Critic Robert Gore-Langton said of him, 'He was an abusive, philandering, self-serving, gluttonous egomaniac with a blind indifference to the thoughts and feelings of others.' Harrison, who wore a toupée in his later years, married six times. Two of his wives, Carole Landis and Rachel Roberts, were driven to suicide by his behaviour. 'Sexy Rexy' he might been to millions of people, but I wasn't keen to be named after him. I suppose it attracted attention and a few jokes.

The South African touring party had arrived in England and they were apprehensive about possible apartheid demonstrations. 'Rex Brian' was advising the *Sketch*'s readers, 'After seeing them I can tell you that fans up and down the country are in for a treat.'

Soon I was taunted by cries of 'Sexy Rexy' from other cricket writers, some of whom were much older and rather cynical, like Charles Bray, the former Essex player who worked for the *Daily Herald*. Bray played ninety-five games for Essex as an amateur and was described as 'a defensive batsman'. When he became a journalist, his carping style of writing upset most of the players. The most ferocious critic was Evelyn Maitland Wellings, known as 'Lyn' to his small number of acquaintances. An off spinner, he played for Oxford and Surrey as an amateur and became the cricket correspondent of the *Evening News* for many years. He savaged the reputations of many cricketers and didn't care. He knew the game better than most and few chose to argue with him. I was sharing a telephone with him once at a Test at Old Trafford and when his last piece had been phoned over by his personal phonist I asked if I could use it. 'Certainly,' he said. A few minutes later I was phoning some copy in the phone booth at the rear of the press box when Wellings yanked the door open and screamed 'Get off that ******* phone!' I decided to ring off and give way.

Wellings was eccentric, like a few other cricket writers of that time. He died at the age of eighty-three. Longevity has long been a feature of cricket reporting – Bray, Swanton, Crawford White, and my *Mail* mentor Alex Bannister all lived into their nineties. When John Arlott died in 1991, a reporter from *The Guardian* rang Wellings for his opinion of the great cricket broadcaster, possibly the best of all time, and he said, 'He was the most evil man I've ever met.' That should have applied to Wellings, not to Arlott. I knew Arlott, a fellow Hampshire man, for many years; he loved cricket, his family, and his wine. Presiding over his dinner table at night, in Alresford and latterly in Alderney, he entertained dozens of his friends and guests with his stories. But when he reported football, which he did for some years, he changed his personality and on many train journeys to matches I found him rather maudlin, almost boring. I soon discovered the reason – he hated football. Hooliganism was ruining the sport and he wrote a piece in *The Guardian* announcing that he would never write another word about the 'despicable game', as he called it. And he kept his word. The death of his young son affected him deeply and he was never the same after his loss.

Watching cricket for six hours a day can be taxing, particularly in the 1960s when too many England batsmen were playing for their averages. Some of the younger journalists liked playing practical jokes on the seniors. One day, when England had been scoring agonisingly slowly, Peter Laker, a *Mirror* reporter and the chief prankster, put a black plastic lump resembling dog excreta on Arlott's working space. It was tea time and Arlott was returning to write his account of the play for *The Guardian* after working on *Test Match Special*. At this time, he had usually drunk a bottle of wine or two and could be emotional. He came into the Edgbaston press box, stopped, stared blankly at the offending lump, and then said, in a pained voice, 'So that's what they think of me.' He turned and walked out, pursued by the *Mirror* man.

Laker – no relation of Jim's – caught up with him down the steps and said. 'It was only a joke John.'

Arlott said, 'I didn't see it as a joke. They think I'm shit!' He drove off to his hotel.

On another occasion, he was commentating on a game at Grace Road and for some time he had the teams the wrong way around. It was some time before someone pointed out to him that Leicestershire were in the field, not batting. By then, he was close to retirement. He soon departed to his beloved Alderney, which had been the most heavily-defended of the German-occupied Channel Islands during the Second World War.

Another prominent personality I sometimes met on the way to football matches while on travelling on trains around that time was Clement Freud, a grandson of Sigmund Freud. He had a lugubrious look about him and his humour was very pointed. We were covering an FA Cup tie together at Bournemouth's Dean Court, which was three miles from the railway station, and we were aiming to catch the 6.10 back to Waterloo. There were no taxis and no buses and we were discussing whether we should walk. Suddenly a taxi drove up and marching towards it was Roger Fitzpatrick, who had refereed the tie. Fitzpatrick, a pudgy, overweight man, was renowned for being able to 'run' backwards just as fast as going forwards. Fitzpatrick started opening the door of the taxi as Freud went up to him.

'Excuse me Mr Referee. My name is Clement Freud and I have covered this match today in my newspaper. There doesn't seem to be many taxis in this place. If you are going to the station, as I suspect, can this gentleman and myself share your cab?'

Fitzpatrick looked at him disdainfully and said, 'I intend to travel alone, thank you.' He sat down in the back seat of the taxi and slammed the door. The driver drove off, leaving us stranded.

Eventually we did get a taxi, but missed the train. When I met Freud again, he told me, 'I found the home telephone number of Mr Fitzpatrick and when I arrived at my home at two in the morning, I rang him. I said, "I am the man whom you rudely refused to let travel to the station with you and I am pleased to tell you that I have now safely arrived at my residence. Good night, Sir!"'

Some readers may not like seeing 'I' in newspaper articles but Sol insisted on it in the *Sketch*. One piece, under the name of Rex Brian, but written with help from Sol, started, 'I saw the 1960 Championship winners at Portsmouth today. The champions? Mike Smith's wiry worriers from Warwick.'

Rex Brian proved to be an awful tipster. Warwickshire finished fifteenth out of seventeen that season. Another embarrassing story appeared under Rex's byline: 'Now Laker chucks – dirt!' I was asked to write about Jim Laker's controversial book, *Over to Me*, which criticised Colin Cowdrey, Peter May, Tony Lock, Freddie Brown, and others. One sentence in 'my' piece was, 'Jim has asked for the muck spreading fork to be passed to him, and in 233 bitter, backbiting pages, he gives cricket another kick.'

I wasn't sure if Jim knew that I was the co-author but when Sol signed him up a year later to write a column, he never mentioned it. 'That Rex Brian used to give you a bit of stick,' I told Jim, and he grinned.

In June, Sol called me in and said, 'You're doing well but we need to get more bite in your pieces.'

I had to say to him, 'As I don't know too many people yet I won't be able to build up contacts if I use my own name.'

'I appreciate that,' he said. 'I've come up with another byline for you for your nastier columns.' He wrote down, 'By the Man with the Chopper.'

My two pseudonyms lasted several weeks before Sol gave me my own byline. I had to take a lot of ribbing, particularly about my alleged sexual prowess. I had letters from girls addressed to 'Sexy Rexy' but sadly it was too soon for the start of Facebook, otherwise I might have laid on a few dates. Now, along with my ghostwriter Sol, I was doing three men's work, and I was just twenty-four. I was the youngest cricket number one on a national newspaper, the number two football reporter (Rex Brian), and the paper's hatchet man (The Man with the Chopper). No wonder that Valdar sent me a letter, saying, 'You have had a tough trial with the *Sketch* and I am delighted that you have come through it so well. As a slight acknowledgement of your efforts, I have increased your salary from £26 10s to £29 a week.'

That summer was one of the most controversial for years. The MCC, backed by Sir Don Bradman, called for tough action against players with questionable bowling actions. England's Harold Rhodes was penalised and the twenty-one-year-old South African Geoff Griffin was no-balled at Lord's in the second Test. 'My' pieces now had huge headlines. One that made me cringe was 'I Stop Griffin'. The story started, 'There is no Geoff Griffin in the South African team at Old Trafford, with splint or without, today. And you can blame me (and a few other Press guys) for that.'

When Sol rang me and read it over there was no mention of the 'other Press guys' and I said, 'We've got to get that in. It could cause ructions.'

Later I was looking out of the press box window towards the away dressing room when Peter Heine, the fearsome Springbok fast bowler, saw me and gave me a 'V' sign. I made a mental note that if I was batting in the nets later and he was around, I would be ready to flee to my car and drive off as soon as possible. Heine, no longer with us, was a real mean man.

Sol relented over the addition of the other pressmen on the 'Stop Griffin' bandwagon, but the next day he was at it again, pumping up my intro about spectators not having their money back when play was abandoned at lunch. The intro was, 'Several hundred people were robbed at Old Trafford yesterday. There's a police station near but the police didn't lift a finger. Coppers watched and all they said was, "Hard luck chaps." I say let's have justice.'

The next morning, the Lancashire secretary Geoff Howard visited the rickety wooden press box and said, 'The committee members are threatening to take action against your newspaper.' Geoffrey was the nicest man I knew in cricket and fortunately he knew the background of the emergence of that firebrand Rex Brian. 'Don't worry,' he said. 'You won't be named in the action!' I made one little slip in my piece – I had mistaken the Salford Council building for the police station, and I couldn't blame Sol for that!

Three months later, the *Sketch* was forced to carry an apology. It said, 'Rex Brian's object was to criticise the practice of not giving free passes for another day to people who had bought tickets in advance and were admitted to the ground. That practice, the Lancashire club inform us, is a rule of the Board of Control, and not the responsibility of the county club. We regret if the article was taken by anyone as imputing unfairness to the club.' Geoffrey was right. My name was kept out of it. It was an enterprising piece of journalism on a day with little cricket to write about. Years later, the Test and County Cricket Board brought in refunds for when a certain amount of play is lost. If Sol had been alive, he would have put a box on the back page with a headline, 'We Were Right!'

Another article said the Springboks were boring, the opposite of what I had written a month previously. Sol put the headline 'Bad Boy Brian' on the top of a page of indignant letters.

One man wrote, 'Your article was in the most execrable taste.'

'Once again we are forced to read a load of trash written by Rex Brian,' said another.

I agreed. Poor Griffin was hounded by the press, the umpires, and the authorities, and his name appeared in massive headlines in the *Sketch* as though he was public enemy number one. It wasn't fair – the reason he couldn't bowl with a straight arm was an accident he'd had as a child; more famous players did far worse. Griffin's brief career ended when Sid Buller kept calling him in an exhibition match after the second Test. Sid was a genuine man who cared for his umpiring colleagues, the cricketers he umpired with, and the game. He was strongly criticised and took it personally. I spent a lot of time with him that year and I felt sorry for him. I think the pressure hastened his death from a heart attack. He was sixty-one, and died while umpiring a match at Edgbaston in 1970. He was in the same class as Frank Chester (the umpire who had one arm), David Shepherd, Alec Skelding (who retired at the age of seventy-two), and Dickie Bird, who almost became a millionaire after the publication of his third autobiography. I wrote his first book, *Not Out*, in 1978. Not wishing to write another one so soon, I gave the publisher a title for his second: *That's Out.* That was what Dickie said when he gave batsmen out. After his retirement, Dickie commissioned a local writer to compose his autobiography, which I thought had been lined up for me, and he boasted, 'My book is the biggest-selling sports book ever in this country!'

I wasn't too bothered being overlooked. Instead, I wrote my own Dickie Bird book, entitled *Dickie Bird: A Tribute to Umpire Harold Bird.* I interviewed 117 cricketers, politicians, and administrators and all of them supplied wonderful new stories about the world's most popular and best-known umpire. For ten weeks, my book topped the nonfiction hardback list.

I was very sad about Griffin's expulsion from Test cricket. He fell off his bicycle when he was at school and was unable to straighten his right arm naturally, so he was certainly not a cheat. He became the first touring player to be called for throwing at Lord's and he also became the first bowler to take a hat trick at cricket's headquarters. His joy was cut short when he was called eleven times by Frank Lee in that match and in the exhibition game that followed, Sid Buller kept no-balling him and he had to finish the over by bowling underarm.

In 2005 I met Geoff on a tour to South Africa and he played for the Willows CC at the Kearnsey College ground near Durban, against the Forty Club, an English club of over-forties whose average age is closer to sixty than forty. He wanted me to write a book about his life but although he was keen, there wasn't enough material to make the project a success. While he was batting, I went for a walk and watched a schools game on the back pitch. I saw an eighteen-year-old bowler with a slightly bent arm take a hat trick. I told him, 'You're not the only one! Geoff Griffin, the first Test player to take one at Lord's, is playing on the front pitch.' Geoff had a young family and a year or so later, he died at the age of sixty-six. Some people have tough lives, and he was one of them.

The headlines were becoming bigger and bigger in the *Sketch.* Maybe that was the reason why its circulation, around 750,000, was fast ebbing away. The *Mirror* sold four times as many copies and it had more money to spend. The *Sketch* was looked on as a peppy little production that appealed to middle and lower class readers, a different readership to that of the *Mirror.* On 21 September 1960, our readers must have been surprised by the gargantuan headline on the *Sketch*'s front page: '£55,000 Soccer Haggle Over Star'. It filled the whole page. On the left side, there was a picture of George Eastham, the Newcastle and England inside forward. Another George Eastham, his father, had also played for England. The byline was mine and the article started, 'The biggest transfer deal in British Soccer ['soccer' should have been lower case: sack that sub!] history was being haggled over last night. It looks as though Arsenal or Spurs will have to pay Newcastle United £55,000 or more for inside forward George Eastham.'

That year the leaders of the Professional Footballers' Association, a trade union, were rebelling against the maximum wage of £20 a week. Fulham forward Jimmy Hill, the chairman, threatened a strike. I knew Hill from covering games at Craven Cottage and was impressed by his sharpness, knowledge, and drive. The *Sketch* team played an ITV team around that time and the television people included Jimmy Hill, Brian Moore, Jim Rosenthal, and Ian St John. The friendly was on a clayey, rain-soaked ground at the Associated Newspapers sports ground in Worcester Park. Jimmy ran the whole show. He shouted instructions to his players and it was like he had a footballing Playstation in his hands. He was much too clever for the industrialists and mill owners in charge of the Football League. George Eastham junior remained a key figure in the dispute. He walked out of Newcastle because he wanted more than £20 a week.

Ernie Clay, a millionaire Geordie, had a factory in Huddersfield and a cork business in Reigate and was a wonderful manipulator. He even stood for President of the League, but lost. Blunt-speaking Ernie gave Eastham a 'job' as a salesman during the three months when he was unemployed and he was the man in the background who was intent on removing the shackles from the professional footballers. He would ring me at eight in the morning and kept ringing me through the day, and often at night. He gave me the news as it happened and my byline became larger and larger, around half an inch in depth.

Today it is difficult for football writers to speak to the people involved in big transfers. They have to go through press officers, who say little. When the deal is done, they call a press conference and after a few questions, the officer says, 'One more question.' You rarely get the real story. That is why so much is written as speculation. Some football people have always told untruths; it is part of the game. The ones who want to stay out of the limelight and hand responsibility to the press officers have something to hide. As with the cricket betting scandals, the villains are still at large.

Clay advised the taciturn Eastham to sue Newcastle, which was another *Sketch* scoop. He also told Eastham to play in a friendly at Brentford, defying the League rules. George was five-foot-seven and less than ten stone. He was just twenty-three, but he was a very determined young man. With a father who grew up as a professional footballer, he was ahead of most young players and he knew what he wanted. Just before Christmas, he signed for Arsenal and the fee was £47,500. George was a good servant of the game, but he wasn't a superstar. He later emigrated to South Africa and I lost contact with him. He was a good man. Early in 1961, the players – or the slaves, as Ernie said – voted unanimously for a strike and Joe Richards, the aged President of the League who loved smoking cigars at the meetings, had to concede. The maximum was removed, but today the pendulum has swung too far the other way. The average weekly wage for Premiership players is now around £50,000, with the biggest earners receiving £140,000 or more.

We enjoyed some hilarious press conferences outside the Ministry of Labour and outside the Café Royal. In one of his more inspired speeches, Jimmy Hill said, 'How much longer will we allow such men to go on damaging the game with their pomposity, their inflated egocentricity, and their blundering inefficiency? Football deserves better.' It took two more years to take the handcuffs away so that players were free to go where they liked.

Alan Hardaker, the former naval lieutenant commander who was secretary of the Football League, was one of my best contacts. I asked him for his views of the League Management Committee members and he said, 'Bloody idiots. I have to tell them what to do and half of them can't even hear what I say.'

He was a tough man, a man who kept his word. The only time I was involved in a libel action concerned him. Hardaker wrote to the clubs and asked them to be more responsible over criticism of referees by managers (a subject that is still coming up today on a regular basis). It was a Chelsea *v.* Newcastle game and David Coleman was commentating for the BBC. Several times he criticised the referee. The next day I rang Hardaker and said, 'Is that what you mean?'

'Yes,' he said. 'Coleman got it wrong and we'll be looking into it. He doesn't know the law.'

I asked him if he minded being quoted. Often something is said as a friend and when it is quoted, the person has to deny it because it was off the record.

Hardaker said, 'Quote me on it.'

The story appeared the next day and shortly afterwards the Associated Newspapers had a letter of complaint. I knew Ken Wolstenholme well and I asked him for his opinion. 'Hardaker is right,' he said. 'Coleman got it wrong. If it gets to court, I'm happy to give evidence of your behalf.'

I rang Hardaker again, expecting he would deny the words, but he said, 'I'll stand by them down to my last piece of furniture in my house.'

It would have been an interesting High Court case but our lawyers agreed to pay around £1,400 damages. Most times newspapers will settle on small amounts, irrespective of whether or not the story is true.

One of my favourite anecdotes about Ernie Clay concerned Robert Maxwell, who became the chairman of Oxford. I invited Ernie to the Football Writers' Association dinner at the end of one season and Harry Harris, my colleague on the *Mail*, invited Maxwell as a guest. Clay and Maxwell disliked each other and we intended to keep them apart on the table. Harry and I were in the deserted bar before the dinner started when the massive Maxwell came in. 'Where am I sitting?' he said in a loud voice. We showed him our table. The only other people in the huge room were the waiters being briefed by their boss. Maxwell sat down and shouted, 'Waiter, bring me the wine list!'

I said, 'It will be another hour before we sit down.' Maxwell picked out the most expensive wine and ordered two bottles. We had to remain at our seats as the room started to fill up.

Clay came in and sat down on the other side. He was talking to me and Harry was chatting to Maxwell as the other guests joined us. After the first course was served, Ernie shouted across to Maxwell, 'Bob, tell me about the episode when you were banned from being a director.' The other guests laughed but Maxwell didn't join in. Ernie chided him. 'Go on, tell us the truth.'

Suddenly Maxwell got up and walked out. Earlier in his career, Maxwell had wanted to take over Manchester United but was rebuffed. He would ring Harry or me to give us stories that put United in a bad light. He was an ogre. After one match at Oxford, a young radio reporter asked him for an interview. 'It's rather late but hop in and we will do it on the way back home,' said Maxwell as he was stepping into his Bentley. Maxwell lived at Headington Hall, a couple of miles from the ground. When the car arrived at his home, he got out and said 'Good night.' He walked through the front door, leaving the youngster to walk back to the city at 11.30 p.m.

Like a number of powerful, dynamic, ruthless businessmen, Maxwell went into football because he wanted, and needed, the publicity. Even joining Oxford, a small club with no resources, got his name into the newspapers. He received far better publicity from football than any of his business activities. Nowadays the American investors are aiming to make profits by following the Manchester United lead and concentrating on the commercial side of clubs. Like Maxwell, they know little about the game. He boasted that he used to climb over the wall to watch Arsenal, but he wasn't really interested in sport. At his size and girth, you couldn't imagine him climbing a ten-foot-high wall.

When Oxford knocked out Everton on their way to winning the Football League Cup in 1986, the journalists wanted to go into the home dressing room to interview Jim Smith and his players. I was among them and a King Kong-sized figure was blocking the entrance – Captain Bob. 'Well you chaps,' he said. 'This is the greatest day in the history of this little club and it won't stay a little club. I will be turning it into a major club, competing with the best in the world. I will give them a stadium our fans will be proud of.' And on and on. Jim Smith was behind him, unable to say a word. None of the players could be interviewed either. It was the Maxwell Show. He exuded power with his booming, guttural voice and his size. In a single meeting of the Football League, he won the support of the other chairmen, most of whom had previously opposed him. He was looked on as the ideas man to save the game. But he conned them just as he conned everyone else. He drowned while cruising about the Canary Islands on his luxury yacht, but we still don't know how he died – was it suicide, murder, or a terrible accident? Betty, his long-suffering wife, whom he spurned after they had produced nine children in forty-seven years of marriage, claimed that more than 5,000 people wrote letters of condolence. They included Margaret Thatcher, Neil Kinnock, and George Bush. They were duped like everyone else. Many people in football knew that he was committing fraud. The FA, the guardians of the game, should have investigated his footballing transgressions.

As for Ernie Clay, he managed to persuade the Church Commissioners to sell Craven Cottage to him and when he sold the club, he made £7 million. But for him, Fulham may well have gone under, but £7 million in those days was a lot of money. These 'benefactors' are considered by the fans as selfless saviours of hard-up clubs, but they usually make big profits from their investments in football.

The volume of copy under my name mounted, but it took eleven months before Sol let me have a picture byline. Again, he overdid it. In the Good Friday edition, he produced a box above my holiday matches preview story that contained the immortal words 'Brian Scovell's Easter Egg' – with my head shooting out of the egg.

In the spring of 1961 he said, 'Do you fancy working in the north?'

'Where?' I said.

'Manchester,' he said. 'You'll love it.'

He offered a sweetener, £5 a week, and I said, 'How long? I don't want to spend my working life up there.'

He assured me I would be writing my usual cricket articles and would be back in the London office within a year, so I accepted. I rang Stratton Smith, known as Tony, who was the chief football reporter, and asked him where I should live. Tony was a good friend of Matt Busby and the United players and he recommended speaking to Dennis Violett. I rang Dennis and he said, 'I haven't got a clue.'

In the first week, the office booked me into a hotel, with the advice that I should find digs by the second week. Looking through the *Manchester Evening News*, I noticed an advert offering 'top class accommodation for young men in Hale'. Hale is one of the poshest parts; I rang the number. The woman who answered seemed pleasant and asked me to call in.

When I turned up, I was taken aback. The house was massive and it had stables for horses at the rear. I knocked at the door and I had another surprise: she was wearing an expensive outfit and a collection of jewellery. She didn't appear to be a person used to taking in lodgers. She invited me into the dining room and a silver teapot and china cups and saucers were waiting. 'I have one other young man who works in the income tax office and he is very quiet,' she explained.

I found it difficult to believe that she wanted to do this work. 'My husband is away a lot and I find it reassuring that someone is around,' she explained.

For a while I thought she in looking for toy boys and was relieved that it wasn't the case. She was an exceptionally good cook and I got on well with her and her horses, but not her husband; I never met him. I think the explanation of my arrival was that she was lonely in a big house and needed the company.

On the Easter Monday Bank Holiday I covered three League matches on the same day, one at Preston in the morning, the second at Sheffield Wednesday, and the third at Manchester City. It must have been a record. The only problem was that I was held up in traffic going to Hillsborough and I arrived a couple of seconds before half-time. The phone, which I hired, rang, and someone from the office said, 'Are you ready to dictate some copy?'

I couldn't say I had only just arrived so I said, 'Hang on for a couple of minutes and I'll be ready.' I put my hand over the speaker and said to another journalist, 'What happened?' Most journalists perform that rescue act for their colleagues and this one didn't let me down.

Two weeks later I was back on cricket and Sol fixed up an interview with Richie Benaud, the Australian captain, who was arriving in London for the Ashes series. My piece was bylined 'By the Number 1 cricket reporter.' Sol made me cringe a number of times and that was probably the worst. I was constantly ribbed by the older correspondents. The story was spectacularly headed 'On A Deck, SS *Himalaya*' and started, 'Here I am five storeys high over Tilburn Docks sitting at the start of the great Aussie invasion. It will make or break cricket because cricket is facing a crisis.' Sol wasn't wholly right because, in the opinion of most experts, Benaud had just led his team to victory in the greatest Test series of all time against Frank Worrell's West Indians. That meeting with Benaud started a lifelong friendship and almost forty years later it was very pleasing that he said some kind things about me in a video from Australia for one of my farewell parties. While rereading that interview on the 'A Deck' I caught this amazing line: 'Richie promised that most of his batsmen will walk when they think they have been caught behind the wicket. He said, "There is no rule about it but we encourage it."' I think that he must have been joking. Keith

Miller was the only one of his batsmen to 'walk' and the last Australian to do it was Adam Gilchrist.

There was no more astute Australian captain than Benaud. He worked as a journalist before he made his name and his PR in that series was brilliant. The shy Peter May was totally outshone. Peter was always reluctant to speak to the press but Benaud seized every opportunity to advance the cause of his team. To win public support when you are the away side is a vital part of any Test campaign and year after year England were second best. They still are, despite recent England captains taking public speaking lessons. The only exception was Tony Greig, who was born in South Africa but led the England team. In the words of John Woodcock, Greig 'wasn't English through and through'. He spoke his mind, behaved naturally, and enhanced his career with frank interviews.

A leader of his mental strength is needed now in English cricket. Kevin Pietersen, another South African, was tried, but his appointment was a calamitous mistake. Just after his promotion, I spoke at a lunch at Trent Bridge at the Nottinghamshire Cricket Society and I asked the audience of 120, 'How many of you agree with his selection?' Not a single hand went up. Most players I meet think he is egocentric, arrogant, and not a good team man. They are right. Andrew Strauss is a far better communicator – he speaks intelligently, and does it with a smile.

Successful Australian skippers like Benaud, Bobby Simpson, Mark Taylor, and Ian Chappell always courted the English journalists, and it helped their team. In 1961 Benaud dominated the back pages with stories about his shoulder problem and his fears about missing matches. On the final day of the decisive Old Trafford Test, England were 150-1 with 106 runs needed to win when Benaud took a gamble and switched to bowling around the wicket into the rough caused by Freddie Trueman's footmarks. He snatched an improbable victory. It took character; he was barely able to spin the ball because of the pain, but the 34,000 crowd were quietened as he removed both Raman Subba Row (at forty-nine) and Ted Dexter (at eighty-four), and then bowled Peter May around his legs. The cocky Brian Close hit a six. Two runs later, he tried another big hit and was caught deep on the legside by Norman O'Neill. On the first day O'Neill was roughed by Jack Flavell, the yeoman Worcestershire bowler who hit him three times in a short space of time, including once in the 'box'. Norm was in such a bad state, he vomited on the pitch. When he recovered to face the next ball, he fell back onto his wicket, trying to avoid another bouncer, and was given out 'hit wicket' by umpire John Langridge. 'I didn't play a shot,' he complained afterwards. 'I shouldn't have been given out!'

Norm was a classic case of the Over Expectation Factor. Some writers called him the new Bradman, but after three hundreds in the build-up to the Test series he showed signs of nerves at the beginnings of big innings. I had brief chats with him at various times and he seemed a confident young man, a typical Australian. But he ended up as a nearly man. Two days after I wrote these words, the news came through that he had died on 3 March 2008 at the age of seventy-one.

The OEF still affects English cricket. Inexperienced journalists exaggerate the qualities of players like Andrew Flintoff, Monty Panesar, and Steve Harmison. To be considered world class, you should be good enough to make a world eleven. None of those three are in that class.

Alex Bannister, the cricket correspondent of the *Daily Mail*, was chairman of the Cricket Writers' Club that year and he made some caustic comments about my cricketing knowledge to his colleagues. 'That bloody Scovell,' he used to say. He was right. My style was too brash for most of the newspapers, but not Sol's *Sketch*. Alex became a good friend over the years and he knew the game better than most cricket journalists. He wasn't a stylist, but was one of the last of the reporters to specialise in obtaining genuine scoops and he never broke confidences. I tried to follow his example.

Bill Bowes, the former England and Yorkshire fast bowler who succeeded Bannister as chairman, was more understanding of my journalistic excesses in those days. 'Don't let it worry you,' he said. Along with Gubby Allen, Bowes refused to bowl flat out on bouncers in the Bodyline series and he was respected for that. He was a gentle, kind man, which is unusual for a fast bowler.

No one doubted that Benaud was a world-class performer and his 6-70 gave the Australians their first win at Old Trafford – a ground they hate – since 1902. He won it from behind because he held his nerve when England's players were losing theirs. It is sad now that Old Trafford has fallen behind other Test venues, but its redevelopment, when it finally happens, should restore its position. Benaud was cheered to the wicket in the final Test at the Oval, proof that he held the esteem of the cricket lovers in England. Early in his career he worked as a reporter and put a lot of time into becoming a rounded sportsman who could express himself in public. He always invited a few English journalists into his dressing room, including me. In my fifty years in cricket reporting, no England captain has ever done that. Norman Preston, the editor of *Wisden* and my former boss, wrote, 'The tour was a personal triumph for Richie Benaud, possibly the most popular captain of any overseas team to come to Great Britain.' Richie, almost eighty as I write, is still commentating on the game he loves. His English wife Daphne, who acts as his secretary, is a wonderful lady who has played a huge part in his success.

At the start of the 1961/62 season, Sol came up with his final interference in my byline. He tried, 'By Brian Scovell (Rhymes with Shovel).' There were hoots all round when it first appeared and for some time I was known as 'Shove'. 'Rex Brian' was still popping out sometimes, also 'The Man with the Chopper'. Thankfully, by the end of the year, they were dying out.

Sol was delighted with one of my stories. The heading was 'Boss Gets the Sack in His Bed' and the intro started, 'Frank Hill, manager of Notts County for three years, was hitting the sack yesterday morning when the sack hit him. He was in bed when his son gave him a letter from club chairman Len Machin. It said "Dear Mr Hill. We very much regret that your employment with this club must be terminated forthwith." Hill wasn't going to take it lying down.'

Hill was known as 'Tiger' because he loved throwing himself into tackles. Before joining Notts County he coached the Iraq international squad. Another Hill, James William Thomas Hill of Balham, had just won the battle over players' contracts against the Football League in 1961, in his role as chairman of the Professional Footballers

Association. Derrick Robins, another self-publicist, was chairman of Coventry City, a team languishing in the Third Division, and he wanted Jimmy Hill as his manager.

The cricket-loving Robins gave Hill carte blanche to run the club and I suggested to Sol that I should have a week with Hill at Highfield Road. Sol was enthusiastic and so was Hill. The *Sketch* gave a page to it every day and it was wonderful publicity for a struggling outpost club. The series was called 'The Wizard of Coventry – day by day with Jimmy Hill'. Heather, the second of Hill's four wives, said, 'I hope you've brought your bed with you. Board meetings usually start at 5.30 and often finish at 3.30 a.m.!'

The Wizard came up with a host of brilliant ideas, including undersoil heating, the Sky Blue commercial concept (which included the creation of the club's own radio station), new stands, and free speech. 'I believe in letting the players talk freely to the press,' he said. At that time there was a rule in the players' contract that no interview could take place without the club's permission. Forty-odd years later, most footballers still cannot speak without permission. Heads of communication tend to select 'safe' candidates, who are programmed to make bland statements. Hill also announced a five-year plan costing £250,000 and he promised that the Sky Blues would be in the First Division after that time. He kept his word. It was an astonishing performance. But because he gave the impression of being big-headed – well, he was! – little praise came his way. His rivals were jealous, of course.

In 1968 he suddenly announced his resignation. 'Players can't keep listening to the same speech from the manager,' he said. 'They lose interest. I've done well to stay as long as I have done.' London Weekend Television made him their head of sport and he made a success of that as well. From humble beginnings as a cornet-playing Boys' Brigade sergeant, he had been a stand-in chimney sweep, an assistant to a City stockbroker, a soldier, a player good enough to score five goals in a game against Doncaster, an FA coach, a club manager, a union leader, a club director, a club chairman, a TV boss, a businessman, and even an emergency linesman at a game at Highbury. He is the complete all-rounder and was still appearing on Sky TV in his late seventies. He should have gone even further in the game and certainly should have been given a knighthood. He would have been an ideal chairman of the FA, running the game from top to bottom. As a disciple of Sir Walter Winterbottom, the man who brought in the FA coaching scheme, he preached good values and was only booked once in his career, for querying a referee over a throw-in. He is one of the most enthusiastic men I've ever met, although his remarkable life was marked by tragedy. His mother lost her first husband in the First World War and his half-sister Rene, who was almost international class in cricket, died in a car accident. Wally, his brother, fell off a crane in Basra and died, and his second wife, Heather, died of cancer. But his stepfather managed to survive on two occasions when his ships were torpedoed. A determined fighter, Hill himself survived cancer of the colon.

Another engaging character with similar qualities, whom I had great affection for, was Lew Kirby, the political editor of the *Sketch* before he became editor of the

Evening Standard and then deputy editor, under David English, of the *Mail*. A Catholic born in Liverpool, one of eleven, Lew had more children than Jimmy Hill and three wives to Jimmy Hill's four. Lew had five children when he joined the *Sketch*, but soon started an affair with a colleague, the delectable Heather Nicholson. I knew both Heather and her sister Joyce, who was also on the staff, and everyone knew about the relationship. Later, he married Heather and fathered two more children. Years later, he interviewed another young lady named Heather, fell in love with her, and they had two children, taking his total to nine. No one knew how he had time to produce so many offspring, but they all loved each other. When he died in 2006, his final father-in-law praised him for his faithfulness!

CHAPTER NINE

The Greatest Goalscorer of All Time

The finest finisher I have seen in football is James Peter Greaves. Most times he passed the ball like a snooker player, right into the corner of the net. He rarely blasted it. He had style and shunned crudeness. His greatest assets were his pace, his anticipation, and his coolness. One day in Stamford Bridge in 1958 I saw him end the career of Billy Wright, the captain of England and Wolves, by scoring five goals. He teased Wright like a matador baffling and humiliating a bull before plunging in the sword. Wolves were the champions and in the previous season they had scored 103 goals and conceded just forty-seven, the best record in the Football League. A crowd of 61,000 turned up to see them and Chelsea were soon a goal behind, scored by Bobby Mason in the third minute. Greaves equalised with a rare hard shot and followed it up with two more goals. He eased the ball over the line, with goalkeeper Malcolm Finlayson powerless to do anything about it.

William Ambrose Wright was born in February, the same month as Greaves, and was in his thirty-fifth year. Greaves was eighteen, half his age. Jimmy's fourth came from a pass from Peter Brabook, the former Chelsea and West Ham winger, whom I still meet at matches (he is now a scout). As Greaves swept past him on the halfway line, Billy stumbled and fell. Jimmy ran on and on and dummied Finlayson before tapping the ball into the far corner, the safest place to put it. He scored again, but it was disallowed as offside. Chelsea six, Wolves two. A few days later, Wright, who was just short of being a great player, mainly because of his lack of height, announced he would retire at the end of the season. He bowed out to hurrahs after 491 League matches and 105 England appearances.

Asked about Greaves, Stan Cullis, the Wolves manager, said, 'What a player! Someone has just said to me he doesn't run enough. He wouldn't have to do that for me. You score five goals and all someone can find to say is, "He doesn't run enough!"'

That apparent indolence of Greaves dogged him through his career. Once he told me, 'The most difficult person to mark is the man who stands still.' That is true. Once Greaves took off, few defenders could match his speed.

Billy married Joy Beverley, one of the Beverley Sisters, at Poole Register Office in 1958 and their happy marriage lasted thirty-six years until he died from stomach cancer in 1994, at the age of seventy. It could have been termed the first celebrity football wedding, because thousands of people turned up. Their honeymoon was a single night at a hotel in Stratford-upon-Avon, because Joy was working in a show in Bournemouth the next day. Teddie, one of the sisters, said, 'There were no gifts, no fuss at all and it was just love from beginning to end.'

When I met Peter Brabook in 2007, he had trouble walking. He was tackled by the toughest left-backs of his time and his bowed and battered legs were often the subject of debate. 'Both knees have gone,' he said. 'I need new ones!'

A year later, when I attended the first game at Colchester's £10 million Community Stadium after advising the club about their facilities, he was smiling. 'I've had a replacement knee on the left leg,' he said. 'Works like a treat and I'm holding back on the other one to see how it goes. I wanted to do it privately but couldn't afford the £18,000 for both knees and I contacted the PFA. They offered a proportion and I was struggling until I saw Joe Cole, who played in the juniors when I coached him at West Ham, and he said, "I'll pay the £18,000." People talk about greedy footballers but there is another side of it. Joe is a diamond, a lovely boy.'

No one coached Jimmy because he was a natural genius and there are few of those around these days, if any. Pelé was the king; others in that class were Bobby Charlton, Eusébio, Alfredo di Stéfano, Tom Finney, Stan Matthews, Diego Maradona, Johann Cruyff, George Best and Denis Law. I've met all of them and they had an aura about them. Cristiano Ronaldo dos Santos Aveiros – he was named after President Ronald Reagan – doesn't have that yet, but it will come when he matures, which may take some time. He stands out because his way of playing the game is unique. He has incredible pace but he can still use his clever tricks at speed. He doesn't just knock the ball behind defenders and run; he can beat opponents at speed by various means. He is a tremendous finisher and can find the bottom corner of the net with explosive pace. A tall man, he is exceptional in the air and when the opponents have a corner, he is often the player who heads the ball clear. He has been crowned by FIFA and his peers a number of times as the best attacking player in the world and if he maintains his form into his late twenties he may well be recognised as the best of all time. But his speed, both at the wheel of his costly, high-powered cars and on the field, could shorten his career. He is definitely the most handsome of the all-time great players, with his looks, his shaven body, and his touched-up teeth. Somehow I doubt that he will still be playing at fifty, as Matthews was, because at his pace he is more vulnerable to serious injuries. He is not much helped by today's referees adopting a soft approach to illegal tackles. Sir Alex Ferguson was always moaning about referees not protecting Ronaldo and in most cases, he was justified. He rarely comes out of a game without a bruise. He comes from the small island of Porto Santo, next to Madeira, one of the autonomous islands in the Atlantic that were ruled by the Portuguese until 1974. He has had an astonishing rise to fame. The son of a gardener who died at the age fifty-one from the ravages of alcoholism, he grew up with only one interest, playing football, and at eleven he joined the academy of Sporting Lisbon.

There are few outstanding headers of the ball in the Premiership these days and Ronaldo is probably the best in the field. But Ronald Davies, a Welshman born in Holywell in 1942, was, in my view, the number one for scoring goals in the air. He was a master of timing his jump beyond the far post and planting a powerful header past the goalkeeper. I was a regular at the Dell around that time and I loved seeing him in action. He had an advantage over most of the big centre forwards of his time, because Southampton's wingers, Terry Paine on the right and John Sydenham on the left, were good enough to deliver pinpoint crosses.

Overall, the standard of football in the Premiership has improved over the years, but there are hardly any wingers now who can match the combative Paine – he always got his pre-emptive kicks in first to frighten his opponents and make sure he would last the ninety minutes – and the speedy Sydenham, who now coaches in Australia. The art of crossing the ball seems to be dying out and instead of buying expensive foreign players, managers and coaches ought to concentrate on young, talented England players and show them how to cross properly. The popular Davies scored 153 goals in 277 appearances for Southampton between 1966 and 1973, and more than half were scored in the air. Like most of his compatriots, he has knee and hip problems, caused by wear and tear and damaging cortisone injections. Recent research has showed that the ankle is the joint that has the worst chance of recovery after these injections. Andrew Flintoff, who has had a number of them, may well have trouble later in life. Ron Davies was one of Southampton's big drinkers and that didn't help his condition. Today he lives with his wife Chris in a mobile van in New Mexico, rejoicing that his first hip operation cost him only $800. It was paid for by the local authorities. He has little money but he loves his new life.

When Ronaldo was first voted 'Football Writers' Association Footballer of the Year', he turned up for the dinner at the Royal Lancaster Hotel in May 2007 and made a nice little speech praising his fellow players. The second time, a year later, the organisers were worried that he might not turn up. He had declined to go to the PFA dinner to receive his 'PFA Player of the Year' trophy some weeks earlier and had also missed the Manchester United dinner. The day before the club dinner he came up with some arrogant comments, saying, 'I am the best.' He was an hour late for the FWA function because the main line from Manchester had signalling problems, and when he turned up he was wearing his dinner suit. The invitation said 'lounge suits', so he had to borrow a suit and a tie. The event was a sell-out and Ken Montgomery, the FWA chief executive, had to hastily rearrange seats at the top table for five of Ronaldo's Portuguese friends. He spoke well and modestly and signed hundreds of autographs, some during the dinner.

You need to be brash and confident to succeed as a top sportsman, but arrogance and indifference to others are negative qualities. After the 2008 European Championships, Ronaldo made some awful gaffes, like agreeing with FIFA President Sepp Blatter's assertion that players are slaves. The full quote from Blatter – 'I think football there is too much modern slavery in transferring players or buying players, and putting them somewhere' – was a ridiculous thing for Blatter to say. The people who move players from club to club are the agents, with the connivance of the clubs. Both parties expect the player's contract to be severed at a whim. Money dictates the lives of famous sportsmen and Ronaldo is no different from the others; they are mostly mercenaries with no loyalties.

Being fabulously rich doesn't necessarily bring happiness. When it suited Ronaldo, he signed for Real Madrid, allegedly for £80 million, but in reality much less, because the whole package, including his wages, was spread over the length of his contract. He left Manchester United a much weaker side, because when he was in the mood he was the fastest forward in modern football and was the most devastating finisher since Eusébio, the Brazilian.

I once met Sepp Blatter at Belfast airport and I sat with him for an hour before we flew back to Heathrow. He is a small, dapper man who worked as a lawyer before going into football politics. A Swiss, he speaks several languages, is polite, and appears to do a reasonable job, bearing in mind that his organisation is never free of accusations about corruption. But now and again, he comes out with an ill-advised blast that damages the image of the game. It is remarkable that he has lasted so long in his job. One could say he is on the way to being gaga at seventy-two, but he is considerably younger than the previous Presidents of FIFA, Joao Havelange and Sir Stanley Rous, were. I knew Sir Stanley when I first started my career and he was very helpful to me. He was straight and honest and at six-foot-four, he had an air of authority. He also had a reputation as a ladies' man.

One great footballer – perhaps the best of all time, but like Bradman in cricket, we can never prove it – still retains his humility. He is Pelé, and his decency is why he is so popular around the world. He is a true champion, with a broad smile and a friendly welcome, a fitting ambassador for Brazilian football, the football that everyone savours and enjoys. He and I were judges for a Man of the Match award at Highbury some years ago and although he had hardly seen any of the players before, he soon picked out the right man. He had strength and balance, the two key characteristics of any great player, but he could be kicked out of a game.

Similarly, I've known Bobby Charlton for almost fifty years and he never changed. He too is a wonderful ambassador for the game. His somewhat serious nature hides a caring and understanding man.

I spent a lot of time with the Portuguese team in the 1966 World Cup and Eusébio, who was the tournament's top scorer with nine goals, hasn't altered either. When I met him four years ago, he had no grey hairs. He was the opposite of Jimmy Greaves. He had the most explosive shot of any superstar and in one game in Portugal I saw him blast in a free kick from near the halfway line. A year before the World Cup, he was a clerk working in a garage in Mozambique, the only earner in a poor family of six: four younger brothers and a widowed mother. A scout saw him and recommended him to Benfica, who signed him on a contract that paid him just £50 a month. Johnny Haynes, possibly the best long passer in English football, told me, 'Phew! I would go on strike if I got only that for such great talent.'

I came across the Argentinian di Stéfano in the Sixties and I thought he was lacking in grace, almost surly. But on the field he was a supremely elegant maestro who brought fans to their feet. He pulled things together and controlled events. He was number one in that decade, yet never played in the finals of the World Cup.

Johann Cruyff, the Dutchman who spoke half a dozen languages, had a similar skill in running his team. I went to see him at the Bank of England ground before the England *v.* Holland game in February 1977 and he was extremely rude, answering questions with evasive answers. After a few minutes, he got up and walked off. I went with him and I asked him more questions, only to be ignored. Cruyff had been sent off while playing for Barcelona three days before and it had caused a riot. The referee was attacked, a TV vehicle was set ablaze, and a mob attacked an ambulance taking injured spectators to hospital. 'I think the referee thought I had insulted his mother,' said Cruyff. 'He didn't understand what I said.' Later I discovered why he had behaved so badly. As captain, he was trying to negotiate better bonuses before the kick-off. After the game he heard that more money had turned up and the dispute was over.

England lost 2-0 and I wrote in the *Mail*, 'Johann Cruyff dominated last night's game as no great player has ever dominated Wembley before. He had sixty-one touches of the ball, and of those fifty passes, thirty were forward passes.' The peerless Cruyff played all over the pitch, dragging English defenders all over the field. If you watch England play under Fabio Capello, there are more passes played across and backward than forward.

Don Revie was honest, for a change, after that Holland defeat. He said, 'They taught us a lesson. We have to go out into the world and find out what it is all about.'

Trevor Brooking, whose book I wrote in four weeks in 1980, called Cruyff 'the best player I ever saw' in an interview in *The Times* in 2008. But when I asked him who his hero was, he said, 'Bobby Charlton.' Not to worry, they are both great players, our one a gent and the other a volatile genius. Trevor told me, 'The Dutch outclassed us. It could have been four or five.' Trevor was never sent off and was cautioned just five times in the 642 first team appearances of his seventeen-year career. And he never swore once. His autobiography was a bestseller and went into four reprints. He still campaigns for young players who are born in the UK to be given proper training and first team opportunities, but he is finding it a tough task against the Premiership juggernauts.

The standard of the England team has deteriorated, despite the vast amount of money the FA bosses have spent on it. The football played in the 2008 European Championships and the 2010 World Cup showed that our way of playing has been left behind. We have forgotten several of the key traits that win matches. The Russians showed us how to pierce defences with midfield players, who dribble the ball with pace instead of using 'safe' passes. They cross accurately, either to the near post or to the far post, and frequently take the ball up to the byline and pull it back to incoming forwards. Charles Hughes, the much derided FA Director of Football, calls it POMO, the Position of Maximum Opportunity, and it is still the most effective way of scoring a goal. The Portuguese showed us how to use centre-backs as occasional attacking players. The Turks, beaten 8-0 twice by England in the 1980s, gave a lesson to Capello's players with their determination and fire to keep going, right until the last kick. But formations, tactics, and non-stop running don't make great teams alone; they need at least one genius to start things off, and if England had a Greaves or a Tom Finney, Capello would be a happier man.

Most players who played with Finney agreed that the Preston plumber was a more versatile all-round forward than Matthews. He played equally well on both flanks and he sometimes played as a striker. He was almost the complete footballer. He hasn't changed; he is still a lovable, friendly man who will always give an interview, even to journalists whom he hasn't met. Even in his late eighties, he is still alert and attentive and he watches most of Preston's home matches. He was lucky to have one of the great marriages. He married Elsie, who worked at a steam laundry in the same town in 1945. She died in 2004, just short of their sixtieth anniversary. 'I was earning 65p a week as a footballer and the wedding cost peanuts,' he said. 'I miss her terribly.'

Matthews had a reputation for being mean, but I found him a wonderful and generous man. When he played the game, the rewards were pitiable and players had to scrap for every pound. Stan was the Beckham of his day – although a better footballer – and without an agent, he often asked for a fee for appearing in friendlies. You couldn't blame him. I took him out for lunch in Edinburgh in 1981 before he played a friendly game at the age of sixty-five – yes, that's true – and he put over more good crosses than the present-day Arsenal side! He hardly ate anything. 'Got to keep fit,' he said. His Czech wife Mila seemed to be in charge and he liked that. She was an intelligent and interesting lady.

I met Maradona in the World Cup in Mexico in 1986 and although he smiled and answered questions, later he turned nasty when someone asked him to elaborate on his deliberate handball, which had robbed England of a semi-final place. If that incident had happened today, FIFA would be under pressure to order a replay or disallow the goal. Bobby Robson barely protested in his after-match interview and Peter Shilton, the victim, wasn't asked his opinion. Four minutes after Maradona punched the ball away from Shilton's grasp, he swerved, like a champion skier, one way and then the other, past Gary Stevens, Terry Butcher, and Terry Fenwick, to score the best goal of the tournament. Steve Hodge was to blame, really. He should have played the ball back to Shilton as the defenders moved up to make Maradona offside. Ironically, Hodge was the first person to approach Maradona at the end and ask for his shirt. It is now on loan to the National Football Museum. Steve won't need a big pension; when he sells it, the income will keep him in good stead for some time. He thinks it will bring in much more than the £157,750 paid for a shirt Pelé wore in the 1970 World Cup. Terry Butcher was one of the most honest sportsmen I've ever met and he said, years later, 'It still rankles with me that he never really admitted that he was wrong. I always said he was the greatest footballer I ever saw but I would just like him to have said it straightforwardly, that it was wrong. He was in the doping room after the game giving it all the high fives and shouts and screams and we sat there next door debating whether to fill him in!'

Maradona could reach the peaks and then suddenly incur the wrath of right-minded football people. He has done some appalling things, yet he is still a national hero in Argentina, as I discovered when I went there in 2006. Forgoing a helmet and a bulletproof vest, I visited the infamous Boca Juniors Stadium in the worst part of Buenos Aires. One of the Boca Juniors' spokesmen admitted that Maradona's favourite club has had more matches abandoned because of riots than any club in the world. Maradona grew up in that environment, and that may explain his behaviour.

Maradona has a box on the halfway line and he sits there like an emperor. When he was appointed coach of Argentina in 2008, I realised that Alf Ramsey was right about Argentine footballers: they're mad!

The cliché 'butter wouldn't melt in his mouth' was often used about George Best and it was very apt. Everyone liked him, including me, and we excused all his excesses. After his premature retirement, he made a living out of being entertained by journalists, who paid him big fees for saying not very much. He was on a path of self-destruction from the first day he arrived at Old Trafford and it was sad that he died so early. Like di Stéfano, he never played in a World Cup final. The fact that he didn't play at that level must provoke doubts over his claim to being the best.

I first saw Denis Law in 1960 and Bill Shankly told me, 'This boy is a genius, just look at his legs!' Denis' spindly legs belied his approach to the game. He was one of the toughest players of his time and he usually got in his preemptive retaliation. That was why he was treated with respect.

All these players share one important quality: they rarely missed a game. Bobby Charlton told me in 2008, 'I never really had an injury in my career.' They all had good balance and could avoid the worst tackles. Greaves was bit of an exception. He contacted hepatitis and failed to regain full fitness before the 1966 final, losing his place to Roger Hunt. But for that, his career would have lasted past 1971, when he was forced to retire at the age of thirty-one. Almost to the end, he filled grounds.

I was tempted to include Manco Castro in my list of all-time greats. Castro was the Uruguayan centre forward who scored the final goal in his side's 4-2 victory over Argentina in the first World Cup final in the Centenary Stadium, Montevideo in 1930. He was described as having lost half of his left arm as a young boy, but pictures cast doubt on that story. Ian Morrison, author of *The World Cup: A Complete Record 1930-1990*, wrote, 'Uruguay could not have been given a better birthday present [1930 was the 100th anniversary of the Uruguayan constitution] than the honour of staging the first competition. The icing on the cake was the winning of the prize. It has been said that other nations have their history and that Uruguay has its football. On July 30, 1930 [the same day of the 1966 final] she certainly had her football and that day will never be forgotten.' There were 93,000 spectators packed into the largely uncovered stadium and most of them travelled in boats across the 100-mile-wide River Plate from Buenos Aires chanting 'Victory or Death'. No one died, but a number of Argentinians hurled bricks into the windows of the Uruguayan Embassy in Buenos Aires.

I followed a similar route to Montevideo in 2006 and called in on the Centenary Stadium, which proudly bears its commemorative plaque. The ground was set in a beautiful park, but the stadium was run-down, as though nothing had been done to take care of it since its inception. The pitch was a different story. As I stepped on it, there wasn't any sign of weeds. The grass was immaculate, similar to the Emirates at Arsenal. Suddenly there was a roar from the other side of the pitch. A man driving a motor mower was shouting in Spanish, indicating that I should leave immediately. I smiled and explained to him that I was an English journalist. He smiled back but insisted I had to get off the sacred grass. I smiled again and retreated to the crumbling terraces. He waved and honour was observed. Such pride is a good sign. Uruguayan football has since been left behind in the World Cup rankings, but at least they still have their pride.

Jimmy Greaves was discovered by a legendary scout by the name of Jimmy Thompson, who later became one of my best contacts. In those days, there were no well-heeled agents, only impoverished scouts, or so it seemed. Small in stature, Thompson nearly always wore a brown bowler, but on some of his expeditions to schools matches he wore a disguise. 'I don't want to be recognised,' he told me. 'If the other scouts know I'm there, they'll try to find out who I'm interested in. Could lose the boy.' He hid behind bushes or trees and rarely stood along the touchlines.

Greaves was born in Manor Park, East London, in 1940. His house was demolished in a bombing raid and the family moved to Dagenham, an undistinguished part of East London that was renowned for producing outstanding football talent. One such talent was Sir Alf Ramsey, although he never boasted about it. Greaves' father worked as a guard on the London Underground and wasn't much of a player himself. However, he was treasurer of Fanshaw Old Boys, a local club that derived its name from a school that boasted Les Allen of the Allen family, Terry Venables, and Martin Peters. When the old leather footballs were close to being thrown away, he would bring them home and give them to his son. That made Jimmy a kingpin of the Blitz boys, the youngsters who played in the streets and on the bombsites. When he was fifteen, he was selected for the London Schoolboys in a representative game at White Hart Lane and in his weighty autobiography *Greavsie*, published in 2003, he admitted, 'I had a pretty quiet game. I was due to leave school and Dad told me he arranged an interview for me for a job at *The Times*. Jimmy Thompson had other ideas.'

The Cockney scout, who was in his late fifties, turned up at the Greaves house a few days later in a bright red Sunbeam Talbot car, with high emissions. His daughter was driving it; Jimmy never drove himself. He introduced himself and asked the boy to 'come up west for a chat'.

Other scouts were watching this prolific goalscorer and Greaves junior said, 'OK, let's go.'

Thompson took him to the art deco Strand Palace Hotel, not a five-star hotel, but enough to impress him, for afternoon tea. 'Chelsea want you,' he said.

After a few brief comments about its manager, Ted Drake ('He scored seven goals in one game and you could do that,' he said) and the prospects at Stamford Bridge, the young man replied, 'It's up to my Dad.'

'Readies', illegal payments to parents who had promising players, was rife at the time, and the Greaves signing was no different. Two weeks later, things were duly sorted out. At the end of the 1956/57 season, Drake, who was well known for not making quick decisions, was dithering over retaining all his 'Drake's Ducklings', a phrase coined by the eloquent Thompson to describe the club's latest intake. One, Joe Baker, had already been sacked – a mistake Drake admitted later – and Greaves could have been as well, despite scoring 122 goals in the South East Counties League. Thompson heard that Drake was thinking about releasing Greaves and stormed into his office. Ten minutes later he came out and told Greaves, 'It's all done. You're on £8 a week in the season and £7 in the close season.'

The next day, Thompson met Greaves' father, who asked, 'What about a signing fee? Other clubs would pay it willingly.'

Thompson put bets on behalf of footballers, which was not allowed at the time, and he was a frequent visitor to racecourses. The day before, he had been to a meet in Ireland. 'Here,' he said, holding out a brown envelope, 'the signing fee is in there.'

In his book, Greaves said, 'Inside the envelope was £50, in Irish fivers. Dad changed the money at the bank but the fact remains that Jimmy Thompson, the man who discovered me, paid my signing-on fee out of his own pocket. I think.' I don't think the scout paid much income tax. Most of his under-the-counter payments from clubs went on horses and greyhounds.

On many occasions, I would be sitting at my *Sketch* desk overlooking the Thames in New Carmelite Street, when the phone would ring and there would be a whisper at the other end of the line. 'It's me,' he said. 'Got a good one. If he doesn't play for England, I'll eat my hat.'

He always marked my card about players going to other clubs and I never paid him for tips. Richer papers like the *News of the World* and *The People*, did, but Jimmy was happy with the odd mention in the *Sketch*. Many of his 'boys' became internationals and he made sure he received extra payments. The cash came from the entertainment accounts of the clubs. Today he would be rich enough to buy a club himself.

Jimmy Thompson and his counterparts have been supplanted by agents, many of whom know very little about players. They rely on videos. The culture of bungs still persists, with some managers still claiming their cut from transfers. In most cases, it is in his contract, but it is almost like embezzling money from the bosses, and the biggest sufferers are the paying public. Several attempts have been made to end this dishonest trade and expose the guilty, but they have all failed.

Ted Drake, who against the expectations of everyone, including the fans, led Chelsea to their first Championship success in their jubilee year, 1954/55, was one of my favourite managers. We were both sons of Hampshire, and we had similar interests, including cricket. He was always willing to have me in his office for personal interviews. As a player, he was one of the most courageous centre forwards of his time. He was fearless and played just nine seasons. Injury stopped him and he went into management. He was a very nice, sensitive man and on one occasion when I was there he was lamenting the arrival of Tommy Docherty in 1961, against his wishes. Suddenly he started crying. I was astonished. The stress had caught up with him and later he resigned. He became a bookmaker before being appointed chief scout at Fulham for fifteen years. I couldn't imagine him handing out brown envelopes.

Another manager I admired for the same qualities was Arthur Rowe, who introduced push-and-run and transformed Tottenham Hotspur into a Championship-winning side in two successive seasons in the 1950s. He twice had a breakdown at Spurs, and when he managed Crystal Palace he was forced to retire after a third breakdown. But his love of the game had a hold on him and in his seventies, he returned as a general adviser to Leyton Orient and as a consultant to Millwall. Alzheimer's caught up with him. He was a very honest man, a rarity in a game where truth is often ignored.

Today's stars – David Beckham, John Terry, Thierry Henry, Ronaldo – complain they are constantly harassed by the press, but none of them will ever undergo the dramas twenty-one-year-old Jimmy Greaves experienced in 1961/62. Chelsea was a bad side and although he had been the first player to score 100 goals for the club in the 1960/61 season, he wanted a transfer. Joe Mears, the wily and much-liked Chelsea chairman, knew his club had massive debts, and he had to reduce them by selling the club's most prized player. The Italian league had lifted its ban on importing foreign players, and AC Milan wanted Greaves. Jimmy was earning £20 a week, was married to his childhood sweetheart Irene, and had a daughter, Lynn, with another child on the way. Tragically, a second son, Jimmy Jr, died from pneumonia at the age of four months, devastating Jimmy and his wife. A new start with more money sounded a good idea. The *Sketch* was one of the first papers to find out that AC Milan wanted him; the chief football reporter Tony Stratton Smith bumped into him outside a London hospital.

'I've been having checks,' said Greaves.

'What for?' said my colleague.

The hospital was owned by Italians and Greaves was kept in hospital for two days before he was declared fit. Tony soon discovered what was happening. A handsome, suave young bachelor, he was close to the Beatles and also to Matt Busby. Later he was rich enough to be a racehorse owner. He was a dilettante and a lover of *objets d'art*. He spent more time in nightclubs than at the office and was rarely seen by his colleagues. Also involved in the affair was Gigi Peronace, a small, multi-talented Italian man who acted as a wheeler-dealer in football, representing Milan. He lived in an opulent flat near Harrods and wasn't the usual football man. For a start, he wore expensive clothes and highly polished Gucci shoes and was always smoking huge Cuban cigars. I spent a lot of time with him and he oozed charm.

Greaves was offered £15,000 as a signing on free, £130 a week, and considerable win bonuses, plus a luxury flat on the outskirts of Milan. The deal was soon struck, with Chelsea receiving £80,000. Jimmy agreed, but reluctantly. After the news came out, Greaves was constantly being asked for his views and with no agent and no adviser, he spoke honestly and naturally. 'My mind isn't in it,' he said. 'I'm thinking of changing my mind.'

Joe Mears, a decent man, showed signs of panic as he called a meeting with Drake, secretary John Battersby, and the bewildered Greaves. Mears was born in the same year as Chelsea, the club his uncle Gus helped to found in 1905, and he served in the Royal Marines. He was once in charge of security at Winston Churchill's underground operations room in Whitehall. Battersby, another good man, told him, 'There's no ifs or buts about it, you gotta go.'

Jimmy Hill, the Professional Footballers' Association chairman who broke the dam and enabled unrestricted football salaries, was called in and he accompanied Mr and Mrs Greaves on the flight to Milan. Also on the plane was Stratton Smith, a self-appointed English wheeler-dealer. Greaves was carrying a very small bag and he joked, 'I'm not staying too long!' They were prophetic words.

Greaves had pleaded with Mears to hire a lawyer to help him get out of the contract, but years later he met Battersby's daughter at a speaking engagement and she admitted, 'The club was so desperate for the money they hired that lawyer to make sure the deal went through.'

Greaves made a bad start to his new career, turning up late for pre-season training because he had remained in London for the birth of his daughter Mitzi. He was fined £50 a day for each day he missed. Italian football clubs were much more strict than English clubs and still are; he should have known that. And then another blow fell – Milan coach Giuseppe Vianni died of a heart attack and was replaced by the fearsome Nero Rocco, a Neapolitan who shouted and screamed at the players and fined them with impunity. He rationed the players with two cigarettes a day and Greaves, who hardly smoked, began smoking more than his quota, earning another fine. I was sent to cover the opening matches and his debut took place in the Romeo Menti stadium in Vicenza, a town on the way to Venice. The temperature was in the nineties and Sol put a headline to my story: 'Yimmi's Wasted in This!' I wrote, 'Jimmy Greaves is tonight a happier little-boy-lost. I have just seen him score a goal in his first Italian league game. His millionaire club Milan, who beat Lanerossi 3-0, have given his wife Irene the match bouquet and Jimmy picked up a big bonus. But I am worried. Today's match in this small wool town in North Italy was so bad that if this is the class of football Greaves is to play in, then he is finished with England. He will be washed up when his well-paid spell of foreign service comes to an end in three years' time. I have seen better games at Shepherd's Bush or on Hackney Marshes.' Sol and I never wasted words.

The Italian newspaper correspondents wrote some vindictive stories and so did some of the English football writers, but Greaves made a joke of it in his regular meetings with the resident English football correspondents – writers like Desmond Hackett (who once took him on a bender at Heathrow, causing him to miss a plane and ensuring yet another Rocco fine), Ken Jones (*Daily Mirror*), Peter Lorenzo (*Daily Herald*), Italian-speaking Brian Glanville (*The Sunday Times*), and the *Daily Mail* trio, Ian Wooldridge, Brian James, and Roy Peskett. He formed The Jimmy Greaves Club and presented a tie to every journalist travelling to see him. It was a good move by Greaves. He was able to speak off the record and give the writers a more rational account of his activities.

Forty-odd years ago, journalists had that kind of access; my successors are now denied it. I mixed socially with the top performers in both football and cricket until the late 1970s, before the drawbridge was pulled up. I remember spending many hours with Test stars like Fred Trueman, Brian Statham, Ken Barrington, Jim Laker, and many others. That is how you learn about your game. For some years I reported England Under-23 matches and can remember visiting the bedrooms of players like Bobby Moore, Greaves, and Johnny 'Budgie' Byrne for chats before games. All three were big boozers; I was stuck on orange juice and lemonade.

One Milan-based reporter often appeared at our meetings at La Tampa restaurant and he rang me with tips. The others were suspicious of some of the 'stories' that appeared in English newspapers, so Clive Toye of the *Daily Express* set a trap. At one of the lunches, he said Milan were going to buy George Eastham. The next day, the *Sketch* used the Eastham story and Bob Findlay, then the sports editor of the *Express*, rang Toye and demanded the reason why he had missed the story. I think the *Sketch* story appeared under one of my pseudonyms, but everyone knew it wasn't me. The Milan players soon turned against Greaves and some of them refused to pass the ball to him. After he scored a brilliant goal against rivals Inter, not one congratulated him, and he gave the double 'V' sign to Rocco. Clearly this couldn't carry on.

During my spell in Italy I moved to Turin to see Denis Law and Joe Baker playing for Torino against Lanerossi. Denis had a car loaned to him and they gave me a lift. What a ride! These days the speed would have qualified him for a six-month ban. The match was explosive and I reported, 'It reminded me of the chariot race in *Ben Hur*. My ears are deaf from the bedlam. I am stunned that this primitive savagery should go under the name of sport. The referee had as much control over the game as the crowd had over their emotions.'

Twenty-one-year-old Baker was sent off for kicking an opponent off the ball, and told me, 'It can't be as bad every week. In my five years in football I have never done a thing like this. I couldn't stand any more of it. One of them poked his fingers in my eye. I had to do something.'

Gigi Peronace looked after Law and Baker when they were in Italy. They lived in a hotel in the centre and were taken to the training ground at nine by a chauffeur-driven limousine. 'It's not true that we are kept in a concentration camp,' said Law.

Not quite, but most of the time they were kept on a lead. When they managed to avoid Torino's manager, they enjoyed themselves in clubs and bars. Not being able to speak much Italian, neither of them fitted in with the more sophisticated life there. Like Greaves, they returned to England having served only a few months of their three-year contracts. There was a trickle of British stars to Italy – the successful ones were John Charles, Gerry Hitchens, Liam Brady, and Ray Wilkins – but it didn't really work. Paul Gascoigne was the biggest failure. Greaves lasted four months. He said, 'At least I ended up the highest score, with nine goals in fourteen games.'

Tottenham manager Bill Nicholson knocked at the door of the Greaves' flat and said to Irene, 'Do you know I am?

'Yes,' she said. 'Our saviour!'

Chelsea said they wanted Greaves back but it was a dodge to placate their fans. They had no chance of outbidding Tottenham. Milan presented so many obstacles that an irate Nicholson said to Andrea Rizzoli, the club's President, 'This is becoming like a scene from *The Merchant of Venice*.'

'You are impertinent,' snapped Rizzoli.

Eventually the clubs settled on a fee of £99,999, to avoid Greaves being known as the first £100,000 footballer. Greaves bought a Jaguar early in his brief stay in Milan, and he chose to drive his family back to London. The car cost £1,000. When they arrived at the customs at Dover he was told he had to pay £400 in duty. 'I don't have any money on me,' he said. The car was about to be impounded when Maurice Smith, the football correspondent of *The People*, helped him out by writing an article in his newspaper about the return from Milan and handing over the £400 in cash.

Tottenham had no provision for a house or flat for the family, so they moved into a two-roomed council house in Dagenham used by Jimmy's in-laws. He was back on £60 a week, less than half of his salary in Milan.

Most people thought Nicholson was chary about taking Greaves because he didn't fit in with the Tottenham work ethic. 'No,' said Bill, 'I always liked his attitude, right from the start. He was friendly and interested in everything, much more than most of our players. And he never bore any malice. I had several several rows with him over minor matters and the next day he was as cheerful as ever. He had a good sense of humour.' Greaves spent eleven years with Spurs and had only four pairs of boots. He preferred rubbers, not studded boots. Both facts are startling. Most players use several pairs every season and they will only use rubbers on dry, hard grounds. Jimmy was unique. He always was.

His experiences in Milan led him to drink heavily, with the encouragement of the English press corps. Before, he was a casual drinker of beer; now he was on shorts. Nearly every footballer drank at the time, and some, like his former Chelsea colleague Peter Sillett, drank up to twelve pints a day without becoming drunk. Sports writers also had big capacities for booze and it is only in recent times that they have found themselves too busy to go on prolonged drinking sprees. Even so, there are few sports writers who are teetotallers and a number still get drunk at the annual dinner of the Football Writers' Association, football's beanfeast night. Football clubs in Britain haven't concerned themselves with the effects of dehydration, unlike continental clubs and managers. Our managers still tend to drink heavily and they have failed to warn their players about binge drinking. Drinking alcohol after an exhausting game – when players can run up to six to eight miles – seriously accentuates the dehydration of the body. Already dehydrated after their exertions, they undergo a second bout of dehydration from booze and that takes some days to recover from, which explains why some players can't repeat their performance in the midweek fixture following a weekend game.

The influx of foreign players changed the emphasis. They recognised the dangers and many don't drink at all, particularly the African players. I think managers and coaches should try to wean their players off any form of alcohol. The first thing they should do is to ban the players from accepting bottles of champagne for being man of the match. I long for the day when a player is given the bottle of champagne and he hands it back, saying, 'I don't drink because it's not good for athletes who want to reach the top of their profession.' If others followed, it might persuade young people to shun binge drinking and enjoy fitter and more rewarding lives.

Not one club in Britain has so far banned its players from drinking, but Phil Simmons, the Trinidadian West Indian Test all-rounder, became the first to do it in cricket in early 2008 when he announced an alcohol ban on the Ireland team for their one-day tour of Bangladesh. 'It has been proven that it does have an effect,' he said.

When Greaves went to Tottenham, he found himself in a big drinking school at the room at the back of The Bell and Hare, a few yards from White Hart Lane. In those days, there was no press room for interviews at White Hart Lane, and the sports writers joined the players at the pub to get lines off them for their reports. We recognised that some quotes had to be off the record, but we had enough material to make our stories more interesting. Dave Mackay was the leader of the drinking brigade and was usually the first to call for a round. Danny Blanchflower was the exception. He didn't drink. Another group of journalists had to wait outside in the car park for Bill Nicholson to come out. Usually it was well past 6 p.m. before Bill emerged, carrying his fawn-coloured raincoat over his arm. 'What are you waiting for?' he asked, as he shook with laughter. He was rather shy about talking in public and preferred talking to footballers, not journalists. But when he started off, he would stand there for up to half a hour, sometimes even longer, talking intelligently about the game.

Towards the end of his time with Tottenham, Greaves realised his fire was nearly out and spent more and more hours in pubs. Nicholson didn't want to keep him and he did a deal with Ron Greenwood to send Greaves to West Ham in exchange for Martin Peters plus £54,000. Greaves found himself with a bigger drinking school, this time headed by Bobby Moore, of whom Greaves said: 'He can drink for England.' By then, Greaves was an alcoholic and his businesses, including a successful box and packaging company, were suffering. Worse still, his marriage was in trouble. Irene could no longer tolerate his drinking habits and he left the marital home and moved into a flat on his own. Soon he was attending AA courses. He took a long time to break the habit and renounce drink.

Half a million people have similar problems and Greaves was one of the few that kept his word and stayed away from booze. To his credit, he has for a long time been back with his wife and family and is living a normal life, speaking at dinners and still putting his name to a weekly column in *The Sun*, which contains much good sense. Another generation of Greaves lovers has emerged and he will never be forgotten. I met him again in 2007, much thicker in girth than he once was, and he was the same old wisecracking Greavsie. He had been through hell, but he was a full and contented man again. A few months later he celebrated his golden wedding anniversary with Irene and a friend who was present said, 'His only slight worry is having to buy two pairs of shoes.' Many years ago he injured a foot in a collision with Jack Kelsey, the old Arsenal goalkeeper, and one of his feet is bigger than the other. He has to buy a pair of sevens and another pair of eights.

According to Martin Peters, he didn't like wearing shinguards, even after he the cut in his leg that kept him out of consideration for the start of the World Cup in 1966. In his book, *The Ghost of '66*, Peters wrote, 'He was his own man and I've always felt that his stubborn refusal to wear shinguards weighed against him when Alf was pondering the make-up of the team. With no substitutes, if we lost a player in the final through injury, we would have to finish the match with ten men. Alf knew that if the cut reopened on Jimmy's shin, England might be playing one short.'

This story should be filed in the 'What if...' file. But for a pair of shinpads, the outcome of England's only triumph in the World Cup Final would probably have ended with much less hassle. The Russian referee wouldn't have needed to get involved in that controversial goal. Had Greaves played, he would have slotted that one in, no problem.

CHAPTER TEN

Danny Boy Was the Outstanding Skipper of My Time

An extraordinary happening occurred during the funeral of Danny Blanchflower at the parish church of St Jude in Englefield Green on 16 December 1993. The former Northern Ireland and Tottenham Hotspur captain died at the age of sixty-seven from Alzheimer's. After the simple service around eighty people, mainly from Spurs, including Bill Nicholson, Cliff Jones, Bobby Smith, and Tommy Harmer – a tiny fraction of the number who watched Danny at White Hart Lane – moved off to watch the committal at the far end of the cemetery. It was a rainy, windy day, with no sight of the sun as we walked towards the graveside. As we approached, the rain started to ease off and a gap appeared in the sullen clouds. The six black-clad funeral men were lowering the coffin into the grave when suddenly a blinding shaft of sunshine hit it. Tommy Harmer, the joker of Danny's Spurs side, said, 'Crikey, I knew he was special but I didn't think he was that special.' It was as though Danny's soul was marching along in tune with the misquoted words of the American Civil War song 'The Battle Hymn of the Republic': 'Glory, glory hallelujah, and the Spurs go marching on.' He was the shining star, with his own spotlight from above.

When I last spoke to Danny, about four years previously, it was impossible to have a proper conversation with him. In 2007 the House of Commons Committee of Public Accounts was told that dementia costs the UK economy £17 billion a year, more than strokes, heart disease, and cancer combined. Many footballers die from Alzheimer's and although the Professional Footballers' Association have helped victims, more should be done to make their lives easier. Danny's early departure was a tragedy because he was one of the best and the brightest of his generation. His wit and vivacity sparkled in any company. He was strong-minded, opinionated, and a leader. Bill Nicholson was the genius who built that legendary Spurs side in the early 1960s but it was Danny who often gave the orders on the field, frequently changing the tactics. Danny was a rebel who railed against the system in football at that time. He wrote a brilliant column in the *Daily Mail* – every word his own – in which he ridiculed those people who treated footballers as second-rate citizens. As I stood alongside the grave, I thought we should reinvent Danny Blanchflower. He could question the awful things which are happening today. You could imagine him saying, 'Why are they paying them £120,000 a week when others are only paid £5.73 an hour? Why are these money launderers being allowed to run clubs? Why should highly paid managers take bonuses when players are transferred? Why are only sixty players from the Premiership qualified to play for England? Why are referees allowing players to crowd round them and argue about decisions?' His powerful advocacy could have started a campaign to sweep away the injustices and crookedness. Peter Doherty, then manager of Northern Ireland, told him before an international, 'If one of their guys are through, don't hesitate to bring them down outside the box.'

Blanchflower said, 'That's a sin. You have to play to the rules.'

Billy Bingham, another Northern Ireland manager, and a friend, gave the main address. 'Danny was my captain and always will be,' he said. 'He had the Irishman's gift of communication with humour and was a born romantic. He was never afraid to face people with truth.'

'He was his own man,' said Cliff Jones.

Danny showed that when Eamonn Andrews lured him to appear on *This Is Your Life*. At the last minute Danny refused to go on. It was the first time this had ever happened. He'd been married several times and seeing some of his in-laws facing him on television was too much for him. 'I did it for personal reasons,' he said. 'If I told you what they were they wouldn't be personal anymore, would they?'

Eight years later there was another bizarre graveside incident. The ebullient Harry Zussman, who was for many years the much-liked chairman of Leyton Orient, died at the age of eighty-four and a large congregation attended his funeral. Short and tubby, Harry was the jolliest and most approachable of chairmen and he ran the Os like a family. His biggest fan was his daughter Delia. They were devoted to each other. A friend who was there said, 'Suddenly Delia tried to throw herself into the grave and had to be held back.'

Harry's favourite manager, and one of my favourites, was Alec Stock, the former Army captain who had fought in Normany after D-Day. His pet phrase was, 'It's a little thing called pride.'

Another mourner at Danny's funeral was Bobby Smith, the centre forward who sometimes shared a room with Danny when they were playing away matches. Danny won most arguments, but failed to talk Bobby out of his habit of betting on horses almost daily. On the field, Bobby was the team's battering ram, but he paid a huge price. Both his knees and hips have gone and he can hardly walk. But he still smiles.

I had some brushes with him when he was at his peak. Once I reported that he was involved in an unsavoury off-field activity and the article appeared next to a picture of someone wanted for murder. Looking quickly at the page, it gave the impression that the murder suspect was Bobby Smith. The day after the story appeared, one of the commissionaires at the offices of the *Daily Mail* rang up to the sports desk to say a Mr Bobby Smith was downstairs to see me. I told the commissionaire, 'Tell him I'm out!' Smith was a cab driver at the time.

Another tricky moment was when I was sent to Ashford, the Kent club then in the Southern League, to report Smith's debut for Hastings Town. Just three years earlier, he had played a sensational game for England against Spain in a rainstorm at Wembley. Also in the tiny Ashford press box that night was my good friend Gerald Williams of the *Daily Mail*, later the tennis correspondent of the newspaper and

Sky television. Gerry was one the best interviewers I've encountered. Unlike most of today's TV and radio journalists, who offer a vapid opinion instead of asking a straight question, he got to the heart of things right from the start. Halfway through the second half of a game, in which Smith had contributed very little, the order came from the bench to get him off. It was humiliating for him. Gerry and I went to the dressing room, knocked, and went in. There was only one person there, Bobby Smith, who was slumped next to the open boiler with his head bowed. Gerry, who like me knew him well, said, 'Bobby, aren't you ashamed of yourself, playing this standard of football so soon after playing for your country?' I glanced around to check that the door was still open for a quick exit.

Smith look up, hesitated, and said, 'Well, I suppose I am.' Crisis over!

When Danny retired, with a knee that was like a shot-up piece of bone on a butcher's slab, I asked him if he fancied playing a social game for the *Daily Mail* football team. We had a string of famous players – like Tommy Docherty, Dave Sexton, Wally Barnes, Don Howe, Tommy Harmer, Micky Stewart, Graham Roope, Arnold Long, and Geoff Arnold – and most of them enjoyed an occasional run out. In one game at our ground in Worcester Park, Docherty clattered into Hugh McIlvanney of *The Observer* and *The Sunday Times*, sending him crashing into the mud. Hugh looked up and said to his fellow Scot, 'Tommy, this is supposed to be a friendly.'

'There's nae such thing,' said Tommy with a snarl. The match Danny played in was against another newspaper and they had a poor side. Unconcerned by his damaged knee, Danny was laying balls all over the field and at half-time, when we were 6-0 up, he started undressing. 'What's wrong?' I said.

'It's over,' he said. 'I'll leave the rest to you and your mates.' So off he went and we carried on with ten men.

He entertained us royally over the years and one of his best stories was about Tottenham's 2-0 FA Cup victory over Leicester in the club's double year. It was one of the worst of the thirty-five finals I have attended. The Duchess of Kent was the chief guest and as she was presented to the players, she noticed that the Leicester players had their names on their tracksuits. The Duchess asked Danny about it and he said, 'Ah well, m'am, you see we all know one another!'

I spent the week before the match interviewing half the Leicester players. Like the other newspapers, the *Sketch* contributed to the team pool a small sum, which was later shared out among the Leicester staff. It was an excellent tax-free perk. The liveliest Leicester player was twenty-one-year-old midfield player Frank McLintock, who was the best talker. I had him down as a future star and I was proved right. Another friend, Wally Barnes, the Arsenal and Wales right-back, worked as a commentator for the BBC and on the Friday he went to the spot at Wembley where he had broken his leg in 1952 Cup Final and was filmed for a piece in the follow day's Cup Final programme. He prophesied that having won the Championship, Spurs' chances of the double might be ruined if a similar accident occurred. Substitutions hadn't been introduced in 1951 and Arsenal had to play on with ten men. Eerily, Wally's forecast almost came true. Five minutes into the game Len Chalmers, the Leicester right-back, was injured and took no further part in the game. It virtually killed the match.

For three years, Tottenham were the finest footballing team in the country and I share the view of Jimmy Greaves that it was *the* greatest of all time. It suddenly clicked into place and the balance of the side was almost perfect. It took two hours to drive the ten miles to White Hart Lane and, after much searching, park the car. When the referee started the game, the swaying of the crowd, the noise, the singing, the passion, the lights, and the glory made it feel like I had been transported to another world. At that time, Tottenham never bored anyone, ever. They thrilled thousands and thousands. Manchester United, with Best, Law, and Charlton, might have equalled it on occasions and Liverpool, with its slick passing and the impassioned noise from the Kop, had justifiable claims as well. But Liverpool's mournful 'You'll Never Walk Alone' never matched 'Glory, glory, hallelujah'.

It is impossible to judge great teams in different eras and say which is the best, but Bill Nicholson only recruited players from Britain. If he had the resources to scour the world, he might well have assembled an even better squad. Some critics thought Tottenham reached its peak on 20 September 1961 when the team beat Poland's Górnik Zabrze 8-1 in the second leg of a European Cup tie. Blanchflower said, 'It was the greatest night in all my years at White Hart Lane. The atmosphere was full of hope and expectancy after we lost 4-2 in the first game. Even when Górnik scored first to make it 5-2, nobody believed they had a chance. The fans began to sing, "Glory, glory, hallelujah." It was the first time I had ever heard it. Yet it had been hanging in the air for some time and now this was their spontaneous contribution. It was virtually a religious feeling. They were showing their faith and they were not denied. Górnik were swept aside with eight emotional goals. Defeat had been transformed into glorious victory.'

Danny Blanchflower was telling us that Spurs would win the European Cup, but the team he feared most was Benfica. Francisco Santos, a freelance journalist and later a Portuguese racing driver, became a friend of mine when we both lived in the Croydon YMCA, and he helped introduce me to Bela Guttmann, the astute sixty-two-year-old Austrian manager of Benfica, as well as several of the players: Eusébio, Carlos Perreira, the articulate goalkeeper, and Germano, the centre half who was reading a book by the philosopher Jean-Paul Sartre. I would recommend any journalist to follow that course. Get friendly with the opposition, because the intelligent ones will be better speakers than the English players. These days our newspapers rarely give big spreads to opposing teams. They gave acres of space to the home side without saying much, but the more entertaining and informative articles are invariably written about the other side, as the *Sketch* proved in the two epic semi-final matches against Benfica. Guttmann had been a member of the 1924 Hungarian Olympic side and had spent four years in a Nazi concentration camp. The first time I met him, in Lisbon, he told me that an English club had offered him a job and that he would be the first foreign coach of a First Division club if the deal went through. But it didn't. 'I speak six languages and have worked in ten countries, but I have never worked in my native Austria,' he said.

I wrote a prophetic interview with him in which he said, 'English football is too proud to learn. Your methods are wrong. We were laughed at in London because we didn't lift weights as the Spurs players did. You don't score goals by lifting weights.

You should have some foreign coaches to improve the knowledge of your players. You should have a two-month break in winter and smaller leagues. You need to mix a different cocktail.' Every word proved to be right.

Like some other big clubs in Europe, Benfica had a reputation for giving expensive presents to the referees and their linesmen. The presents went well beyond the customary value. When Spurs lost 3-1 in the first game in the Stadium of Light, hardly any of the critics mentioned that two of Spurs' goals had been disallowed in suspicious circumstances. Blanchflower told me that one of them was definitely not a goal. 'Greaves pulled the ball back to Smithy to score but the linesman told the Swiss referee Muellet to change his mind,' he said.

Before the return leg in White Hart Lane I found myself being praised by Sol for my Benfica stories. That was because I spent the three days before the game sticking with Guttmann and his players, who were staying in five-star luxury at the May Fair in Piccadilly, which was owned by Arsenal director Guy Bracewell Smith. I sat in on his team lecture on the first day and it was most impressive. The bald Guttmann was as much a psychologist as he was a coach. I reported that wingers Simões and Augusto had filed a complaint about their beds: they were too soft. Guttman also tipped me off that his players would not be paid if they lost. Their reward for meeting Real Madrid in the final was £180, compared with their monthly pay of £56. In a first-person interview, Guttmann said, 'I am worried about Dave Mackay. He is so hard. Smith is hard too, but he is easy to stop in comparison. I hope the referee is strict.'

Thousands of fans were locked out and the noise was almost unbearable. Guttmann thought his players would crumble when they went out to warm up and he told them to stay in the dressing room until summoned by the referee. Whether his PR campaign worked or not I don't know, but the Danish referee Aage Poulsen disallowed a 'goal' by Jimmy Greaves, the third in the two matches, and Benfica went through on an aggregate of 4-3. I attended the party afterwards and Blanchflower said, 'I don't think there was any underhand nonsense but that linesman was incompetent and Benfica had more luck than us.'

Most big clubs had their special ticket touts, but Tottenham's was by far the most entertaining. Their players did plenty of business with the likes of Johnny 'the Stick' Goldstein, One Arm Lou, and Stan Flashman, whose favourite club was Arsenal who never let that stand in the way of business across the North London divide. They went on all the big trips abroad and made good money, but they never bought any decent clothing or shoes. Johnny the Stick always slept in Spurs shirts passed on to him by Jimmy Greaves. The FA were always calling for bans on the touts, but they knew the players were the ones who handed the tickets on. They never took any punitive action until many years later, when the Government passed a law prohibiting the sale of tickets at enhanced prices. Touts are still in action: no one is jailed for it. Strong leadership would have stopped it much earlier. In his latter days, Stan Flashman was one of my informants. It was rather naughty to be mixing with a dodgy character, but he never asked for a brown envelope. It was good for my business and his.

I rated Danny as the best all-round captain I have seen, but he wasn't far ahead of his teammate Dave Mackay. Having two great leaders in one side was a tremendous advantage to Tottenham and Mackay inspired his colleagues with the way he performed. Now he is seventy-four and still looks like Braveheart. In his best year, in 1963, he was five-foot-eight and just over eleven stone, yet he somehow towered over his opponents, who were intimidated by his barrel chest and his show of defiance. The picture of him grabbing Billy Bremner by the shirt in the third minute of a League game at White Hart Lane in 1966 stills rates as one of the most expressive football pictures of all time. Bremner had dived in on Mackay and, realising that Mackay was going to go for him, the Leeds captain started to raise his hands in surrender. Norman Burtenshaw, the number one official of that time, always kept up with the play and he can be seen in the pictures as well, while Terry Venables approaches with admiration on his face. I asked Norman, 'What did Dave say?'

'I don't know,' he said, 'they were both jabbering away in Scots and I couldn't understand a word.'

When Norman retired in 1973, I wrote his book, *Whose Side Are You On, Ref?*, which was the first referees' book to expose the many evils in the game. Norman, whom I still meet on occasions, detested the way Don Revie's team played, and his descriptions of their shady tactics created an immense amount of interest.

Norman sent George Best off on 18 August 1971 and it was the start of the big clampdown. Alan Hardaker ordered the referees to be stricter and that night thirty-eight players were booked in the First Division and three were sent off. There were 54,763 spectators inside Stamford Bridge and many of them wanted to see the genius Best, not Norman. Before the kick-off, he came into both dressing rooms and spoke about the Hardaker letter and mentioned several points including Law 12, about swearing directly at officials. 'I spoke slowly when I came to that bit,' Norman told me. 'It's laid down in the laws and you have to act on it. Up to then I hadn't sent a player off for it.' In the forty-first minute, Peter Osgood – one of my favourite players, now sadly no longer with us – headed across the goal and Tommy Baldwin (dubbed 'the Sponge' for his ability to hold his drink) headed in. United players erupted, claiming there was a push and Willie Morgan chased Norman back to the halfway line. Norman cautioned him for dissent.

Best approached the referee, looking very agitated. 'My recollection,' said Norman, 'was that he was looking right at me when he said, "You are a f****** disgrace!"'

'I said, "What did you say?"'

'Best replied, "I wasn't talking to you."'

'"Yes you were, what's your name?" I said. When Best was shown the red card, he sat down on the pitch, holding his head.'

Norman was a hated figure for the rest of the night. Not a single player shook his hand at the end and I remember chasing him down Fulham Broadway to get an exclusive interview. It was an hour and a half after the end of the game and the street was still busy. It needed courage to travel on the Underground on your own in those circumstances but Norman, who was paid just £10.50 for his night's work, showed it. He was a very principled man. Today he might have been beaten up. Today's referees all travel in unmarked cars and are always accompanied. The problem was that attendances were falling and the game was attracting a lot of bad publicity. Banning the best footballer of the day for twelve weeks – which would have been a possible penalty – sent shivers down the spines of the game's administrators. Norman owned a sweetshop in Great Yarmouth and the next morning a boy of about ten came in and said, 'Ain't you the feller who sent George Best off?' Norman replied that he was, and the boy said, 'Well, I ain't coming in here anymore.' He never came back. Photographers besieged the shop, where one of the jigsaws on sale had Best's face on it. They offered him £50 for a photograph and he refused. Thousands of letters arrived in the next few days, all in sacks, mainly addressed to 'Burtenshaw, referee, Yarmouth'. Only one supported him.

I attended the FA Disciplinary Committee hearing at the Great Western Hotel, an imposing Victorian building next to Paddington Station, a month later. There were around 100 media people there. The Football League had its meetings there and I spent hundreds of hours over the years waiting for decisions to be announced in the lobby. The reason why they chose that hotel was that some of committeemen lived in the West Country and they would be the first to catch a train home. Meetings rarely exceeded two hours. Most were of pensionable age and they had to be on time for dinner. Norman told me afterwards that there was a farcical moment when he was asked by Cliff Lloyd, the kindly PFA secretary who was defending Best, to say where the Subbuteo men were positioned on the green board when Best was sent off. The Subbuteo men were always used in these cases.

Norman pointed to one and was asked, 'Are you sure?'

'Yes,' he said.

Lloyd said, 'So you weren't facing Mr Best at the time.'

'Yes I was.'

'But you have placed that player facing the wrong way.'

'I wasn't aware that Subbuteo men had faces.'

There was no one to act for the prosecution and when Best was asked to speak, he mumbled something that most people in the room couldn't hear. No one asked him a question. I had joined the committee of the Football Writers' Association and when I met Football League and FA officials I said to them they should open these hearings to the press, like a normal court. The Best case was a typical miscarriage of justice. The verdict was, 'Having heard all the evidence the Commission is not satisfied beyond reasonable doubt that George Best directed the words complained of to the referee. We were satisfied that the sending off was sufficient punishment.'

Denis Follows, the FA secretary, was at the match and he should have backed his referee but when Norman rang him a day later he said, 'If you had asked me I would have given evidence.'

Norman replied, 'They've completely chickened out of their responsibilities.'

The result was that the referees' clampdown went into reverse. The players were back in the saddle. Lord David Triesman, the first independent chairman of the FA, tried to re-establish law and order, but Norman recently told me, 'It won't change. They've given the players too much power and they're being paid obscenely high wages. The people in charge aren't going to see them sent off, and if they are, they will be defended by expensive QCs. Referees are still being treated abominably.'

One of the many critics who attacked Norman was Danny Blanchflower, whose article in the *Sunday Express* included this: 'Burtenshaw is not my favourite referee and he irritates my instincts for the game. He has caused more trouble than most players but never been suspended.' Norman was so angry that he spent £80 on getting advice from a QC to find out if it was defamatory. The expert told him not to bother.

In his erudite book *Double and Before* Danny Blanchflower wrote critically of the press, saying, 'In this competitive business it is not difficult for a young ambitious man to go wild and insult the outside world for the sake of a good story. He won't be bothered too much by what is written as long as his name is big enough on top of it. If I were the chairman of a football club, I would not want hooligans in my team, I would not want hooligans in the crowds, I would not want hooligans where they could do most damage to the club, in the press box. I would not ban any newspaper but only the irresponsible journalist whom I thought was over stepping the mark. I do not think the press is all irresponsible, probably the majority of pressmen are not. But there are a few figures in high places of sport who do not get my vote.'

I would agree with that. Richard Desmond, the owner of the *Daily Express* and the *Daily Star*, had to pay out £550,000 in damages in 2008 after admitting that his newspapers had published a series of concocted articles about the abduction of Gerry and Kate McCann's daughter Maddie. Other editors have had to pay large sums in recent years and it acts as a powerful deterrent. But it is not so easy for sportsmen to pick up damages, because the newspaper can plead fair comment. The facts have to be proved untrue and often it is a matter of opinion. In football, the administrators are now keen to ban offenders and take away their accreditations. The journalists are fighting for their rights and they claim that having to sign up for a licence would lead to censorship and infringe free speech. One writer I used to work for was threatened with having his accreditation withdrawn by a press officer at a Premiership club for being 'rude'. All he did was laugh at the way the team were playing.

Blanchflower also raised one important issue: the way some journalists exchange stories after games to make sure they have the same story, to protect themselves. He wrote, 'The wide boys of Fleet Street have realised this and sometimes there tends to be collusion on their part. They gang up and arrive at the angle of the story that they will all report. It is a frightening ploy and it leaves me bewildered when I read them and try to form a picture of the event. Worse than this are the fiction writers, the beat the drum brigade, all ballyhoo and bloodthirsty sensationalists.' There is not so much fiction writing these days and overall standards are much higher. Reports are better written and supported by stats and the other interesting details, and the press is giving millions of pounds' worth of publicity to the game without receiving too much comfort in return. The reason why some younger journalists write the same story is the fear factor. If someone chooses a different story, he can be reprimanded by his sports editor, who will ask him why he has missed the other one. He needs to be bold. If you think you have a good line, you should persevere with it. Originality will win admiration and promotion, but the same mundane stories won't.

In 2004 the Middlesex Wanderers invited me to speak at their dinner at the splendiferous Café Royal in honour of Dave Mackay. Opened in 1891, the Café Royal is being transformed into a hotel that will make more money than it did when it only staged dinners, business conferences and entertainments. Normally I would be delighted, but the place brought back bad memories of the time when I spoke at the FWA Footballer of the Year dinner there in 1985. As chairman, I had to deliver the introductory speech, thank the chief guests and others, and present the trophy to the winner, who that year was the Ipswich midfield player Franciscus Johannes Thijssen. Before making my necessarily formal ten-minute speech, the MC said, 'We have a short break after you speak and you should lead the way to the toilets.'

I didn't really need a pee but I went there and as I was standing at a urinal I heard a loud voice saying, 'Listening to that guy Scovell is worse than being incarcerated in a Japanese prisoner-of-war camp.' I had to laugh.

In 2004, I was sitting next to one of my heroes, Dave Mackay, and we were striving to think of good stories to entertain an audience of 500. Dave came up with a long, rambling anecdote about a taxi drive in Portugal, which I have to say didn't sound too funny, and as he was speaking I noticed the banner on the far wall, which said 'The Mid Sex Wanderers Tour of Japan'. I thought that was a good, amusing way to start my speech. 'Gentleman,' I began, pointing to the banner, 'I've just been looking at that sign over there. I didn't realise you are a mid sex team. Boy George will want to sign you.' There was hardly a laugh. Political correctness had taken over one of soccer's oldest established clubs.

I needed a Dave Mackay with me an hour or so earlier as I walked around Piccadilly Circus towards the Café Royal. It was 6.45 p.m. on a Saturday and the pavements were packed. Suddenly I heard a man saying 'Speed up you c***, I want to get by!'

I turned to a smartly dressed man in his late twenties, not a hooligan or a potential knifeman, or so it seemed. 'You can see it's crowded,' I said.

'Get out of the f****** way, otherwise I'll give you a slap,' he said.

All I could think to say was, 'Hold your tongue my man!' I realised that was foolhardy and it could have been dangerous. He could have pushed a knife past my ribs and no one would have known. I looked around and there was no sign of a policeman. If Dave had been there, he would have seized him by his shirt and lectured him.

Dave Mackay was the toughest and bravest footballer I have seen and in his time there were plenty of challengers. Ron Harris, known as 'Chopper', was a feared tackler, but off the field he was one of the calmest, most softly spoken players I've met. A real gent – off the field. Surprisingly, he was never capped by England.

Similarly, Tommy Smith was presented with just one cap. Years after he retired, he brought out an entertaining, lengthy book, *Anfield Iron*. He was an iron man of a tackler, a master of sledging, but he paid a high price. He has difficulty walking these days.

Norman 'Bite Yer Legs' Hunter carried out Don Revie's instructions – 'Let him know that you're around! – to deter the opposition's star man, but his international career capsized when he made a mistake on the halfway line at Wembley in the match against Poland, when England were knocked out of the 1974 World Cup and Alf Ramsey was cruelly sacked.

Vinnie Jones? Not in the same class as these men.

CHAPTER ELEVEN

'Get Back on the Field, You Coward!'

Appointing a brigadier or even a general to lead an international cricket squad is not a good idea. In the wet summer of 1962 the Pakistan Board of Control chose two military men to head their second tour of England, six-foot-six Brigadier Ghazi Hyder, an outstanding polo player, and five-foot seven Major Rahman. The Pakistanis were 2-0 down going to Headingley for the third Test and I followed my policy with the Portuguese football team of the year before. I stayed at the foreign team's hotel, the Majestic, a four-star establishment in Harrogate with a well-equipped sports room. I got to know the younger players pretty well because they loved playing table tennis, particularly Mushtaq Mohammed. Mushie was the youngest of the five Mohammed brothers and four of them, Hanif, Waqar, Sadiq, and Mushtaq, all played for their country. He still lives in the Midlands and is a popular figure. Most days we played table tennis. Mushie was by far the best player, and the fittest. The least fit of the players, as it proved, was the suave twenty-two-year-old fast bowler Mohammed Farooq, who, like Mushie, settled in England. The handsome Farooq was tall and lean and his bowling was just as fast as Fred Trueman's. But unlike Trueman, he had various ailments and was only declared fit at the last moment.

Just before lunch on the second day, Brigadier Hyder marched to the edge of the pitch and as Farooq was carried off injured, he shouted, 'Get back on the field, you coward!' The medical men who had helped Farooq off released his arms and the startled bowler hobbled a couple of steps on to the ground and the game resumed with him 'fielding' at third man, the position some of today's captains seem to have forsaken. When the umpires called for lunch, Farooq was helped to the away dressing room to wait for a doctor. When the doctor turned up, he decided that Farooq wouldn't be fit to take any part of the Test. It was the last time Farooq played in that series, which England won 4-1. If that had happened today the player would sue the Brigadier, or the Board of Control.

Javed Burki, the Oxford-educated captain, aged twenty-four, decided to put England in. It was the first time Pakistan had ever asked the other team to bat first. The Pakistanis had loved batting first up until then. But Burki was right to field on the first day because England only reached 194-6 and the only highlight of a miserable day was a six struck by Micky Stewart off the first ball delivered by Farook. Munir Malik, an electrician by trade, had been bowling non-stop from 3.30 p.m. on the first day until lunch the next day and Farook had also bowled twenty-eight overs. In short, both men were knackered.

The Brigadier sent for two replacements from home. He should have sent for half a dozen, because most of their players were always breaking down. Twice in his two innings, when struck by deliveries from Brian Statham, Burki collapsed to the ground holding his left shin. His pads must have been made with paper, because on both occasions he was carried off without being accused of cowardice by his manager. Hanif Mohammed, who held the world record of the slowest Test innings and the highest individual score of 499 at that time, was handicapped by severely bruised knuckle and he dropped down the order to five. Hanif was a national hero in his country and had the same reputation and looks as Sachin Tendulkar. His bat was virtually impassable and he was an unerring judge of the line and length of the ball.

In 2005 my friend Qamar Ahmed told me Hanif's eleven-year-old grandson was on holiday with him in London and wanted to play for the Woodpeckers, my wandering side. 'We've had a couple of ten-year-olds who did well,' I said. 'With a name like that he will be even better than them.' I rang Hanif in the flat where he was staying near Oxford Street and we fixed up a time to pick his grandson up outside the block of flats. The traffic was almost gridlocked as I approached the rendezvous. Twenty or so yards ahead, I saw Hanif and the boy stepping into a car and moving off. It turned out that the driver was one of those rogue taxi drivers. I gave pursuit and my car was half a dozen cars behind in the slow-moving queue as we went round the one-way system. The other car stopped and I saw them get out. The driver accelerated away and when I stopped, I said to Hanif, 'I thought you'd been kidnapped!'

He laughed. 'I hadn't seen you for many years and didn't realise it was the wrong man,' he said.

Hanif had a painful knee and didn't want to go to the Avorians CC ground in Cobham, near the Chelsea training ground, so I drove his grandson along with another of my players. The boy was very confident and intelligent and I asked him what he thought about his grandfather as a batsman.

'I think he was boring,' he said.

'You never saw him play,' I said.

'Well I heard others saying that,' he said.

As we arrived at the ground, he asked, 'What position will I bat? I like opening.'

I had to explain that we had other, older openers available. 'You go six,' I said.

When he eventually reached the crease wearing men's size batting pads, he appeared so small that the first delivery, no more than slow medium, passed over his helmet. With an older player it would have been waist-high. That caused a debate with the umpires. Was it a no ball? We decided to let that go.

On the next ball, he played a firm shot to mid-on and called for a run. The other batsman hesitated. 'Come on,' said the lad, 'that's a run.' I wondered who was in charge. Certainly not the other batsman. He faced nine balls before he was given out, caught down the legside by the keeper. He protested loudly, saying, 'That came off my thigh pad. Can I continue batting?'

The umpire said no. 'You go and have a shower,' he said.

Later, the umpire told me, 'He's a cheeky bugger.'

Hasib Ahsan, the ever-smiling Pakistan off spin bowler, was another injury victim in that Headingley Test in 1962. He was sent home not because of injury, but because the umpires thought he was a chucker. At the time, my scant knowledge of cricket was summed up by a comment in my piece before the Test at Edgbaston, which said, 'Their attack has no genuine pace and a so-called leg spinner Intikhab, who has so far taken only one wicket for 168.' That was Inti, one of the greatest leg spin and googly bowlers of all time. He was a jolly, roly-poly man, and he expressed his personality with his bowling. He could bowl immaculately for over after over and then toss up a short one, which the batsman would dispatch to the boundary. Either that, or the shot finished up in the hands of a fielder. Cricket was never dull when Inti played.

The finest Pakistan leg spinner in my view was Abdul Qadir, who took 236 Test wickets at thirty-two apiece, and in some respects he was better than Richie Benaud and Shane Warne, thanks to his extra versatility. He had the lot – leg spin, googlies of different types, a flipper, and two different top spinners. While Warne concentrated on his stock leg spin towards the end of his career, his googly was rarely used. Qadir kept wheeling away right to the end. All three of these great bowlers had shoulder trouble, but Qadir retired from Test cricket at the age of thirty-nine for other reasons. Like England's reluctant Steve Harmison, he did not enjoy travelling abroad, yet he continued playing in domestic cricket for several more years. I had several interesting conversations and he was always helpful and polite, but he upset the authorities too often to have a long and happy career. He was sent home from New Zealand in 1985 for 'disciplinary reasons' after taking 2-212 in the first two Tests and making a half-hearted effort to stop a shot at Wellington. Zaheer Abbas, the acting captain, ordered him off the field. That's the worst thing anyone can do to a struggling cricketer.

Fazal Mahmood, the green-eyed former police officer who bowled Pakistan to victory in England in 1954, was hurriedly flown in to improve the accuracy of the bowling in the 1962 campaign. At thirty-five, he was well past his best. The Brigadier and Burki never learned the lesson that if you bowl someone all day, they will eventually break down. At Trent Bridge, Fazal bowled forty-five overs in the day of England's first innings and finished the next day up with 3-130 off sixty overs, not taking his sweater off until the sixtieth over was completed. The innings lasted seven and a half hours and he bowled all but half an hour. Today fast bowlers rarely bowl more than twenty overs in a day. Perhaps they are mollycoddled too much?

One military man who impressed me was General Tauqir Zia, the chairman of the Pakistan Board of Control who represented Pakistan on the ICC Board in the 1990s. I once sat next to him after a meeting of the Asian Cricket Council in Edgware Road and he spoke perfect English and had a wide knowledge of the history of the game. He sat on my left and on my right was Jagmohan Dalmiya, then the President of the ICC. The General played first-class cricket and knew the game intimately, including the dirty part of cricketing politics. If he had stayed in charge, Pakistani cricket might well have had a better future. But like other decent men in that part of the world, he was soon supplanted by another set of military people. Dalmiya was a very shifty person, unable to answer a straight question. He talked a lot but it was difficult to understand what he was saying. Some of his dealings over contracts, including television ones, were investigated and he managed to stay ahead of his pursuers before he handed over to Malcolm Speed, the Australian lawyer who eventually retired himself when he knew that he couldn't beat the rat pack – those with suspect backgrounds.

The most unusual cricket manager I ever met was the Duke of Norfolk, who took the England team to Australia in 1962/63. Acting on what appeared to be sound information, I had written several articles saying that Billy Griffith, the assistant secretary of the MCC, and a popular figure, would be the manager, with Colin Cowdrey as skipper. I was wrong on both counts. The old school tie still held the reins at Lord's and Cowdrey and Ted Dexter, both public school boys, were vying for the captaincy until Reverend David Sheppard, educated at Sherborne, was talked into making a comeback. He had previously quit in 1956, and he became the first ordained priest to play Test cricket. Sol christened me 'the Sheppard correspondent' as I followed the Reverend's dismal return to the Sussex side.

Just before the selectors sat down to pick their squad, he scored 112 for the Gentlemen against the Players. Sol obviously liked my piece, which started, 'David Sheppard, like Psidium in last year's Derby, has come from nowhere to flash past the post first. It will push him up the gangplank to Australia and I expect the selectors will announce tonight that Sheppard has the captain's job.' He stuck a headline on it, saying, 'Gangway for the Rev – 112 passport to Australia.'

Sheppard was picked, but not as captain. Ted Dexter, his teammate from Sussex, beat him to it. Sheppard and Cowdrey were similar people, devoted Christians who wanted to do good things for their neighbours. Cowdrey brought the Spirit of Cricket campaign into international cricket and it still acts as a check on bad behaviour.

On a few occasions, Colin gave me lifts back to South London from Test matches in the north. Sitting in his Jaguar with its prominent registration number, 'MCC 311', it was like having a private tutorial. I learned so much about the game from him. He was loved by almost everyone. The exceptions were those who thought he was dishonest about being a 'walker'. Another England captain told me, 'He doesn't "walk" when it is a tight one!' I think he was wrong. There was no finer sportsman in England than Colin Cowdrey. With a little of David Sheppard's steeliness, he would have added many more Tests as skipper to his total of twenty-seven, compared to Sheppard's two, Dexter's thirty, Mike Smith's twenty-five, Brian Close's seven, and Ray Illingworth's thirty-one.

Sheppard was a tougher character than Colin and if he had continued to play, he could have been England captain again. Several times during his comeback he confided to me, 'My fielding isn't up to it. At thirty-three you need to be fit and athletic. I'm not.'

When he played in that tour Down Under, the crowd barracked him when he misfielded, provoking a wonderful comment from Fred Trueman: 'It's a great pity that the Reverend don't put his hands together more often in t'field.' David scored a gutsy 113 in Melbourne, but he quit the game and returned to the full-time saving of souls.

The day after the announcement of the England 1962/63 squad, the MCC called a press conference at Lord's, supposedly to appoint Griffith as the tour manager. Ronnie

Aird, the MCC secretary, came in, followed by Griffith. Next to them was the figure of the Duke, who was President of Sussex CCC. I thought he was there to support his friend Griffith, but Aird said, 'And the manager for Australia is... the Duke of Norfolk.' Everyone was staggered. The whole of the cricketing fraternity down under were delighted. The Duke, full name Bernard Marmaduke Fitzalan-Howard, the sixteenth Duke of Norfolk and the Earl Marshal of England, was fifty-four and he looked older. He said his wife had talked him into it. 'I was tentatively offered the job by an MCC committee but I told them I had a lot to do at home. When I got home I told her about it and she said, "Why don't you go?" She insisted I would enjoy it. I woke at five in the morning worrying about it and then I decided to go, if certain difficulties could be overcome.' The Duke would often wore plus fours – tweed trousers tucked into thick socks just before the knee. The Aussies loved that.

The Duke loved cricket but he didn't really understand the politics of it. He was the titular manager of the tour, with the ninety-five per cent of the work being undertaken by the assistant manager, Alec Bedser. 'It worked,' said Alec years later. 'These days they appoint dozens of them for these tours. I don't know what they do. I did it almost on my own.' There were legions of amusing stories about the Duke and one of the funniest was about his butler. His team, Sussex Martlets, were playing at his ground at Arundel Castle – my favourite cricket ground in the whole world – and they were short of an umpire. The Duke sent a message to his butler, Meadows, to take over, although he knew little about the laws. Meadows was given a white coat and went out to the middle. The Duke came in with seven wickets down and was at the non-strikers' end, with Meadows at square leg. The other batsman called for a run to give the Duke the strike and set off saying, 'Come on, your Grace.' But the Duke slipped and was run out yards short of the wicket.

'How's that?' shouted the fielders.

There was a delay as Meadows deliberated. Then, with his two hands in front of his chest, as butlers tend to stand, he said, 'His Grace is not in!'

Another classic story was about one of his many visits to race meetings in Australia. He was in the paddock one day and noticed that a trainer had slipped something into the mouth of a horse. As a leading figure in the Jockey Club and the Queen's representative at Ascot, he said to the trainer, 'What's that you've given to the horse?'

The trainer said, 'Oh, your Grace, not to worry. It was a lump of sugar. Here, have one yourself. I'm having one myself.'

The Duke popped the lump of sugar into to his mouth and ate it, and the trainer did the same. Just before the start, the trainer was heard giving the jockey his instructions. 'With two furlongs to go,' he said, 'let him go and give him all you've got. If anyone passes you after that, it will either be myself or the Duke!'

On one occasion I had to ring him at Arundel Castle and he was quite brusque but answered the question before wishing me a good evening. It was awkward addressing someone 'Your Grace'.

One of the reasons for his appointment was that the MCC wanted to have better relations with the journalists – not me, I have to say! Dexter had upset some of them with his infrequent habit of walking past them without speaking. Someone at the MCC came up with the idea of inviting the Duke to come along to the Test at the Oval and have a drink with the correspondents who were going to Australia.

One of wittiest stories on the theme of Dexter's indifference concerns Robert Walter Vivian Robins, the former England captain. He was known 'RWV' or 'Walter'. He was chairman of the selectors and early in the tour he was walking in the lobby of a hotel when Lord Ted walked past him without saying anything. Later that night, he sat down and wrote a short note to Dexter. 'Dear Ted. I am that small git with a bald head who walked past you earlier today and I am your boss. This is to introduce myself to you!' Dexter had several jousts with the older cricket writers, accusing them of writing scandalous stories about the private lives of the players. He felt drawing the series was creditable but some critics lambasted his captaincy. Later, of course, he became the cricket correspondent of the *Sunday Mirror*. Most England captains finish up as cricket writers and the latest one is Mike Atherton, the correspondent of *The Times*, who succeeded Christopher Martin-Jenkins, the doyen of cricket journalism. Atherton is now the highest paid cricket writer, with an annual income reputed to be around £250,000. He still works for Sky and is a very busy man, and a thoroughly capable individual. He is a far better writer than the correspondents I worked with in that era, maybe with the exception of Brian Chapman of the *Daily Mirror*. Of the twenty-seven England captains I have worked with since my career started, fifteen became cricket writers or television commentators. So far, not one pukka journalist has graduated to become a Test cricketer.

Despite his almost saintly reputation, there was one occasion when I upset Colin Cowdrey. A friend rang up to say he went to the annual dinner of the Caledonian CC in Dartford and heard Mike Denness, then aged twenty-three and in his second season with Kent, making a speech in which he said that Cowdrey should be replaced as Kent captain. I rang Mike, a good man and a Scot, and he said, 'Yes, it's true. I made the point because I believe you can't build a team if the leader is often not there. Colin is one of the world's greatest batsmen but he has so many calls with Tests and everything that the side frequently has to be led by someone else. You can have the best players in the world in your side but there has to be unity. I think some of the other players feel the same way as I do. Year after year we finish about twelfth in the table. There must be some reason.'

The story proved to be a scoop and the other correspondents rang Cowdrey to get his reaction. He was very unhappy. He called me and said, 'That was a private dinner and you shouldn't have reported it.'

'I don't think so,' I said. 'If people pay to go a dinner it's in the public domain. A lot of people heard it and what Mike said was fair comment.'

It didn't really affect our relationship. Even today, sporting people complain when their speeches are reported in the newspapers. If the speech is complimentary, they don't mind, but if it is critical, they claim their privacy has been invaded. There is no such thing as privacy when others turn up to listen to speeches. If the speaker is upset he can resort to the law. But 'fair comment' is a defence against libel.

Colin Cowdrey's wife Penny, daughter of the former Kent CCC chairman Stuart Chiesman, was a bubbly, thoroughly nice lady who often accompanied him on tours.

But their longstanding and happy marriage sadly ended, and Colin married Lady Herries, one of the Duke of Norfolk's daughters. In his later years, Colin and his new wife lived at Arundel and he spent a lot of time telephoning cricketers to congratulate them or give them advice about problems. He was a kind of Good Samaritan for the game.

Just before he died, I met him at a reception at the South African Embassy as I checked in my black leather briefcase at the cloakroom. We had a good chat, inevitably about cricket. He had a gentle, mischievous sense of humour. I picked up my briefcase and drove home, but when I went into the house to open it, I realised it was Colin's, not mine. They looked very similar. I rang him on his mobile and explained the mistake and he said, 'I've read through your documents and I'll be passing the information to the *News of the World*.'

I replied, 'Your material is already with MI5,' and he laughed.

He said he would drop it at the *Mail* offices the next day. 'Don't worry,' I said. 'We'll leave it to the next time when we meet.'

'No,' he said. 'I insist. I'll drop in at the office around midday.'

He and his chauffeur arrived on time: he was that sort of person. When he died in 2000, the service of thanksgiving for his life was packed with 2,000 worshippers. Former Prime Minister John Major, who often invited him to 10 Downing Street for a late night chat and a tipple, gave the address. I have attended four services of that nature in Westminster Abbey and this was by far the best and most uplifting. John Major summed Colin up beautifully: 'He left us too soon but it was a gem of an innings,' he said. 'He lived life with a clear eye, a straight bat, and a cover drive from heaven. He was a true Corinthian.'

CHAPTER TWELVE

Lord Ted Reaches One Pinnacle
But Fails as the England Boss

In the 300 or so Test matches I have reported around the world, I must have seen almost 10,000 Test innings. Which was the best? I watched a number of Brian Lara's greatest innings, particularly in the West Indies when he took on the Australians almost single-handed, the 125 by Graeme Pollock at Trent Bridge in 1965, Viv Richards' epic 291 at the Oval in 1976, and some of the finest of the innings scored by Sachin Tendulkar, Sunil Gavaskar, Gary Sobers, Javed Miandad, Colin Cowdrey, Gordon Greenidge, David Gower, Adam Gilchrist, and one of my favourites, Barry Richards. But the accolade goes to Ted Dexter's seventy out of 102 in eighty minutes at Lord's, in what was termed 'the greatest Test match of all' in 1963, which ended with a stupendous draw. Ian Wooldridge, the Bradman of sports writing, sat near me in the press box in the Warner Stand, and we agreed on this. Years later, he said to me, 'I never saw a better one.'

In his book *Cricket, Lovely Cricket*, Ian wrote, 'To clear the decks for Dexter it must be explained that England have rarely come closer to totally and disastrously disappearing from a series than they did in the remaining twenty-five minutes of that Friday morning. Edrich was out to the first ball he received, Stewart to the last ball before lunch, and Griffith and Hall, like two huge hired assassins, seemed set for a bloodbath.

'This was the background, then, against which Dexter's innings must be measured in the years to come if we are someday to assess whether it was the greatest he ever played. All I can say is that not for a moment could I drag my eyes from that splendid, Olympian figure. He struck seventy off seventy-four deliveries, but even those startling statistics tell next to nothing. It was the manner of their making that transformed his deed into the dream of all schoolboys and the fireside romance of old men. For me the second Test and the earth itself seemingly stood still as he played one of the truly great innings of all time. He simply stood and smashed anything that Hall and Griffith could hurl at him. The faster they bowled, the more savagely he cut and drove and pulled them. This was Dexter, the enigma of even his own generation, rising head and shoulders above all his contemporaries.

'Dexter was once an infantry subaltern and it seems that these attitudes might well have been learned from the Small Arms Manual. He treats his bat like a tommygun. Hall and Griffith, the most volatile fast bowling attack in the world, simply had no idea where next to bowl at him. When he was out, lbw Sobers, there was just one more remarkable scene before he disappeared. All along the Nursery balconies, down the length of the ground, and across the three tiers of the pavilions, there was a sudden upward movement as though Lord's itself had risen two feet off its foundations. It was an illusionary effect for it was nothing more than every man, woman and child, coloured and white, standing to applaud him each yard of the way. Anyone who did not feel some tiny tingle down the spin must have been soulless, or very, very cynical.'

If it had been a bright sunny day, and a flat, dry pitch, it would still have been a great innings. But the day was sullen and murky and the pitch, yet to be purged of its dangerous ridge, helped the bowlers, who were aided at the pavilion end by a 'sightscreen', which was no bigger than a double bedsheet. There were interruptions through rain and the stops gave the West Indian fast bowlers a chance to recharge and roar on again. On the final day, Colin Cowdrey's left arm was struck by a brutal delivery and he went off to hospital where an X-ray revealed that a bone had been broken. When Dexter, nicknamed 'Lord Ted', was lording it, he wore the minimum of protection: a pair of pads, a box, and a pair of batting gloves. His bat was really his protection. I wrote in the *Sketch*, 'He showed that a great cricketer can hit any bowling, however fast, on any type of pitch. Wes Hall, world's fastest bowler? Dexter straight drove him so hard that the ball was gaining speed as it crossed the boundary. Charlie Griffith? The same story. Blows of such velocity that one wondered how a two-pound-eight-ounce piece of wood could generate such energy. A cover drive off Griffith rang out like the crack of a ringmaster's whip. I spent some time with the barrackers in front of the Tavern and rarely have I seen a cricket crowd so spontaneously roused to enthusiasm. This was his way of fighting out of a crisis. Not for him the hunched shoulders and the hesitant bat and pad shuffle up the pitch. Exploding violence was met with even more explosive violence. The ball hummed, the crowd roared. Dangerous? Yes, but gloriously thrilling. This is what cricket is all about. This is what 31,000 people want to see. It couldn't last and everything after his departure was like a hangover.'

Dexter was similar in some ways to Douglas Jardine, England's most misunderstood and disliked captain. Both men were tall and angular with their caps jutting out, seemingly in defiance. Born in Milan, Dexter was the last man to captain the Gentlemen against the Players, which signalled (or should have signalled) the end of class distinction in cricket. He was almost as aloof and disdainful as Jardine, who was born in Bombay and died in Montreux at the age of fifty-seven. Dexter went to Radley and moved on to Cambridge; Jardine was educated at Winchester and went to Oxford. Jardine was the more practical of the two. Dexter was more of a theorist. He was a single-figure golfer, and he flew aircraft, drove fast motorbikes, modelled clothes, ran a PR company, owned horses and greyhounds, and stood unsuccessfully as a Conservative against the local MP James Callaghan in the Cardiff constituency in 1964. He lost to the future Prime Minister, but not disastrously. Dexter was never bored, or if he was, he would move on to something else. Both men ignored pain and Lord Ted showed his stoicism when his car ran backwards over one of his legs, breaking it. Jardine retired at thirty-three to became a cricket correspondent. Dexter gave up cricket at thirty-four to do the same. For all his years in the game, he never really mastered the art of putting over a good image. He would come up with comments that upset people. He was a hero, but he wasn't a lovable one.

In 1989 he must have thought he had reached the pinnacle in his cricketing life. He became chairman of the England Committee and chairman of selectors. He had a host of good ideas, but some were not so good, and he fell calamitously from power after an interview at a losing Test match against the Australians at Lord's, when he made a remark that he thought was funny – he blamed the defeat on Venus being in the wrong part of the Solar System in relation to the moon. It would have come out as funny if he had delivered it in a different way, but a majority of the press men mocked him and called for his resignation. He never really got on with the press, but I liked Lord Ted and still have a great regard for him.

This small incident explains why his PR wasn't as good as his batting. At a Lord's Taverners dinner in 2005 I asked him if he could supply an anecdote for my imminent book commemorating the fiftieth anniversary of Jim Laker's world record 19-90. He said, 'I'm off duty' and walked off to his table.

'It would only take a minute,' I said, but he carried on walking.

It reminded me of the story about Alf Ramsey, when some journalists came to see him the day after the World Cup and congratulated him. They were hoping to get some happy quotes from him, but Alf just said, 'It is my day off.'

On the last day of the 1963 Lord's Test, England needed 118 on 116-3, with two of their gutsiest players, Ken Barrington and Brian Close, at the crease. Barrington didn't fancy Griffith, as a man or as an opponent. He told me that Griffith occasionally threw the ball when his lethal yorker was delivered and in the Surrey *v.* West Indies match in May he said to umpire Dusty Rhodes, 'Watch out for this fella, one minute it's fast medium and suddenly the ball comes at you like a high philosophy bullet!'

The deeply loved Kenny was the master of the malapropism. Once he said to Mike Brearley, 'It's a good job we had those helmets, otherwise there could have been some fertilities.' In a disturbance at Bangalore, he told the players, 'It was sorted out because the police sent in 200 plain clothes protectives.' His favourite phrases were 'he didn't know whether to stick or twist' and 'you've got the batsman in two man's land now'. Asked to comment on the Trevor Chappell underarm bowling incident, he said, 'I think I'll twist on what the manager said.' In Australia, he umpired a practice session under lights and gave three lbws, saying, 'I caused a commotion, I can tell you. It raised a few eyelashes.' Shown a photograph of him when he was in his teens, he said, 'I look like one of those guardsmen outside Buckingham Palace. What's it they have on their heads? Fuzzbies or something!' When it was raining hard, he used to say, 'It's coming down like pea pods.'

Kenny wasn't joking when he scored his 110 for Surrey against Griffith at the Oval. Griffith hardly spoke during the tour, certainly not to most English journalists. Sol told me to go to Paddington and meet the team early in April and my job was to ask him, 'Are you a chucker?'

When I put the question to him, he glared and said, 'No.' He walked off with a scowl reminiscent of Sonny Liston. Having not seen him bowl in person, I decided he wasn't and concluded my article saying, 'A chucker? Never in a thousand years.'

Cricketing friends Jim Laker and Kenny Barrington told me, 'You watch his yorker. His chest opens up and it's blatant.'

In that Oval match, Kenny drove one of his few bad deliveries for four, and Griffith said to him, 'Wait until I get you on a fast pitch!'

'What's the matter?' said Kenny. 'Aren't I supposed to hit the ball, stand back, and let you have a free go?'

Despite being peppered with short balls and yorkers, Kenny survived long enough, somewhat luckily, to score eighty and sixty in that Lord's Test, and he managed to avoid being put in a hospital. But Close, who scored seventy, was hit more than a dozen times on the right side and on the back of his body without flinching. When his book came out in 1978, it was titled *I Don't Bruise Easily*. A great title, but somewhat contentious, because at Lord's in 1963 and the Old Trafford Test in 1976, after facing the Hall-Griffith and the Roberts-Holding duos respectively, he took his shirt and vest off in the dressing room and on both occasions revealed a mass of bruises. It made for damning photographs in the newspapers, and the umpires were criticised for not taking sterner action. Today no batsman would face that type of bowling without wearing chest protectors, arm guards, and helmets.

Close was a heroic figure and a brilliant captain. He should have captained England many more times than seven (his record of six wins and a draw was the best record of any) but at Lord's the game's rulers didn't like him. After leading England to success against India and Pakistan in 1967, he was ready to take on the West Indies in the Caribbean when he slowed the over rate in a county game at Warwickshire to save champions Yorkshire from defeat. Only twenty-four overs were bowled in the last 100 minutes, just about the minimum over rate now permitted, and he had a brief row with a spectator. The affair was referred to Lord's and he and his team were severely censured. Most people thought he would never play for England again. Ten years later, at the age of forty-five, he and John Edrich, aged thirty-nine, took on Holding, Roberts, and Wayne Daniel on a dank and wet day on a spiteful pitch. It was like a coconut shy, with the veterans ducking and diving and being knocked down and still getting up. I was there and it was an incredible show of courage. The Test and County Cricket Board, who ran the match, might have been charged with violation of their human rights had the EU law been in force.

I spoke to him in 2009 when I asked him how he managed to skipper the Yorkshire Colts side in his early seventies. 'Keep fit,' he said. 'I've had a hip replacement and two dodgy knees but I still play golf most days. I use a buggy now but I still do a lot of walking. I go to the gym at four every day and spend an hour and a half there, in the sauna, in the Jacuzzi, when I do my stretches, and swim in the pool. If you don't keep exercising, you'll seize up!'

One of the weaknesses of English team selection over the years has been the insistence on picking players to suit the conditions, instead of players with class. The Lord's Test of 1963 was a typical example. The selectors dropped Brian Statham on a pitch that eminently suited fast bowling and brought in thirty-nine-year-old Hampshire medium pace bowler Derek Shackleton. In the selected twelve, only three players were under thirty; the average age was thirty. Shack was one of my early heroes when I first watched a game at Portsmouth's United Services ground. He was the finest medium pace seam bowler of his time, just ahead of Tom Cartwright, but he was miscast in this dramatic match. 'Brian should have played and we needed quick bowlers and we let the West Indies off the hook,' Close said to me afterwards. 'The top went and with the ridge, the chucker and the weather, it wasn't easy.' With wickets falling, Close decided to advance down the pitch to Hall and Griffith. 'When I started coming down, Griffith's eyes popped like chapel hat-pegs,' said Close. 'He shuddered to a stop and Frank Worrell had to coax him to go back to his mark. He was wasn't the same after that. Then he got me caught behind with a very, very fast bouncing off cutter and it was thrown. No one on earth could have bowled at that speed from that approach.'

Kevin Pietersen, similar to Close in many ways, tried to come down the pitch and attack the bowling of Glenn McGrath and Brett Lee in the 2005 Ashes series, and he collected a bruise on his chest, off McGrath, for his impertinence. Close was out to a risky sweep shot in the Old Trafford Test, which eventually cost England the series in 1961. I was there. If Close had kept his head, England might have been the winning side.

Eight were needed from the last over at Lord's in 1963, with Shackleton joining David Allen. Shack was run out on the fourth ball and Cowdrey, his arm strapped, came in to a tremendous standing ovation. Allen, on strike, blocked the remaining two deliveries. If Cowdrey faced, he was going to bat left-handed to save any more damage to his arm. Hall bowled for three hours and twenty minutes without a rest, one of the most magnificent fast bowling performances of all time. Tired from his exertions the day before, he overslept and had to depart on the coach without having breakfast. Frank Worrell had two hard-boiled eggs in his hand. 'Here,' he said. 'That should keep you going!'

His book was called *Pace with Fire*, and he was writing a second one when I last met him in Barbados in 2006. He became a priest, then a Government minister, and at seventy-two, he swims up to a mile a day. He has battled through a serious illness and two car crashes and his courage, like Close's, is undimmed.

You can imagine seeing Wes Hall's gold necklace jangling as he tears up to the crease, straining every muscle and sinew. I was at Hove on 18 June, two days before the Lord's Test, when the West Indies bowled out Sussex for fifty-nine with Griffith warming up with 3-14. Kenny Suttle, the left-hander who was one of the most popular players ever to play for the county, came in at first wicket down and Griffith caught him on the side of his head with a ferocious bouncer, knocking him to the ground. The press box was no more than sixty-five yards from the pitch at square leg and we could hear the crack of leather on unprotected skin. Everyone thought Kenny would have to go to hospital and be detained for checks. He managed to stagger to his feet with Griffith not showing too much concern, and was helped off. Half an hour later, he came back and Griffith unleashed a few more bouncers. But Suttle battled on to forty-two before the West Indies won.

Three years later, history repeated itself when a bouncer hit Suttle in the jaw. It was his first ball, from Griffith. Again, Suttle was helped off, but as the West Indies had been bowled out for sixty-seven, the game soon ended with a nine wicket win for Sussex. 'That ball was the fastest I ever faced,' said Suttle. 'The blow knocked me half silly. All the West Indians came in to ask me how I felt before I went to hospital, with the exception of Griffith. That hurt me more than anything.'

The last time I met Griffith he was still bowling, but at medium pace in a seniors' game in Barbados. His first words were, 'I remember you, you used to give me a whole lot of ****!' He's not a bad guy and he has put a lot back into the game he loves.

Kevin Pietersen has the same confidence and arrogance of Dexter and as those qualities are needed to become a great player, he should be on the way to becoming an all-time great, but he has fallen short. Yet having seen several of his innings, his overconfidence has led on several occasions to the team's failure, like the occasion at Edgbaston in 2008 when he stepped down the pitch and drove on ninety-four and was caught by AB De Villiers, aiming for a six. If England were 300 ahead, it wouldn't have mattered so much. But the team needed a big innings, not a minor explosion. That caused one of the rows he had with coach Peter Moores that eventually led to the latter's dismissal. He was a novice as a captain. One of his most unprofessional acts was at Sabina Park in 2009 when after hitting two sixes, he lashed out and was caught on ninety-seven. Afterwards he said, 'I am a happy boy' – overlooking the fact that his duty was to ensure a very big total and deny the West Indies victory in the first Test. Instead, England crumpled to fifty-one, their third lowest total. His best asset is his wife Jessica Taylor, the pop singer. When he was appointed, Mike Atherton interviewed him on the Lord's ground and he started talking about 'his wonderful wife'. 'She supports me all the way and she gives me tips,' he said. 'She's been in the public eye more than me and she can help me a lot.' I've never heard a sportsman talk about his wife in those circumstances and I was really excited. They are obviously in love and when there are stressful times, which will always happen in sport, he won't need a team psychologist or a counsellor; he has Jessica. Alas, Jessie failed to restrain her headstrong husband when he overreached himself.

I have always opposed the selection of anyone who is not English-born and will never change that view. Pietersen qualified by having an English mother, born in Canterbury, and a four-year stay in the UK, but his father is an Afrikaner. Most other countries do not poach players from other countries. How many English players have been capped by South Africa? It is patently wrong that England recruits foreigners. So many South Africans occupy key slots in the England lineup and it has gravely hampered English cricket.

When South Africa was banned by the ICC in 1970, Graeme Pollock was the top player of the day and was young enough to qualify for England, had he served the necessary seven years residence, which he hadn't. Every time I meet him now, he always gives me a hearty welcome. Perhaps that is because on 5 August 1965 at Trent Bridge I wrote, 'Robert Graeme Pollock played one of the great innings of Test cricket to save South Africa in the second Test – 125 in 140 minutes. England were roaring to victory when South Africa were 80-5 when their bowlers were suddenly Pollocked. Like a mad infantryman who leaps from his trench and charges the enemy single-handed, twenty-one-year-old Pollock routed England almost single-handed. They panicked, and almost cracked. This blond, six-foot-two left-hander is now king of the world's batting empire and he has the time and ability to develop into a Bradman.'

Wisden said, 'It is one of the finest Test displays of all time.' Any high-quality batsman can score a rapid century on a hot, sunny day on a flat and dry pitch, but this Test was played on a slow pitch, often in poor light, and frequently sawdust had to be used to hasten the drying process. In England's attack were three arch exponents at the top of their profession: John Snow with pace, Tom Cartwright with medium pace, and Fred Titmus the off spinner. Pollock almost treated them with contempt. His heavy bat, weighing three pounds and four ounces, sent the ball skimming along the ground with beautifully timed, effortless shots. According to his father, who had played for Orange Free State, Pollock was walking at the age of eight months, and there was plenty of evidence at Trent Bridge that day to indicate that his batting was precocious, too. On the Monday, Peter Pollock, three years older than Graeme, rushed England to defeat with 5-34 to follow his 5-53 in the first innings. While Graeme was a gentle, nice man, Peter, at the time, was the opposite. But later in life he took up religion and was a changed man.

At 6.14 p.m. the match was over with a day to spare. Reading the *Sketch* the next morning I thought Bob Findlay had touched up my introduction. He had a nasty habit of doing that. It now read, 'We slunk out of Trent Bridge last night ashamed of the batsmen of England as a breed of men worthy of the trip to Australia after the South Africans had won the second Test by ninety-four runs.'

He rang me at the YMCA and before I was about to complain about his unwarranted interference, he said, 'You've missed a good story! What's your explanation?'

'I haven't read all the papers yet,' I said.

'Well,' said Bob, 'Ian Wooldridge has a good scoop in the *Mail*. He said the South Africans celebrated their win by coming out onto the pitch and peeing all over it.'

'Good luck to Ian,' I said. 'He was probably the only journalist who was still at the ground at eight o'clock. He is not the fastest writer around. If I was still writing then, my piece would have missed the first edition.'

Any chance Graeme Pollock had of catching Don Bradman ended when South Africa was expelled from international cricket, but up to until recently, his average of 60.97 was second in the Test career averages behind Bradman's 99.94. He played only twenty-three Tests and scored 2,188 runs. Without apartheid, he could have proved one of the all-time greats.

Barry Richards, born in Durban, was in the same position. He only played four Tests. Many judges believe he would have been the outstanding right-hander of his generation, or of all time. I first met him when he joined Hampshire in 1968, when foreign players were admitted to the county championship. Peter Presence, who had a sports agency, First Features, wanted him to write a worldwide cricket column and asked me to write it. Barry was twenty-three, hadn't made much money, and was keen to do it. He was a diligent provider of information and always contacted me on time. He had plenty of ideas to improve English cricket. The main one was, 'Take some chances, give it a go!'

He thought English cricketers were too cautious and he showed the way, dominating

Hampshire's innings with his vast repertoire of shots. He scored a century before lunch nine times and few batsmen bettered that. 'Until I came here, I rarely hit a six,' he told me. 'I thought it might be a risk, might give a chance. Now with these smaller grounds, I've been giving it the gun.'

He pioneered going down the pitch to off spinners and hitting over extra cover. 'English players don't do that. They were schooled to work the ball to leg.'

He also used the tactic of advancing out of his crease to drive the medium pacers and in his book, ghostwritten by soccer commentator Martin Tyler, he said, 'Word spread around the circuit about it and Ken Higgs of Lancashire was ready for me. When I started going up the pitch he bowled the ball on the full, straight at my head. I just hit the dirt and should have been stumped. I decided not to try it again against Ken.'

Richards had to tighten up his game on turning pitches and was a master of handling spin. He reckoned his most treasured innings was seventy out of a total of 122 at Harrogate, on a pitch that was damp at one end and firm and bouncy at the other. Fred Trueman said to him, 'Ee, lad, bowling's not all beer and skittles.'

The next finest bad-pitch innings he played, certainly the best I have ever seen of that type, was his half-century against Ray Illingworth and his Yorkshire champion side at the United Services ground in Portsmouth, out of another low total. There was a hole at one end and Illingworth kept finding it. Barry managed to evade the ball when it jumped chest-high, or else played it in front of him. Technically, his game was close to perfection. Sometimes, when he was bored, he virtually surrendered his wicket. He wasn't an averages man. Gordon Greenidge had just earned a place in the Hampshire side and being at the other end to Richards, he matured quickly into a world-class opening batsman.

Hobbs and Sutcliffe, Bradman and Ponsford, Hutton and Washbrook... They were all record-breaking opening partnerships, but I believe Richards and Greenidge were even better. Barry is one of the most expert commentators on television and is still closely involved with the game. He is a good man.

If Denis Compton had two good knees, he would have broken most of the Test batting records. Modern methods of treatment would have given him a chance of doing it, but he wasn't a man to covet records. He loved entertaining his audience and delighted them with the most audacious shots. I was too young to see him in action other than on 19 August 1953, when at seven minutes to three, he swept a boundary to win back the Ashes after nineteen years of Australian dominance. The first four Tests were drawn and the two boards agreed that the match should be extended to six days. I bought my ticket, which cost 10s, well in advance, and I was praying that the game went into Monday. Jim Laker and Tony Lock hustled the Australians out in their second innings, taking nine wickets for 120 from their thirty-seven overs. Without Bill Johnston's services, England only needed 132 to win, so I only saw half a day's play. Arthur Morris, the Australian opening batsman, bowled, and Compo, who was limping badly, hit the ball very fine with his left leg stiff, crossed over his right. It must have troubled him, I thought. A collision with a goalkeeper at Charlton just before the Second World War had left him with a serious weakness in the joint, which was exacerbated when the kneecap was removed. I sat in the Vauxhall stand and most of the 30,000 crowd rushed on to the ground as the ball sped towards the rope. The police lined up to allow Bill Edrich and Compo off the field. It was well worth leaving home – then the Isle of Wight – at 6 a.m. to see history made. It was the same year as the Coronation and Sir Edmund Hillary's conquest of Everest.

I got to know Compo when he became a 'journalist' working for the *Sunday Express*. He wasn't hot on facts and he was always asking questions like, 'How many fours and sixes?' Late in life, after hip surgery, he had to walk with a stick. The second operation failed and he needed a third hip operation. When I spoke to him a month before he died on St George's Day 1997, he was in a maudlin mood, almost as though he knew his last innings was about to end. 'Can't get about, old boy,' he said. 'Can't even use a buggy.'

He started talking about helmets – he hated them! – and the state of the game, the state of the country, and the current politicians. Everything was in a mess, he said. Half an hour later, he cheered up a bit. It was the old Compo, talking excitedly about the talents of a new generation of batsmen.

These great sportsmen paid a heavy price for their success. His loyal friend and comrade, Keith Miller, who attended Compo's memorial service at Westminster Abbey, also went through hip surgery. He had cancer of the face and ear as well. Keith's body was ravaged, but his spirit was unquenchable. His eyes lit up when he was asked for his memories of his great friend. 'He used to ring me most weeks, or me him,' he said. 'I spoke to him a couple of days before he died and we arranged to meet for a pint at Lord's. He often used to ring in the middle of the night. He never did get used to the time difference.'

All 2,086 tickets had been taken up for the service and more than 1,000 applicants were disappointed. It was, said officials, the most oversubscribed memorial service held at Westminster Abbey since Richard Dimbleby's. John Major should have been in Hong Kong to see the handover of the colony to the Chinese, but he preferred to honour Denis Compton's memory instead. 'I think I made the right choice,' he said. 'To watch Denis play cricket on a good day was to know what joy was.'

Just before the service, a familiar face appeared near the two rows set aside for the press in the nave. It was Dennis Skinner, the Labour MP known as 'the Beast of Bolsover' because he riles both the Government and the Opposition. Spotting an empty seat next to Henry Blofeld, he said, 'I'll sit there with Henry.' I was sitting on the other side. Technically he should have been sitting elsewhere, but no one complained.

'Mr Blofield is one of my heroes,' said Dennis. 'I love listening to him.' Henry beamed.

'I used to play cricket myself – a medium pacer who swung it,' said Skinner. 'I got off school to watch Denis when he played at Derby. He was a genius, a natural. Never needed to practice. I could watch him all day.'

After a series of salvoes at the expense of the absent Geoffrey Boycott, he proceeded to tell us about his early life. 'I was a miner,' he said. 'Came up from the pit and went straight out there to play, like a lot of players in that part of the world.'

William Hague had just been elected to succeed John Major as the leader of the

Conservative Party and I asked Skinner why Hague hadn't been likened to E.T. 'He has,' he said. 'Someone shouted out "E.T." when he rose for his first speech as leader but the press missed it.'

Henry and I were left in no doubt that he had a low opinion of Hague. 'He's a lightweight,' he said. 'A short-term appointment. They're just waiting for Michael Portillo and Chris Patten to get back in the House and they'll choose between them.'

He was partly right on Hague, but not Portillo and Patten. He had an engaging niceness that belied his fierce reputation in the House. He was frank about Europe. 'We're more split than they are,' he said. 'But we don't come out in public about it. I'm a Eurosceptic and always have been. A federal Europe will never happen. You can't get a set of nations all agreeing on the same things. They are destroying it now and all we've got to do is let them get on with it.'

One of the highlights of the magnificent service was the elegance and style of the reading by Jim Swanton of a passage from *English Cricket* by Sir Neville Cardus about Lord's. I congratulated him later and he beamed with pleasure. It was a considerable achievement by an extraordinary man in his ninety-first year. Standing outside the abbey, I saw Alex Bannister, who was also well into his nineties. I mentioned Swanton's performance. Alex had a cynical slant on life and he said, 'I've been trying to get away from that man's voice all my life, mate.' They weren't good friends; they were two very respected cricket writers from entirely different backgrounds.

CHAPTER THIRTEEN

The Cobbold Brothers –
The Last of the Corinthian Chairmen

John and Patrick Cobbold were the kindest, funniest, most outrageous chairmen in the history of English football. There will never be any more Cobbolds, and that's not just because they were bachelors. They were unique. When Ipswich won the Championship for the first and last time in 1961/62, John Cobbold, known as 'Mr John' to the staff and 'Johnny' to his friends, was asked what his role was in the club's astonishing, unexpected success. 'Well, it's like being after the Lord Mayor's Show,' he said. 'Tottenham won it last season like kings and our boys came along on their tractors and snatched it away from them. Do you know, more than half our supporters work on the land. As for what I do, I pour out the drinks in the boardroom. But I did invite Alf Ramsey in and gave him the key to the drinks cabinet. He took it away but as far as I know, he never used it.' (Byron Butler, the BBC football correspondent for many years, wrote of Ramsey's title-winning squad, 'Alf stitched a collection of remnants into a quilt of quality.')

I went to the celebration dinner at the Savoy Hotel on the Embankment in London and the menus were beautifully printed in French with the names set out in full – names like Horace Millward, Edward John Phillips, Raymond Crawford, John Cavendish Cobbold, Patrick Mark Cobbold, and even the groundsman, Frederick Blake. It was the Cobbold's idea and they also invited a group of bunnies from the Playboy Club, dressed in their skimpy black-and-white outfits, with tails. Both of the Cobbolds swore in almost every sentence. The girls took exception to Mr John's coarse language during his speech and fled. The Cobbolds called Ramsey 'Old Stoneface', and when the manager got to his feet and droned on in his monotonous voice, a voice could be heard from behind a window saying, 'C'mon Ramsey, stop boring everyone. That's enough, Alfie.' It went on for some time until someone realised it was John Cobbold.

After the speeches, I congratulated Mr John on his success in organising such a great night. 'It could have been more successful if I didn't have to sit next to that ****,' he said as he pointed to Bob Lord, the Burnley chairman.

Burnley were runners-up and Lord was supposed to rise and congratulate the winners. But he said, 'Ipswich only won it because Burnley threw it away.'

The two men had been enemies since Lord had made a racist remark at a game at Turf Moor. 'I hate racists and I won't have them in my boardroom,' said Mr John. A butcher, Lord had no sense of humour, and he ignored Cobbold throughout the evening. 'He's ******* deaf and couldn't hear what I said anyway,' said Cobbold.

Mr John appeared on a live television interview at Anglia TV before an East Anglian derby between Norwich and his club and the interviewer asked him, 'What do you know about the Norwich team Mr John?'

'F*** all,' he said.

That was earlier in his reign as chairman, well before Kenneth Tynan was supposed to have been the first person to use the 'F' word on live TV. I attended his summer barbeques for the staff at Glemham Hall, his fifty-room fifteenth-century country house near Woodbridge, and one of his party tricks was to slide down the bannisters to the hall below. The guests knew when he was ready to go to bed. He would change into his pyjamas and his silk dressing gown for his final slide, saying 'I'm off to bed. Help yourselves to Patrick's best wine!'

The brothers went to Eton and neither of them was an outstanding scholar. John was first to arrive in the world, in 1927, the son of Captain John Murray Cobbold, who was often called 'Ivan the Terrible' as a family joke, and Lady Blanche Cobbold, the daughter of the 9th Duke of Devonshire. 'Ivan' was brother-in-law to Prime Minister Harold Macmillan, later the Earl of Stockton. Lady Blanche was sister to Lady Dorothy Macmillan, the Prime Minister's wife, who had a long-term affair with another Tory minister, Robert Boothby. Macmillan made Boothby, who had a relationship with one of the Kray brothers, a peer. These things happened a lot in the previous generation! Macmillan often went shooting with Captain Cobbold at Glemham Hall and also at their 40,000-acre estate at Rannoch in Scotland. Captain Cobbold took over the amateur club Ipswich in 1936 and turned it into a professional club. He also went shooting with George VI and was a close friend of Winston Churchill. The Captain worked alongside the wartime Prime Minister in the War Cabinet Rooms in Whitehall, helping to direct the war effort. He was blown up in 1944 along with 120 other people when a V-1, called the doodlebug, landed on the Guards Chapel near to Buckingham Palace when he was attending a service.

One of the players asked Patrick, 'Is it true that you and John are from aristocracy, blue blood and all that?'

'You could say that,' he replied. 'We play in blue.'

In their youth, the Cobbolds often stayed at Chatsworth House at Christmas. John, in particular, loved kicking balls up and down the immensely long corridors. 'Actually, he kept falling down,' said Patrick. 'He started drinking at a very young age!'

On a visit to Barnsley's Oakwell Stadium, Patrick told one of the home directors, 'I've just arrived from Chatsworth Park. I stayed in my usual bedroom.'

The director said, 'You can't be. It's closed for the winter months.'

'You f****** idiot,' said Patrick. 'I stayed because I am a member of the family!'

When another director at Hull was announced as the local MP, Patrick said to him, 'Which part of the Labour Party are you f****** up?'

Patrick, who was born in 1930, left Eton to join the Scots Guards and was a lieutenant in charge of a platoon when he was accidentally shot in the leg while on exercises in Pickering, Yorkshire. Harold Macmillan was speaking at an election meeting in his Bromley constituency when a message was handed to him. He told the audience, 'My nephew Patrick has been shot in the leg and it looks serious. I hope he is alright.'

Fortunately he survived. John served briefly in the Welsh Guards and had a good time in Egypt before he joining Patrick at the family brewery, Tolly-Cobbold, on the banks of the Orwell. Neither of them were good businessmen and when someone asked them what they did with the brewery, they chorused, 'Drank it dry!' There were 270 Tolly-Cobbold pubs around Ipswich between the world wars and by 1961, the total was down to 110. 'I've drunk in all of them,' said Mr John.

He fought three Parliamentary elections as a Conservative candidate and lost all three. I wrote up a story when a casually dressed Mr John – in his suede shoes and tweed coat, looking like a spiv – went into the throng of fans in the street outside Portman Road to try to stop touts selling tickets for an FA Cup tie. 'I don't like it and I want to stop it,' he said.

He made no progress. Most of the tickets came from his own players. John told me, 'One of these fellows went so far as to threaten me. It was all rather splendid.'

Sol inserted a picture next to the story captioned 'Mr John Cobbold', but it certainly wasn't John Cobbold. I rang to tell Mr John the news. 'I know that fellow,' he said, 'he farms my ducks. Better looking than me and better fed.' He also liked Sol's headline: 'Soccer boss threatened in Cup tie town'. It was hardly a riot.

Mr John was banned twice for being drunk at the wheel. It would have been more but for lenient police officers. Finally he gave up driving and employed a full-time chauffeur, Roger Nightingale. When he died in 1983, from cancer, he left one of his properties to Nightingale, who looked like the late Hollywood star Richard Widmark. 'I worked for him twenty years and it was the most exciting, the funniest and the most frantic twenty years I've experienced,' he said. 'He had a great sense of humour and could pick up little comments and turn them into big jokes and have everyone rolling around with laughter. He was an exceptionally kind person. After a time, he gave me a deposit to buy a house and in his will he left it to me. It could be a twenty-four-hour day job and it was very difficult to fit a life around – a marriage. In the end it cost me two marriages, but I never regretted it. Sometimes he would invite people back to Capel Hall when there was no one left to serve dinner. One of the guests was Prince Michael and his wife and I had to cook some beef and dumplings and afterwards he said, "Those ******* dumplings were burnt. You're fired!"'

Often Mr John would be on his own at his imposing mansion and found it rather lonely. He found solace in drink and frequently woke up with a sore head. On another occasion he invited Peter Hill-Wood, the chairman of Arsenal, to visit Capel Hall and have dinner. When they arrived, he opened the fridge and said, 'Good gracious, there's nothing left to eat and only one bottle, champagne. That will do!'

The brothers were the most generous of hosts and some occasions, when the club was hard up, they would pay the players' wages. 'They always picked up the tab for drinks,' said Terry Butcher.

Once, they were the guests of a leading football writer at the Football Writers' Association dinner at the Café Royal. A year later, Mr John said, 'I'm not going again. The wine was awful. We've hired a room at the Dorchester and we are having our own party, with proper drink.'

One of his friends often flew his own aircraft and on one flight, with Mr John as passenger, he ran into bad weather and it crash-landed, with the plane ending up nose-down in the mud. Mr John's first comment was, 'Where's my f****** drink?'

He was the youngest director to join the Ipswich Board at the age of twenty-one and he was made chairman in 1957 before handing over to Patrick in 1976. Patrick died from a heart attack in his bath at the age of sixty, in 1994. Between 1957 and 1990 they had shared the chairmanship. No other club has had such long service from one generation of a family.

I telephoned them most weeks and they loved having chats about almost everything except football. 'I know little about it,' John would say.

After matches, they would invite the journalists still on the ground to come into the boardroom for a drink. It was hard to get away, especially for a teetotaller like myself. They often brought their dogs, which would pee on the carpet and cause mayhem. Once Robert Oxby, the Welsh football writer working for *The Daily Telegraph*, had been drinking heavily at the club and showed no sign of being able to stagger back to the nearby railway station. 'I've got to go home and I don't know how I can do it,' he stuttered.

'Don't worry Robert, we'll take you home,' said Mr John. 'Where do you live?'

'Streatham,' said Robert. The chairman and his chauffeur drove the 186-mile round trip and deposited the tired writer back safely at his door.

On a trip to Blackpool, the Cobbolds went for a walk on the Golden Mile before a game and started talking to a man with a monkey on a chain. 'Do you want to buy it?' said the man. 'Cost you a fiver.'

Mr John's imagination began to go into overdrive. 'Yes, I'll buy him,' he said. He turned to Patrick and said, 'I'll introduce him as our new director.'

The Blackpool directors were taken aback when they saw this monkey charging around the Ipswich boardroom, but the Cobbolds kept the joke going for some time until the monkey jumped out into the window and made off – probably back to his trainer.

At a South Eastern Counties dinner at the Great Eastern Hotel, the younger Cobbold was asked to speak. It was past 11 p.m. when he rose to his feet, waving backwards and forwards like a reed in a swirling wind. He started to say something and slowly collapsed into the table. Lawrie McMenemy tried to grab him but he slid under the table. Everyone in the room got up to clap and cheer vociferously. 'They thought it was the best speech of the night,' said Lawrie.

Mr John fancied himself as a skier and visited St Moritz most years. 'I can only pretend I can ski,' he admitted. His last run down the feared Cresta Run ended with him having twenty-six stitches around his mouth.

He flew back to Heathrow with his gear and a taxi driver said, 'You look as though you've been in a car crash mate.'

'Came a cropper on the Cresta Run,' said the chairman. 'That's the last time I'll do that. I used to go on it because it was good for a hangover.'

When he arrived at Liverpool Street to catch a train back to Ipswich, he discovered he had no cash. The driver was annoyed but the battered football chairman said, 'I know. Take my skis.'

The driver agreed. 'That's a fair exchange,' he said.

There were only five full-time members of the Ipswich non-playing staff when Ramsey took over as manager in 1955 and took the Third Division club to the First Division in six years with a team valued at £25,000. The first time I met him, this small, gnome-like man was sitting in his spartan office in a wooden building that had been built in the First World War to accommodate soldiers. A bucket was positioned to catch rainwater because the roof was leaking and there was one telephone, placed on a small shelf behind him at head height. He smiled and offered me a cup of tea. He appeared to be rather shy and stiff and spoke in a somewhat posh voice as though the Cobbolds had given him elocution lessons. All three men denied it, but a lot of people who had met Ramsey in his early life swore that he had been coached by a speech expert. He spoke in clipped sentences with pauses and used stilted phrases like 'in as far as' and 'in respect of'. You realised that they were delaying devices. The words didn't gush out.

One of the more excitable wives of the players had a habit of coming into his office to complain. David Rose, the long-serving secretary, said, 'Alf was getting upset about it and he made arrangements to evacuate. There was a pile of coke outside the window and when he heard her voice, he opened the window and jumped down the coke and made off.'

Ted Phillips, his leading goalscorer – who now has knee replacements – turned the hosepipe on him once and soaked him while he was wearing his best suit. Alf shook himself, got into his car, and drove off without a word. 'He never lost his temper,' said Ted. 'Once one of the players threw a boot at him and he ducked and carried on without remonstrating him. He kept his feelings in check. Alf was the best I worked with and most people would say the same. He won the World Cup for England, no one else. He knew the game inside out and spoke sense.'

Alf had a fantastic memory for matches. He would recall moves and who passed to whom and which of the players were at fault when the move broke down. It was tragic that he contracted Alzheimer's in his final years and started to lose that memory.

This singular and much-admired man was helped in his career by his remarkable marriage to a beautiful brunette from Southampton who had been married previously. Her name was Victoria and he called her Vic while she called him Alfred. She came to all his early matches and shared his love for vaudeville shows and the quiet life. The place where he was happiest was at home with his devoted wife. Victoria had a daughter named Tanya from her previous marriage, who married and went to live in the USA. I have met Victoria several times over the years and she is a lovely lady. She lives alone in the same detached house in Ipswich where Alf first moved to from North London. Some of Alf's memorabilia has been sold but there is enough to remind her of the happy days when they were together

In those days journalists were able to dial the number of club managers and speak directly to them. I found Alf extremely courteous but he never said much and avoided controversy. Mr John said, 'I leave it to him. All I do is be sociable to everyone and make them welcome. I never tried to correct him. Well, just when we sat together at a match on a very cold night. I kept chattering away and he didn't say anything. "Have you anything to say?" I said to him. He finally said, "It's a not a very good night." I said, "If that's all you can come up with you might as well shut up."'

Ramsey believed in teamwork and balance and wasn't so keen on big-name players. Roy Bailey, one of his first goalkeepers, was invited to look around Portman Road before he signed from Crystal Palace. As he was going around the ground, he saw what appeared to be an old man sitting in an outhouse toilet with the door open. 'Who's that?' he said.

'That's our star player James Hunter Leadbetter,' said Mr John. Leadbetter was in his mid-thirties and looked like a dosser. He had a wonderful footballing brain and played in a deep role on the left. Ramsey fooled Tottenham in the Ipswich championship year by introducing a new tactic of withdrawing his wingers and using longer passes, and twice he finished up on the winning side.

I interviewed Leadbetter forty-five years later at the reunion dinner at the ground and I said, 'You look younger now than when you were playing.'

A Scot from Edinburgh, he said, 'Aye, I lost some teeth and the dentist told me it would be better to have the lot out and give me dentures so I took his advice. I looked a different man.' He was still playing local football in Edinburgh in his fifties.

As a reward for the players, the Cobbolds arranged a short tour to the continent in May and the idea was for them to enjoy themselves. The chairmen led the drinking expeditions in Copenhagen, Berlin, Rostock, and Kosice. Many of the players were drunk and insensitive.

In a game against Vejle Boldklub, some of the players were accidentally locked in the dressing room. There were only six players out on the field when the second half started. No one pointed out that you need seven to make it legal. A few minutes later, the match was abandoned, with an official saying, 'The cycling race is about to start so the footballers have to give way to it.'

Ted Phillips captained the side against Offenbach Kickers and lost the toss. 'Toss again,' he told the home captain.

The referee said, 'We have had the toss and you lost it.'

'But in England, it's best of three tosses' said Phillips.

The German skipper relented and Ipswich won the deciding toss.

In the next season, Ipswich fell apart, finishing seventeenth. Mr John said to me, 'We've won the second and first championships and who cares if we've been relegated? It's good fun going up and down!' His club's glory had been short-lived and it was time for Ramsey to go. After Jimmy Adamson rejected the FA's offer to succeed Walter Winterbottom as the next England manager, Sir Stanley Rous, the former FA secretary, recommended Ramsey. Mr John said, 'You are a silly **** but we will not stand in your way. If England calls, we have to respond.' The deal was swiftly concluded with Ramsey on £2,000 a year. Some players called him 'the General' but although they made fun of Ramsey, they had immense amount of respect for him.

In 1966 I was flitting backwards and forwards from reporting the Jules Rimet World Cup and the England v. West Indies Test series. At the same time, I was ghostwriting the copy of Sir Learie Constantine, who had been hired as the cricket expert for the *Sketch*. My friend Bob Findlay had taken over from Solly Chandler at the *Sketch* and he liked big names. Learie was never late and I usually drove him to games. He came from humble beginnings; he was descended from an African slave and was born in Diego Martin, near Port of Spain. He rose to eminence in England as Lord Constantine, Baron of Maraval and Nelson. He performed astonishing feats as a Jessopian batsman and as a fast bowler who could bowl almost everything from extremely hostile bouncers to leg breaks, but his most extraordinary work was done as a fielder. His contemporaries rated him the best of his day. When he joined Nelson CC as a professional, he transformed league cricket in the north with his dynamism and popularity. If he were alive today, he would be one of the first signings by the Indian Twenty20 organisers and he would have commanded the highest salary.

There are very few people who are genuinely happy in their lives, but Learie was one of them. I spent four wonderful summers with him and whenever people went up to him, before they could say anything, he would smile and say, 'How are you?' and start asking them about their lives. He spread joy and sunshine wherever he went. He had no bitterness about being turned away at hotels and restaurants as a black man; he only wanted to prove that those responsible were wrong and that they had to change their approach. In the Second World War, he was refused a room at the Imperial Hotel in Russell Square. As a qualified barrister, he took legal action and won the case. He was paid £5 in damages. Often racism gives rise to hate, but Learie never hated anyone. He and his wife Norma got on well with everyone – with the possible exception of former Trinidadian Prime Minister Dr Eric Williams – and their marriage was long and ecstatically happy. They were delighted when Audrey and I invited them to become godparents of my daughter Louise.

I learned a great deal about cricket and life from Learie. He had strong views, especially about the way England played the game. 'They are too frightened to express themselves,' he told me. 'They strive to build a position where they think they are safe from defeat. The West Indian philosophy is to attack from the start and try to win the game. Dominate, not occupy the crease. England make heroes like Boycott. It's all wrong.'

Learie died in 1969 and his beloved Norma died shortly afterwards. His words still apply. England are still too cautious even today. When he was sixty, I asked him to play in a charity game near Chelmsford. His appearance drew a large crowd and he spent a lot of time signing autographs and having friendly chats. The opposing side had some reasonable bowlers, but even at his age, and not having played for years, he smashed seven sixes in a rapid half-century before getting himself out. That's a real hero. I attended his memorial service at Westminster Cathedral and it was packed – proper recognition for a man who changed the lives of so many others.

One of his best friends was C. L. R. James, the Trinidadian writer and intellectual who wrote some of the most oft-quoted words about cricket. I met him a few times and although he was still in his fifties, his hand would be shaking so much that half of the contents of his cup of tea would end up in the saucer. A friend told me, 'He was like that earlier in his life. He drank spirits a lot and didn't eat much. C. L. R. (everyone knew him as C. L. R.) spent much of his life in England and lived until his late eighties.

John Cobbold was one of the first people to ring Alf Ramsey at the Royal Garden Hotel in Kensington after England had won the World Cup on 30 July 1966. He refrained from using his nickname, 'Stoneface' although he must have seen Alf's stern demeanour on television when he was sitting on the bench at the final whistle. Everyone else jumped into the air while Alf stayed put. That summed him up – totally unemotional, or so it seemed. Bob Findlay had given me the job of being at the Royal Garden Hotel in the evening to write a piece about Bobby Charlton and Franz Beckenbauer cancelling themselves out. Bobby was helpful, but it was difficult to get hold of Beckenbauer, who was totally gutted. I spoke to Wilfried Gerhardt, the press officer of the German team, and he gave me some quotes from Beckenbauer. Gerhardt was by far the best press spokesman I encountered; there is no one of his class around today. He spoke perfect English and always came up with stories and angles and quotes from the best-known players and Helmut Schoen, the manager. The FA should have hired Gerhardt. The problems they had after the appointment of Don Revie as Alf Ramsey's replacement would have been handled in a much better manner. Beckenbauer, primarily an attacking midfield player, was upset because he had been given a more defensive role. If Schoen had stuck to the tactics that had brought his side to the final, it might have ended in a German victory. I watched the game from the 400-seat press box underneath the roof and it was an enthralling match, although not a classic. The drama and controversy compensated for that. The fitness of Ramsey's players, particularly Alan Ball, made the difference in extra time. Managers rarely mention luck, but England had luck that day, particularly with the disputed goal by Geoff Hurst and the help of the Russian linesman Tofik Bakhramov. If technology had been used, the goal might well have been cancelled. More than forty years later, FIFA are still resisting the help of technology. Recently they came out with the idea of having four extra line judges. You can imagine what reception they will get from opposing fans if a contentious goal is scored.

Bob Findlay wanted a big name to comment on the match and he made an odd choice: fellow Scot Billy Liddell, the Liverpool left-winger who had played 490 League matches in a fourteen-year career at Anfield. He gave Billy two tickets in the stand opposite the royal box and Billy rang me the day before to say that he wasn't bringing anyone. Audrey, who had never seen a football match, took the spare ticket and sat next to him. 'He was a delightful man,' she said. I don't think Billy's views brought in any new *Sketch* readers. I had a spare ticket for the 1968 European Cup final at Wembley when Manchester United beat Benfica and Audrey was there as well. She only saw two football matches in her life.

It was a mistake to believe that Alf Ramsey didn't have a sense of humour. In private he could come up with mischievous quips and one of my favourite anecdotes about him was at Wembley in 1969 when England beat France 5-0. I had to do the after-match interviews and there was no interview room at that time, so a group of journalists were allowed to come into the tunnel and stand outside the two dressing rooms, North and South. There was little space because the England coach would be parked there with the engine running and the fumes almost asphyxiating us. We kept telling the FA that this wasn't the right way to treat the members of Her Majesty's

Press, and they always laughed it off. For some unexplained reason, Alf gave an exclusive interview to ITV for a future programme. We had to stand and watch before we started interviewing him. At last, it was our chance. I thought it would be a good opportunity to start with a cheeky question. I said, 'Is that revenge for the our defeat at the Battle of Hastings?'

There was a glimpse of a laugh from him before he said, 'When was the Battle of Hastings?'

Some of the best anecdotes about the Cobbold family came from the FA Cup final, when Ipswich upset Arsenal by beating them 1-0 with a goal from Roger Osborne, who was nearly knocked out when his teammates threw themselves on him.

Lady Blanche Cobbold was made President of Ipswich FC in 1965, but her sons banned all women from the boardroom. 'It's a male preserve and we want to keep it,' said Patrick.

But ladies were admitted to the royal box at Wembley. Before the Cup final kick-off, an official said to Lady Blanche, 'Ma'am, would you like to meet the Prime Minister, James Callaghan?'

Lady Blanche looked dismissively at the man and said, 'I would prefer a large gin and tonic.'

The Cobbolds called her 'Mama' to her face and 'The Old Grey Mare' behind her back. They arranged to have 'The Old Grey Mare Ain't What She Used to Be' played by the Coldstream Guards Band, which was under the direction of Major Andrew Napier, Patrick's best friend. As Lady Blanche emerged into the royal box, the music came on and the Cobbolds were convulsed with laughter. No one else knew it was a joke, certainly not her ladyship.

Sir Bert Millichip, the FA chairman, and his wife Barbara were following her as she went down the steps. Sir Bert told me years later, 'To my astonishment I noticed that her knickers was slowly falling down her legs and ended up around her ankles. John Cobbold nipped in and bent down and picked them up and shoved them into his pocket. She carried on as though nothing happened.'

Some months later, Lady Blanche had a puncture in a wheel and changed it herself. Harold Smith, the longest serving director at Portman Road, told me, 'Not many women of eighty would have done that. She was a very tough nut.'

She outlived her sons by some distance. She drank, although not as heavily as her sons.

Shortly after Bobby Robson was appointed manager of Ipswich, Manchester United were the visitors and George Best scored a hat trick, and the crowd booed the new boss. Later on, after a copious number of rounds, Mr John told the directors, 'I have fixed up a meeting tomorrow starting at eleven. Please be present.'

Next morning they turned up and the chairman said, 'Right, first on the agenda, the subject of Bobby being barracked. I have apologised to Bobby and I have said that if it happens again, I will resign. Everyone in favour? Yes, that's fine. That will be the end of it, I hope.'

The local newspapers carried the story and Robson was never treated that way again. He said, 'They were wonderful people and they never interfered. When things were tough, they would invite Elsie and me out for dinner on the Sunday. Later, when we were winning, they rarely invited us out.'

One of the Cobbold pranks concerned an incident at a restaurant in Spain on a UEFA trip. 'You ought to have the lobster,' said Mr John.

'Oh, all right,' said Bobby.

When it arrived he started picking at it and Patrick said, 'How is it, Bobby?'

'Fine, yes, fine,' said Bobby. They had taken the meat out of the lobster and replaced it with bread crumbs. They crumped up with laughter when their manager realised he had been tricked. Before the club bought a team bus, the Cobbolds usually hired the dining room on rail journeys. The chairmen often threw bread rolls at each other, at the fellow directors, and even at Robson. They didn't really grow up.

Bobby Robson's happiest days were working under the Cobbolds and the last time I met him, at the 2008 Football Writers' Association dinner, he said, 'They were the last of the line.'

Bob – I called him that – emerged to become the most respected football manager of modern times, for his honesty, his passion, his love of the game, and his raw courage. He survived five bouts of cancer and never moaned about it. His willpower was unequalled. He has proved that mental strength can overcome serious illness and keep it at bay. His wife Elsie was the pillar that kept him going. A former nurse, she knew how to treat him and when to let him get on with it.

CHAPTER FOURTEEN

A Leg Up to the *Daily Mail*

In the spring of 1971, the *Daily Sketch* was ailing. The circulation was dropping fast, money was short, and the staff attended regular union meetings calling for higher salaries, more expenses, and better conditions. Lord Rothermere and his directors worked out a salvage operation under the leadership of David English, who had been appointed editor in 1969. His predecessor was the foppish-looking Howard French, who always travelled on buses. White-haired with droopy shoulders and a luxuriant grey moustache, Howard was a relic from the 1890s, and he called everyone 'old boy'. He boasted that no one on the staff came from universities or public schools and that the staff were rapscallions. It was amazing that he survived so long. Associated Newspapers said their two national newspapers would be merged, but that wasn't strictly true. The *Sketch* was swallowed up by the *Mail*, which was also having financial problems. I have a picture in my study of 'the Night of the Long Knives'. It shows eighty-nine members of the *Sketch* team in the editorial room, waiting to hear their fate. The time was 8.34 p.m. Only one person smiled. The rest looked as though they were sitting on the top deck of the *Titanic*, about to be told to jump. Only two were smoking, which was unusual. In those days, most journalists smoked.

The desks were covered with paper, worn-out Remington typewriters, and untidy files. Dozens of old-fashioned lights were hanging from the ceiling. One tall man was standing on a desk near a window, possibly preparing to throw himself out. Right in front of him was Laurie Pignon, my friend, who had a close relationship with David English. David loved Laurie's booming voice and charisma. On the left was Rod Gilchrist, my right-winger in the *Sketch* football team, and the only man wearing a sharp suit and a waistcoat. The managing editor tolled out the sad news. The *Sketch* had folded. Long live the new *Mail*. Letters were addressed to everyone. They could be taken now, or posted to homes. Most of the staff wanted to know their fate immediately, but I told Laurie, 'I'll wait for the post to arrive tomorrow. If it's bad news I don't want to ruin a nice evening,' I was happily married with two very young and bubbly children to whom I read stories most evenings. They particularly liked stories about Dick Turpin and the Bow Street Runners.

When I arrived home Audrey asked me about my prospects. 'I just don't know,' I said. 'But David English likes my enthusiasm and he likes hard workers. But I suppose it will be down to money. They are trying to cut costs.'

Next morning the mail arrived and I was in the bath. Audrey rushed up and handed me the letter. It was good news. More than half of the better-paid *Mail* staff had been axed, including Brian James, the outstanding football reporter. The order of play in the football section was now Jeff Powell, who had been promoted after starting his career as a sports sub editor, Laurie Pignon, who preferred tennis to the rough game of football, the late John Parsons, whose first love was tennis, and me. As one might have guessed, David was another tennis fanatic and he particularly liked hopping off to Wimbledon for the championships. Changing from broadsheet to tabloid size did not seem to bother our readers. It was easier to read it on the Underground and in trains. Sales went up while the number of union meetings holding up production were less frequent. Like most of the others, I resigned from the National Union of Journalists.

One of my first trips for the *Mail* was to report on Tottenham's UEFA Cup tie against Keflavík in Reykjavík. That was a very funny trip. When the players and press got on the coach to go training, a young woman staggered on and found it hard to stand up without falling into the players. They were laughing and shouting encouragement to her and it took some time to persuade her to get off. In the three days we were there, we discovered that many young people were under the influence. It was a precursor of today's binge drinking in the UK. Iceland was a fascinating place and I made another football trip a few years later. The young people were drinking even more booze, but there was little or no bad behaviour. Why do so many of our young drinkers want to misbehave and cause problems?

David English retained a high proportion of the *Sketch* writers. He hired Ken Barrington as the voice of cricket, with me as Ken's ghostwriter. Ken tried to scribble a few thoughts down, but he was unable to follow the lead of his former Surrey colleague Jim Laker, who wrote his own words. One of the first big-name cricketers to be interviewed in my other role as back-up cricket reporter to Ian Wooldridge was Zaheer Abbas, the elegant Pakistan batsman. Looking at my cuttings, I noticed we had him down as 'Zahir'. Zaheer was in the bath when I passed through the dressing room into the shower room and I always thought that was the best way to conduct an interview. It is the relaxed way to do it, and if the interviewee became fraught, he couldn't stepping out without any clothes. Zaheer had just scored 274 at Edgbaston and he told me, 'I have an uncle who is a dentist and he gives me 100 rupees every time I scored a century.' That year he didn't stop scoring hundreds.

The headlines in the hybrid paper were more restrained. David liked original ideas. I think he felt the old *Mail* had been rather stuffy and needed a injection of pep.

Wilf McGuinness was a failure as manager of Manchester United in 1971 and Sir Matt Busby had to return for a season, but he wasn't fit enough to do it. So the club put an advertisement in the *Mail* and said the applicant should mark his letter 'private and confidential'. I suggested that I write a spoof application that wouldn't be confidential. I wrote, 'I am taking the liberty of applying for the job because things are very tight in Fleet Street these days and the last journalist to be a manager of a First Division club was George Allison, and he was a big hit, wasn't he? These are the facts Sir Matt and the Board will want to know – Managerial experience: Ten years in charge with the *Sketch* side that won the World Tabloid Championship in 1963 and still retains it (few other tabloid papers can raise eleven players). Record: We've only lost once in the last season because they had ten men to our nine.' I listed eight other points but the directors made the wrong decision. They gave the job to Frank O'Farrell and he only lasted one season before handing over to my mate Tommy Docherty, who is still barking on.

David English had little interest in football, but he knew all about Malcolm Allison, who had just been made manager of Crystal Palace. I was given the task of reporting his debut and I had just put my piece over – Crystal Palace won in a drab match – when the sports news editor rang and said, 'He wants half a page on Allison.'

I replied, 'Well if he thinks I can summon up 750 words on that I'll do it but it was a terrible game.'

'He wants to know what he said at half-time to transform the team,' he said.

So I rang my friend Mel Blyth, the talkative and personable centre half. 'He hardly said a word,' Mel reported 'He sat there not saying anything. Then he told the back four to push up more. Not very inspiring stuff.'

I was about to play cricket for my wandering side the Woodpeckers at Beddington CC but I managed to knock out the necessary words. Half an hour later, I was at the ground and had been bowled out for another low score. The phone at the rear of the pavilion was ringing and I answered it. 'He wants 1,500 words and he's insisting on blowing up Allison's half-time speech,' the sports news editor said.

'I've told you, Big Mal barely said anything,' I said.

I started writing the new piece and forty-five minutes later I phoned it over. The phone rang again. 'Where are you?' he said. 'He wants you to come in to do it the way he wants it done.'

Could be trouble, I thought. I gave my apologies to the rest of the team and drove to Carmelite House. There was no sign of David English, but my friend said, 'Don't forget. Tell it through the words of the great messiah, Allison!'

I belted out another 1,500 words. I realised that David was a perfectionist. The sports news editor looked at it and said, 'I suppose that'll be OK.'

The next morning I rushed to see the 'new' version. There was a single column report, around ten paragraphs. I had refused to make up interviews, so the piece had been restored to its original state.

Allison was revered by a number of journalists but not by me. There was no doubt that he was an outstanding coach. An exhibitionist and self-publicist, he smoked huge show-off Cuban cigars and wore a fedora hat at Palace and he had a large ego. Part of being successful in any sport is self-discipline and Allison had very little. He got drunk, lost money on dogs and horses (once losing £4,000 in a day at Kempton Park), was a womaniser who pleasured and let down scores of young ladies, and was an inveterate nightclubber. Palace chairman Ray Bloye, a very odd man who led Palace into deep financial problems, let Allison run the club. Palace finished up being relegated to the Third Division in Allison's first season. Not a man to accept criticism, he blamed the previous manager Bert Head for leaving him 'a rotten edifice'. After three seasons, he departed after Fiona Richmond, a model and actress with enhanced breasts, was pictured naked in the team bath. When he played at West Ham he had taken to the younger players out drinking, including Bobby Moore. Halfway through that season, Ron Greenwood put Bobby on the transfer list after sixteen years and sold him to Fulham for £25,000. Bobby was then on the winning side at Palace in April and that defeat confirmed Palace's demotion. Allison finished up as one of the many ex-footballers with dementia, and his final years were spent in a nursing home in the North East.

That summer the West Indies were touring and an incident at a Test at Edgbaston yielded one of the best stories of the year. Today it would never have appeared in print. It would have been kept quiet. Late in the day, when most of the cricket correspondents were writing their reports, I noticed that umpire Arthur Fagg appeared to be very upset after he turned down an appeal for a 'catch' taken by wicketkeeper Deryk Murray against Geoff Boycott off the bowling of Keith Boyce. Several West Indian fielders, headed by skipper Rohan Kanhai, complained. Kanhai threw down his arms in disgust and turned his back on Fagg. For the rest of the final session, Kanhai kept chuntering away, and Fagg was looking more and more agitated by the minute. My best cricketing friends in the press box were Chris Lander of the *Mirror* and Ian Todd of *The Sun*. I said to them, 'We ought to go and see Fagg about it after the close of play. Could be a good story.'

Today the procedure is to ask the ECB press officer and ask for permission to interview the umpire. A statement might be passed from Fagg to the journalists, likely denying that there had been a spat. The answer would doubtless be, 'It's all been smoothed over.'

The umpires' room was on the right side of the dressing room and the interviews with the captains were held in the players' dining room on the left. They had been completed. 'Crash' Lander and Toddy followed me into the corridor by the umpires' room and Dickie Bird, who had made his debut earlier that summer at the age of thirty-nine, came out and said, 'Arthur has shot off!'

We ran out to the pavement and Arthur was walking slowly towards the car park. We caught up with him and I said, 'Arthur, we've seen what happened over the Boycott business. Can you tell us what happened?'

We were expecting to be fobbed off. Umpires usually don't talk about controversial decisions. Now Arthur couldn't stop taking, and he said, 'If they won't accept decisions, there is no point in carrying on. Why should I? I am nearly sixty. I don't have to live with this kind of pressure. I've had to live with it for more than two hours out here. People don't realise how bad it is. I don't enjoy umpiring any more. There is so much at stake. The players shout for things and when they don't get the decision, they react the way Kanhai reacted today. The game has changed and not for the better. The players have to learn to accept decisions otherwise there is no point in continuing. We are human, the same as everyone else, and we make mistakes, as players make mistakes. It doesn't matter whether it was out or not, it is the umpire's decision. When players are trying it on, they don't look at you. I did not see any deviation.'

The three newspapers used the story on their back pages and it was a shock to spectators, administrators, and players to read that an umpire was about to quit. Fagg was a fine batsman for Kent, exceeding 1,000 runs in thirteen seasons. He had been one of the best umpires in the previous eighteen years.

The next morning, Dickie was panicking. He told me later, 'I would have been the senior official and I've only just started. I ask you!'

A succession of people in power trooped into the umpires' room to ask Fagg to change his mind, but he refused. 'Only if I get an apology from the captain,' he said.

The ground was filling up and efforts were being made to get another umpire, Charlie Elliott from Chelmsford, but time was against it. Leslie Deakin, the Warwickshire secretary, a kindly man who was revered in the Midlands, suggested that Alan Oakham, the former England and Warwickshire player who had had a short period on the umpires' list, should take over. Alan was reluctant, but with time running out, Esmond Kentish, the West Indian manager, and Alec Bedser, the chairman of selectors, made one final attempt to talk Fagg round. Again, Fagg refused. Having finished his packing, he was ready to leave. Oakman agreed to go out, and with Dickie taking both ends, the match started. One over was bowled and suddenly there was a roar – Fagg was walking out to the middle. He hadn't been given an apology from Kanhai, but Kentish assured him that there wouldn't be a repeat of the Friday night trouble. The promise was kept.

The days of journalists who can approach a player and start asking him questions have long ended. Today they must go through agents and PRs and these people choose the person to be interviewed and guide his answers. It is controlled journalism, to eliminate controversy. And it doesn't really work. The readers and the viewers, the people who contribute a large percentage of the wages of the sportsmen, like to see pungent and interesting interviews with the subject speaking naturally, not hiding behind clichés and 'you knows'. No, we *don't* know – tell us. A recent development is the sponsored interview. A famous cricketer will be interviewed and at the bottom a line says, 'This article is sponsored by... [whatever it is].' Or it will mention a book that has just been published. The interview is only published if it has a 'plug' attached to it. It is very difficult for today's journalists to become good friends of sportsmen. They are treated with suspicion. On the continent and in North America, journalists are mainly looked on as honourable, professional people.

David English wouldn't have liked these modern trends in English journalism. Winning friends and influencing people was his game and that made him to the greatest editor of his generation – in the words of Lord Rothermere, Paul Dacre, and William Hague. Tony Blair, who shamelessly exploited journalists in his rise to fame, said of him, 'I counted him as a friend and he was a truly outstanding journalist. He never lost his love and enthusiasm for his chosen profession and never lost his eye for a good story.'

David English was born in 1931 and grew up in Bournemouth and started out with a local newspaper. He had a similar background to Ian Wooldridge. He was twenty when he started working with the *Daily Mirror* off Fleet Street and his experience as a reporter in the USA give him an advantage over other aspiring editors. He never lost his sense of humour. At parties, he would josh with the diminutive Jack Tinker, the *Mail* theatre critic, and occasionally Jack would turn up dressed in women's clothing. Most editors are miserable and have a pained look about them, but he was an exception: always smiling and saying something positive to people. Not everyone agreed with that. One well-respected feature writer was fired at the *Mail* and said of English, 'He was a spiv.'

The *Daily Express* was still the leader in the field when he joined the *Sketch*. It sold over 2 million copies more than the *Mail*. He was editor of the *Mail* until 1992, but by then the circulation of the *Express* had dropped to under a million, with the *Mail* at 2.4 million. A devoted family man, he realised that half the population, namely women, wanted to read about subjects that would appeal to them. He was first to devote more space to women's interests and Paul Dacre, his successor, has carried out the same policy. He also came up with the phrase 'creative tension'. Often he would put two members of staff on a story and see who came up with the better piece. It was cruel, but sometimes it worked.

He was chairman and group editor-in-chief at Associated Newspapers when he suffered a severe stroke in June 1998. He died at St Thomas' Hospital a few days later. He was sixty-seven and his wife Irene was too ill to attend. His memorial service at St Martin-in-the-Fields in Trafalgar Square had 800 mourners, and was an extraordinary affair. Politicians always court the editors of national newspapers and David had enjoyed good relationships with Lady Thatcher and the Blairs; all three turned up. I was sitting about ten rows back when five members of OutRage! walked up to the front holding up placards accusing Sir David of being a 'Gay Baiter', a 'Queer Basher', and a 'Homo Hater'. Stewards seized the placards and the men were escorted out of a side door. One protester escaped and walked back down the aisle, still holding his message. In a statement afterwards, OutRage! Said, 'English promoted prejudice, intolerance, and discrimination against lesbians and gay men. He encouraged news stories and editorials that stereotyped, vilified, misrepresented and demonised the homosexual community and he contributed to an atmosphere of intolerance that led to a massive increase in queer-bashing attacks and murders. He had blood on his hands.' As Christians, many *Mail* readers would have shared Sir David's beliefs about the excesses of some exhibitionists among the ranks of homosexuals and lesbians. Sir David would have deplored the antics of Peter Tatchell and his supporters.

David was looked on as a tough, almost ruthless editor but he went soft over one of the untold cricketing controversies of his reign. The Australian swing bowler Bob Massie, known as 'Ferg' because of the Massey-Ferguson tractor, suddenly took sixteen wickets for 137 runs in his debut in the Lord's Test in June 1972, but within eighteen months, his meteoric Test career had ended. He was twenty-five and was extremely fit, although asthmatic, and yet he only played six Tests in all. Ken Barrington said to me, 'They've put something on the ball to make it swing.'

He didn't want to put his name to the story and the Australian manager Ray Steele, a real gentleman, told me, 'Certainly our boys haven't used this and I don't believe England's bowlers have either.' I think he was being diplomatic. Interfering with the ball – using the thumbnail, bottle top removers, Vaseline, Murray Mints, resin, plain dirt, and lip salve – has been a part of cricket since the game began. Now, with better pitches, bowlers are still seeking ways of redressing the balance. Mike Atherton was caught at Lord's with dirt in his pocket and was fined by Ray Illingworth, the chairman of selectors in 1994, but the Australians always escaped. No one owned up about the Massie affair. It was a team effort.

David English wanted a follow-up and Richard Gwynn, a bowler I played with for a time, rang me and said that he knew how Massie had achieved his staggering feat. I met with Ron Fortune, a *Mail* photographer, and Richard explained, 'It's all down to his action. I can imitate almost any bowler's action. For his outswinger, his bowling arm is close to his head but with the inswinger, his arm starts further away.' The editor was excited about it and gave a page to it, including two strips of pictures to illustrate the story. The headline was 'Massie's Secret – This is how to pick that swing'. It was a good projection, but the Aussies must have been laughing when they saw it.

Illingworth had a shrewd idea that the real explanation was the application of lip salve from a phial. The day before the final Test, when England were 2-1 up, I met Illingworth along with Chris Lander and we asked him about the lip salve. 'Don't quote me,' he said, 'but they're at it. I don't mind if the story is used as long as I'm not quoted.'

My report was headlined 'Illy's Alert – Watch out for suspect shine'. The intro started, 'England skipper Ray Illingworth has told his batsmen to watch out for using artificial aids to shine the ball in the final Test at the Oval.' Massie had figures of 2-147 in that match, vastly different to his 16-137 at Lord's. Illy's warning worked, but a world-class bowler who didn't need any assistance, Dennis Lillee, won the match to square the rubber with class bowling, taking 10-181. Today someone would have been offered a large sum for the Massie story, but David English wasn't up to that game. Well, not in sport.

Around that time, the *Mail* gave a luncheon to celebrate one of Ian Wooldridge's awards, Best Sports Writer of the Year. I was invited and sat not too far from David English and Lord Rothermere, the father of the present chairman. Vere, as he was known, was a chummy, likeable man, and halfway through the lunch the conversation began to sag. I had just read Paul Ferris' book, *The House of Northcliffe*, about Alfred Northcliffe, founder of the *Mail*, and his family. Vere was the son of the 2nd Viscount Harmsworth, the brother of Lord Northcliffe, and I said to him, 'I've just finished a book about Lord Northcliffe and is it true that he died of syphilis?'

There was stony silence from the Viscount and everyone else for some seconds until he said, 'Well, that's right.'

No one said anything. Then he turned and whispered to Sir David, 'Who is this cheeky young man?'

Later I told Audrey about it. 'You could have been sacked, or demoted,' she said.

'To the contrary,' I said, 'every time I see him he says hello!'

When we celebrated our tenth wedding anniversary that year, I took Audrey out for dinner at the Savoy, courtesy of Vere. I put the chit in, claiming I had entertained Paul Ferris. On the actual date, 1 October, I was covering Ipswich Town's 2-0 UEFA Cup win against Feyenoord and I gave her £100 and ten red roses. I wrote her a letter saying, 'Dear Big A [she was slightly bigger than in 1965 but still in a class of her own]. A small present because I can't think of what to buy that would be appropriate. At

£10 a year, it represents the best bargain since the white settlers bought the West from the Indians for a couple of dozen shirt buttons. I was coming home in the car the other night and after hearing Roger Whittaker's latest single, I thought of buying that because it said all the things I would like to say about you, like "you are so beautiful" and "I love you more than words can say" but I thought the title "The Last Farewell" might give you the wrong idea! Anyway, thanks for saying Yes in 1965, thanks for ten ecstatically happy years, thanks for making me a fuller person, thanks for feeding me so excellently, thanks for trying to educate me, thanks for giving me two little kiddiewinks and thanks for putting up with cricket and my occasional moods. The best thing I ever did was get married and the second and third best things were Little Woman and Little Man. I love you... forever and forever.'

Mike Brearley was considered by many to be the best England captain, but in my view Illingworth was a better skipper, and a superior all-round cricketer. Douglas Jardine was the toughest and won the Ashes in the Bodyline series by using unfair methods. Both Brearley and Illingworth have put a tremendous amount of work into the game since they retired. Brearley is still serving on committees and was President of MCC, while Illy acted as the groundsman at his club Farley, near Leeds, for many years and was President of the Yorkshire CCC.

Brearley is fiercely protective of the spirit of the game. The only time I upset him was the day at Westcliff on 19 July 1972 when he was one of six Middlesex players who were dismissed for a duck and bowled out for forty-one in 19.2 overs in a Gillette Cup tie. Essex responded with 43-2 in eighteen overs and by 2.20 p.m. the match was over. The Southend arterial road was blocked and I was caught up in a massive traffic jam. It was 2.40 p.m. when I arrived at the almost empty ground. Nigel Fuller, who reports Essex's matches, said, 'You've missed it. It's all over.'

Some of the players were coming out and I saw Brearley. When I asked him what had happened, he said, 'We batted badly, which didn't help, but this was no pitch to play a match of this kind. It was under-prepared and dangerous.'

Brian 'Tonker' Taylor, one of my favourite cricketers and wits, was the Essex captain and when I told him what Brearley said he was furious. He took me out to the pitch and said, 'What's wrong with it? It makes me sick when I hear a team bellyaching and make excuses when they are beaten.' Tonker always told it straight!

The next day, the phone rang and it was Brearley, saying I had got it wrong. 'I hadn't reported the pitch to Lord's,' he said. If it wasn't reported, it should have been.

CHAPTER FIFTEEN

The Frighteners

Do you need to be nasty to win? Personally I prefer our sportsmen smiling and having a joke, not trying to intimidate their opponents. If they are enjoying it, the spectators are enjoying it as well. Between 1976 and 1994, the West Indies introduced, from boxing and wrestling, an element of mock intimidation into cricket and changed the game. Skipper Clive Lloyd and his successors used four fast bowlers who bowled at least twenty overs every day. They were all giants, and never smiled but glowered as though they were about to explode in anger. The spirit of cricket? There wasn't much around. Larwood and Voce, Miller and Lindwall, Statham and Trueman, Lillee and Thomson... These great fast bowlers were normally good enough to bowl most sides out. Now the duos were replaced with quartets, mean-looking men who bowled plenty of bouncers which, without helmets, would have led to a rash of severe head injuries. Someone might have died.

Possibly the most hostile of the West Indian bowlers was the former pilot and teetotaller Colin Everton Hunte Croft, whose tally of 125 Test wickets at 23.30 was the seventh best return by a West Indian bowler when he retired in 1981. He bowled wide of the crease up to 90 mph and angled the ball sharply into the batsman. The ball followed his victims and frequently they were hurt, or might have been. I played with him a couple of times in friendly games and although he was much slower, he discomforted ordinary batsmen. We had him down for another game for the Cricket Writers' Club, which he had agreed to play, but he failed to turn up. His opponents cheered when they were told he wasn't coming.

I asked him once, 'Was it really necessary to go through a whole tour scowling and looking nasty?'

'It was part of the act,' he said. 'To be intimidating you have to look intimidating. It is no use going around smiling at people all the time. You won't frighten them that way.' West Indians are nice guys – most of them – I told him. 'That right,' he said. 'But it was something we had to do. We were here to do a job, bowl out England's batsmen and win Tests. We did that and we were world champions. That meant more to our people. We were the best.'

Almost as nasty was six-foot-eight Curtly Elconn Lynwall Ambrose, who when first asked by an English journalist for an interview, replied, 'Curtly don't give no interviews! To anyone!' He said it with such force that the word soon spread round the cricket reporting world. No one, or hardly anyone, spoke to him. His reputation for being a sullen, unhelpful person persisted right up to the end of the 1996 season, when he began talking as a normal human to his Northants teammates.

Some of them were astounded. 'We never suspected he was such a friendly guy,' said one.

When David Lloyd took over as coach to the England team in 1996, he spoke about adding some menace to the players' performances. 'Controlled aggression, I call it,' he said. 'The Coach', as we call him, is a good man with a great sense of humour. 'Put them back into the hutch without too much damage!' he once said.

Duncan Fletcher wanted a similar approach and the nice man who took over from him, Peter Moores, didn't discourage controlled aggression. Stuart Broad has been giving batsmen 'the stare' without success. So why is it necessary? The truly great performers – Brian Lara, Michael Johnson, Cristiano Ronaldo, Adam Gilchrist – generally acted in a gentlemanly manner. Sonny Liston was probably the most menacing sportsman of all time but where did he end up? In a mortuary, the victim of a shooting! Mike Tyson, one of his successors, never gives the impression that he enjoys life.

The West Indian fast bowlers of the previous generation may have been the best of their type, but they probably didn't win too many friends outside the Caribbean. They were accused of brutalising a great game and by doing so, deterring young people from taking it up. That might have been true in the West Indies then, but now more and more young men are taking up cricket. Before Kerry Packer's World Series – which, mercifully, was soon ended – started in 1977, it was possible for spectators to identify the batsmen because helmets weren't obligatory. Today the faces of batsmen are hidden and it is almost impossible to see who is actually facing. Incidentally, why don't the authorities let batsmen have a name, or a number, on their helmet?

If I had to nominate a quartet who were quicker, better, and more fearsome than any other, I would name Andy Roberts, Michael Holding, Colin Croft, and Joel Garner, who took part in the World Cup in England in that year. Malcolm Denzil Marshall was in the West Indies squad and wasn't picked, but he took more Test wickets, 376 at 20.94, than any of them. He was, in my view, the greatest of his type, although he was an inch under six feet. He followed the Derek Shackleton tradition at Hampshire: he never bowled a bad ball. I attended his funeral at St Mary's Church, Southampton, and it was a desperately sad day. He died of cancer of the colon at the age of forty-one and was down to a third of his normal weight at the end. Garner and Croft were giants and made the ball rear alarmingly. Roberts and Holding, a shade quicker, were just over six feet. They shared a wonderful, rare gift: they could pitch the ball in such a way that the batsmen were never in control. They were.

I first met Sir Clyde (after the river) Leopold ('I don't know where that came from,' he told me) Walcott in the 1960s and thirty years later I wrote his book *Sixty Years on the Back Foot* when he became chairman of the International Cricket Council, succeeding Colin Cowdrey in 1993. Few cricketers have done more for the game of cricket than Sir Clyde. He was respected throughout the world and his loud laugh, accompanied by his heaving, broad shoulders, soon ended any tensions on or off the field. It is difficult to run a major world sport even when incorruptible men like Sir Clyde are in charge, but now the ICC is almost held in contempt. Power has moved to the East, where 'fixed' matches brought the first serious investigations into match fixing. With Twenty20 competitions taking over, there are more temptations for cricketers. The ruling bodies of other popular sports face similar problems and none of them, including FIFA in soccer, the IOC in athletics, the FIA in motor racing, and the ITF in tennis, have escaped criticism. Firm, responsible, and inspirational leadership is needed, and I see little sign of it.

Sir Clyde was manager of the 1979 West Indies squad and although strict, he was always fair. I asked him whether it was possible for the *Mail* to take a close-up picture of the Roberts-Holding-Croft-Garner quartet that would illustrate their menace. 'By all means,' he said, 'we love a bit of menace! I'll tell them to report at five.' Cricket has become so commercial that if such a request had been made today an agent would probably demand a fee of thousands of pounds, with a clause covering the players' images.

Accompanied by a photographer, I arrived at the hotel in Knightsbridge a few minutes before the appointed time. As we got out of the lift on the third floor, I told him, 'They may not be happy about it, so watch out!'

I knocked at the door of Andy Roberts, the most senior player, and he emerged unsmiling. 'Clyde has said it's OK to do it now,' I said. He grunted. In later years, I got on well with Andy. He is a genuine man.

Michael Holding, the nicest, most charming of the lot, a fervent horse-racing man, was standing behind him. 'Can we have you out in the corridor with the other two?' I said.

Andy wasn't too pleased but he knocked at the next door and Garner ducked his head out, just missing the beam above the door. He looked as though he was about to send a bouncer hurtling straight at us. But he shouted out to his roommate Croft, who came out, again with no greeting. All four were in the corridor on time, a tribute to Sir Clyde's expertise in handling top, temperamental sports stars.

'How do you want them lined up?' I said to the photographer.

'Why don't we line them up with their sleeves pulled back to show their muscles?' he said.

Croft laughed and pointed to Roberts 'What muscles?'

The others started rolling around, convulsed with laughter. Even Roberts smiled. Suddenly they looked far less menacing. The photographer positioned them in a compact row, all looking backwards, unsmiling behind clenched fists. The effect was frightening and there was no need to tell them to look menacing. If a chambermaid had come around the corner at that precise moment she would have screamed and fled. It made a great picture in next morning's *Daily Mail*, and was captioned 'The Force Four Hurricane Squad'. My story started, 'As they say in the calypso, if Holding and Roberts don't get you, Croft and Garner will.' When I saw Sir Clyde at breakfast he was smiling broadly.

Two years earlier, Geoff Boycott had just completed his 100th century, at Headingley, and I was there to interview him. He had upset many of my colleagues but they gave him credit for joining Herbert Sutcliffe and Len Hutton as the first three Yorkshiremen to go past the coveted total. I always had the belief that Boycott had set out to outdo Sir Len, but he failed. Len's Test average was 56.67 to Boycott's 47.72, and this was the true test for any great batsman. Typical Yorkshiremen, they looked after their brass and became rich men. Boycott was involved in so much controversy it was inevitable he became a long-serving TV pundit.

Well after he retired from playing, I saw him in the press lounge at Lord's and he came in to collect his usual plastic box of fruit and started eating it. I was talking to David Manasseh, Brian Lara's then-co-agent, and David pointed to the fruit and said, 'Is it all right for me to have a couple of strawberries, Geoff?'

'No,' said Boycott. 'Get your own food.'

A few minutes, having eaten the lot, Boycott summoned up a second box and began tucking in. 'Go on,' said Manasseh, 'just one.'

'I told you,' said the great batsman, 'fetch your own!'

That summed him up. He was not the most generous of men. But when he contracted cancer of the throat, he battled through it and resumed his television career and he was a changed man.

In 1979 Boycott was one of the first batsmen to experiment with using a helmet. Mike Brearley was one of the pioneers, but his 'helmet' would never have passed a rigorous test. Patsy Hendren was the first batsman to claim that he introduced helmets. Raymond Charles Robertson-Glasgow, known as 'Crusoe', the brilliant cricket essayist, wrote of him, 'He excelled in the hook shot off fast bowling and I cannot remember any batsman who played it more boldly or with such a fierce and violent relish.'

I met Crusoe a few times and was enchanted by him, by his humour, his courtesy, and his laugh. Alan Ross, a fellow essayist and cricket writer, wrote of him, 'The first thing you noticed about him first, apart from his resemblance to Alastair Sim, was his reverberating laugh. It was a laugh that penetrated all corners of a pavilion and there was no gainsaying it.' *Crusoe on Cricket* was one of my first cricket books and it cost me 45d. I still value it. It is a classic work. Ross said he and Cardus raised cricket reporting into an art and he was right, except that Crusoe was a better writer and an honest one. Sir Neville Cardus had a habit of making up 'quotes' for famed cricketers. The bursting enthusiasm of Crusoe brought to life the actions of the outstanding cricketers of his time in vivid words, but this wonderful man suffered from depression and on a dark day in 1965 he took his own life. He was sixty-four.

In the following year, the West Indies were back for a full tour, managed by Sir Clyde. Messrs Roberts, Holding, Croft, Garner, and Marshall were denied a whitewash, a 5-0 win, mainly by the weather. At a morning conference early in the summer, held at Northcliffe House off Fleet Street, then the headquarters of the *Daily Mail*, someone brought up the subject of the extreme speed of the ball when it was delivered by these bowlers and asked how it could be portrayed pictorially in terms that would be understandable to anyone, even a housewife. The *Mail* being a newspaper that based its appeal on women's interests, it seemed a good way to approach it.

'I've got it,' said one of the executives, 'why don't we get them to bowl at an ordinary fridge so it can show up the damage?'

Sir David, a great enthusiast, liked it. 'Get your best men on it,' he said to the sports editor.

Later in the morning, when I rang in to the sports desk, I was told about it and was given the task of putting it into practice. 'I can foresee some problems,' I said. 'Once we get a fridge out in the nets all the other papers will be on to it.'

'It's your job to prevent it,' said the sports editor. 'Don't let them get a sniff of it.'

Another problem, of course, was to get the players to agree to do it for nothing.

Fortunately Sir Clyde was keen on it. The West Indies Board had appointed an agent to handle the team's affairs for the first time and the first offer of £500 was accepted without argument. Clyde's status in West Indian cricket was such that whatever he said, went. 'Can we do it the day before the first day's play in the Test at Old Trafford, after practice finishes?' I asked him.

'Certainly,' he said. 'And I hope it's not raining. I played league cricket up there for many years and I know what it is like.'

The next problem was finding a suitable refrigerator and transporting it to the ground without being detected. Mike Forster, a cameraman based in the North, was charged with buying an old model and hiring a van to convey it to Old Trafford. He rang me the night before to say that he had bought an old, second-hand Prestcold model, some six feet in height, for £6. He had been assured that it would dent under the onslaught. He planned to drive the van into the car park at around 9 a.m. and enlist the help of the groundstaff to unload it and take it over to a practice net on a trolley. When I turned up at 10 a.m. this tall, forbidding object was there, covered by a black tarpaulin, placed on a batting crease. The players started arriving in the four adjacent nets and as the morning wore on, more and more reporters and photographers arrived. To my amazement, no one asked what the object in the unoccupied net was. Surely, I thought, someone was bound to go into the net, lift the tarpaulin, and discover our secret. Mike Foster had painted the shape of a life-size cricketer on the front of the fridge door.

While the West Indian fast bowlers were bowling into the normal nets, I stood right behind the net, only three yards from the batsman. I wanted to imagine that I was facing them and work out the reaction time. Lifting the bat too high seemed a luxury. There would not even be time to aim a defensive shot, I thought. Half the deliveries would have smacked me into the chest, or forced me to duck to avoid being hit. Graham Gooch, who opened in that Test with Geoff Boycott, told me, 'It's hellishly difficult to take runs off these guys. You could wait all day for a half volley and you'd never see one. You've got to be patient. They've got a ring of fielders in the slips and they don't drop many.' I realised that this was a new ball game. How would Sir Don Bradman have handled it? You had to admire the bravery of Gooch, Boycott, Peter Willey, Mike Gatting, and Bob Woolmer, all renowned for their skill and technique in facing sheer pace. Joel Garner, at six-foot-nine, was the meanest of the four, averaging one maiden every three overs in that series.

After another hour of practising, black clouds started to appear and some of the batsmen were cutting short their sessions. Suddenly I noticed Alvin Kallicharran, who still plays club cricket in his early sixties, going into 'our' net to retrieve a ball. He went up to the covered object and started to fumble with the tarpaulin. He lifted it a couple of feet and I was beginning to panic. But he didn't bother to lift it all the way up and he turned around and moved off. By noon the players were ready to return to the dressing rooms for a shower. Our fast-bowling models were sweating profusely and I realised it might be difficult to persuade them to carry on bowling after a punishing session. I said to gangmaster Roberts, 'Can your lads stay on for a while until everyone has gone and we can start? It won't take more than ten minutes.' Andy's face wore a mournful expression. I mentioned Clyde's words and reluctantly he told the others to remain.

Eventually the last of the thirty reporters, photographers, and radio men departed and the path was finally clear. Mike pulled away the tarpaulin and I explained to the bowlers that we wanted them to bowl at the top half of the 'batsman'.

Croft, in particular, was rebellious. 'That's made of steel,' he said. 'A cricket ball won't make much of an impression on it.'

'He's right,' said Holding. 'Why don't we bowl full tosses, that will mean the ball hitting it harder.'

'Good idea,' I said. Holding bowled his first delivery and it made a slight dent, not really enough to notice. But I had a marker pen with me and promptly filled in the indentation.

A few months previously, Holding's bowling speed had been timed at 87.76 mph in Melbourne and he was rated the fastest bowler in the world. Croft and Roberts were timed at 86.45, and Garner 85.32. England's fastest bowler of the day, Bob Willis, was timed at 75 mph, but he will query that. When a radar gun was used at Lord's in 1996, the fastest time achieved was by Waqar Younis at 82 mph, well ahead of any of the English bowlers.

After each of the four West Indian fast men had bowled at the fridge, with varying degrees of minor damage, I noticed that in the distance one of the pressmen was walking back towards us. 'Quick,' I shouted to Mike Forster, 'Cover it up! Someone is coming!' The fast bowlers were unhappy at the delay. 'I don't want anyone else muscling in on our idea,' I explained. At least two of them wanted to go. 'We haven't quite finished yet,' I said. 'Do you mind hanging on a couple of minutes while I put this guy off?'

No one went, thankfully. The pressman was closing in fast. 'What's going on here?' he asked.

'We've just been doing a few head and shoulder pictures,' I said.

'What's that?' he said, pointing towards the covered fridge.

'Something to do with the groundsman,' I said. 'I don't really know.'

Luckily he accepted my explanation and turned to go towards the car park. Spots of rain were falling. 'Let's get going again,' I said as he disappeared.

The bowlers bowled three more balls each and then posed, with arms linked, for a Liston-style picture.

In the next day's *Mail*, the heading read, 'Chilling power of the squad who can dent our Test hopes', but the pictures were not used too well. These days, pictures are displayed much more effectively, and in colour. But it was a good idea and the high command at Northcliffe House pronounced it a reasonable success, although they would have preferred to see a softer metal fridge being smashed into pulp.

When I arrived at the old press box perched on a stand to the right of the pavilion, hardly anyone mentioned Operation Fridge except for the West Indian journalists. West Indians love a joke and that is why I keep going back to the West Indies. They play the game with flamboyance and style.

One of my rivals said to me over coffee at the hotel, 'I hope you didn't have to pay for that rubbish.'

'No,' I said. 'They like a bit of fun, these West Indians.'

As a contribution to the reporting of Test cricket, it hadn't amounted to much, but the miracle was that we had been able to pull it off without the opposition knowing about it. That was the only bit of fun the tourists had in that Test. Rain and bad light cut ten hours off the playing time and it ended in a dull draw. Robert injured his back bumping into a fridge in the dark, and Croft didn't have a chance to come thundering down the runway. He was dropped and replaced by Marshall.

Before Sir Don Bradman died in 2001, he nominated the fastest trio of bowlers he ever saw – Frank 'Typhoon' Tyson, Harold Larwood, and Jeff Thomson. I knew all of them. For two years in the late 1950s, most experts thought Tyson the fastest. Some of today's experts agree, and that includes Shoaib Akhtar, the first man to go through the 100 mph barrier, and Brett Lee, who was not far behind. After Tyson retired, I played with him in a charity game in Leeds and he opened the bowling to a tall man, a member of the MCC, who faced the first ball. Julian – I think that was his name – was about to pick up his bat to shape up for a defensive shot, and the ball, which was short of a length, reared up and hit him in the heart. Julian collapsed as though a sniper had picked him out from a nearby building. I thought he was dead, but after some time he came round and was helped off the pitch. The remarkable thing about it was that Tyson was bowling off no more than ten yards. His normal run was three times longer than that. He had huge shoulders and bowled almost like a javelin thrower. It wasn't a classic delivery and that accounted for the fact that he played only seventeen Tests. Injuries soon curtailed his career and he emigrated to Australia and finished up as a headmaster, author, and cricket coach.

I met Harold Larwood on several occasions when he returned home to see relatives in Nottingham. He was still in good shape in his eighties and was a gentle, modest man who was very popular in Australia, which was where he migrated with his wife and five daughters. Douglas Jardine ordered him to bowl short to Bradman and his batsmen and he took thirty-three wickets in the Bodyline series at 19.51 apiece. 'No one blamed me,' said Harold. 'I just did what I was told.'

Under six feet, Larwood came off an eighteen-yard run like a long jumper and there was a suspicion that sometimes he threw the ball. Later, film showed there was something odd about his action, but he was never penalised.

Jeff Thomson had a similar effect, in reverse, when he captured thirty-three wickets at 17.93 in the 1974/75 Ashes series. That was when John Edrich, Dennis Amiss, and David Lloyd all broke bones and Boycott declined to go on the tour, saying that he 'couldn't do justice' to himself. Thomson was quoted as saying that he liked to see blood on the ground and came over as a thoroughly objectionable person. On the next Ashes tour to England, in 1977, I sat next to him at a dinner and my opinion was confirmed. He was very boorish, and was living up to his 'Thommo' image. I suspected that he played up to that reputation and that he wasn't quite as bad as he appeared. His bowling action resembled a javelin thrower's and he delivered the ball at a frightening pace, made worse by the way his arm suddenly came from behind his back, giving the batsman less chance to pick it up. He could get the ball chest-high from only a foot or two short of a length and for a time, he was the most feared bowler in the world.

He certainly troubled the Sri Lankans in a World Cup tie the Oval in 1975, which I reported for the *Mail*. One delivery struck Duleep Mendis in the head and put him into a ward in the nearby St Thomas' Hospital and not long afterwards Sunil Wettimuny was dispatched to the same hospital after he was hit on the foot. On neither occasion did Thomson offer any sympathy. Wettimuny was struck four times by deliveries from Thomson, twice in the rib cage and twice in the foot. Thomson called his yorker 'the sandshoe crusher'. The second time Wettimuny was struck on the foot, Thomson picked up the ball and tried to run him out. There were jeers from the crowd but Wettimuny wasn't out because his runner had stayed in the crease. I reported Wettimuny's comments the next day: 'After the first ball I felt shivers down my spine. He seemed to be swearing and grinning at me at the same time.'

David Montague, the Surrey physiotherapist, said of the Mendis blow, 'If he had been hit on the temple, he could have been killed. He was very lucky.' Four years later, everyone was wearing helmets, courtesy of Kerry Packer.

Kerry Francis Bullimore Packer was responsible for World Series Cricket in 1978/79 and he, too, was a boorish man. I organised the English Press XI *v.* Australian Press XI at Harrogate in 1977 and Ian Chappell was the captain of the Australian team. Four days before the game, Chappell rang me and said he had another player to put in.

'Who is it?' I said

'Kerry Packer,' he replied.

'We can't have him,' I said, jokingly, 'he's upset the top brass in the UK and half the journos.'

'He's been to Harrod's and bought pads, box, helmet, everything, and is ready for action,' said Chappell.

I relented, saying, 'We need the publicity and I'll get it in the Harrogate paper straight away.'

Twenty minutes before the start of the game there was no sign of Packer and his friends. He flew in on a light aircraft and drove in just in time. He said, 'Look [a favourite word in Australia], we're all here for a civilised afternoon. Cricket is a very civilised game. I haven't played for eight years but I've just had a net.'

One Yorkshire correspondent said, 'Civilised my arse! He's in the process of brutalising the game and turn it into a bull fight.'

Packer was down as eight in the batting order and with Chappell scored sixty and his side passed the 200 mark with only four overs remaining. The TV and radio people were panicking. Chappell sent the twelfth man a note addressed to me, saying, 'Can we extend the overs to forty-five?'

I said, 'Tell him we can't.'

But as the man started to leave, I said, 'OK, but make sure he gives me a free trip to WSC!'

Packer finally arrived at the crease with two overs left. He faced seven balls and every time the ball hit the pad, we appealed all around the ground. Another delivery came off the pad for a single and in the scorers' book it was scored as two for Packer. After tea he came out as wicketkeeper and held a smart catch off the bowling of his enemy David Lord, the agent. The victim was Peter Lush, the Test and County Cricket press officer who topscored with fifty-two.

Packer and his group went off for dinner at the Dragonara Hotel in Leeds – and didn't thank me or anyone else. In the bar afterwards, John Parker, the ITV sports correspondent, found that £50 had been taken out of his pocket. I checked my wallet. My only fiver had gone as well. I'm reasonably certain it wasn't Kerry Packer.

The following year I managed to persuade Robert Alexander QC, who acted for Packer in the High Court, to play for the NatWest side against the English press in Norbury. Robert lived half a mile from Lord's and I often met him on his way to the ground. He loved art and was a most engaging man. He turned up without any kit and proceeded to open the innings wearing dark blue trousers. He blocked a few before turning the ball behind square for a single and then declared his innings closed. 'I've got another engagement and I am extremely sorry,' he said. The contrast between him and the bullish Packer was extraordinary. One was a gentleman and the other wasn't. Packer died on Boxing Day 2005 at the age of sixty-eight, forty days after Lord Robert Alexander of Weedon had died at the age of sixty-nine.

The finest duo of opening bowlers I have seen were Wasim Akram and Waqar Younis. I was at Old Trafford at the start of the season in 1988 when Lancashire unveiled Wasim at a press conference. He was a very confident young man who spoke English well and Imran Khan told me, 'He will be as good as Alan Davidson.' No disrespect to Davo, one of Australia's most popular cricketers, but Wasim was better. He was taller and he could get extra bounce and more swing. No batsman faced him with confidence, not even Brian Lara. Waqar claimed that he was born in 1971, meaning that he was five years younger than Wasim. That was disputed; he looked much older. But what pace, what menace! His 'sandshoe crusher' was far more damaging than Thomson's and he swung the ball prodigiously, mainly into the right-hander. Good-looking and personable, he collected just as many conquests in the bedroom as wickets on the field. Growing up on flat, unfriendly pitches in Pakistan, 'the two Ws' learned how to make the ball swing more and more and graduated to masters' degrees on reverse swing. Opponents claimed they interfered with the state of the ball and that was true. They would rough up one side and shine the other. Whether bottle tops were used has never been proved, at least not to the satisfaction of the ICC and its umpires.

Will sportsmanship and fair play survive? With vast amounts of money now being paid out in the short form of cricket, many of today's players say a loud 'no'.

But I disagree. Money is ruining the spirit of professional football in this country and I believe there should a balance between being over-competitive, forcing a win at all costs, and being too chivalrous, letting the other side win. In today's international games, the teams walk past each other offering limp handshakes and not looking in the eye of the opponents, particularly in football. But a true sportsman would look his peer in the eye and smile – firstly because he knows his own talents and secondly because he enjoys what he is doing. We shouldn't lose track of that.

My confidence that sportsmanship will live on was suddenly lifted by an incident on the early morning of 7 January 2009, when the deep freeze and the credit crunch had given the new year a depressing start. I switched Sky on to see the final overs in the third Test at Sydney. South African skipper Graeme Smith went out to do a Colin Cowdrey and bat for several overs before he was finally bowled, and Australia won by 103 runs. Smith had a broken finger on one hand and an injured elbow on his other arm. When he was bowled, Ricky Ponting came up and congratulated him and patted him on the back. Players on both sides were shaking hands and hugging each other and former Australian captain Mark Taylor said, 'It's been a great day for cricket... and for sportsmanship.'

Like many cricket lovers, I never thought that Glenn McGrath was a true sportsman. He was one of the worst sledgers and he was in a number of nasty rows, one with Ramnaresh Sarwan, which plumbed the depths. But on that day at Sydney, McGrath made a gracious and emotional speech, thanking his fellow cricketers and everyone else at the ground for their part in raising A$500,000 for the Jane McGrath Foundation. In my previous meetings with him I found him as a pleasant man and wondered why he behaved so aggressively on the field. Now we have seen another side of his personality. His wife Jane, a former English air stewardess, died of cancer at the age of forty-two on 22 June 2008 after ten years of brave resistance. You could see that his overwhelming love for her had deeply affected everyone in that Test match, especially when the third day was dedicated to Jane and everyone was asked to wear something pink. Most of the Australian batsmen had pink rubber grips on their bats. 'Jane was a wonderful, fantastic person,' he said. 'Every day she thought it was a beautiful day. Let's go enjoy it.' I feel the same way.

CHAPTER SIXTEEN

I Share the Top Table with the Reverend Canaan Banana but Not Robert Mugabe

I must have made more than 250 trips to eighty-eight countries in my life and the funniest was the one I made to Zimbabwe in 1980 to celebrate the country's independence. Glen Byrom, a Zimbabwean journalist and businessman who lived in London for a while and played for my Sunday wandering side the Woodpeckers, was by then living in Harare. He rang and asked if I would like to speak at the dinner of the Zimbabwean Sports Association in Bulawayo on 8 November.

'We can offer you a first class air tickets both ways, sponsored by Air Zimbabwe, and we'll put you up,' he said. 'It will make a nice break. The people are lovely and you'll enjoy it.'

Audrey wasn't available and I didn't take long to accept. Ipswich were playing in a UEFA second round against the Czech side Bohemians on 5 November and I told Glen I would be ready to fly to Harare the next day. Ipswich were bidding to become the first club to win the League, the FA Cup, and a European competition, and Bobby Robson reckoned his side reached its peak around that time, partly thanks to the inspirational Dutchmen Arnold Mühren and Frans Thijssen. They finished second to Aston Villa in the League, lost 1-0 to Manchester City in the semi-final of the FA Cup, and beat AZ Alkmaar to win the UEFA Cup.

The temperature on the day of the game in Prague was –16°C and we feared that the match might be postponed for the next day or even the second day, which would scupper my exotic trip to Africa. I remember Kevin Beattie playing a sterling game wearing his short-sleeved shirt. Everyone else had the long-sleeved version, two vests, two pairs of shorts, and gloves. Paul Mariner insisted on a rub of olive oil all over his body to keep the heat in. It didn't really work, but Ipswich managed to hold on to qualify for the next stage and the charter aircraft departed on time.

I went on all six away trips that campaign and they were some of the toughest I have encountered. In Salonika the local press had convinced the volatile home supporters that their team had been cheated in the first leg at Portman Road, when Ipswich won 5-1. Portuguese referee Antonia Garrido awarded the team three penalties and ace penalty converter John Wark scored all three. Eric Gates was the player who was brought down and none of the 'fouls' looked clear cut. Robson told me later, 'Gates didn't throw himself down. Defenders commit themselves against him and he goes over their foot and that's why he gets a high proportion of penalties.'

'You sure!' I said with a smile. Cristiano Ronaldo uses that technique but what he gains in converting penalties he loses when referees look at questionable incidents and decide he has dived.

In the second leg, played on a pitch full of ruts and potholes, the 40,000 screaming supporters kept chanting 'Garrido' and drawing forefingers across their throats. Now things were being balanced, with the new referee awarding two goals to the home side – although neither went over the goal line. Robson's apprehensive players scraped through on a 5-4 aggregate and a brick was hurled through the coach window, just missing George Burley's head. 'It's relief to get out of the place without being killed,' said Paul Mariner. His oil rub wouldn't have saved him.

The opponents in the third round were the Poles of Widzew Łódź, whose manager Jacek Machciński went up to Robson before the kick-off and said, 'Will you be betting on the result? I fancy a bet on 2-2.' Robson had to tell him that betting by managers and players is illegal in England.

A 5-0 win in the first game eased any fears there might be an upset in the return match in Łódź. David Rose, the Ipswich secretary, had to ring the Foreign Office to find out if the team could travel. The newspapers were full of stories that the Russians were about to invade and there were demonstrations by workers. The FO gave the go-ahead.

If Prague had been freezing, Łódź was far worse. The pitch was a mixture of snow and ice and when I sat down at a desk just behind the touchline in lieu of a press box and put down my notebook, I noticed that that ice was forming so fast that I couldn't pick it up again. It was stuck to the desk. Neither side risked a tackle and Łódź won 1-0.

The night before, our group of journalists dined at the hotel because there was nowhere else to eat. There was plenty of cheap booze available and one redtop reporter said, 'I've hired a few ladies and everyone is invited to my room.' It was my bad luck to be in the room next door and the noise was deafening. I locked my door because some of the tipsy correspondents were shouting for me to join them.

My phone rang and a stern-sounding woman speaking English said, 'There is a message for you. Your friends want you to join them. You must cooperate.'

I said, 'I do not wish to join them. Please tell them to quieten down. I want to sleep.'

A few minutes later there was a knock on the door. A man in a white coat unlocked the door from the outside, rushed in and pointing at the next room, he said 'You must go there. Get out of bed!'

For a moment I thought I was being taken away to a concentration camp. 'Please leave the room immediately,' I said. 'If you don't, I will call the police.' He turned and left.

When I arrived in Harare, the temperature was in the eighties and the wide streets were filled with beautiful jacaranda trees originally imported from Brazil. Harare gave the appearance of a clean, orderly city and everything worked. Cecil Rhodes was the man who initiated it and he had done a fine job, except that only one section of the population, the whites, mainly descended from the English, enjoyed most of the benefits. The non-whites were left behind. The man who was going to change things was the new Prime Minister of the country, fifty-six-year-old Robert Gabriel Mugabe. He was born in Matibiri village north-west of Salisbury, as the capital city was known before it was called Harare. Both of his older brothers died and his father Gabriel, who was a carpenter, abandoned the family in search of work in Bulawayo. Mugabe was brought up as a Roman Catholic and qualified as a teacher. He graduated with a Bachelor of Arts degree in 1951 in Fort Hare university in South Africa and mixed with future African leaders like Julius Nyerere and Kenneth Kaunda. He went on to gain six further degrees; two of them were acquired when he was in prison after being found guilty of making a subversive speech. Ian Smith ruled the country and during Mugabe's ten years in prison Smith refused him permission to attend the funeral of his three-year-old son.

Mugabe won control over Joshua Nkomo's Zimbabwe African National Union and played a key part in the guerilla warfare against the white minority rule in the Bush War of 1964-79. Henry Kissinger and South African President B. J. Vorster put pressure on Smith and at a meeting at Lancaster House in London in 1978 an agreement was reached to set up a democratic government dominated by blacks. Mugabe was looked on as a hero and Bob Ogley, who lives near me in Bromley and worked for *The Rhodesia Herald*, wrote in the *Kentish Times*: 'He came over very intelligent, very likeable and determined. The sort of person you might like to know. His great hero was Mahatma Gandhi. He wanted to free Rhodesia of white rule and give black people an opportunity to advance in government, commerce, industry and education, similar to the achievements of India. I even remember how we used to reverse the syllables of his name and adopt a northern accent – E-ba-gum. He was all for one man, one vote because there were almost 8m Africans and only a few thousand whites. He felt it was his country and that was fair.'

In my first conversations with Glen, I asked him whether Mugabe would be appearing at the dinner in Bulawayo. 'Difficult to say,' he said. 'It's going to be live on television and he likes good exposure. We've only gained independence and it's early days.'

Glen took me to the nicest parts of the country – Victoria Falls, racing at Borrowdale Park, a cricket match, a game park, a sensational golf course, and a tobacco auction. The Victoria Falls were spectacular but not in the class of the Iguaza Falls on the border of Brazil and Argentina. I heard that Mugabe had waged a violent campaign against homosexuals. He said, 'If you see people parading themselves as lesbians and gays, arrest them and hand them over to the police.'

The day before the dinner Glen told me that someone from a Government department had called, saying that eighteen tickets on the top table were needed for ministers. 'We haven't got eighteen seats,' said Glen. 'I don't know where they are coming from.' Eventually the original top table guests, excluding Glen and myself, were moved to other tables, making room for the ministers.

'Is Mugabe going to be there?' I asked.

'They haven't come up with all the names yet,' said Glen.

Later in the day a hand-delivered letter arrived at the hotel with the list. At the top was the Reverend Doctor Canaan Sodindo Banana, Zimbabwe's first President, who was, I discovered, six months older than me. He was from the Ndebele minority, like Joshua Nkomo, and he was chosen to provide a balance for Mugabe and his Shona majority. Ordained as a Methodist priest, he wrote a book, *The Gospel According to the Ghetto*, and his version of the Lord's Prayer had these lines: 'Teach us to demand our share of the gold, and forgive us our docility.' On 8 November, Mugabe must have been busy grabbing his share of gold; he wasn't going to be present.

The seating plan had the President on my right and Deputy Sports Minister Dr Joyanya on my left. All the people on the top table were highly educated people who spoke excellent English. Most of them were educated in England, America, or South Africa. I had jotted down a few notes, but not knowing much about sport in Zimbabwe, I asked Glen for guidance. 'They like being given some praise,' he said. 'There are some excellent sports facilities and you can talk about them, and about a few personalities like Bruce Grobelaar and some of the leading football, cricket, and golf players.'

I spoke for seventeen minutes and it wasn't exactly riveting for the TV audience at home. There was polite applause, but it would have been better with a question-and-answer rather than a formal speech. I found it was rather difficult to talk to the Reverend Banana. He obviously wasn't a sportsman.

Nineteen years later, he was charged with sodomy, non-consensual sex with gardeners, cooks, and bodyguards, and assault. He denied everything, saying the charges were trumped up in a conspiracy designed to bring him down. But the evidence was overwhelming and in May 2000 the Supreme Court in Harare upheld his conviction on eleven counts and sentenced him to ten years in jail, nine of them suspended. He spent most of his prison term under house arrest. Mugabe knew about his predilections but despite his hatred of homosexuality never did anything about it. Banana died of cancer at the Charing Cross Hospital in Hammersmith on 12 November 2003.

The next day, Glen and his family took me to watch Zimbabwe draw 1-1 with Malawi. I sat just behind the directors' box, which was designated for Government officials, including Banana and Robert Mugabe. Twenty minutes before the kick-off, an announcer told the 20,000 crowd to rise and applaud the arrival of Mugabe. A cavalcade of black limousines came into the stadium and drove around to the side where I was sitting.

I noticed that several Americans were strategically positioned and asked one of them, 'What are you doing here?'

One said, 'We're here to protect Mugabe and his men. They're not taking any chances.'

I counted around twenty-five security men, all armed. Mugabe and his henchman sat down at the front, about twenty yards from me. If someone starts firing I will be a prime target, I thought. Grobbelaar was nineteen and he looked like a good player, pulling off spectacular saves. His best work was coming far out of his area to take high crosses – no other goalkeeper I saw ever did that – but I remember he dropped one. Just before the final whistle, there was an announcement saying, 'Do not leave your position until the procession has left the stadium. Stay seated.' The referee blew and it was all over. There were six vehicles, all Mercedes I think, and their engines were running. As the first group, including Mugabe, got into the first one, it accelerated away. The second one, which was still being filled by bodies, began to move off as well. Only one person had got in, yet it started to drive off to keep up with the leading car. Bodies were flying everywhere, including politicians, guards, and drivers, as the other cars shot off. It was a scene from a Keystone Kops film. People were shouting orders. The leading cars went out into the road and raced to Mugabe's residence. The others were gathering up the survivors. I looked around. Few of the blacks were laughing, but in the stands the whites were hooting. It could be seen as a precursor of future events: if they couldn't get that right, what chance had they of making a success of this beautiful country?

I haven't been back to Zimbabwe, sadly. Like most people, I wonder how Mugabe got it so badly wrong. If he was so intelligent, why did he let inflation go berserk, wrecking the nation? In 2008 it rose to 100,000 per cent, making it impossible to conduct normal life. Most people who remained in the country were kept going by money sent from relatives in other countries. Mugabe virtually destroyed the farm industry and his country came to rely on aid from abroad. He owned three farms himself, all seized from its owners. His 'freedom fighters' were keeping the populace in check as though they were in an open prison. Zimbabwe had the highest inflation in the world and the lowest life expectancy, thirty-six years for men and thirty-four years for women. If he had any compassion or sense, he would have stood down after the 2008 election, which was won by Morgan Tsvangirai's Movement for Democratic Change. He has ruined his own country, and also its cricket, which he professes to like.

Early in the 1990s, the Zimbabwe Cricket Union were lobbying the ICC to become a full member, despite not having the numbers and resources to justify it. I reported on an ICC meeting at Lord's, and England opposed the country's membership. It was partly seen as a race issue, with non-white countries supporting Zimbabwe's application. There was also a dispute about which countries were staging future World Cups, and England had to compromise, moving its intended tournament forward to 1999. Not all the newspapers cover these meetings, but this one was going to be newsy, I thought; for most of the day a number of correspondents were left to stand outside the Grace Gates hour after hour. You can gauge the quality of news by the way journalists are treated. If we are invited in, it will be an easy-ozey PR exercise. If you are kept outside, the signs are it will be a hard news story and the organisers will try to minimise any damage.

By early evening, most of the correspondents had given up and only one other journalist, from the Press Association, remained. I sensed that it might turn out to be a back-page story so I stayed on, like a guardsman on duty out on the pavement. Some of the delegates left the meeting at 7.30 p.m. for a half-hour break and went into the Lord's Tavern for a drink . I recognised a member of the Kenyan delegation – I played cricket against him in Nairobi some weeks earlier – and I asked him how it was going. 'It might last all night,' he said. 'Very stormy!' He pointed to a rather large black lady who was fast asleep on a bench. 'She's got the crucial vote on one issue,' he said.

'Is she a cricket person?' I said.

'Not at all, she doesn't know anything about cricket.'

The meeting resumed and by this time I was alone. At 11 p.m. John Stephenson, the MCC secretary who was also secretary of the ICC, came out and said, 'You still here?'

I said, 'What's the result?'

'Come into the committee room,' he said.

I followed him and he went up to the drinks cabinet and said, 'What do you want to drink?'

'I'm not too bothered about having a drink,' I said, 'I want to put over a story. If it doesn't reach the *Mail* before 11.30 p.m. it will miss the first edition.' He started briefing me about the decisions while pouring out a gin and tonic for himself and a coke for me. He told me that Zimbabwe had been accepted and England had to back down on the next World Cup. I ad-libbed 500 words and my account made the back page. No one else touched the story until the next day. I was quite satisfied about it – a scoop of some importance – but my feet were aching.

Peter Chingoka, the head of the Zimbabwe Cricket Board, was the key man in the affair. He is still in charge, but Zimbabwean cricket has virtually disintegrated. According to one English administrator, he owns a flat in London and on 22 July 2008 his name was put on a list by the EU of those who have had their overseas assets frozen and been refused visas. *The Times* claimed that Chingoka supported the terror campaign in the election. Zimbabwe shouldn't have been admitted to the ICC from the start. It was a calamitous mistake.

Over on the west coast of Africa, Charles Taylor, the President of Liberia between 1997 and 2003, was placed for some time on Interpol's 'wanted list' for 'crimes against humanity, grave breaches of the 1949 Geneva Convention including murder and genocide'. At the time of writing, he faced 650 counts at the European Court at the Hague. His reputation is such that only one country has agreed to jail him if he is convicted – Britain. Margaret Beckett, the former foreign secretary, said it would need legislation.

I never met the Liberian President – whose second name was McArthur, after the US General – but in 2003 I received a telephone call from a prison in Monrovia. Speaking from his cell was the Dutch-born photographer Teun Voeten, who does much of his work in war zones, and is a friend of my daughter Louise. He said that along with a number of foreign journalists, he had been arrested and they had been threatened with death by shooting unless *The Daily Telegraph* published a retraction on their front page of a story that President Taylor was a cannibal. It seemed like a scene from 'Carry on Monrovia', but it was authentic. *The Telegraph* had published the story and Tim Butcher, the respected African correspondent, had vouched for it. 'You do work for *The Telegraph*?' said Teun. 'Can you speak to someone high up and get them to do something about it?'

I had worked with Jeremy Deedes, the son of William Deedes, at the *Sketch* in the 1960s and knew him well, so I told him I would contact him immediately. Finding Jeremy turned out to be a difficult task. I finished up speaking with the sports editor, who promised he would pass on my message to the foreign editor. Teun had told me that three American warships with 2,300 marines were patrolling offshore ready to seize Taylor and his supporters. President George Bush had told Taylor to quit or else.

The next day, the phone rang and it was a relieved Teun on the line. He said Taylor had agreed to release the journalists and the pressure was off. 'I'm catching the first plane home,' he said. Within hours, Taylor and his cohorts left for safe conduct to Nigeria. The US Government then passed a bill detailing a $2 million reward for his capture. Teun has had a very adventurous life, and I don't think I could do what he does. I'll stick to sports writing.

One of the most intimidating and depressing trips I went on was to Tbilisi in Georgia in November 1973. Tottenham reached the final of the UEFA Cup that season. The match was an irrelevance, with Spurs happy to draw 1-1 against the home side Dinamo Tbilisi. The flight from Heathrow was a tiring, punishing one in an old Aeroflot, and when the aircraft thudded into the runway it was like being dropped on a corrugated road. It was the worst landing I've ever experienced and the players said the same thing. We were driven at high speed to the team hotel, which looked like a prison, and the players, officials, and press sat down for dinner at 1.30 a.m. It wasn't worth waiting up for; the food was inedible.

I have always liked walking around foreign cities, but on this occasion I felt threatened. Georgia was part of the USSR at the time and the place was run by the secret police. Stalin, who presided over the elimination of more than 20 million people, was born in Gori, west of Tbilisi, and the country has never recovered from his insane legacy.

After walking around some extremely drab parts in the centre, a young man came up to me and said in English, 'Can I speak to you about the politics of this country?' He looked round to see if anyone was close by and said, 'It is safe here to talk.'

As we walked on, he told me how he and his colleagues barely existed and how they were continually harassed by the authorities. It was like a scene in George Orwell's *Nineteen Eighty-Four*. I gave him a football book that I had with me, but there was no point giving him English money. When I returned home, I rang the office and told the features editor I intended to write about my meeting with this brave young man. He agreed and I wrote an 800-word feature for the foreign page.

On the day of the match, the Georgian FA laid on a banquet for the officials and the press. There was practically no tasty food, but plenty of the local brew. Every few minutes, a succession of tubby, florid-faced men rose to propose a toast. After three hours, most of the Tottenham directors were so drunk they were also toasting the health of various political figures, both in Tbilisi and Moscow. Several of them had to be assisted to their taxis, but the Georgians were still going strong.

With the exception of a couple of cricketing trips to Guyana, one part of the world I hadn't been to was South America, but in November 2006 I went on a five-country tour to look at some of the most famous football grounds. I was advised to take maximum insurance. Our group was walking along a street in Valparaíso in Chile when a man on a motorcycle stopped in front of an elderly man, snatched his expensive camera, and drove off.

After spending a few days in Lima, including a rundown by the elderly courier, Lucy, of all the corruption and stupidity of the Government, we flew off to Cusco, the capital of the Inca people, which is 9,000 feet above sea level. I learned that the football club, called Cusco Donkeys, were playing the Young Boys. Despite their unusual name, they were the South American champions in 2004. I asked the courier, a young lady, 'Will there be a problem getting in?'

'The ground stadium holds 40,000 and I am a rabid supporter,' she said. 'Just turn up and buy the most expensive seats on the halfway line. It will cost you the equivalent of £3.'

An hour before kick-off, the streets were almost deserted except for ticket touts. One, who was holding a bunch of tickets, approached me and said, 'These are the very best seats.'

I worked out the price in English. It was three times the figure mentioned by the courier. 'Don't bother, I'll go to the main office,' I said. 'Where is it?'

'There isn't one,' he said.

'So where do I buy a ticket?' I said.

He pointed to a slit in a wall at head height about the size of a small case. 'There,' he said.

Nervously I tendered my money, fearing that it might be snatched, and I was relieved to be handed a ticket. Inside we were shown to an area behind the directors' box, a prime spot protected from the sun. The ground looked as though it had been built in the early 1930s and no alterations had been made except for the installation of floodlights. The standard of play was very high, with the players showing wonderful control. Most of our group found it difficult to walk more than half a mile in those humid conditions at 9,000 feet, but the players maintained a good pace until they flagged near the end. Some of them would be stars in Premiership teams.

In the five days we stayed at the hotel, I paid the bill every morning using US travellers' cheques, but on the final morning a young girl presented me a bill for the whole sum. 'I've paid on the first four days,' I said. 'I only owe for one day.'

'Oh no,' she said, 'this is the bill, and we have no record of any other payments.'

I said, 'Yesterday I cashed a US$50 cheque to pay and was given $25 in change. Where is it?'

She denied any knowledge of it. A man behind the counter started nodding his head and I asked to speak to the manager. He wasn't there, I was told. By this time our coach was ready to go to the airport and the courier was anxious for us to depart. I felt like Bobby Moore in Bogota when he was accused of stealing jewellery. It was a put-up job. The other alternative was for me to stay on and call the police. The total was just under £100 and I reluctantly decided to pay up and not hold up the others. The girl I had dealt with looked at me and said sheepishly 'I am sorry' and averted her eyes. The journey to the airport lasted fifteen minutes and we sat in the lounge for three hours before the domestic flight back to Lima. I could have stayed on to argue my case. When I returned home, I wrote to the travel company and complained. They sent me a cheque for £69 – it was better than nothing.

For some reason we flew into Buenos Aires at 6.30 a.m. and were assured that our rooms in a classy, four-star hotel on Avenida del Libertador, the seventeen-lane street in the city centre, would have rooms ready when we arrived. No such luck. We spent nearly eight hours in the lobby before we were given our keys. Eventually I showed my *Daily Mail* card to the manager and within minutes I was shown to our room. I should have tried that from the outset.

The next day, we went on a day excursion across the River Plate to Montevideo, a quieter, cleaner and to my way of thinking, more interesting place. My aim was to see the football ground where the first World Cup Final was held in 1930, as described in chapter nine. On the way back we visited the museum that housed memorabilia of the scuttling of the German battleship *Admiral Graf Spee*. The German captain sank his own ship after the British conned him into thinking that three English cruisers were in position to block his vessel's escape. They weren't.

Back at the airport we waited for the final flight to Buenos Aires, which was due at 9.21 p.m. We took fifteen flights on this fantastic trip and none departed on time. The average delay was two hours. Now we were being told that the flight would be rearranged for 11.21 pm. A member of staff rang a friend at the Buenos Aires main airport and was told that with only twenty-eight people left they wouldn't be sending a plane for the last flight. We made strong overtures to members of staff, but no one seemed to be in charge. Meanwhile we organised an impromptu game of skittles using tennis balls and plastic bottles in the now-closed departure lounge. Some of the Argentinians had never heard of it and joined in enthusiastically. Suddenly a police officer arrived and ordered a ceasefire. 'It is not permitted,' he said. We were the only people in the lounge, except for two staff. We had to concede and an Argentinian rang someone at the Buenos Aires airport and explained that there would be a diplomatic incident if these British tourists were left stranded overnight. At midnight a plane landed and we were ushered on for the joyous return journey. Everyone was laughing and joking. That's the only way to behave in these situations!

I wanted to visit the Boca Juniors Stadium in a poor part of Buenos Aires. It is the club where Maradona made his name and where he still presides. I asked for the chief press officer and a middle-aged lady appeared. I showed her my *Mail* card. She spoke good English and invited me into the President's room. I can't imagine an Argentinian journalist turning up at most Premiership clubs and asking to look around. Her assistant conducted me around the ground and I was astonished by the lack of space.

'It is a small ground because of the dictates of the local authority,' he said. 'The area is very built-up and it is impossible for us to expand. We are making it all-seater and that has reduced the capacity of 57,000 down to 35,000. But it helps make the atmosphere, which is the best feature.'

I asked him, 'Do you ever get games abandoned because of hooliganism?'

'Sometimes,' he laughed. 'It is an excitable crowd and sometimes things go too far.'

I asked to see the press box. It was situated on a corner of the ground and it had 296 seats, more than any club in Britain. It has a great view of the corner flag at that end but it wasn't so good a view of the far end. And it is filled at every match.

Then he took me to the interviewing room on the same floor. It had 180 seats, again far more than any ground in Britain. 'We need every seat,' he said. 'It is always filled. Sometimes the coach drivers lose their tempers and depart.'

On the last stage of my trip, I watched a Flamengo *v.* Fluminense game at the Maracanã Stadium in Rio de Janeiro. Luiz, our courier, said we would be given the best tickets on the halfway line, costing £5. I didn't bother to apply for a press pass, which might have been difficult to obtain. In its heyday, the capacity at the Maracanã was 200,000, but now it is being rebuilt and the capacity will be 90,000. I am acutely disappointed that they have retained the same elevation instead of knocking down much of the ground and starting afresh. The view was similar to the 1923-built Wembley Stadium. We didn't make our target of a position on the halfway line. Instead, we were given seats about fifty metres from the corner flag, where you needed binoculars to see the action at the far end. The sun was setting and in the half light it was difficult to pick up the numbers on the backs of the players. The standard of play was unexceptional. The temperature was 32°C and there was high humidity, so no one was moving particularly fast. One Brazilian explained, 'All our best players are in Europe and that has affected the standards. And you don't see so many children playing football on the beaches. Those who do play are very skilful and entertaining but we wonder whether we can keep producing so many fine footballers.'

All twenty-two players were Brazilian. They don't go for foreigners. As for the fans, they rarely stop chanting and shouting, and waving huge flags in front of people. It was early evening and there were many mothers with babies. The ground was only a third full, despite the match being a local derby. I noticed that the two teams came out about fifty yards apart and that the referee had his own entrance, over at the other side of the ground. When the officials emerged, they passed through two lines of about sixty police officers holding their shields high in the air, obviously designed to stop missiles hitting them.

The night before we flew home we were awakened by gunfire from behind the twenty-five-storey hotel near the Copacabana Beach. At breakfast I asked one of the locals about this and he said, 'It was the police shooting at the gangsters who sell drugs and weapons. It happens regularly. There is a kind of shanty town built on a hill behind and that is where they hang out. It is nothing to worry about.'

It was my birthday and the journey home via Madrid lasted thirty-six hours, including two delayed flights. On leaving Rio, we were told it was possible to buy duty-free goods and take them home, but at Madrid the customs officers said, 'No that is not true.' They started grabbing the bottles of perfumes and spirits and hurling them into large bins, with glass smashing everywhere. Trying to help, I picked up a piece of glass and cut my finger. An English lady, who was protesting about having a £100 bottle of perfume being confiscated and destroyed, lost her temper and picked up a wine bottle and threatened one of the customs officers with it. In most countries she would be arrested, but the Spanish people are much more tolerant than they used to be under General Franco. On the way out to Santiago for the start of the tour, several people had their luggage tampered with and the same thing happened on the return flight to London. Some bags were missing, presumed lost. A few weeks later, the Argentinian airline went bust – not surprising. It sounds as an awful trip, but it wasn't. It was good fun.

My second visit to Georgetown in Guyana was in February 1999, and I loved the place and its people despite it being probably the untidiest, dirtiest place in the world. It may have improved since then, but there was rubbish everywhere. There were a lot of shootings between Indian and indigenous gangs and Shivnarine Chanderpaul, the crablike left-handed batsmen with the peculiar stance, was caught up in one incident. He was approached by a man whom he thought was a villain and the pistol he had in his hand went off, hitting the man in the hand. But it was a policeman, not a rogue. Chanderpaul, like a number of famous people in Guyana, is given diplomatic status, and wasn't prosecuted.

Mark Ramprakash's father Deo came from Guyana, and Mark, born in Bushey, Hertfordshire, was very keen to make a big score in front of his Guyanese relatives. And he did, scoring ninety-eight in his two innings in a low-scoring match, a third of England's runs. He should have been the Peter May of this era. He had all the qualities and he is still proving it today. Maybe he needed a more understanding mentor or manager. He finished top of the England averages on that tour and coming in at number six he scored 154 in his only innings at Barbados, ending a dismal run of only two fifties in his previous twenty-one centuries. He looked set to blossom into greatness and I wrote, 'Such was his mastery he is now being talked about as a contender for the England captaincy if Mike Atherton, who is averaging a paltry thirteen in the series, fails in his remaining three innings.'

Sadly, it didn't happen, and Atherton went on to fame and fortune while Ramps made his fortune from ballroom dancing. I interviewed him at the Pelican Hotel in Georgetown before the fourth Test and he came up with an unusual reason for his lacklustre appearance – air conditioning. 'I didn't feel well in Port of Spain and wasn't fit to play,' he said. 'It was 85°F through the night and with mosquitoes queuing outside you are reluctant to open windows. I am susceptible to air conditioning.' In most hotels where the England team stays, it is not possible to open the windows. It may not be the whole story, but a good night's sleep is good for calming the nerves.

CHAPTER SEVENTEEN

Contradicting Mrs Thatcher at 10 Downing Street

Margaret Thatcher invited twenty-four of the leading football writers and several of her officials to attend a meeting at 10 Downing Street on 31 August 1985, and I was among them. The purpose of the meeting, the first of its kind, was to come up with some solutions following the death of thirty-eight spectators, thirty of them Italian, in the Liverpool *v.* Juventus European Cup Final in the Heysel Stadium, Brussels, on 29 May. There had also been the Bradford City fire on 11 May and several other outbreaks of hooliganism that year, all of which had horrified the sporting world. I sat on the left side of the huge table, one up from the Iron Lady, Britain's first female Prime Minister. Sir Robert Walpole, known as 'Sir Blusterer', is generally recognised as the first British Prime Minister; after forty-eight men in charge, male dominance had been breached, and how!

The football writers had been asked to arrive by 9 a.m. and were shepherded into a side room before Mrs Thatcher marched in at a fair pace. My former *Sketch* colleague Ferdinand Mount, who later became an adviser to Mrs Thatcher and helped write her speeches, described her distinctive walk in his book *Cold Cream: My Early Life and Other Mistakes* as 'a waddle'. Having seen her at close range, I had to agree.

'Now I'm taking you upstairs,' she said. 'You will see the pictures on the walls of my predecessors.' We showed interest and as the tour ended and we sat down, she gave a short preamble about the current problems and her thoughts about changing matters, including an identity scheme for football clubs, banning alcohol at matches, more closed circuit TV, and tougher penalties for hooligans. Soon we soon realised that she knew very little about football and at one time during the ninety-minute meeting she chided me about the money the clubs were making when they should have spent more on building better and safer grounds.

'That's not strictly true Prime Minister,' I said. 'Gary Lineker has just gone to Everton for £800,000 but that money doesn't stay with the selling club, Leicester. The Leicester directors will be buying other players to strengthen their team and so it goes on. The cash spreads down to the lower clubs. Without big transfers, the small clubs will die.' I quoted a recent report saying that only thirty-six out of the ninety-two League clubs were out of the red in the previous season. (Today that total is much lower.)

Mrs Thatcher turned to Neil Macfarlane, the Sports Minister. 'Is that right?'

Macfarlane looked shocked. 'Ah, yes, that's right, Prime Minister,' he stuttered.

He started to say something else but she interrupted and said, 'I don't think we need to go into that.' She treated him like a headmistress admonishing a naughty boy. I was struck by her eyes – bright and shining, exuding power. I have been close to the Queen at her visits to the committee room at Lord's and she has the same luminous eyes. Mrs Thatcher's officials, dotted around the room, seemed fearful of her, and she dominated the proceedings throughout. Metaphorically, she was wearing the trousers, although she was hardly ever seen wearing any. Having so many people at this 10 Downing Street mini-conference was a mistake. Half of them would have been much more beneficial. Brian Glanville of *The Sunday Times* tried to make a comparison with Italian clubs – the Juventus fans had been the innocent victims of the Heysel Stadium disaster three months earlier – and she soon changed the subject.

I think I was better briefed than some because in the previous eighteen months I had been ghostwriting the book of FA secretary Ted Croker, *The First Voice You Will Hear Is...* The title came from the first words uttered by the BBC football correspondent Bryon Butler when he presided over the FA Cup draws held at 16 Lancaster Gate, the previous home of the Football Association. Byron was at the meeting along with another great friend of mine, Brian Moore, the ITV commentator. Both men were top of their field. They died just as they were about to go into semi-retirement and they are sadly missed.

In the final chapter of his book, Ted wrote, 'My impression was that Mrs Thatcher was being given the wrong advice at an earlier meeting and it was confirmed when I was told that one of the people who was called in – in all probability he volunteered his services – was Robert Maxwell. The Oxford chairman was running a campaign against the football authorities and was responsible for some dubious statements. As we had done at her previous meeting with the FA people, she was bullish, almost hectoring, giving the impression she thought football was responsible for these tragic events through its negligence. She seemed to have no feeling for the game whatsoever and did not seem to appreciate that it brought great pleasure to millions of players and watchers every week for forty weeks a year. I was left with the feeling that she would not have thought it a loss to the social scene if football was stopped altogether.'

Croker was bitter because he felt the Government was at fault for not taking up the recommendations of the Norman Chester Report in 1968, which included setting up a football levy board similar to the one in racing, with the income being devoted to modernising the Football League's grounds. He said, 'I told her the tax on football pools, which was twenty-five per cent, had been increased to forty per cent by successive Governments and then 42.5 per cent by her Chancellor of the Exchequer, Sir Geoffrey Howe. If a football board had been created, the Bradford fire might not have happened as the old stand would probably have been replaced. She didn't reply to that point or my claim that while football was providing the Exchequer with £220 million in tax every year, racing, the sport of kings and queens, was being favourably treated and attracted only a minority audience in comparison.'

So now we know: Sir Geoffrey was the man to blame. Five years later, he made the damning speech in the House of Commons that provoked the rebellion of the Tory elders who refused to back Mrs Thatcher, leading to her tearful resignation.

Significantly, Mrs Thatcher devoted just sixty-two words to the Heysel disaster in her 1993 book *The Downing Street Years*.

Croker, who died on Christmas Day, the same day as Audrey, was right about a football levy board. Once I asked him, 'How are the relations now between the press and the FA?'

He answered, 'The councillors are petrified about the press and always have been. Whatever they say, we tend to follow. We should have kept pressuring the Government to bring in a levy board but the journalists didn't really support it.'

From my experience, that was true. A levy board would have brought massive improvements to the archaic grounds, but I didn't share Croker's views that Mrs Thatcher didn't really care whether or not football survived. In June I wrote to her with some ideas about combating hooliganism and she wrote back saying, 'Thank you for your letter and the suggestions you make for dealing with the problem of football hooliganism. I am very grateful for the response from people in this country who were shocked and shamed by the dreadful events at the Heysel Stadium, and who have taken the trouble to write to me. I also found it enormously helpful to meet representatives of the press, including your colleague Jeff Powell, to hear their first-hand account of the tragedy in Belgium. I will certainly give careful consideration to the points you raise in your letter. You will be aware of the initiatives the Government has already taken and will take to stamp out this dreadful menace. Let me assure you that we are determined to restore this great national game as a source of family entertainment and pleasure. Yours sincerely, Margaret Thatcher.'

Neil Macfarlane, whom I got to know and recognised as a decent man but a 'wet', was the first Sports Minister to write a book while in office. A few months later, he was sacked. He preferred cricket, the gentlemanly game, to football. I worked with most of the Government's sports ministers in my time and most of them were totally unsuited to the job. Successive Prime Ministers have handed the task to the wrong people, giving the impression that they don't have much regard for sport. Colin Moynihan was the only one from the Conservative ranks who had any sound ideas; he had a sporting background and did a reasonable job. Richard Tracey was appointed as Macfarlane's successor and he wasn't up to it. The best Sports Minister in my view was the former Football League referee Denis Howell, more famous for supposedly ending a drought than for his work in football. He knew the game from the inside and he had the right instincts to act on them. A latter-day Howell could have campaigned against the corruption in the game, the illegal payments to agents, players, chairmen, and others, the money laundering from abroad, and the squeezing out of English players that has seriously weakened the national team.

Alan Simpson, the rebel Labour MP from Nottingham, would have been a sound choice for that job but Tony Blair soon excommunicated him for speaking out against the party line. I went on the Fleet Street tour to India in 1999 under the dynamic leadership of Mihir Bose, the BBC's sports editor. Simpson, a useful all-rounder and an enthusiastic footballer who was with us in the touring party, told an extraordinary story. 'Soon after Blair took over I spoke in the House and made a few cheeky comments about him and there were a few laughs but as I left my pager rang and one of the whips told me that if I repeated that or similar, I would have the whip taken off me. I realised that Blair was intent on everyone agreeing with his views, and not letting anyone else give an opinion.'

Blair held on to his job for a third term, a record for a Labour leader, and this was the main reason for his longevity: keeping his MPs on a tight rein. He was aided by his Rottweiler, Alastair Campbell, Labour's director of communications and strategy, whom I used to play against in *Daily Mail* matches with the *Mirror*. Campbell was an aggressive player and just as nasty in politics.

Teamwork usually brings success, whether it is in sport or politics. Mrs Thatcher was deposed in 1990 because too many of her lieutenants were 'not one of us'. Paul Johnson, a former colleague on the *Mail*, called her 'the greatest Prime Minister, along with Winston Churchill, since WWII'. Many people would agree. She won the battle over the unions, brought in privatisation, and helped Mikhail Gorbachev to end Communist rule in the USSR. But the majority of people think she was too divisive and I agree. She created too many enemies.

She had few close friends. Her greatest supporter was her husband Denis. I met him on numerous occasions at cricket dinners and he was a lovely man with a wonderful sense of humour. His wife lacked that essential quality. He loved a tipple and if he trusted you, he would come out with his real opinions, condemning the 'wets', the Commies, and the cheats in sport, particularly golf and cricket. He wasn't a football fan but he had strong views about hooliganism. 'Stick them in jail and throw the key away,' he said. He was so popular among the journalists that hardly anyone wrote anything nasty about him, even though he often came out with a few indiscretions.

In the 1980s, I sometimes met Carol Thatcher, the Iron Lady's bubbly daughter, who wrote occasionally articles for the *Mail*. In one taxi ride across London, she kept two journalistic colleagues and me in stitches of laughter. She has the same qualities as her father, except that Denis kept his indiscretions in-house whereas Carol was caught out when she called a tennis player a 'golliwog' in the privacy of a 'green room' at the BBC. When two colleagues, Adrian Chiles and Jo Brand, snitched on her, she was sacked from *The One Show*. If her mother had a sense of humour, she might have lasted as long as Sir Robert Walpole. The Thatcher twins, Carol and Mark, were born six weeks premature on 15 August 1953 while their father watched Alec Bedser beat Maurice Tate's record of thirty-eight wickets in an Ashes series at the Oval. Australia were bowled out for 275 and Bedser, who started out bowling a rare full toss, had figures of 3-88; Fred Trueman just beat him with 4-86. Has England ever had a better, and more varied, attack than the one that played in that match – Bedser, Trueman, Trevor Bailey, Lock and Laker? When Denis went to inspect the new arrivals later in the day, he said, 'My God! They look like rabbits. Put them back!'

The first woman to hold the job of Sports Minister, Kate Hoey, was popular among the sports administrators and press but not with Blair and his cohorts. Kate, a former athlete in Belfast who once served on the Surrey CCC committee, was too independent for Blair's liking and he ditched her.

In the last days of Sam Hammam at Wimbledon FC he invited me to join a buffet lunch before a game at Selhurst Park and I was surprised to see Gordon Brown, then the Chancellor of the Exchequer. He came over as an agreeable man with a ready smile and I was impressed by his knowledge of football, even though it was mainly restricted to Scottish football. He said he was a fan of Raith Rovers. When we shook hands, I discovered that his outstretched hand was limp. The last person to extend a similarly limp hand in my direction was 'Bubbles' Harmsworth, Lady Rothermere, the wife of the late Lord Rothermere. Audrey and I were being introduced to her in a long queue at the entrance of the main dining room of the Dorchester Hotel and she was sitting in a high chair. As she held her right hand toward us, she turned away as though we were 'lower than vermin', to quote Aneurin Bevan. She must have had a bad day. She was a J. Arthur Rank starlet before she married into the Northcliffe dynasty. The Prime Minister who probably had the weakest handshake of all was Harold Macmillan, the Earl of Stockton, who was MP for Bromley from 1945 until he retired in 1963. He had a beautiful, distinctive house a mile away from our house and a good friend, Neville Holtham, who was sports editor of *The People* for some years, lived and died in a flat next to it. Macmillan was shot and injured twice in the Battle of Loos in 1915, the first time in the buttock and the second in the right hand. 'I never regained strength in my hand but my bottom did,' he wrote in his memoirs. He finished up with five war wounds and it was remarkable that this most radical of Tory premiers, who was known as 'Supermac', lived until he was ninety-two. His record of longevity was later beaten by Jim Callaghan.

Kate Hoey was also at the Wimbledon lunch and I sat next to her. There was an empty seat on her other side and Brian Glanville approached with his full plate of meats and salad and said, 'That seat is free, isn't?'

Kate looked up and with a haughty expression, and said, 'Oh no it isn't!' Glanville had to retire to another part of the room.

A short time before, Kate and Glanville had appeared on a TV programme and the hawkish *Sunday Times* football correspondent accused Hoey of being cowardly by not repeating in public what she had said in a Commons debate. She was furious. An advert came on and in the background they exchanged unpleasantries before the chat resumed. Glanville has been one of the most capable and aggressive football writers of his time and he is still going strong in his seventies. Like Mrs Thatcher, he made plenty of enemies.

Hammam made a fortune by selling Wimbledon to two Norwegian businessmen, who clearly didn't know the whole story about the club. When he moved to Cardiff, he encountered more financial problems but there were no foreign millionaires to bail the club out. I liked Hammam, a Lebanese who talked and talked, and by the end of the conversation you still didn't know what he meant. Occasionally he let slip a good story and I always appreciated that.

A revealing story about Peter Ridsdale, the former Leeds chairman who succeeded Hammam as chairman at Cardiff, illustrated the troubles at Ninian Park at the end of the 2006/07 season. I was covering the Cardiff v. Hull match in the final game of the season and when I arrived the man in the kiosk was supposed to be giving out press passes. He said, 'The press officer is off today but if you go over to the room over there, someone will give you a ticket.'

As I approached the door, a burly man with a shaven hair shouted, 'F*** off!' He turned out to be a steward and he was talking to someone else, not me. Normally, one would expect an apology, but he didn't offer one.

Dean Windass scored the late winner to keep Hull up in the Championship and everyone wanted to interview him. However, the Hull press officer told the press corps, 'It's not his turn to be interviewed. We've got someone else.'

The writers protested. 'Windass is the story,' I said. The press officer went off without changing his mind.

Half an hour later, I was in a group of six journalists outside in the corridor when Windass, normally a very talkative man, walked over. One of us said, 'Can I speak to you Dean?'

'I'd love to,' said Windass, 'but they've blocked it.'

This is not uncommon with football people. Too many of them have no idea of how to promote their club and their players. Quoteless, we were discussing other options when a steward came up to us and said, 'You lot out! You've got to leave the ground.'

I asked why. 'The players are upset from the previous game,' he said.

'Which players?'

'Roy Keane,' he replied, 'and he wrote a letter to our chairman about it.'

Of course, this was nothing to do with the home players or even the Hull players, and I asked to speak to the chief steward, a friendly West Indian who produced the first smile of the affair. I explained I was on the Football Writers' Association committee, which deals with Football League facilities, and I asked to speak to Mr Ridsdale. Ten minutes later, he returned to say that the chairman wasn't available, but the chief steward was sensible enough to rescind our expulsion order.

The FWA sub-committee had just met League President Lord Brian Mawhinney, and this would be a good subject to bring up at our next meeting. I also wrote to Ridsdale, saying he ought to improve his club's press relations and treat professional people in a proper manner. He didn't reply. I wrote again. No answer. After my fourth letter, Ridsdale finally wrote to apologise and said it wouldn't happen again. 'Sorry about the letters,' he wrote, 'but I don't have the luxury of a secretary and on occasions correspondence is not answered.'

He is hated by many people in Leeds because of his handling of the club that Don Revie built, but he transformed Cardiff and a new ground has been completed.

Kate Hoey is still campaigning against the closure of sports grounds and swimming pools; she is the alternative voice in sport. When she was Sports Minister, I was invited to attend a function at a school in the East End to promote sports facilities and what happened turned out to be a farce. Half a dozen Government cars were parked outside because there was no space and all six were clamped.

I came out of the school and spoke to a warden and explained these were Government cars.

'That doesn't matter, they are parking illegally,' he said.

'One of the cars contains the Sports Minister, Kate Hoey, and another minister, and they are due to be at the House of Commons in an hour for a debate,' I said

'Bad luck,' he said. I was clamped as well and had to pay up.

Ninety-two per cent of the school's children were Bangladeshi, a remarkably high proportion. One of the teachers told me, 'Behaviour is excellent and they work extremely hard.' It reminds me another incident some years later, when I gave Lee Bowyer a lift home from the Football Writers' Dinner at the Royal Lancaster Hotel in Lancaster Gate. He had an agent who wanted to improve the images of young players and invited Bowyer and Jason Euell to dinner. Bowyer was eighteen and impressed me as a nice young man and when I was driving through the East End I noticed a school with very high fences. 'Are the fences keeping out the hooligans?' I asked him.

'No, keeping the pupils in!' he said.

One of Sol Chandler's ideas at the *Sketch* was for me to ring Harold Wilson, the Prime Minister, and ask him about the subject of hooliganism. I thought it might be difficult: an unknown football writer in his twenties trying to speak to the Labour Prime Minister person-to-person. It turned out to be easy. I rang someone at the press office at 10 Downing Street, explained what I wanted, and left my number. Three hours later, I was about to go home when the phone rang on my desk in and it was Mr Wilson. He was very polite and friendly and our conversation lasted more than fifteen minutes. I was amazed that someone as busy as the Prime Minister should devote such a long time talking to someone like me. My article failed to appear the next day. The reason was that the *Sketch* supported the Conservatives. The last time I covered a game in Huddersfield I came out of the station and saw Harold's statue. I felt like apologising.

Wilson was renowned for his talent with facts and figures. His memory was phenomenal, but he contracted Alzheimer's after he resigned in 1976. He was one of the first Prime Ministers to realise the importance of football in English life. When England won the World Cup in 1966, he was at the hotel that night to join in the celebrations. I was there as well, but I was outside in the large lobby downstairs waiting to interview Bobby Charlton and Franz Beckenbauer. Sol told me, 'That's your story – how these two great players cancelled each other out!' It was true. But Bobby finished on the winning side because he had an explosive shot, whereas Beckenbauer rarely scored goals. And while Alan Ball ran and ran, his opponents would start flagging. Big events are usually won in the mind, and Ball was a classic example.

During the World Cup in 1982, I was sitting in the huge press box in the Vicente Calderón Stadium in Madrid watching France beat Austria in a drab game and I turned round and sitting right behind me was Henry Kissinger, who two months earlier had had a triple heart bypass. Between 1969 and 1977, he was one of the most powerful men in the world. During the administrations of Richard Nixon and Gerald Ford, he advocated a policy of détente, first with the Russians and then with the Chinese. It was said of him, 'His foreign policy record made him a nemesis to both the anti-war left and the anti-communist right alike.' But despite the criticism he faced throughout most of his career, he survived.

Kissinger was born in Furth, Bavaria to Jewish parents in 1923, and fled to New York to avoid persecution. He studied at the George Washington High School at night and worked in a shaving brush factory during the day. He became a US citizen in 1943, but never lost his German accent, as I discovered later in the evening when I met him in a club along with Ian Wooldridge, Tom Clarke, and Jarvis Astaire. 'I love soccer and I see as many matches as I can,' he said. 'And I loved watching the New York Cosmos.' He showed that he knew a lot about the game. He had his second wife Nancy with him and I noticed that she was wearing a dental brace.

The tournament was fraught with political problems that even a Kissinger wouldn't have been able to solve. The Falklands War was raging when England arrived at their hotel, Las Tamarises, eight miles outside Bilboa where ETA, the Basque separatists, are mainly based. Sixteen marksmen were on duty round the clock and the players were often kept awake by the sound of their soldiers walking about on the roof. Around this time, *The Sun* and the *Mirror* were competing with each other to come up stories that would embarrass Ron Greenwood, the reluctant manager who had been persuaded to succeed Don Revie. One of them published a photograph of a dead dog on a tatty nearby beach, ignoring the fact the picture was taken several months ago and that the dog had long been removed. An agent rang up and said a ballet group was in the city and that it would make a good picture with the players. The FA agreed, but the ballet girls turned out to be topless models. An angry Greenwood took these slights personally. Two days before the opening game against France – won by England 2-0 in a temperature of 100°F – an official rang to confirm that the party was going to the reception of the mayor of Bilbao at 12.30 p.m. FA secretary Ted Croker said, 'We never received an invite. Most of us were going to play golf.' Croker, Greenwood, and Geoff Hurst had to drop golf and turn up at the function. Later there were stories that England had snubbed the mayor's drinks party.

One of the players tipped me off that Kevin Keegan was unlikely to take part in the first three matches because of a bad back. When the redtops wrote that he was going home, Greenwood was livid. Keegan told the manager he wanted to see his specialist in Hamburg and borrowed a Mini owned by a receptionist at the hotel and drove the 250 miles to Madrid-Barajas Airport on his own and caught a plane to Hamburg. After his meeting with his consultant, he flew back to collect the car. Neither Keegan nor Brooking played in the first four matches; Greenwood brought them on twenty-seven minutes from the end of the 0-0 draw against Spain at the Bernabeu Stadium. It was too late; England were out without losing a game. It was a regrettable end to Greenwood's career.

The funniest thing I experienced on that trip was a four-hour trip from Bilbao to Valladolid to see France draw 1-1 against Czechoslovakia. Some of us put our names down for the press coach and the trip was enlivened by a heated discussion between Brian Glanville, David Miller, and my friend Harry Miller of the *Mirror*. Our coach was the first to arrive three hours before the kick-off and I said to Glanville, 'Make sure that it waits for us after we finish.'

The stadium was miles out of town and the huge car park was covered in what appeared to be dust from the moon. After the game I had to obtain a quote from Michel Platini about England's prospects and when I came out to find the coach, I suddenly realised dozens of coaches were moving off in a cloud of dust at the same time, almost blinding everyone on foot. Where was our coach? They all looked the same. Twenty minutes later I still hadn't seen Glanville or the coach, the car park was virtually empty, and I had to return to the press room. How would I get back to Bilbao?

Three friendly Danish reporters were the only people left and I recognised Steen Ankerdal, a good friend. 'Any chance of a lift?' I said.

'Certainly, we're ready to go,' said Steen.

It was a pleasant return journey, interrupted by a stop in Burgos to have drinks. It was now approaching midnight and we were watching the highlights of the match on TV. I suddenly realised I had put over the wrong goalscorer – Soler, not Didier Six – the cardinal mistake of any football writer. None of us had mobiles; no one had them in those days. I went to the toilet and behind the door was a miraculous sight, a telephone. I picked it up and dialled the 'Sportsmail' number and spoke to the chief sub who altered the mistake in my report. Saved at the last minute.

At that time, I was writing Trevor Brooking's column for the *Mail*. Everyone knows he is the most gentle of men, but when I saw him at Navacerrada, the 6,000-foot-high training camp, he was very angry. He said, 'I've just read an article in the *Mail* TV page saying that I don't sleep with Hilkka!'

I had to placate him. 'I don't know anything about it,' I said, 'but you ought to ignore it. I'll tell them to get it corrected.' They never did.

Not blessed by extreme pace, Trevor was one of the most skilled players this country has ever produced. How they need a Brooking in England's midfield today. When I wrote his book, he said he learned mastery of the ball by taking a tennis ball to and from his school. 'I would flick it against the wall or whatever and that's how you acquire a good touch,' he said.

Since very few English tennis players ever reach the highest standards of the game, we might as well give the country's tennis balls to young children to kick about. It would certainly teach them better control than senior-size plastic footballs.

CHAPTER EIGHTEEN

A Chat with Lady Di

In 1985 I was starting my three-year stint as chairman of the Cricket Writers' Club, which with more than 300 members is the world's premier cricket journalism organisation. The Princess of Wales was the patron of Gloucestershire CCC and we thought it was a good idea to invite her to one of our ceremonies. Late in the summer, our members voted Gloucestershire's fast bowler, twenty-one-year-old David Valentine Lawrence, 'Young Player of the Year' after he took eighty-five wickets. Courtney Walsh was bowling at the other end, which helped. Although born in Gloucester, Lawrence's parents came from Jamaica and he was the first Afro-Caribbean-descended cricketer to win the award. I wrote to Lieutenant Commander Richard Aylard, the equerry to the Princess, to ask if the Palace could let her present the trophy. A few weeks later, he replied that she would be pleased to do it. The date was fixed for 11 April 1986 at Gloucestershire CCC's headquarters on Nevil Road, Bristol. In a chat with David Collier, the club secretary, I asked him if Diana was willing to make a short speech. 'I don't think so,' he said. 'You can do that and she will hand the trophy over.'

Experiencing coincidences is a regular feature of my life and this was another one: England was sending its Under-21 side to Pisa to play the Italian Under-21s on 10 April and I was asked to cover the match. Fortunately the aircraft bringing the party back to Heathrow – the players, officials, and press – was timed to arrive mid-afternoon, enabling me to be picked up by Audrey and taken to Bristol, ready for the date with Lady Di. On the second day in Pisa, I was one of several football writers who stayed in bed with stomach problems. Dr John Crane, the much-liked FA doctor, produced the right tablets to cure the problem on the day of the match. In the afternoon, we were walking around the Piazzo next to the Leaning Tower and we noticed that there was a large number of police officers and spectators on the other side. 'Prince Charles is visiting the Tower,' explained a policeman.

When he was told that some English journalists had turned up, the Prince came over and said, 'Who do you work for?'

'The *Daily Mail*,' I said, 'and we're football writers, we're not news chasers! And I'm meeting your wife in Bristol tomorrow on a date.' He guffawed and seemed not to know about her whereabouts.

He was limping and another writer asked him about it. 'I came off my pony playing polo,' he explained. He was very cheerful but twitched a lot; he was continually tapping his foot on the ground. With a cheery wave, he turned and said, 'Have a good game,' as he hobbled off.

England lost the match 2-0 with a weakened side. Gianluca Vialli sidefooted the second goal past David Seaman. Charles, not a football fan, would have hated it.

Royal visits are timed to the last second, and Audrey and I were supposed to be at the main pavilion at 9.30 a.m. the next day with the statuette at Gloucestershire's county ground in Bristol. Diana was accompanied by her lady-in-waiting, Anne Beckwith-Smith, when the official party arrived an hour later. Anne turned out to be a very lively, bubbly lady. For some reason, Audrey was left behind while I was taken into the committee room and the three of us sat down exchanging small talk. Diana was twenty-four at the time and her sons, William Arthur Philip Louis and Henry Charles Albert David, were nearly four and almost two respectively. In terms of doing the job royalty wanted, producing male heirs to the Crown, her task was over. It was well known that Prince Charles had affairs with older, more mature women. Diana was apparently chosen because she was a member of the Church of England, had an aristocratic background, and was supposedly a virgin. Their engagement was announced in February 1981 and Charles gave Diana a £30,000 ring consisting of fourteen diamonds and a sapphire, much more valuable than the one Dodi Fayed bought her much later. She was twenty when the marriage took place in St Paul's Church, watched by a worldwide TV audience of 780 million. She wore a gown costing £9,000 with a twenty-five-foot train made of lace. It didn't look like a love match from the start, and in the late 1980s the marriage crumbled. The divorce was finalised in 1996, and she received a settlement of around £17 million, the cost of an above-average international Premiership footballer.

In our meeting she was wearing a royal blue suit and a striking blue and white scarf. I noticed that she wore flat shoes because she was almost as tall as me: I am five foot eleven. She was pretty, very pretty, but appeared extremely shy, often looking down and avoiding eye contact. She said she didn't really know much about cricket and when I asked her if she was going to say anything, she said 'Not really, just a few words to congratulate him.' At that time of her life she wasn't confident about public speaking.

I tried to keep the conversation going, asking her about her interests. She liked music, she said, but not classical.

'Ballet?'

'Not really.'

'Opera?'

'No.'

I learned that she didn't like cats. Not wanting to have awkward silences, I said, 'Is it possible for my wife Audrey to be allowed to join us? I'm not very knowledgeable about these matters, whereas she is.' Diana and Anne Beckwith-Smith both nodded their heads in agreement. Audrey soon lit up the proceedings, talking animatedly about many different subjects. By then Diana was warming up. She was smiling but out in the Upper Grace Room a few minutes later, when she met the dignitaries, she was soon back to her nervous state.

I sat next to her and someone asked if she wanted a glass of wine. 'Just a glass of water,' she said.

At 12.25 p.m. I was scheduled to make my speech, with a limit of five minutes. I went on for seven. 'This is only the second time one of our functions has been graced by the presence of the royal family,' I said 'The first occasion was in 1948, the year after our formation, when Prince Philip presided at a dinner in the City of London in honour of the Australian cricket team. Sir Donald Bradman spoke so eloquently that his speech, broadcast to the nation on the BBC, delayed the start of the nine o'clock news. I don't think I am going to stop the news today. Gloucestershire's excellent young fast bowler David Lawrence is a deserved winner of the award and I hope he won't mind me repeating a snatch of the conversation when my newspaper, the *Daily Mail*, arranged for him to pose for pictures at Lord's last summer with that other fine ambassador of British sport, Frank Bruno.

'Frank said to him, "Where did you get that name Syd?"

'David replied, "Syd Lawrence the band leader."

'Frank snorted. "Syd Lawrence!" he said. "Never heard of him. I thought you were named after Sid Vicious!"'

Diana laughed along with everyone else. It broke the tension, which she had obviously been feeling.

I went on. 'David's bouncers can be a little nasty at times but everyone knows him as a delightful and dedicated young man. Most of the previous winners of our award – thirty-three out of thirty-seven – have gone on to play Test cricket. I am sure David will eventually join them. Her Royal Highness might be interested to learn that the statuette was made by the same jewellers who recently were responsible for a certain engagement ring – Garrards of Regent Street. By coincidence, I was in Pisa yesterday, covering a football match and Prince Charles was there and along with some English football writers, we had a pleasant chat with him. Unfortunately, for security reasons, he was one of the few tourists to visit Pisa and not go up the Tower. However, I was assured that his injury, caused by a polo fall, won't stop him doing his duty as an off-break bowler when the young princes require him to bowl to them!'

She clapped demurely. She then handed over the statuette and congratulated Lawrence, saying, 'Keep up the good work and keep playing hard.'

Earlier, the party had visited the indoor school to watch a bowling machine delivering the ball at 95 mph. She asked Lawrence how fast he bowled. He said, '85 mph with a strong wind blowing behind me.'

Diana said, 'You need to bowl fast with those broad shoulders.'

Someone suggested that the machine should be named after her but she said, 'No, it would probably break down.'

The players' wives were invited to the reception afterwards with their children and we saw another side of Diana. Julie Graveney, the wife of David Graveney, introduced her to the wives and she was laughing and joking with the young children and picking them up. Her kindergarten training had come into its own. The confidential programme had the time of departure for the party as 1 p.m. but it went into overtime. She was enjoying herself and she probably would have liked to stay on.

'Syd' Lawrence did play for England. He appeared in five Tests but despite his tremendous enthusiasm and bull-like strength, he never established himself in the side. He had a similar problem to Andrew Flintoff: he was too heavy. In his prime he was six-foot-three and weighed fifteen and a half stone. Thundering down at such speed took a toll on his knees and on 10 February 1992 he was bowling against New Zealand in the third and final Test when he fell, splitting his knee cap. He let out an excruciating scream of pain as he collapsed on the pitch. Thirteen days before, he had turned twenty-eight. His first-class career came to an abrupt end. Manfully, he tried to regain his fitness, but cracked his patella again. He played club cricket for a while. He was an unlucky cricketer.

The day before the presentation at Gloucestershire, I was reading the *Mail* and on the front page the leading story was headlined, 'My Life as a Disciple of Satan'. Underneath there was a picture of Ian Botham and his wife Kathy. The picture wasn't connected to the main article, which was about a meeting in Antigua when Botham had to explain to his wife why the *News of the World* had published a story the previous week saying that the all-rounder had had an affair with Lindy Field, daughter of a wealthy family in Barbados. It was suggested that Botham, who weighed the same as Syd Lawrence, had been instrumental in the collapse of a bed. Botham explained to his wife that it wasn't true; his teammate Les Taylor shared his room and broke the bed, not him. In his latest book, *Head On: The Autobiography*, he said, 'Ms Field was a good-looking woman but beyond a few bland pleasantries on the drive to the restaurant I hardly spoke to her and spent the evening chatting with Mick Jagger about cricket. I went back to our hotel with Gerry (his father-in-law) and Les and forgot all about Ms Field. Later, one of our friends told me some interesting news about her: it turned out that she had a very expensive cocaine habit to support, suggesting a strong motive for her to want to concoct a lucrative story of the Press.'

After a big row in which he said their marriage was over, the Bothams woke the next day in a different frame of mind. The marriage was back on and Kathy was reported to have said, 'Everyone has been wonderful, friends and family, everyone.'

According to the *Mail*, Botham gave her a big hug and said, 'Now I just want to get on and play cricket.'

A few years later, Audrey and I were having dinner in a new restaurant in the centre of Dulwich Village. The owner was a rather tubby, attractive lady in her late thirties, and she spoke with a Bajan accent. I asked her, 'Do you come from Barbados?'

'I certainly do,' she said.

We had a lively conversation and she told us that she was about to give birth. Apparently, the father was the tall young man who was waiting on the tables. I suspected that the proud mother may well be the former Barbados beauty queen Lindy Field. 'You're right,' she said.

'Is it true that the bed collapsed?' I said.

'Yes,' she said. 'And I'm going to mention that in my book, which I am going to write about the whole matter. There were many other things that happened, other people involved.'

We had a pleasant meal and wished her and her boyfriend a successful birth. The restaurant was obviously unsuccessful and shortly afterwards it was taken over by another owner. But there was a happy end to the story. Some months later I read a small paragraph saying that Ms Field had won £200,000 in the National Lottery. That might explain why she hasn't written the book. If she had, it would have run into legal problems.

In 1984, Botham foolishly signed up Tim Hudson as his agent, replacing Reg Hayter, the former cricket writer who ran a sports agency. Reg played cricket until his seventies and was universally liked; the Cricket Writers' Club paid for a commemorative plaque for him in the Lord's Media Centre, the only person to be so honoured. Getting rid of him and substituting Hudson, a bizarre character with links to drugs, was like taking off David Beckham and bringing on Pete Doherty. One of Hudson's most quoted remarks was about cannabis: 'Doesn't everyone smoke pot?' He convinced Botham that he would be a star in Hollywood and dressed him up as a cowboy wearing a stetson and carrying two pistols. The trip to California was a disaster. Undaunted, Hudson launched several more ventures, one of them dressing up his clients, including Botham and Viv Richards, in gaudy blazers to invoke Rastafarian culture. He wanted Botham to wear a pirate-style earring and a headband with St George's flag on it when he went in to bat. Hudson was living in an odd, sprawling house in Cheshire named Birtles Hall and it had its own cricket ground and pavilion. I got to know him over the summer and you couldn't take him seriously. He invited me to play against his all-star team and nearly all the players were Test players of repute. It must have cost him a lot of money to assemble them. His American wife Maxi was wealthy and maybe that was the explanation.

I faced the bowling of Franklyn Stephenson, the former West Indian fast bowler and professional golfer who bowled the finest slow delivery of all time. No one matched it. He could run up fast in his usual manner with his right arm whirling over and the ball appeared to come at you as a fast beamer aimed at the head. Instead, it was a very slow lob, and countless batsmen were taken unawares, particularly Chris Read of England and Nottinghamshire, who was made a fool of in one match. As a believer in not moving your feet until the ball is on the way, I was able to swing the bat at the gentle delivery and it flew low and straight to Phil Simmons, the West Indian and Trinidadian all-rounder. Phil was standing four yards away at point and caught the ball effortlessly close to his ankles. There were so many famous players thronging the tiny pavilion that it was impossible to return to the dressing room, so I took off my gear and put it into the boot of my car.

Audrey was having a conversation with Maxi about art. 'I've got a wonderful collection at the Hall,' said Maxi. 'Do you want to come and look at it? The door is open.'

Audrey was keen to see it and we set off up the hill on foot to the Hall. As Audrey started to open the door, Maxi drove her car up and with tyres screaming, skidded to a halt. She jumped out, shouting, 'Get out! Don't go in! Clear off!' We were rather surprised, especially as she had made the offer a few minutes earlier. We had to walk back to the pavilion.

'What's all that about?' I asked Audrey.

'Well it might be the pungent smell coming from inside,' she said.

Eventually, Botham realised he had been foolish and asked his lawyer to end his relationship with Hudson. He admitted it had nearly cost him his marriage and that he was in danger of becoming an international joke. Since then, Botham has prospered and has done a tremendous amount of work raising money for charity. He was knighted for that work, not for the self-indulgence encouraged by Hudson.

Sarah Ferguson, the Duchess of York, was good friends with Lady Diana for a while. Like Diana and Charles, Fergie's marriage to Prince Andrew didn't last. Fergie had a very different personality to Diana, as I discovered when I met her on 7 October 1999. Her father, Major Ronald Ferguson, invited me to a press night at his indoor cricket school in Dummer in Hampshire, where he was born in 1931. A company was advertising a cure for arthritis and as a sufferer, he wanted to do his bit to promote it. I remember it cost £199 and I told him, 'I've got arthritis but I'll wait a year or two before lashing out on that.'

He was sixty-eight and still opened the batting for his village side. One of the players present on that press night said, 'He stays at the crease but he doesn't hit it off the square. He's very keen though.'

Fergie showed her exuberant nature as she went around the building introducing herself. She laughed at the slightest thing and when Arthur Edwards, the *Sun* photographer who made his name snapping members of the royal family, arrived, she squealed with delight and gave him a smacker of a kiss. 'I've got someone to bring along a beautiful birthday cake for you,' said Arthur.

It was Fergie's fortieth birthday and he wanted a picture of her lighting the candles. After the short speeches, the cake, inscribed with the words 'Fergie Fab at Forty', was carried in and Fergie was handed a box of matches. She lit one and began to light the first candle. Suddenly flames shot high into the air, scorching her eyebrows. She jerked her head back and roared with laughter. 'You naughty man!' she screeched. They were trick candles. If it had been Princess Anne, it might have provoked anger. But she took it as a practical joke.

Known as 'the Galloping Major', Ronald was polo manager to the Duke of Edinburgh and later the Prince of Wales. After Sarah's marriage in 1988, the *News of the World* printed a story about his membership of a massage parlour in London whose female employees performed sexual services. He was sacked as polo manager to Prince Charles and moved on to working for the Royal Berkshire Club. Caught having a relationship with a young polo events manager, which was also reported in a newspaper, he was dismissed. He said, 'Men get carried away sometimes.' I found him a nice, engaging man and was sad to hear in 2003 that he had died of heart attack after contacting prostate cancer. Prince Charles showed his loyalty to his former polo manager by attending the funeral. The Major had wanted to have a cricket ground next to his cricket indoor school, but he ran out of time.

Sometime later I wrote to Lieutenant Commander Aylard asking if Charles would be interested in speaking at one of our dinners. He wrote back, saying that the Prince of Wales had a busy programme and that the prospects were not good. Charles isn't a cricket lover, unlike his father. Prince Philip played a number of matches after the Second World War, including several in front of large crowds at Arundel. He was an off spinner. He has been patron of the Forty Club, the club of veteran cricketers who take on the public schools, since 1961, and in 1985 he wrote to the club congratulating it on its first fifty years. He wrote, 'Human civilisation can only survive if the older generations are willing to pass on the fruits of their experience to a younger generation willing to learn. Cricket can only flourish if it is played by civilised people with the highest standards of sportsmanship and humour.' Some of today's Test stars all around the world should take note of those last three words!

Above: 36. The *Wolverhampton Express & Star* cricket team in 1958 with Don Howe (back row, second from left) and myself (far right). Both of us had hair then! (*A. Higgins*)

Below: 37. Roughing it in the open air 'press box' in Arad, Romania. (*Carleton Photographic Services*)

Left: 38. Interviewing Eusébio, the Portuguese star of the 1966 World Cup.

Below: 39. A better class of press box in Spain. Left to right: Derek Potter, Jeff Powell, me.

Opposite: 40. On duty as Dave Sexton leaves Chelsea on 3 October 1974 in the shadow of the new £2 million stand. (*Sporting Pictures Ltd*)

Above: 41. With Pat Godbold, Audrey, and Bobby and Elsie Robson at Bobby's book launch. (*Daily Mail*)

Below left: 42. Kerry Packer, with arms crossed, waits to hear the Mayor of Harrogate's speech at the English Press XI *v.* Australian Press XI in 1978. David Lord, his enemy, stands with his hands in his pockets. I am pensive.

Below right: 43. In Zimbabwe. I am apprehensive as I look past President Canaan Banana.

Opposite: 44. The last time I reported on Stan Matthews, he was sixty-seven! Here he is at Grangemouth on 19 April 1981. (*Brian Fair*)

Above: 45. With Philip Webster, *The Times'* political correspondent, in Delhi.

Above: 46. Relaxing with Ron Greenwood, Steve Tongue, and Bryon Butler (of BBC Radio) in Madrid, 1982.

Below: 47. With Trevor Brooking and Michael Hart of the *Evening Standard* at the 1982 World Cup.

Above: 48. The first cricketing engagement for the Princess of Wales at Gloucestershire CCC in Bristol. On the right is secretary Graham Parker.

Below: 49. Jimmy Hill confronts the *Mail*'s Jeff Powell in Guadalajara, Mexico, during the 1986 World Cup.

Above: 50. David Lawrence becomes the Cricket Writers' Club's 'Young Cricketer of the Year' in 1985. (*John Walters*)

Below: 51. Ashley Metcalfe (left) and James Whitaker (right) are joint recipients of the CWC's 'Young Cricketer of the Year' award on 23 April 1987. (*John Chapman*)

Above: 52. With B. S. Chandrasekhar and Alan Simpson MP in India.

Below: 53. Revving up to start Sir Gary Sobers' autobiography in Barbados.

Above: 54. Bobby Robson ponders a question in the old Wembley Stadium

Below: 55. Bob Findlay, at various times the sports editor of the *Daily Sketc*
on his eightieth birthday.

Above: 56. Sir Len Hutton walking off the Oval, the scene of his 1938 world record, just before he died in 1990.

Below: 57. Ready to take on Wandgas CC with former Australian Test opening batsman Michael Slater in 2005.

Above: 58. Brian Lara with his father, Bunty.

Below: 59. Celebrating my sixtieth birthday at the Oval with Audrey. Two great sports writers helped to shape my career – Ian Wooldridge (second from the left) and Laurie Pignon (right).

Above: 60. Speaking at a Middlesex Wanderers dinner honouring Dave Mackay.

Below: 61. The Fleet Street XI touring India. Back row, from left: Alan Simpson (first on the left), Nick Hewer (sixth, Alan Sugar's PR man), Phil Webster (seventh, *The Times'* political correspondent), Nick Wood (eleventh, *The Times*), Michael Cockerell (thirteenth, BBC), Mihir Bose (fourteenth, *The Daily Telegraph*), Michael Evans (fifteenth, *The Times'* defence correspondent), myself (sixteenth), Richard Heller (seventeenth). Front row: The WAGs.

Right: 62. At the Lord's Nursery with the Media Centre in the background, 2009.

Below: 63. Opening stand of 96 for the Stoics at the new Test ground at Dambulla in Sri Lanka with former Pakistan Test captain Aamir Sohail.

Next page: 64. Frank Wiechula glancing at my scoop, 21 September 1993.
(*Dave Shopland*)

CHAPTER NINETEEN

Three Lives Too Many!

Most people experience a near-death experience in their lives and I've had twelve, plus a few near misses. I have been very fortunate; nine lives is normally the limit. The most terrifying incident took place at the airport in Nagpur, one of the dirtiest, most disorderly cities I have ever visited. On 20 September 1989 I was reporting on Manchester United's 3-2 win at Portsmouth's archaic Fratton Park when Cammie Stewart, the *Mail*'s assistant sports editor, rang to say that Peter Johnson, the paper's number one cricket writer, had to go into hospital for a heart operation. 'We're sending you to India to cover the Nehru Cup,' he said.

I've toured India four times, three as a player with various clubs, and this turned out to be the most sapping trip of all. When I arrived at Heathrow, I discovered I had left my passport at home, but Air India let me through without one. Their generosity continued when I landed in Bombay. I was whisked off to a VIP room and after the usual presentation of garlands and a soft drink, I was invited to join the coach for the early morning practice. They thought I was a player or an official. Micky Stewart, the England manager and an old friend, said, 'What are you doing here? You better get your bowling boots on.'

Nasser Hussain, born in Madras, was at the age of twenty-one the youngest in a strong England squad, but he wasn't given a game, which upset him. Everywhere he went, he was pestered for tickets. 'I am related to you sir,' they would say. 'Please sir, please!'

Every two or three days, we were flying beat-up airplanes transporting up to four international cricket squads all over the country, with the insurance cover adding up to millions of US dollars. Halfway through the tour, en route from Hyderabad to Bhubaneswar via Nagpur, several of England's seventeen-strong team were suffering from the inevitable Delhi belly. English players tended to accept the advice of their medical people and take precautionary tablets, but Bobby Simpson, who was in charge of the Australian squad, said, 'I've been on four tours to India and I've never had Delhi belly. I ate the local food, avoided water, and stayed fit.'

A four-hour wait at Nagpur – short by Indian standards – was spent trying to make abortive telephone calls back to the UK. The Boeing 737 was refuelled and eventually we were herded back on, escorted by vast numbers of soldiers carrying First World War Lee Enfield rifles. All safely strapped in, the captain welcomed the famous passengers as the fully laden aircraft started taxiing down a side runway towards the main runway. Most of the players were dozing or not paying attention, but looking to my left from my window seat I suddenly saw a turbo-prop aircraft just landing. To my horror, it was on a collision course with our 737. Allan Border, the Australian captain, shouted, 'Geez, look at that!' The heads swung round and the suntanned faces turned a different hue. Panic stations! There was no time to bend to the recommended position, hands around the back of the head, no chance to slip off our shoes. The pilot slammed on the brakes and we crashed into the back of the seats in front. The other airplane roared past less than thirty yards away.

'Wow, that was hairy,' said Wayne Larkins. We straightened our hair, released our safety belts, and stood up to look around to see if anyone was hurt. No one was.

The pilot, rather wizened and grey-bearded, was coming slowly down the aisle. I asked him what happened. 'Everything is under control,' he said with a wan smile.

Peter Lush, the England manager, said, 'It was slightly disconcerting at the time but you have to accept you are in good hands and the pilot reacted in the right way. Obviously it wasn't the best confidence booster but the players are all fine.' In good hands? Someone should have seen that airplane much earlier in the proceedings!

It was late in the evening, and I was sitting on the best story of the tour, unable to phone it over to *The Mail on Sunday*. When the plane landed at Bhubaneswar, there was an announcement over the Tannoy informing us that the pilot was celebrating his seventieth birthday and would be presented with a commemorative trophy. All the players wanted to do was to get to the hotel and get some sleep before the match against Pakistan, which was due to start six hours later. Eventually I found a telephone in the hotel lobby – the one in my room wasn't working – and at 10 p.m. English time I phoned over the story – a scoop because none of the other writers had managed to get through. Ted Dexter, the TCCB chairman, was with the squad and was suffering from laryngitis. He was speechless.

Few of the journalists were able to provide any scoops or even uneventful stories to their newspapers from Kanpur, the grubby, ghastly city that was famously besieged during the Indian Mutiny in 1857. The phones never worked and we had to walk through smelly streets covered by cow, dog, and monkey excrement – in preference to the ultra-dangerous three-wheeler tuk-tuks – to the communications office in the centre. The friendly manager welcomed us in. 'There are sixty fax machines available, all manned,' he said. 'Unfortunately only one is working.' I started to type out my message. Suddenly the power was cut off. It took an hour to be restored. At the hotel, the lights were coming on and off all day and night, mainly off. These trips are the best, because it's fun and you never know what is happening next. And the majority of Indians are so polite and helpful.

My son Gavin had a similar experience at Nagpur. He was directing the ESPN television coverage of the India *v.* Pakistan series in November and December 2007 and was on the plane taking the Indian and Pakistan squads to its next destination when an eagle crashed into an engine. With an engine out of action, the pilot had to turn back and execute a successful emergency landing. 'It was pretty scary,' said Gavin.

The second scariest air flight I experienced was on 18 March 1980, when Arsenal were on the way to playing a second leg European Cup Winners' Cup tie in Gothenburg. They won the first leg 5-1 and the players were blasé about visiting a snowbound city just emerging from a severe winter. Most of them were playing cards when the pilot started making his announcement just before the landing. 'If you look over on the right side,' he said, 'you will see the emergency services lined up on the runway.' The cards were suddenly stilled and those on that side looked out of the windows and were able to see the fire engines and other vehicles.

'Christ,' said Graham Rix. 'What the hell's going on?'

The pilot continued on the intercom. 'We have a slight problem with the landing gear,' he said. 'We will be coming in low to check things but may have to go up again. But there is nothing to worry about.'

Worry? They all looked as though these were their last minutes on earth; they appeared ashen-faced and wild-eyed. One or two called for stiff drinks but with the safety belt signs switched on there was no chance of that happening. The chartered aircraft began losing height and even the loquacious manager Terry Neill hardly spoke a word. Time was dragging and it seemed an interminable amount of time before the plane was low enough for someone with binoculars to check from the control centre that the wheels had been lowered. A steward said, 'I was told that they had to lock as well. The light has to light up to say it's OK, but it wasn't showing.' What that meant was that the plane could hit the tarmac and the wheels could collapse. Coming in at 160 mph on an icy surface could easily have resulted in another 6 February 1958 – when BEA Flight 609 crashed on its third attempt to take off at Munich-Riem Airport, killing twenty-three of the forty-four passengers, including eight Manchester United players. As our plane swept over, the pilot eased it back up again and circled around before coming in for his final descent.

The tension, for some, was almost unbearable. The players were leaning forward with their heads bowed and their arms behind their heads, ready just in case the landing went wrong and the plane burst into a fireball. There was total silence. What do you think in these moments? Rather surprisingly, I wasn't wracked with fear and my hands were not sweaty. Oh well, I thought, no one can do anything about it. There is no point pumping up one's blood pressure unnecessarily.

We were almost down and there was a huge thud as the wheels landed, accompanied by roars from the players behind. 'Good one,' said John Hollins, the calmest of the lot. Chairman Peter Hill-Wood promised to pay for a round for the whole squad in the hotel bar. He did, and he included the aircrew.

The next evening, we were greeted with a rock-hard pitch before the kick-off. The game ought not to have been played. The temperature was below freezing when it kicked off. Today's health and safety experts would have intervened and asked the referee to call it off. Hollins cut his knee on the rutted ice and had to go off for stitches. Fred Street, Arsenal's physio, said, 'It didn't bleed because it was so cold.'

The Swedes were the first to introduce compulsory stretchers to carry off players around that time and Holly didn't want to be carted off. He preferred to walk off, but they insisted he had to lie on the stretcher and be picked up. Sven-Göran Eriksson was the manager of the Gothenburg side. There were two little huts on the halfway line to house the teams' staff and there were strips of heating above, so it was quite warm. Even at that stage, Sven had a look of strength, and people respected him. I wasn't surprised when he became an international manager. He didn't talk a lot, but he carried himself well.

I was in other flights when aircraft suddenly dropped, losing hundreds of feet without reason. The worst was on a twin-prop Herald taking forty-five passengers from the Canary Islands to Tunis on an air cruise. They were fashionable in the 1960s. We were crossing the Atlas Mountains when the noisy, bumpy plane fell like a meteor, or so it seemed. The panic lasted several seconds and we wondered whether we would come out of it. Luckily we did, but we were trembling. It was time for prayer. Gavin experienced a similar free fall travelling in Pakistan in 2009. The aircraft was a Boeing 747 and they are not supposed to do it, but this one went hurtling towards the ground before it pulled out of its terrifying free fall.

When I was three, our family were sitting on the crowded beach in Ventnor enjoying the sunshine. Our picnic had finished and I was toddling around in the shallow water. None of them took any notice when I started sliding down the steep bank of sand a dozen or so yards further up the beach and disappeared under the water. But a nearby sunbather was watching and he said to my mother, 'Your son has gone under. Is he a good underwater swimmer?' She was horrified. The man ran into the water and pulled me out. He banged a hand on my back a couple of times and there were no side effects.

More than thirty years later, Audrey and I took the children on a holiday in the Mediterranean, a week in Propriano in Corsica followed by a week in Santa Theresa in the Costa Smeralda in Sardinia. The Corsican holiday was rustic and we had to climb over beds to get to the toilet in the cramped hotel room. There was no shower and we were allocated just one towel between the four of us. After two days, I asked the courier if we could have some towels. 'Here,' he said. 'Borrow mine!'

The day we were leaving for Sardinia, we were turfed out of the rooms at nine although the coach wasn't due to pick us up until eleven. So we went on to the beach to play Scrabble. Another family arrived and their children were the same age as ours. We started talking with them and they told us they came from Ipswich. Just before we were setting off, I saw their three-year-old daughter run down the shingle, straight into the sea, and disappear. It was an uncanny rerun of my own experience at Ventnor. I shouted to the father, 'Your daughter has gone under.'

'Oh my God,' he said as he started running into the sea. He yanked out the child, who was breathing hard. When things calmed down, he thanked me and we exchanged addresses.

We didn't contact each other but ten years later I was in a pub near Ipswich with Bobby Robson, interviewing him for his ghostwritten book, aptly named *Time on the Grass*, when a familiar figure arrived, went up to Bobby, and congratulated him on his latest UEFA Cup success. I realised it was him. 'This man saved my daughter's life,' he said to Bobby, pointing to me. 'And I'll never forget it.' I asked him about his daughter and he said, 'Sadly, the marriage broke up and it's not the same.'

There are two other occasions in my life when I nearly drowned, both in the West Indies, where I have spent around a dozen very happy holidays and a few working trips. The first saga started on Good Friday, 9 April 1993. One of my front crowns had fallen out at Bromley South station and Audrey had a bad cold. When I returned home from covering Crystal Palace's 4-0 defeat by Wimbledon at my least preferred football ground, Selhurst Park, the phone rang. It was Cammie Stewart again, the portender of surprise foreign trips. 'Four Pakistan Test cricketers have been arrested in Grenada for supposedly taking drugs and Pakistan are threatening to call off their tour of the West Indies,' he said. 'Get out there!'

He never asked about my health or my tooth. I would be travelling with a big gap in my top front teeth and it was too late to arrange a temporary tooth. The next morning, I caught the 10.50 a.m. flight to Grenada and when I arrived in the Spice Island I was taken in a battered old taxi to the $150-a-night Ramada, nowhere near the hotel where the Pakistan squad was staying. I looked up the number of the Coyaba Beach Resort, which was housing the angry Pakistanis, and booked myself in. You need luck on these solo trips and I had it. I discovered my room had been used by Khalid Mahmood, the Pakistan manager, who had moved to another room. When the phone rang, the calls were for him, not me. A very helpful police officer told me what was happening. 'By tomorrow night we will be able to make a decision on whether the players should be charged or released to go off to Trinidad for the Test starting in four days,' he said.

There was another break for me. Trinidadian human rights lawyer Ramesh Lawrence Maharaj was also staying in the hotel and he told me that skipper Wasim Akram, Waqar Younis, Aqib Javed, and Mushtaq Ahmed were due to appear in court for a preliminary hearing on charges of 'constructive possession of marijuana'. He explained that the 'whiffs' were found near the players on the beach in front of the Grand Anse Hotel the previous evening, and said, 'I think they have been framed.' Eight hand-rolled cigarettes were found on beach chairs and two English women and a Grenadian were also arrested. Mahmood, a Harvard law graduate, said, 'I haven't the slightest doubt these boys are innocent. There isn't a scrap of evidence.' The police commissioner, Nestor Ogilvie, refused to accept the players' explanations. If the tour had been called off, massive court actions would follow.

Aqib, who had a season with Hampshire and was much later banned for betting on matches, said, 'It was crazy what happened. Someone gave us a bottle of rum and we drank from it which I know we shouldn't have done. A man came up and asked us for money and we gave him some and then two others arrived, grabbed us and said, "We've found this!" We were taken away by the police and Akram cut his head as he fell in the cell. They didn't help him and made nasty comments.'

The next day I sat outside my room waiting for calls, which were many. At 6 p.m. a young policeman came up and, thinking I was Mahmoud, said, 'They've got clearance. The Test will go ahead.' I thanked him and went inside to telephone the story to the *Mail*. It was a very satisfying scoop.

The Pakistanis were playing against a West Indies XI the next day. I delayed my departure and decided to use the swimming pool to do some exercises. Everyone had left and as I checked to see the depths of each side of the pool I noticed the sign 'five feet deep'. I clambered in and swashed towards the middle of the pool. Shock horror! Suddenly I had found myself in the nine-foot-deep section, well out of my depth. The notices were the wrong way round. Shouting for help was a waste of time. I was now ten yards from the nearest side of the pool and found myself sinking to the bottom. I struggled up again, only to fall to the bottom once more. If panic had set in I might have drowned but for some reason – help from above I think! – I didn't and managed to reach safety. I dried myself quickly and rushed to the reception, more than thirty yards away.

'You could have killed me!' I said to the clerk. 'You've got those signs around the wrong way.'

He smiled like a typical Grenadian. 'Maybe,' he said. 'But you're all right so what's the problem. Just relax. Have a good day sir.'

Still agitated, I said, 'If I were an American I would sue this hotel and pick up thousands of dollars.'

He laughed. 'Well, you're not a Yank so you're unlucky.'

I was completely disarmed. 'Have a drink,' he said and I did.

The following day I joined the Pakistan team on the flight to Port of Spain and had my first look at Brian Lara. He was twenty-three and should have played much earlier but for politicking in West Indies cricket. He scored ninety-six in the second innings while fifteen of his colleagues mustered forty-six runs with none of them passing ten. His technique, self-taught, was amazing, and his strokeplay was audacious. In my report I neglected to mention him because all the space was devoted to Desmond Haynes, who scored 143 and wasn't clapped by the Pakistanis when he reached his century. Three years before, he had called Akram a cheat and these things are rarely forgotten. After he was cleared of the drugs accusations, Akram sold his story to *The Sun* and when I arrived at the ground an irate Vic Robbie, the *Mail's* sports editor, called me, saying, 'You've let me down. You haven't got any quotes from Akram.' I had to explain that the great all-rounder had taken cash for his first-person story and although I had a nice chat with him at breakfast, he declined to be quoted. But I still had the best story about it.

The Port of Spain pitch was the lowest bouncing pitch I've ever seen. There were seventeen batsmen given out lbw, a world record, and six of them were given out by Dickie Bird. 'They're all out, you know,' Dickie kept insisting. I was toying with the idea of bringing out a tribute book to him and thought that this would make for a wonderful chapter. Three years later I brought it out and it topped the non-fiction bestsellers' list. It was extremely pleasing to see that Sebastian Faulks' book *A Fatal Englishman* was in eighth position. He wrote a nasty review of one of my books and I wrote back criticising his lack of cricket knowledge. His letter to me was written in copperplate script. I admired his writing.

Dickie lives in a white eighteenth-century cottage where John Wesley stayed for a while. Geoff Boycott, who has acquired similar wealth from his writings, used to live across the moor. 'I don't know where he's hidden his money,' Dickie would say. After the Test against Pakistan, I took the overnight flight from Port of Spain and arrived at

Heathrow at 9.30 a.m. That evening I reported on Arsenal *v.* Nottingham Forest, 1-1. Yes, that was life in sport's faster lane. It is called unbridled enthusiasm.

The closest I have been to drowning was on 29 April 2003, covering the West Indies series against Australia in the Caribbean. The day before, Tony Cozier held his usual pre-Test party at his wooden property in Consett Bay, on the more rugged side of Barbados. He usually invites most of the TV commentators, including two of the more macho men of Australian cricket, David Hookes and Jeff Thomson. I don't know if it was because they were drinking a lot of beer, but both of them kept tripping over my stiff leg as they walked past where I was sitting. It happened a number of times and neither of them apologised. What do you say? Do you come up with a smart retort or do you ignore it? I decided to keep quiet. Both were aggressive types, rather boorish in manner, and like everyone, I was shocked some time later when Hookes was struck in the face by a nightclub bouncer. He fell, hit his head on the ground, and died.

The next day, Jillian and Tony Cozier and a group of friends went for a swim at the most popular beach in Barbados. Accra Beach was next to the hotel where the Australians were staying. When we first visited Barbados, in 1967, Audrey and I often called in on Accra. The waves were always high and even a non-swimmer like me could be swept towards the beach for a vast distance without touching the bottom – very exhilarating. On this occasion, the waves were higher than usual because it was a neap tide, and I should have been more cautious. Around thirty-five yards from the beach, I jumped up ready for a big wave to carry me in, but this time a wall of water sent me flying. I found myself facing the opposite way, being bundled along under the water at great speed. I panicked, taking in huge gulps of water, and tried to locate the sand below with my left leg, the strong one, but failed. My heart was beating like a frenzied drummer. I feared that I might have another heart attack, which would have been the end. I've never encountered such a feeling. I could have died without anyone noticing what had happened. I found myself hitting the sand for a split second before another huge wave tumbled me over, head first. Suddenly, I saw a glimpse of a rather tall man nearby as I went under again and screamed, 'Help!' He dived in and picked me up in his arms like a child. It was a member of our party, a six-foot-six Canadian named John. In the trauma, I never found out his name, or his address. I was in such a state that I was hardly able to speak. It was some time before my heartbeat returned to normal.

'You all right?' asked Jillian.

'I am now,' I said. 'But it could have been dicey.' I have been back to Accra several times but I will never go into the sea there again. My recklessness might have stopped me seeing a wonderful innings by Brian Lara.

I must have driven more than a million miles and I have experienced dozens of near misses on the road. One of the most mystifying happened while I was coming home from a football match in the North at around 1.30 a.m. when a driver of a car coming in the other direction kept flashing his lights. There was only one other vehicle in sight and in those days the motorway wasn't lit up. I was driving at around 80 mph and wondered whether he was giving me a warning: it might have been a speed trap, so I slowed down to 50 mph. Out of the dark I saw a lorry blocking all three lanes right in front of me. Fortunately I had my light on full beam and was able to stop in time. There was no one around – no sign of the driver or any damage. Rather mysterious! I managed to squeeze past on the hard shoulder and continued my journey. But if the other driver hadn't flashed his lights I might have smashed into the lorry with possibly fatal consequences.

Another incident followed a Test match at Trent Bridge, which ended midway through the second session of the fourth day. This time I knew nothing about it until it happened. From my teenage years, I had suffered from hay fever and none of the treatments had really worked. Ted Dexter was standing in the press box that day, watching me sneezing. He was a sufferer as well and said to me, 'Try some of these. They work for me.' I swallowed a couple and in a short time, I was back to normal: no more sneezing. It was a very hot day and I had the roof open and some of the windows as well. Traffic was reasonably heavy and driving along at 80 mph I suddenly found myself waking up after falling asleep and seeing my sturdy brown Rover 2000, sold to me by Ken Barrington, bouncing off the near side barrier and lurching into the middle lane, just missing another car. For a few seconds it was rocking precariously and I feared it might overturn and crash. After a few hundred yards it stabilised and the other drivers alongside and behind were looking at me in astonishment. The vehicle was still going, but it was impossible to see the damage. The next motorway café was coming up and I drove into the car park and got out to inspect the damage. The whole of the far side was roughed up as if it had passed through a giant mangle, but amazingly no windows had been broken. It must have been a glancing blow. A few hundred yards further, the motorway barrier had come to an end and a line of trees was close to the motorway. If I had been rudely awoken a second or two later, I might have gone straight into them. When I took the car into a garage the next day, the owner said, 'You were very lucky to survive that.' The bill for the repairs came to £1,500.

Ken Barrington died of a massive heart attack in Barbados during an England tour of the West Indies in 1981, so he never knew what mischief I had wrought on his prized car. He was the most fastidious of men. He ran a garage in Great Bookham for a while and the day after I bought the Rover 2000, he rang and said, 'I hope you're looking after it. Keep it clean and drive carefully.' He was a wonderful man and the course of English cricket might have been different had he survived. He was like a guardian angel for the England cricketers of that era. As for my escape from a life-threatening experience, I jokingly 'blamed' Ted Dexter. They must have been the wrong tablets. From that day on, I never had any trouble with hay fever.

Besides my heart attack in 1997 and the accident in 1943 that left me in intensive care for two weeks, there was one other occasion when my life was threatened, although I didn't know about it until two weeks later. My right hip had been painful for more than thirty years and by my late fifties I was having problems walking. Like my mother, who had a deformed leg after contracting poliomyelitis at a young age, I kept putting off surgery, but Audrey kept urging me to do something about it. The health insurance took care of the £7,000 cost of a total hip replacement, a Charnley joint invented by Dr John Charnley. John Woodcock of *The Times* had one and it was thirty-five years, twenty years longer than it should have been, before he had a second replacement. My operation, undertaken by Dr Thomas Bucknill in King Edward VII's Hospital for Officers near Baker Street, went painlessly, or so it seemed. When I woke up a nurse asked me how I felt.

'Fine,' I said.

'What about getting up?' she asked.

Alhough a little dozey, I started to sit up and slid gingerly off the bed with the weight of my body on my left leg, the stronger one. It was a remarkable that anyone could rise from a four-hour operation and actually stand up. They offered me painkilling tablets but I rejected them. They did insist on inserting a rectal suppository.

After two days, they gave me sticks and I was walking up and down the corridor. Within twelve days I was discharged and starting physiotherapy in a local hospital. Liz Richardson, the lady in charge, gave me a list of exercises, and I still do them every day, either on the bed while watching the BBC News at 7.30 a.m. or in the swimming pool in Beckenham Spa. Most people with hip replacements do hardly any exercises afterwards, not realising the joint has to be protected by strong muscles. They give up most of their sporting activities and that is another mistake. Keep moving, I tell them.

A month later I was in the clear, beautiful sea of Negril in Jamaica, courtesy of Butch Stewart, the owner of Sandals Resorts and Air Jamaica. Butch sent one of his chauffeur-driven Mercedes 420s to pick Audrey and me up from Kingston Airport. Espe, the trainer at Sandals, was a class one football referee who had been in charge of a number of international football matches, and she took charge of my rehabilitation. Despite much effort on my behalf, I still couldn't learn to swim properly. A few days after the operation, I noticed a front tooth had been displaced. It must have happened during the anaesthetic work for my hip surgery. I saw my dentist after we returned home and he explained, 'It was one of your ten crowns and the post was bent. It would be impossible for normal masticatory forces and I think it is caused by the use of a laryngoscope during general anaesthesia.' He reckoned it would cost £300 to put right.

I applied to BUPA for a rebate but it was turned down. The anaesthetist, Dr Richard Langford, was a very amenable man and I wrote to him about it and suggested that he should waive his bill of £259. A few days later he rang to say he was agreeable. 'What sometimes happens is that the patient's eyelids start going blue and the laryngoscope has to be whipped out,' he said.

I asked Robin Torrance, my dentist, about the chances of expiry during an anaesthetic and he said, 'Once the lids go blue you have to act very fast.' So I owe a lot to Dr Langford for his alertness.

It wasn't a near miss, but there was an occasion when I could have been bumped off by the Ministry of Defence. In 1954 I saw a short article in a newspaper appealing for volunteers to attend the Porton Down research station near Salisbury, all expenses paid for a week plus a reasonable sum. I needed a holiday and called to get the details. Someone told me the boffins at the research station wanted to do tests that would help cure the common cold. The only downside was that you might catch a cold. But young, fit people probably wouldn't. I was quite tempted. Except for going on a cricket tour with Newport CC in South Devon, I hadn't been away on holiday. Fortunately I declined. On 31 January 2008 I saw an item on the *ITV News at Ten* concerning the survivors from the Porton Down experiments. The announcer said they were to be paid £8,300 each after suffering the effects of being administered the nerve gas sarin, as well as CS gas. Some actually died and others were never the same. One sixty-nine-year-old man was interviewed, and he was remarkably calm about this scandalous affair. Many victims would hire lawyers and claim millions of pounds.

The next day *The Sun* reported, 'Forces veterans and others used as human guinea pigs to test poison gasses last night won a £3m payout from the Ministry of Defence. A total of 360 will receive around £8,300 each after being duped into agreeing to the experiments during the Cold War. They were told they were helping to find a cure for the common cold at the Government's infamous Porton Down Research Station. It was set up in 1916 to test chemical and biological weapons. The Government apologised last night to the men and their families, who campaigned for justice for years. But the MoD refused to admit liability for any injuries or ill health the veterans claim to have suffered, fearing massive lawsuits. Defence Minister Derek Twigg told MPs, "The Government accepts there were aspects of the trials where the life of health of participants may have been put at risk." Between 1939 and 1989, the men were offered money and extra leave to be exposed to the gasses. The group's lawyer Alan Care welcomed the settlement, adding, "This is a good deal for the veterans."' I wouldn't have thought so – £8,300 for fifty years of not being in full health!

On my fourth cricket tour of Sri Lanka, with the Stoics Crusaders in February 2008, some of the wives were apprehensive about being there because bombs were going off after the civil war had flared up again. The week before we left, Kshenuka Senewiratne, the High Commissioner of Sri Lanka, whose embassy is just round the corner from Tony Blair's much-protected property, assured us that there would be no losses among the tourists. 'We've never lost a tourist,' she said with a laugh.

Our second match was at the new Test ground at Dambulla and on the jungle road from the hotel we saw a bus that had impacted with a large lorry, blocking the road. We thought it was an accident, but we soon discovered that it was the bus that had been blown up by a bomb three weeks earlier, causing twenty deaths. A former police superintendent, who was in charge of the Dambulla ground, explained: 'We are having forensic tests on the bus and it is still there. It was unfortunate that it happened because a judge had ruled that security was too oppressive and the Government withdrew some of its security people. Now the Government has re-imposed the strict security. They should have ignored the judge. It will be back to normal, you can be assured of that fact.'

Sadly he was wrong. Eight days later, another bus was attacked at Mount Lavinia, six miles south of Colombo. We were staying at the nearby Mount Lavinia Hotel, built in 1806 and named after the beautiful Lavinia, the Portuguese-Sri Lankan exotic dancer who was the mistress of the English governor. He had a tunnel built beneath the hotel to rendezvous with her in secret. We booked out the day before an explosion happened not far away. A parcel bomb was planted by Tamil Tigers – the rebels from the north of the island fighting for independence – in a privately owned bus.

'Casualties would have been far greater if an alert passenger had spotted the booby-trapped package and shouted at people to get out of the vehicle,' said Brigadier Udaya Nanayakkara.

A passenger named Mervyn Silva said, 'I noticed the package on a vacant seat [a rarity – Sri Lankan buses and trains are nearly always crammed] and when no one claimed it I alerted the bus crew and shouted to the passengers to get off and run.'

A spokesman from the Ministry of Defence said, 'The bus was evacuated and as the crew rang the nearby police station, the bomb went off. The terrorists' beastly intention to commit carnage against civilians was foiled due to the vigilance of the civilians themselves. The bus was totally destroyed.'

Eighteen people were injured and later the Ministry reported that 1,487 terrorists had been killed in the first seven weeks of the year. The conflict has raged, on and off, since 1970, with upwards of 75,000 people dying, mostly Tamils. Early in 2009, the war was finally ended.

The most famous Tamil in the country is Muttiah Muralitharan. He lives in Kandy and I met his brother, who looks similar in appearance but does not have the same bowling action. 'I do not bowl the doosra,' he said. This beautiful island – called Serendipity, then Ceylon, then Sri Lanka – is blessed with niceness yet it had the bloodiest, most enduring internal war in the whole world. The islanders love cricket but even Murali, their most popular sportsman and a Tamil, couldn't solve it.

My son Gavin seems to follow my precarious path, dodging close encounters with danger. On 3 March 2009 he was about to join the rest of his Ten Sports TV crew, who were covering the Pakistan *v.* Sri Lanka Test match in Lahore, when he learned that Waqar Younis, one of his commentators, was still in bed. Thanks to Waqar's lateness, Gavin left ahead of the Sri Lankan team. Otherwise, he would have been in the convoy when terrorists started firing at the team coach, injuring most of the players and killing the driver of the umpires' minivan.

I had just woken and turned on the 7 a.m. Sky News. 'Terrorists have shot at the Sri Lankan players in Lahore today...' intoned the announcer. My heart jumped like a gazelle.

Seconds later I heard Gavin describing the scene. Few people have ever had such a dramatic change of feeling; one second I feared the worst, a few seconds later he was alive and safe. Mark Nicholas told me later, 'He ought to become a foreign correspondent. He was great!' I felt a great surge of pride. Audrey was with him in spirit.

Three weeks later Gavin had to go into hospital, the impressive Charing Cross Hospital near Craven Cottage, to have a lump in his throat checked by the doctors. Like Audrey, he has had problems in that part of his body. He was becoming frustrated with his progress, and his medical insurers insisted that a 'previous medical condition' wasn't covered. Peter Rhys-Evans, one of our former Woodpeckers bowlers, rang me on the same day. Peter is an ear, nose, and throat consultant at the Royal Marsden Hospital and the President of Tillingford CC. He was inviting me to play in his 'President's Match' at his village club. I told him about Gavin and he said, 'I would love to help. Get him to ring me tonight and I can arrange to see him tomorrow.' It was astonishing timing. I hadn't spoken to Peter for two years. Now on the day when a throat consultant was urgently needed, the right man was there. But Gavin, Louise, and I weren't really surprised. This was further proof that Audrey was watching over us. Peter told me he had been having similar psychic experiences since his mother-in-law had died.

CHAPTER TWENTY

Pay Up or We
Don't Play at Wembley!

In February 1991 the Sports Council's British Sports Journalism Awards gave me a citation – 'Highly Commended in the Sports Section' – for my mini-scoop that Bobby Robson was to become manager of PSV Eindhoven after the FA had declined to extend his contract as England manager. He had taken England to the semi-final of the 1990 World Cup in Italy and but for two missed penalties he could well have matched Alf Ramsey's record of being the only English manager to win the trophy. The FA made a terrible mistake by rushing in and appointing Graham Taylor as the new manager before they knew whether England would fail, or, as it turned out, be hailed as heroes. The *Mail* gave the story only a few paragraphs and it wasn't exactly an earth-shaker. In his speech, my good friend John Bromley, the chairman, described me as 'a stalwart and the backbone of the *Mail* sports writing team', which was kind. The BAFTA of sports writing should be one of the highlights of the sporting year, but the presentation, held in a large room in the City, turned out to be rather demeaning. Lots of people turned up to drink, eat, and smoke, and many of them continued talking during the ceremonies. Naturally, I was pleased that I had been recognised, but the way the evening was almost ruined by loudmouths didn't encourage anyone to enter subsequent Sports Journalism Awards.

I entered a year later because I thought another scoop, much more substantial, was far superior to the Robson story. It was about the Cameroon footballers – saluted in the 1990 tournament as 'the Lions of Africa' for raising the profile of African football – refusing to play against England in a friendly at Wembley in February 1991 unless their players were each given envelopes containing £2,000 in sterling, the dreaded 'bung' before the game. The match was in danger of being called off until David Barber, an FA official and historian, arrived at Wembley in a taxi carrying the money with little more than an hour before the kick-off. When they saw the money, the team agreed to go out and play on a freezing, inhospitable night in front of an expectant 61,075 crowd. Their expectations were soon dashed. It was a dreadful game, won by England 2-0. Graham Taylor said, 'I felt a bit sorry for the fans. It was bitterly cold and they were looking for a game from two teams not frightened to lose and they didn't get it.'

Roger Milla, the thirty-nine-year-old centre forward who collected most of the headlines in Cameroon's World Cup campaign, partly because of his habit of wiggling around corner flags to celebrate his goals, refused to play because he thought he deserved a bigger 'bung'. I always believed in spending time with the away side before internationals – some newspapers still don't do it – and this time my orders were to stick with the Cameroon squad. The late Barrie Gill, the agent handling the Guinness sponsorship of the Cameroon squad, was a friend from years back and he gave me a full run-down of what was happening from the time the party had arrived on Sunday. No other journalist tried to court him and the team were happy to attend the press conferences. If I had stayed with the pack, the scoop would have been ruined. The day after the match, most of the newspapers didn't have a line about the financial skulduggery, except one or two, who lifted a few paragraphs from my story. They were unable to follow it up because the Cameroon squad flew from Heathrow at 7.45 a.m. for home. They were almost uncontactable.

I felt sorry for the Cameroon players because there were stories that they hadn't been paid all the money they were owed from the World Cup. Some prominent officials of the Cameroon Federation were sacked for their part in misappropriating the money made from Italia '90. The new officers promised £2,000 a man to appear against England, and half an hour before the team coach left Grosvenor Square, they were still in a team meeting waiting for their cash. The FA's problems started at 3.30 p.m., when one of their officials, Brian Scott, their travel man, arrived at the hotel with the money, US$125,000 made up of $25,000 in cash and a cheque for $100,000. Njikam Simon, the President of the Cameroon Federation, told the players he didn't have enough cash to pay them and the players responded, 'No cash, no game.' The general manager of the Britannia InterContinental Hotel was asked if he could raise the cash to honour the FA's cheque. He rang all the InterContinental Hotels in London without success. Scott contacted the nearby Thomas Cook and arranged for the money to be collected by Barber. The crisis had eased: the coach and its police escorts departed just before 6 p.m. and the eight-mile journey took almost an hour. What would have happened if the game hadn't gone ahead? It would have made history: the first international game to be called off because the 'bungs' hadn't been handed over!

Guinness regretted its decision to sponsor the team and Ken Bruce, the head of sponsorship, told me afterwards, 'Good riddance to them. They ruined all the goodwill they created in Italy. From the time they arrived here on Monday it was one long hassle. Every time we were in the lobby they would come up and ask for money for taxis, physios – you name it and we had to pick up the tab. Our £150,000 sponsorship soon jumped to £250,000. Cameroon TV couldn't afford to buy satellite time for the live coverage of the game back home and we had to pay for that as well.'

On Monday the squad were late for training and Milla rejected an invitation to appear on the Terry Wogan programme. He wanted more than the £150 fee he was offered. At 6.30 p.m. Milla went to the BBC studios in Shepherd's Bush on his own and was refused admission. Wogan didn't want him. The next day, he refused to train and went to Oxford, where a room at Magdalen College was named after him. Asked if he was playing the next day, he said, 'Only if I get a proper fee.'

He refused to say how much he wanted but Roy Mantle, another of Gill's team, said, 'I heard anything between £5,000 and £30,000. Basically he was just trying it on and we told him we weren't going to pay any more than the £2,000 than the others were getting.'

On the day of the match, the Cameroon players refused to train at Roehampton, saying it was too cold, despite the fact that Guinness had given them an extra £10,000 for Yves Saint Laurent coats that cost £300 each, plus thermal underwear, gloves, and shoes. After the game, Philippe Redon, the new coach, said he would be looking for amateur players who would be less temperamental. A good proportion of African players play in English football, but so far only two countries, Cameroon (in 1991 and 1997) and Nigeria (1994), have appeared at Wembley to play against England. The explanation may well involve money, as Guinness discovered.

A month later, I visited South Africa and interviewed Johnny 'Budgie' Byrne, the former Crystal Palace, West Ham, Fulham, and England striker, only one of five players from outside the top two divisions who were picked for England. I lived near him in Croydon in the 1960s and I named my Sunday League side after him – Byrne Nitonians. We were promoted in the first season and relegated in the second. Budgie said, 'Your mob better pack up. I don't want my name associated with failure.' So the club was wound up.

John Joseph Byrne was nicknamed 'Budgie' because he never stopped talking. When I saw him in Cape Town he was coaching the top club Hellenic and he told me, 'The players have plenty of skill but if they played in England they would struggle to beat Woking. They don't travel too well.' Byrne coached a number of clubs in the Cape but although he loved his work, he found it difficult to cope with the financial machinations behind the scenes. Corruption is still rife throughout Africa and that hinders progress towards world recognition.

Budgie was a big drinker and by the time he was fifty his weight had ballooned to twenty stone. 'I'm on Diet Coke now,' he said. Tragically, he died at the age of sixty.

Budgie swore a lot, but hardly anyone complained. He was such a character and swearing is part of the game, almost throughout the world. In 1991, Gordon Taylor, the long-serving and dedicated chief executive of the Professional Footballers' Association, started a campaign to curb swearing. My story about it was headlined 'Players warned: The swearing must stop!'

Paul Gascoigne was sent off for swearing at a referee and I rang Gordon Taylor for his reaction. He said, 'Whatever the provocation, players must hold their breath, count to ten, and walk away. Swearing used to be part of the game and referees like Arthur Ellis and Gordon Hill would let them get away with it. It was the repartee of the game. But now referees are stricter.'

That isn't true now, and far too often we see players of all countries, including those in Africa, say to an official, 'F*** off.' The offending word isn't normally used in their own countries, so how do they pick it up? I blame the managers. Nearly all of them swear to build up tension and make players try harder. If Sir Alex Ferguson and his mates gave the order, 'No more swearing or else,' the problem would fade away. In any other workplace, you don't allow the employees to insult the bosses like that. Lord David Triesman, the first independent chairman of the FA, tried to persuade the managers to set an example, but the results might take generations.

One manager who always set an example was Alec Stock, who managed Yeovil, Orient, Arsenal, Roma, QPR, Luton, and Fulham. He rarely swore. When he was eighty-two and living in a nursing home in Ferndown, I went to see him. Alec was wounded in the Normany landings in 1944 when the tank he commanded was blown up, and he still had the shrapnel in his leg to prove it. 'Going through that experience gave me an ideal training for my life as a manager,' he said. 'It's all about getting the best out of people, isn't it? And it's about a little thing called pride. In my thirty-one years in management I had just four players sent off – four of the nicest guys in the history of the game, Bobby Moore, George Best, Alan Slough, and dear old Les Gore. If someone was show a yellow card it was almost a boardroom matter. Now cards are thrown around like confetti.'

Mohamed Al Fayed paid the expenses of a testimonial match, Yeovil *v.* Fulham, to commemorate the fiftieth anniversary of the greatest result in the Somerset club's history, the 2-1 win over Sunderland in the FA Cup. I wrote, 'Mohamed Al Fayed is unlikely to be at the game, nor is another former Fulham boss, Kevin Keegan.'

Michael Cole, Al Fayed's PR and friend, sent an extraordinary letter to me afterwards. 'I read your piece on Alec Stock with interest,' he wrote. 'I noticed that in the testimonial match at Yeovil the visiting team was not Orient, Arsenal, Roma, QPR or Luton but Fulham and yet at the end you chose to take a swipe at Mohamed Al Fayed because, in your judgment, he was unlikely to attend the game. Why did you do that? Who do you think gave approval for Fulham to play the match and underwrote the cost, in order that Mr Stock might benefit the greater? The answer has to be Mr Al Fayed, so what reason could you possibly have for being snide about him, unless or course you are responding to some directive I know nothing about? I have always respected your work and I shall not let this uncharacteristic lapse change my opinion but I do feel that such a gratuitous comment should have been beneath you. I have been a Fulham supporter since 1954 and it is as a fan of fair play of forty-five years that I write this letter.'

The fact that Al Fayed had another engagement wasn't worth such a pained response. When Fulham moved out of the bottom three in 2008 after their chairman gave them a pep talk, *The Mail on Sunday* reported that Al Fayed 'promised them a hamper full of caviar and Viagra worth £5,000 and I think it must have worked'. I should have written to Michael to complain about Al Fayed's behaviour – leading footballers astray!

Some of my better stories were obtained in car parks. On the evening of the first day of the Lord's Test in 1995 I was returning to my car near the Regent's Park Hilton when I saw Alan Smith, the former Crystal Palace manager, sitting in the front seat of his car with the door open. He waved out and I went over to greet him. He is an intelligent, understanding individual who earned a lot of public sympathy that year over the way he was allowed to leave Selhust Park. He is now an agent. 'Gareth Southgate is joining Aston Villa,' he said. 'I've just been speaking to him. The deal has been done and he'll sign in the morning.'

Southgate was Smith's captain at Palace, a confident young man with a much more lively personality than the average footballer. Although uncapped at that stage, he was rated as one of the outstanding all-round English players in the Premiership. Once Smith departed Palace, he and several of his colleagues asked for transfers. He was one of the first to go. Southgate has since emerged as one of the most promising young English managers, although he is now working as a TV analyst.

When a contact gives you a cracking story, you have to check whether it can be printed, including quotes. I checked with Alan and he said, 'Certainly, but don't connect it with me. But it is definitely going to happen in the morning.' We chatted briefly about the Test match. England had scored a slow 255-8 against some hostile West Indian bowling. It had been a good day for serious cricket watchers such as Alan. 'I'd much sooner be sitting at Lord's with a glass of wine than going to half the football matches I have to go to,' he said. Only a few cars remained in the car park and there was no sign of rival journalists. I thanked him for the tip and drove off. Later, I ad-libbed ten paragraphs and the *Mail* put an exclusive tag on it. No other newspaper had it. Heartening news.

The next morning, I arrived at the car park and a voice shouted, 'Everything I see under your name, it's got exclusive on it.' It was Micky Stewart, the former England cricket manager and England and Surrey cricketer.

'Have you got an exclusive for me?' I asked.

We laughed and exchanged pleasantries before heading off toward the Grace Gates. Eight years later, I was leaving Lord's after a Cricket Writers' Club annual meeting when I noticed one of the pillars at the gates was covered in a tarpaulin. I said to one of the groundstaff, 'What's all this about?'

'A lorry backed into it and it's going to be rebuilt,' he said. 'But it should be ready for the start of the season.'

I rang the office and the sports news editor showed minimal interest. 'Put six pars over,' he said.

'Get a photographer up there,' I said. 'It's a good story: exclusive, too! The most famous cricket ground in the world has its gate knocked over right at the start of the season! Got to be worth more than that.'

The photographer was unable to take a good picture because the tarpaulin was still in place and not a line appeared in the *Mail*. By then I was working as a freelance and I called *The Daily Telegraph* sports desk and they appeared to be keener. I filed twelve pars. Next day, the same. Not a line. I gave the story to the *Evening Standard* and they didn't use it either. It must have been a conspiracy by MI5 acting on behalf of the MCC Committee!

These days freelance sports writers have a hard job surviving. Not me, because I have Associated Newspapers, but I do feel sorry for them. Match fees and payments have been reduced, and expenses have been pruned. One leading commentator, recently retired, told me, 'I've been told that the golf correspondent has been told he can't stay in a top hotel at the Ryder Cup. He's been told to hire a caravan! And it's not a joke.'

CHAPTER TWENTY-ONE

It Might Have Been
Prime Minister John Redwood

The Lord's Test in 1995 yielded a near scoop, and I still blame myself years later for missing it. If I had been more persistent, I might have cracked it. The truth is that John Redwood MP, known among satirists as 'the Vulcan', may well have taken over as leader of the Conservative Party and perhaps become Prime Minister in place of John Major.

The story starts with yet another car park conversation. David Evans, then a maverick and outspoken Conservative MP, had parked his car near mine and we walked over the road to Lord's together. He introduced me to his wife Janice and she said, 'I remember you, you helped me out in a very awkward incident at Wembley a few years ago. Some yobs were making life nasty for me.' I had to say I couldn't recall the incident, but it seemed like a good story.

I first met David Evans in the mid-1970s when he became a director of Luton Town before becoming chairman. A good cricketer, good enough to captain the Club Cricket Conference team, he loved cricket more than football.

During the Packer Affair – a war between the Australian TV mogul Kerry Parker and the international cricket boards – English cricket faced the problem of losing its best players. Money was needed to preserve the standards of Test cricket. It was a situation similar to today's incursion of the Indian Premier League, with its massive salaries and often poor-quality cricket. At least Packer's matches were of a very high standard. Evans announced in the press, 'I'll sponsor Test cricket and I'll pay these cricketers what they deserve. If a couple of other businessmen join me in putting up the money , I'll pay them £1,000 a Test and they won't have to sign up with Packer.'

Through Evans' promotional efforts, Cornhill Insurance started negotiations with the Test and County Cricket Board to sponsor home Test series. I had several talks with their executives and sensing that a deal might be in the offing, I rang the number of their head office and was put through to the boardroom. To my amazement, I found myself talking to Brian Schofield, probably a relative of mine (if you meet a 'Sco' in the UK, chances are they can trace their family back to Escoville).

'We're talking about it now,' he said. 'How did you get through?'

'By perseverance!' I told him.

He didn't actually confirm it, but it was enough for me to write the exclusive story. Two days later, Cecil Burrows, the chairman of Cornhill, announced that his company would be paying £1 million for a five-year deal. The players were now having their salaries trebled. The man who clinched the deal was Doug Insole, a man of immense qualities who has done so much for the game he loves. He never pushed himself forward and I've always admired him.

The day before I met Mr and Mrs Evans, Prime Minister John Major quit as the leader of the Conservatives to allow his MPs to vote for the man they wanted – i.e. him or another candidate. There was so much criticism of his performance as premier that he had decided to end the uncertainty by challenging his opponents to 'put up or shut up'.

'What's going on with your leader?' I asked David as we approached the Grace Gates.

'God knows,' he said. 'Most of us didn't know anything about it. They are far from happy about it, I can tell you.' Evans was a member of the 1922 Committee, the group that wielded considerable influence behind the scenes. He had been close to Mrs Thatcher and was known as a hardline right-winger.

'Is anyone going to stand against him?' I asked him.

'Dunno,' he said. 'Might be. We'll know more later on.'

He was more interested in talking about cricket. As we parted, he said, 'I am in box twenty-six. Come over and have some tea later.' The boxes in the new Mound Stand were on the opposite side of the ground to the old press box and it was a long walk, especially when you had to fight your way through thousands of milling cricket fans during the intervals. It never crossed my mind to take up his invitation.

Just before the tea break, the *Daily Mail* phone in the front of the press box rang and it was the deputy news editor. 'We want you to find John Redwood,' he said. 'We've been told that he is in a box at Lord's. He's the Welsh Minister and he is the only member of the Cabinet we've not been able to contact. All the others have pledged their loyalty to John Major. He's the only one who hasn't.'

'Fine,' I said. 'One of my mates, David Evans, is in box twenty-six and he'll know.' I set off for the Mound Stand.

At the time I didn't know that Evans was Redwood's parliamentary secretary. My press medallion allowed entry to any part of the ground, or should have done, but the two attendants at the bottom of the steps leading to the Mound boxes refused to let me pass. 'You need have a proper pass,' one said.

I explained that I had been invited by David Evans in box twenty-six and if they wanted to check it they could ring him.

'There're no phones in the boxes,' said one of the attendants.

I must have been persuasive because after a few minutes they relented. I knocked at box twenty-six and David answered it. He looked taken aback.

'I've come to take up your offer for tea,' I said. 'The office want me to find where John Redwood is and have a chat with him. I thought you might know.' By this time, I was starting to walk into the box. Sitting on the balcony, having tea, were several people, one of whom I later learned was John Redwood.

Evans stood in front of me, barring my progress any further into the box. 'I don't know where he is,' he said, adopting the look football club chairmen and managers have on their faces when they say something that doesn't approximate to the exact truth. He was still shaking me by the hand as he said it and I realised he was slowly propelling me towards the door. 'I can tell you this,' he said. 'He will be making a statement on Monday.'

'What about?' I said.

'Ah, you wait and see.'

Now I was almost in the corridor. The door was about to close. That was the moment a major scoop was disappearing into the ether. I mumbled, 'I've got to find out which box he's in. I'll look at the lists.'

The door closed and I walked to the end of the corridor and scanned the lists, looking for names with Conservative connexions. There were several and I knocked at a few doors, unsuccessfully: no sign of the Vulcan.

Back on the thoroughfare outside, I bumped into Roger Knight, the MCC secretary. 'I don't think he could be here,' he said. 'If we get a member of the Cabinet visiting the ground we are always advised because they will have their own security.'

That finally made me abandon the search. I rang the news desk and told them the news. They didn't seem too interested.

On Sunday, the newspapers were full of stories that Redwood, a club cricketer, was intending to stand against John Major, another cricketer. And my dismay was compounded a day or two later when Michael Cockerill, a friend who accompanied me on one tour to India, wrote in *The Times* that Redwood had been a guest of Evans and during the Test match Evans had talked him into standing. 'It's your one chance,' Cockerill reported him saying. 'Heseltine will bottle out. Portillo will bottle out. If you stand, you'll have a clear run.'

David Evans never got on with John Major and every time Evans was invited by the Surrey committee to lunch at the Brit Oval he would also ask, 'Is Major coming?' If the answer was 'yes' he would decline.

Redwood was playing cricket in Oxfordshire that Sunday and the journalists failed to find him. Cockerill said of his cricketing prowess, 'He's not a normally gifted player but is the triumph of determination over talent. When I played against him for the BBC recently he displayed a style of backing away and hitting full length balls with a cross bat. When I faced his bowling, it was deceptive. He was much quicker than he appeared from the outfield.'

He sounded like a marginally better player than John Major, who on the Friday of the Lord's Test was a guest in one of the MCC boxes. Redwood confirmed on the Monday that he was indeed standing. When the election took place, he polled eighty-nine votes, a quarter of the parliamentary party. Major, who polled 214 votes.

Six years later, Evans invited me to lunch at the Savoy Grill before it was demolished in the 2007/08 refit, and he told me an astonishing story. He said that Major should have lost that election and if he had done so, the history of the Conservative Party would been vastly different. Tony Blair might not have been elected as Prime Minister in 1997. Evans was not an admirer of Major. 'Too weak,' he said. 'Another eleven votes for Redwood would have swung the second ballot against Major.' He challenged Sir Marcus Fox, the chairman of the 1922 Committee, to open the sealed ballot box to check how many slips had been placed in it. He claimed the vote was rigged. Sir Marcus was very angry. He said his honour was at stake. After a heated conversation, the decision was taken to open the box. It was empty.

A couple of years later, Evans invited Sir Marcus, who was then very ill, to lunch and he accepted. During the meal, Sir Marcus put a hand on his and said, 'You know, you were right about that business and I was wrong. They backed the wrong man.' Sir Marcus died in 2002. Now 59, Redwood remains a firm Eurosceptic, as Evans was. He is co-chairman of the Conservatives' Party Policy Review Group.

I average about three or four coincidences a week, most of them stunners, but there was a sensational one the day I finished writing the Redwood story. I picked up the 106-page *Mail* on 6 May 2008 and on page twenty-three there was a large picture of a Vulcan bomber!

Evans died on 21 October 2008, Trafalgar Day. That would have pleased him: he was born on St George's Day. A self-made multimillionaire, he upset many people with his views, but he was honest and didn't duck issues. I liked him. When I heard of his death, a friend told me, 'You know how he died? He contacted asbestos poisoning and knowing that there was no treatment for it in England, he flew to America and he died there.' It was yet another coincidence. The day before, there had been an item on *BBC Breakfast* about asbestos, and they interviewed a victim. The programme said that 4,000 people die every year, 1,000 more than die on the road. Nearly all of them are exposed to asbestos because of their work. Evans made his wealth by setting up an industrial cleaning business; he and his wife started the business by scrubbing and cleaning themselves. In the end, it killed him.

Another potential 'scoop' went awry on 16 March 1999 when Rachael Heyhoe-Flint, England's greatest female cricketer, finally broke down the male dominance of Lord's after seventy-three years of struggle. I first met Rachael when I worked on the *Express & Star* in Wolverhampton and she had a winning way, both on the cricket and hockey pitches and with people. She was the best PR English cricket has ever had. After being appointed captain of the England team in the early 1970s, she campaigned for the right to play an international ladies game at Lord's. Every year she was rejected. 'They said the pitches were being overused but it was obvious it was a symbolic thing,' she said. 'Women had never played there before and they didn't want us to start.'

In 1976 the Women's Cricket Association were celebrating their Golden Jubilee and the Australians were touring the country. Yet again the MCC rejected their request to play at Lord's. The second one-day game of the One Day International series was scheduled for Sunbury, a ground I have played at on a number of occasions. It was a pleasant ground with a reasonable pitch, but it wasn't Lord's. Middlesex were favourites to reach the quarter-final of the Gillette Cup, but they lost, so Lord's was available. The members of the MCC Committee, pressured by the persistent ladies of the WCA, relented, and the first women's game went ahead there. Rachael led her team out through a side door because she thought the members would object if women walked through the Long Room. 'Walking out I almost blubbed,' she said. 'Such a good crowd turned up and it was a beautiful day. And we won by eight wickets, so that was marvellous, and I was not out at the end.'

I was there at the Oval when she batted for eight and a half hours, reaching her top score of 179 against the Australians. It was supposed to be a three-day game but on an excellent pitch and with no result in sight, the two sides agreed to play a further day. The result was still a draw, with Rachael scoring more than half of England's second innings of 326. Asked how she felt, she said, 'Knackered. Oh no! Just say I'm tired.'

Cricket's suffragettes now wanted membership of the MCC and each year Rachael applied in the name of R. Flint. 'If I used my name the letter would be binned immediately,' she said. Each year her application was turned down. She sought to change the MCC constitution to allow female membership. A two-thirds majority from 18,500 male members was a stiff hurdle to clear and year after year her application failed. 'I suppose I could have chained myself to the Grace Gates and gone on a hunger strike but that might have alienated the men,' she said.

In 1999 a special meeting was held to debate the issue and the women won. Eleven honorary life members of the MCC, all women, were going to be admitted and she was one of them. Some of the others were in their eighties, and there was even a ninety-year-old. They were the original cricketing suffragettes. On 16 March the eleven were invited to Lord's to be presented with their membership cards. It was a momentous day in the history of women's sport.

I was there to report the event and I spoke to her in private after the lengthy press conference in the Long Room – yes, the citadel had fallen at last. I suspected that some people within Lord's might still be awkward and I said, 'How did you come in today?'

'I drove up to the Grace Gates and you can't believe it, but they turned me back,' she said. 'An attendant said, "You can't come in this entrance. Go to the North Gate." I ask you, on that day of all days.'

'Have you told anyone one else, pressmen etc.?'

'No,' she said. 'That's a scoop for you!'

When I got back to the *Mail* office in Kensington High Street, I told the sports commander-in-chief, 'I've got a good intro for the women's cricket story – Rachael Heyhoe-Flint was told she couldn't drive her car in through the Grace Gates.'

He was rather noncommittal, not convinced by the importance of the story. 'The news desk put Barbara Davies on the story and it will be on a news page,' he said. 'They can marry up the two stories.'

'I hope they're not going to ruin the intro,' I said.

Ms Davies rang me later and asked to check a few matters. She hadn't been at Lord's. The next day I looked for the story, but there was nothing in sport and on a news page there was a large article written by Barbara not mentioning Rachael's snub. And no sign of my byline. Urghh!

A few years earlier I was invited to take a press team to play against the England women's team in La Manga as a consolation, but world cricket was sadly disrupted; the ladies' tour to Jamaica was cancelled because of the West Indies' opposition to apartheid in South Africa. We had several famous players including the England and Yorkshire spin bowler Don Wilson, the Sussex batsman Mike Griffith, and David Green, the Lancashire and Gloucestershire opener. The pitch was artificial and

I noticed that the women's opening bowlers swung the ball prodigiously, always outswingers. Don Wilson coached the groundstaff youngsters at Lord's at the time and I asked him why this was happening.

'It's to do with their anatomy,' he said. 'With their bosoms, they can't swing the ball in to the bat. Most of them only bowl outswingers.'

The first match was a declaration game and Enid Bakewell, the left-handed Nottinghamshire batslady, batted for more than three hours for her fifty. Most of the time she faced the bowling of the supremely fit Wilson. I was fielding at slip and after bowling his twentieth over in succession, Don thought he had her caught. The ball came off the glove over my head and it would have been a simple catch. I tried to turn, but my right boot caught in some webbing alongside the end of the artificial pitch. Instead of completing an easy catch, I fell over and missed the ball by inches. 'Christ!' shouted Don, 'I've bowled my guts out against this woman and you bloody drop a dolly!'

That evening we had a team dinner in the main restaurant. Rachael had a bad stomach and she didn't play. Don was scheduled to make the speech and as he was about to rise to his feet, a group of elderly people of both sexes came in to fill the table next to ours. I thought they were Germans but I was wrong. Halfway through his speech, which was hilarious, Don called on us to join in the words of the 'Horst Wessel Song', the song adopted by the Nazi Party in 1930. Suddenly the diners on the other table started jabbering away, and then they all got up and walked out.

I asked a waiter, 'Are they upset with our boisterous behaviour?'

'No,' said the young man, 'they are Dutch and they were Resistance fighters in the Second World War.'

By this time Don was starting up another anecdote and he was standing on his chair rolling backwards and forwards. He toppled backwards and fell into a door which burst open and crashed down a dozen steps before reaching the stone floor. Within a minute or two, and not having been helped by our group (they were splitting themselves with laughter) he climbed up the steps, got back on the chair again and carried on speaking.

In the next match I opened the batting with David Green, who was renowned for his powerful strokeplay. 'It's forty overs a side and we can't afford to sit about and take a look at things,' he said. 'We don't want anyone sitting on the splice.' I think he had heard of my reputation.

The first bowler was very accurate and I was unable to beat the field in her first five deliveries. Greeney was looking distinctly unhappy. Off the sixth ball, I drove the ball straight to a deepish mid-off and called 'One!' He was shocked, but seeing me careering down the pitch, he ran.

I just scraped in and as the over was called, he went up to me and said, 'Listen mate, neither you nor I are McDonald Bailey, especially you. Cut that out!' McDonald Bailey was the former Olympic 100 metres sprinter.

I still see Rachael, either attending charity dinners or Wolves' matches (she is a director of the club and advised Sir Jack Hayward, the previous owner). In 2004 she was the first woman to be elected to the full committee of the MCC. These days she can drive through the Grace Gates without impediment. Twenty years ago, she told me, 'What I really wanted to do is to be the secretary of the MCC. I actually applied but didn't have an interview.' She would have made a good one.

Until the MCC and the Cricket Writers' Club agreed to cut down the number of visitors to the Media Centre, there was a stream of celebrities, relatives, and others who were allowed in – and also into the earlier, smaller press box in the Warner Stand at fine leg. One of them was probably the most pretty – Linda Lovelace, the American porn star who made her name in the hardcore 1972 film *Deep Throat*. No one seemed to know how she got in. Dressed demurely in white, with a low-cut top, she came in with two overweight, middle-aged men, one her agent and the other a PR. I asked her if she knew anything about cricket. 'No, but it looks exciting, better than baseball,' she said. 'And I love London.'

She was whisked out before anyone else could speak to her, and continued her tour of the ground. Her real name was Linda Boreman, and she was born in the Bronx. She was paid only $1,250 for *Deep Throat*; the film earned $500,000 worldwide. In her autobiography, she claimed that her manager Chuck Traynor beat, raped, and exploited her. She later contracted hepatitis and needed a liver transplant. That's a connection with Audrey: my wife also contracted hepatitis, supposedly from eating seafood while we were holidaying with our friends John Shepherd, a cancer surgeon, and his wife Alison in Tampa in 1982. Audrey was offered a liver transplant and turned it down because in those days there was only a fifty per cent chance of survival. Linda Lovelace died after a car crash in 2002 at the age of fifty-three.

I was in the Media Centre on the Friday of the South African Test in 2008 when a flustered-looking David Cameron suddenly came out of the lift right next to me. He didn't appear to be the smooth salesman who would later become Prime Minister. I think he was behind schedule. Jonathan Agnew was due to interview him on the lunchtime *Test Match Special* programme and he was looking rather harassed. Aggers had made the transformation from cricketer to superb radio commentator, and he told me he was allotted twenty minutes to grill the Conservative leader in the upstairs studio; it went on for an hour. I wondered whether Cameron knew much about cricket. 'Oh no,' said Jonathan, 'he was very knowledgeable.' It will be interesting to see if John Redwood becomes one of his ministers.

That year I discovered that I was one of the few to take Sir Allen Stanford's dollar and cash the cheque. Tony Cozier rang me and said he wanted 1,200 words on one of the Middlesex players for the brochure being prepared for the Stanford Super Series in Antigua and Trinidad.

I picked on Tyrone Henderson, the South African all-rounder and called his mobile. I said to him, 'I notice when you started your ODI career for South Africa, you failed to score a run or take a wicket. How did you get called up for your third appearance with that record?'

'I was sitting in the Odeon cinema in Leicester Square watching a film when my mobile rang,' he said. 'I rushed outside and it was a call from a mate in Johannesburg. He said, "Do you know, the selectors have picked you for the next ODI on Friday? You'd better get down there!" I thought he was joking. The Middlesex players were always ribbing me. He convinced me that it was true and I rang the SA Board and they confirmed it. They hadn't been able to get hold of me.'

I asked him how he first played in England and he made another astonishing comment. 'Someone from the Edinburgh Heriots Former Pupils CC said to me did I fancy a summer of cricket in Edinburgh?' he said.

'Well, you wouldn't have earned much from that,' I said.

'That's right, only expenses. The following year I played for Marlborough 1870, a club on Dulwich Common, and they didn't pay me either. I just love playing cricket.'

It was a refreshing story. He wasn't chasing fortunes. As Middlesex lost, he didn't make much out of his Stanford debut. Soon afterwards, Stanford was exposed as another Robert Maxwell – same height, same bluster, and same conmanship. He gave a donation to Barack Obama and he also gave one to President Bush. They were duped, the ECB chairman Giles Clarke and his board were duped, and so were Michael Owen, Andy Murray, and a few others. I know Giles Clarke and have played against him and he was unfairly pilloried. He didn't get paid as chairman of the ECB; he's another Henderson: he does it for love of the game. And he has played a part, along with the MCC President, in persuading the professionals that they should be sporting and fair, and so set a good example to the next generation.

A few days after England regained the Ashes in the final Test at the Oval in 2009, I met one of cricket's top administrators and he told me an amazing story about how England won the match – by 'doctoring' the pitch. Normally the Oval Test pitch is flat and easy paced because the commercial people want the game to last five days. The days leading up to the game were sunny ones and the day before it started, the sun shone brightly and the temperature was high, in the seventies. England included two spinners in their squad, although only Graham Swann played. He finished off the Australians by taking 8-158 in the two innings, compared to his six wickets at eighty-six apiece in the previous Tests. Few people thought the pitch would help spinners. Ricky Ponting and the Australian selectors didn't think so and they left out their spinner Nathan Hauritz. But the day before, someone from Lord's had arrived and told groundsman Bill Gordon to take the covers off to 'bake' the pitch. Usually the pitch is covered in these circumstances to ensure that it lasts. My friend said, 'The pitch dried out much more than usual and that was why dust started appearing on the first day.' There is no law against the home side preparing a pitch so that it suits their bowlers, but this seemed to be a blatant case of not playing the game in the sporting way. Of course this story will be denied, but it is true.

CHAPTER TWENTY-TWO

Dickie's Last Stand

Considering that it is such a nostalgic game, it is remarkable that there have been few really memorable farewells by cricketers. Sir Donald Bradman's at the Oval in 1948 was an exception. Also Adam Gilchrist's. Brian Lara's might have been, but many of the spectators had left when he started his lap of honour at the end of the 2007 World Cup. One of his heroes, Sir Viv Richards, had a reasonable departure at the Oval in 1991, but it was without much ceremony. The final exits of these great players did not compare with Dickie Bird's last Test at Lord's in June 1996. Lord's groundsman Mick Hunt said when it was announced that the world's best umpire was quitting, 'I feel sorry for anyone who gets a hundred. It will be swamped by all the publicity Dickie gets.'

Sourav Ganguly scored 131 in India's first innings and it received scant recognition, as Hunt had forecast. Dickie dominated the news coverage of the match from the day before it started until the day after it ended. There were countless jokes about Hunt not needing to water the pitch – Dickie would have done that for him with his tears. 'Aye,' he said in countless interviews, 'I'll be shedding a few tears but when I get out there I'll have to get a grip of myself. Flippin' heck I will!'

He was sixty-three when his retirement was confirmed, two years before the official retiring age. Did he want to carry on? Sure he did. He loved the job so much that it came as a severe shock to him when Tony Brown, the TCCB official responsible for umpires, told him the Umpires' Committee thought it would be a good idea if he went while still at the top of his onerous profession. Although he was religiously doing his half-hour stretching exercises every day, he was not as fit has he had been. His back caused him problems for some years.

Earlier in the season, when he was officiating at Chelmsford, Sachin Tendulkar kept hitting the ball out of the ground and replacement balls had to be found. Tired of sending for more, Dickie said, 'Can't we do something about his?'

One of the Essex players said there was scope to put some balls in the covered hole housing the fielders' helmets. 'That'll do,' said Dickie. 'We'll use those. Save stopping the game.'

When Tendulkar hit another six and a further ball was required, Dickie went towards the covered hole and started to bend to lift the cover. Halfway down, he felt a sharp pain in his back. Several times he tried to bend over far enough to reach the ball, each time pulling back and rubbing his back. The Essex players gathered around him with smiles on their faces. 'Can't you lads to it?' he asked plaintively.

'It's your job,' said one. They stood back and let him have another unsuccessful go before finally giving up.

The Essex players had a reputation for playing the most practical jokes on Dickie over the years. 'That Ray East, he were a one,' Dickie once recalled. 'Never stopped appealing.'

The title of my ghostwritten 1978 book about Dickie, *Not Out*, was very appropriate The slightest doubt was always given to the batsmen, which is why he was termed a 'not outer'. In his late fifties, his eyesight started to deteriorate and he had to wear glasses. The players respected him, and most of them still thought he was the best in the business, but holding on to that eminent position was proving a difficult task. As cricket became more competitive, relationships between umpires and players were bound to suffer. Strict regulations about dissent, with tough penalties, had kept order, and the traditions of the game were still intact. But the pressures were mounting. After reflecting on what Tony Brown had said, Dickie agreed that it was time to go. 'Lord's is my second home,' he told me. 'It'll be great to end my career there.'

Pre-match interviews were restricted to a staged press conference two days before the start of the match, but Dickie insisted on doing many more on his own. One writer from *The Baltimore Sun* even interviewed him. The day before, he was remarkably calm for someone known for his excitability.

He attended the launch of my book *Dickie: A Tribute to Umpire Harold Bird* and he said, 'I'll sign 'em, don't worry. Tell 'em in the MCC shop. Tell 'em to order more!'

Some of England's best-known captains turned up, including Sir Colin Cowdrey, Ted Dexter, and Mike Brearley. Mike said to him, 'It will be a good time for someone to get his pad in front in the first over Dickie! With all those tears you won't be able to see to make a decision.'

'Aye,' said Dickie. 'I'll be shedding a few.'

By the following morning, officials were wondering whether the great umpire would be in a fit state to take the field. Would he need chaperoning? Was there enough Kleenex to cope? Would his fellow umpire, the magisterial Australian umpire Darrell Hair, be able to calm him down?

Appropriately, there was an Indian steward on guard at the end of the corridor leading to the umpires' room. 'Mr Dickie,' he said, 'I would like to have a picture taken with you.'

'No problem,' said Dickie. 'But we'll have to do it later.'

Next, Dickie approached Mick Hunt to find out the day's forecast. 'Same as always when you are here,' said the groundsman. 'It's going to rain cats and dogs.'

Dickie claimed he woke up in the middle of the night and dreamt that he gave out England's captain in the first over. Before he went to bed he prayed, as he always does, for fine weather. His prayers weren't answered. The opening day dawned drizzly and wet. 'Doesn't look too bad,' said Hair. The umpires went out several times to inspect the pitch before announcing that play would start half an hour late.

The new, enlarged Lord's covers ensured not too much time would be lost. By 11 a.m., the normal start, the ground was almost full. At 11.25 a.m. the players filed through the members in the Long Room and down the steps. The umpires were in their room waiting for the call. TCCB secretary Tim Lamb appeared, saying, 'Where is he? The players are ready.'

He dashed towards the stairs, almost colliding with Bird and Hair. 'Must be some kind of presentation going on,' said Dickie to his colleague. As the umpires turned into the room that houses some of the most highly valued cricket paintings, the members stood aside to let them pass and applauded, even cheered. Older members said it was totally unprecedented.

Dickie looked up as he started going down the steps and the noise was taken up all around the ground. No batsman could ever have received such a salutation. He shook hands with all the players who were lined up in their respective teams and Mohammed Azharuddin embraced him. Those closest thought they saw tears in his eyes. But his eyes weren't streaming. The old showman had come through like the professional everyone knew him to be. He pulled out his handkerchief to perform the gesture the photographers were waiting for, a wipe of the eye. His glasses remained on. The feared waterworks had not happened.

'I'll take the first over if you like,' said Hair.

Officials had suggested that to Dickie but he had been noncommittal. 'No, I'll take the pavilion end,' he said, 'that's my end.'

Javagal Srinath, the lead bowler for the Indians, handed him his sweater. 'Right arm over,' he said.

Dickie looked towards Atherton at the far end. 'One leg?' asked Atherton.

It was just like the start of any Test, except for the emotion. Srinath bowled, Atherton played defensively forward. Dickie transferred a red barrel into his other pocket. He did that every ball to confirm to himself that six balls had been recorded. The fifth ball of the over cut back up the slope and Atherton, neither forward nor back, was struck on the front pad in front of middle and leg. Srinath and his colleagues went up with loud appeals. Dickie peered down the pitch. For a second or two he waited before pointing his right forefinger into the air. 'That's out! Aye, that's out.'

Atherton, who had survived countless lbw appeals deliberated on by Dickie in the past, burst into a broad smile. The unthinkable had happened: H. D. Bird, known throughout the game for giving the benefit of the doubt, especially in the first over, had fingered England's captain in the very first over. Up in the press box, the seventy or so journalists turned toward the TV monitors to check the replay. The radio and TV bosses they were doing the same. The general view was that it might have missed leg. Still, it is a brave man who gives the skipper out in the first over. Back in the pavilion, Atherton said to David Lloyd, 'The bugger's given me out!'

A few overs later, Alec Stewart padded up to another delivery from Srinath, which seamed back sharply. The impact took place several inches outside the off stump and it seemed to clear the stumps. 'Not out,' ruled Dickie. Two lbws in the first fifteen minutes would have been too much.

'Did your finger quiver a bit with that one?' I asked him later.

'Not really,' he said. 'I don't know what all the excitement is about. I was part of a world record for lbws in Trinidad not so long ago. Seventeen there were and I gave six of them. All out. No doubt about it. They were out, the lot of them. All six.'

Interviewed after close of play, Dickie almost broke down on three occasions, choking back the tears. Each time he recovered to make another heartfelt point and each time he won approval from nodding journalists.

On the Sunday of the Test, when play was turgid and the near-capacity crowd was bored, the great umpire won his final battle – he actually managed to quell the Mexican wave. When the first wave swept round the ground – but not in the pavilion, which was filled with members – he looked agitated. Anything that might put the batsman off is a mortal sin in his eyes. 'What d'ya think?' he asked the facing batsman, Alec Stewart.

'I don't mind them making a noise, but when they leap up and down behind the arm it is a bit off-putting,' said Stewart.

Dickie held up play and turned toward the Compton and Edrich Stands, where the disturbance was at its height. Like a politician imploring his audience to be seated, he motioned to the 8,000 or so people. The wave suddenly stopped, as though he had switched it off with a remote control, but a minute or two later, with no more runs having been scored, another, much louder wave started.

Dickie was apoplectic. He turned round angrily and on TV he could be seen mouthing the words, 'Let the man bat for God's sake!'

To everyone's amazement, the demonstrators sat down and were quiet. Dickie had become the first umpire to give the Mexican wave out. 'The batsmen weren't happy about it,' he said. 'It's not right, is it?'

After the end of play, I had to deliver some material to him and finish off my account of Dickie's historic day for the *Mail*. In my experience, during Tests no journalist has ever been admitted to the umpires' room at Lord's, situated around a corner from the away team dressing room. But on this special occasion, Richard Little, the TCCB media manager, said, 'Go on in, no one will mind.'

It was a smaller room than I had expected. Clothing, newspapers, congratulatory cards, and other items were strewn around the floor and furniture. Darrell Hair, several inches taller than Dickie, as broad as a rugby player, seem to fill half the room. There was also a police sergeant present. 'He's been with me the whole of the game,' said Dickie proudly.

He asked me about the wave. 'What do you think?' he asked. 'I was right, wasn't I? They don't like it here, you know.'

The Indian steward came in unannounced. 'Excuse me Mr Dickie,' he said, 'can I have a picture with you? I must have another picture with you.'

Dickie looked up, agitatedly. 'Just a minute, just a minute,' he said. 'I'm busy. I'll do it later.'

The steward withdrew, crestfallen. I asked Dickie what he had said to the crowd. 'Just told them to be quiet and give the batsman a chance,' he said. 'That's all.'

There was a perfunctory knock on the half-open door and the steward burst in again. 'Mr Dickie, my £600 camera has disappeared and I now have another one. I must have this picture with you.'

Dickie was upset. 'Can't you see I'm having a private meeting?' he said. 'I'll do it later.' He ushered the man back through the door and closed it behind him. 'He's a persistent beggar,' he said.

Dickie was already in his National Grid blazer and flannels, ready to attend the usual after-match drinks. These days the drink sessions have been drastically reduced for economic reasons. I followed him out of the door, with the policeman in front. 'Mr Dickie!' shouted the steward, lurking outside in the corridor. 'Please, I must have my picture.'

'All right,' said Dickie. 'Just one.' The steward passed his replacement camera to me. The two men stood together and as I pressed the button, the flash didn't go off.

'Oh dear,' said the steward.

'Hurry up man,' said Dickie. 'I've got an appointment.'

'Just one, just one,' said the steward. 'It won't take a second.'

Normally Dickie is most accommodating with autograph hunters and those wishing to take pictures of him. He loves it really. But there was irritation in his voice as he said, 'Goodness me, man, I can't wait all day. Get on with it!'

The steward fiddled with the camera before passing it to me. He stood next to Dickie, who by this time was not his usual smiling self. I pressed the button, the flash went, and that should have been that. 'One more,' pleaded the steward.

'No more,' shouted Dickie. 'That's enough!'

'Please sir, just one,' said the Indian. 'Just one more in case the other one doesn't come out.'

Again I lined the pair up and took another one as Dickie was about to turn and disappear around a corner. As we went downstairs, an MCC official approached and said, 'Dickie, there are hundreds of people outside waiting for you to sign. Shall I take you out the side entrance to avoid them?'

'No,' said Dickie, 'I'll sign the lot. I never turn people away. Wouldn't be right, would it? No, I'll do the lot.'

And with the police officer by his side, he walked out the main door to be thronged by his fans. 'Line them up; in an orderly line and I'll do the lot,' he said.

And he did. He has put his name to six books with sales in the millions and I reckon he has signed more autographs than any cricket person in the history of the game.

Later that evening, a journalist from the *Daily Mirror* was rung by someone in his office and he was asked to investigate a claim that Dickie had told the people doing the Mexican wave, 'Sit down you wankers. Let the man bat.' At 10 p.m. he finally contacted Dickie in his hotel room, just as he was about to turn the lights off. It was a tricky subject to broach and the journalist started with softball questions including one about why it was necessary to have a police escort. Had there been any threats to him?

'Threats?' said Dickie. 'Threats? Goodness me, no threats at all, why should there be?'

The journalist asked him what he said to the crowd. 'I just told them to sit down and give the batsman a chance.' The journalist gently brought up the word 'wankers' and Dickie was aghast. 'Good gracious,' he said, 'I never said that. It's a word I never use. It's insulting.'

Some newspapers still make a story out of something that isn't true by quoting the person and saying he has denied it. Fortunately for Dickie, the *Mirror* didn't follow that route. The story was spiked. His sixty-sixth and final Test was a happy, memorable occasion, not one that needed to be soured by controversy. David Bairstow, the former Yorkshire wicketkeeper who committed suicide, had a business producing ties and to commemorate the occasion, he ran 1,000 off, all bearing the motif 'Dickie's Last Stand'. They were sold out within days and a further consignment was produced. Dickie was rightly given an unprecedented send-off because he is one of cricket's most-loved personalities. He revelled in every moment of it.

Mohammed Azharuddin skippered the Indian touring side on three occasions in England and in 1990 I was involved in a very humorous incident. The day before the Lord's Test, I arrived late for the official press conference and saw the Indians returning to the dressing room after practice. Azharuddin was one of the last to leave and I asked him if I could interview him alone. I noticed he had a pretty limp handshake, but that didn't matter. 'OK,' he said, and we walked across the ground to the pavilion.

The MCC bars all people besides the players and MCC officials going onto the ground in these circumstances. But we got across to the pavilion without trouble. We were sitting on a bench outside the Long Room when a highly agitated Colonel John Stephenson, the MCC secretary, approached. John was universally known as 'the Colonel' and was liked by everyone. 'Brian,' he said, 'what is going on? You know that you can't interview the Indian captain in front of the Long Room. The press conference has already taken place. I must ask you to leave immediately.'

I explained that Azharuddin was quite happy to spend a few minutes with me. 'It's not going to cause any problems, is it?'

'Yes it is,' said the Colonel.

I had a very good relationship with him and I joked, 'It's not going to give one of your members a heart attack seeing me talking to Azharuddin.'

'You are obstructing the view from the Long Room and I must ask you to leave at once.'

I turned around and said, 'But John, there is not a single person in the Long Room. It's deserted.'

'Never mind,' said John. 'Someone might come in.' Azharuddin was very amused but we had to leave.

On another occasion I said to John, 'It's about time we had a proper press box at this ground. The one we have is at backward square leg and we can't see what is happening out the middle. What about having one at the top of the pavilion, or even at the Nursery End.'

John looked shocked. 'We will never have a press box in the pavilion. That's certain. As for the Nursery End, one will only go up there on my dead body.'

A few years later the UFO-like Media Centre, designed by a Czech architect – who won an award for her work – was constructed at the Nursery End. The Colonel was still alive. Sadly he died a few years later, too soon to do the many things he wanted to do in his retirement. He was a giver, and gave pleasure to so many.

My tribute book to Dickie sold well, but it might have been in the top ten longer had David Hopps of *The Guardian* not brought out his unauthorised book *Free As a Bird* at the same time. His book was also in the bestsellers' list for a time, which proved just how popular Dickie had become. I discovered that Hopps' book was being planned when I rang the former Yorkshire and England bowler Don Wilson and asked if he had any funny stories about Dickie. 'Someone else is up to that game,' he said. 'Hoppsy rang me with the same question.'

Hopps, who often covered Yorkshire's matches, had been one of the people I wrote to requesting for Dickie anecdotes. He didn't reply. I rang him and asked if he could confirm that he was writing a book on Dickie's career. At first he was evasive. 'It's nothing that will affect yours,' he said. Anyone can write a book about anyone else; I wasn't too bothered. But if it came out at the same time as mine, it would be damaging.

When I told Dickie he was upset. 'He's not, is he?' he said. 'I don't want him writing a book about me. He once wrote something in his paper which I didn't like. How can I stop it?'

I explained there was no law to prevent a person writing a book about someone else, even if it failed to meet his approval.

'I'll not cooperate with it,' he said.

I gave him the number of Robson Books, who were the publishers. Dickie duly called one of the executives and was told that no book of that nature was being planned. That pacified Dickie, but shortly afterwards a bulky envelope arrived at his house, addressed to him and containing a contract between Hopps and Robson Books for 70,000 words about Dickie. It had clearly been sent to the wrong address. Like football managers, publishers have to be somewhat coy over their plans, but that was duplicity on a grand scale. The next time I saw Hopps I told him about it. 'Mine won't be out until the end of November,' he said. 'It won't clash with yours. I'm not as fast a writer as you.'

While Dickie pondered how to stop publication of this unauthorised book, I pressed on with mine to make sure it would be out in time for the Lord's Test, and it was. Hopps wrote an article about his book in *Wisden Cricket Monthly* and one sentence stood out: 'Dickie deserves something better than a collection of anecdotes compiled by Brian Scovell.' That was an unnecessary jibe. I had made no public comment about his book. I called Tim de Lisle, the editor of the magazine, and asked for the right of reply and he readily agreed. My letter was in the style of *Private Eye*, ending, 'Surely some mistake!' Hopps, who is one of sports journalism's most humorous writers – well, sometimes – did not see the joke. In the following issue of the magazine he wrote a vitriolic letter accusing me of 'grossly misrepresenting the truth'. He claimed Dickie had given him full support and was regularly signing copies of the rogue book. He had gatecrashed my book launch at Lord's and now claimed, in his letter, 'I wandered into the room by mistake.' Some mistake! Some Long Room! By now Hopps *v.* Scovell was being built up into an amusing literary spat and items appeared in various cricket diaries about it. Charles Sale, writing in the ailing *Daily Express*, devoted part of his column to the subject. Reluctantly, I called de Lisle yet again and asked for a second right of reply. 'Your man has called me a liar and I have to respond,' I said. A nice, pleasant man, de Lisle OK'd it and I went into action yet again.

Hopps and I didn't speak for several weeks, although we were covering the same Test matches and sat in the same press boxes. It must have irked him that my book was outselling his, but it also had better reviews. Jonathan Rice, one of the leading cricket reviewers and the brother of Sir Tim, said he preferred mine to Hopps'.

A few weeks later, we were sitting in the Trent Bridge press box – the best of the lot, with its calmness and orderliness – when Hopps read the Rice piece. He came up to me and said, 'He must be a friend of yours.'

I replied, 'I know him. He is not a friend but he appears to have good judgment.'

On the Sunday morning of the Headingley Test, the journalists were disturbed just before the start of play by the raising of voices at the back of the darkened box. Hopps was having a row with his *Guardian* colleague Matthew Engel, who was then the editor of *Wisden*. Engel, a superb writer, has a quirky sense of humour and can easily lose his temper. The previous day, Hopps had wrote an article for his newspaper saying there were political undertones to the disturbances that occurred on the Western Terrace – the hooligan part – at Headingley. Ten people were arrested and 100 ejected.

'You are a Marxist-Leninist patsy,' screamed Engel.

'I will not have you call me a Marxist-Leninist patsy,' shouted Hopps.

'Yes you are,' said Engel.

'Don't say another word,' replied Hopps, 'I don't wish to talk to you anymore.' With that, he walked out.

Half an hour later, I was standing by the scorers at the other end of the press box when a sheepish Hopps approached. Half smiling, he said, 'I have just had a major row with Engel and I can't stand having two feuds. Can we end ours?'

I burst into laughter and we shook hands, but not before I admonished him for calling me economical with the truth when it was really him who was distorting the facts.

'Anyway,' I said, 'you've done pretty well out of all the publicity. You've been in the bestsellers list as well as me.'

Later in the day, Engel came up to me and said, 'You know I've had this bust up with Hopps.'

'Yes I know,' I said. 'He's a Marxist-Leninist cad, I understand.'

'Well,' he said. 'It's all over now and we've shaken hands, so can you restart your feud?'

Happily I didn't. These press boxes are full of men who love cricket, but they can be temperamental.

My report of the day I spent at Dickie's last Test match was, I think, the kind of journalism my readers like to read; they prefer it to comment pieces. They would love to spend a day with one of their heroes and the next best thing for them is to read someone else's experiences. Before the final Test at the Oval in the West Indies series in 1991, I asked Micky Stewart, then the England manager, if I could talk through a day with one of his batsmen, particularly a newcomer. I suggested Hugh Morris, the Glamorgan left-hander opener who had just been capped. Hugh is now the deputy chief executive of the England and Wales Cricket Board; he was the man who years later had to announce the news that Kevin Pietersen and Peter Moores were sacked. Hugh was twenty-seven and he was keen to do it and Micky thought it was a good idea. The West Indian pace quartet was Curtly Ambrose, Patrick Patterson – the closest to Wes Hall in terms of terror – Courtney Walsh, and Malcolm Marshall. I introduced my article like this: 'Sportsmail asked Hugh to talk us through his first day at the Oval and the result is a fascinating insight into life in cricket's fast lane, where the ball is coming at you like a speeding vehicle on a motorway.'

When Hugh was out and showered and changed, I came to see him and he proved a very fine interviewee. He faced 130 balls, thirty of which were bouncers, batted for 188 minutes, and hit four fours. He scored forty-four and finished his Test career after only three Tests, totalling just fifty runs. He will never forget his debut. There was plenty of bounce in that Oval pitch; Mark Ramprakash had to go to hospital for an X-ray when he was struck in the arm and Alec Stewart had a bruised finger. There were 555 deliveries bowled on the opening day and 102 were bouncers. Many of them were lethal.

The first thing Hugh said was, 'Curtly got me out for a pair at Swansea this season and that's a good start! And I knew I was only in the team because Derek Pringle wasn't well.'

On the strike of midday, Curtly hit him in his chest protector. So far so good, and he was congratulated by his teammates when he came in for lunch. He sat in the dressing room and had only vanilla ice cream and orange juice. At 2.35 p.m. a vicious bouncer from Ambrose hit him on the side of the visor of his helmet. Luckily there was no damage except that the strapping broke. 'You're a lucky Welshman,' said skipper Viv Richards, who had played for Glamorgan in the previous year. 'You're used to worse than that, playing all those rugby games!' Ten minutes later, Curtly hit him in the arm guard. When he was out, a catch off Curtly's bowling, he sat in the dressing room for fifteen minutes before he could speak.

Later he said, 'It makes me realise just what a remarkable Graham Gooch is and how incredibly fit he is to stand out there as long as he does.'

The next morning I wasn't expecting to be showered with praise for what I considered to be one of my better pieces, but I was taken aback when some of the other correspondents complained that they hadn't been allowed to interview Morris. Some moaned to the press officer. Today it would be virtually impossible to interview a Test star in these circumstances, which is sad. It is a competitive business and the race ought not to be run by everyone switching on their cruise control and going at the same pace. There should always be winners and losers.

The previous year I spent a day with Ray Lewis, the FIFA referee, and the match was Wimbledon, the roughest side in the First Division, against Arsenal. It was interesting to be next to Lewis and his officials through the day, and one of the linesmen was a fireman who pulled Norman Tebbitt and his wife out of the rubble in the Brighton hotel that had been bombed by the IRA. The feature didn't really work out because it was a quiet match, not typical of Wimbledon. But it did prove that Ray Lewis, a part-timer – he was paid £100 for his work – can do a good job, or better, than a professional.

CHAPTER TWENTY-THREE

A Cheese Sandwich
Stops Play at Molineux

I've had dozens of work experience boys accompanying me on reporting jobs. Once one asked me, 'What is the most important part of the job?'

'Good question,' I said. 'First, arrive not on time, but before time. Second, be patient. You could spend hours in a street waiting for the news to happen. It can be boring but you've got to stick it out.'

In the summer of 1995, I had a fifteen-year-old wanting to come to Lord's to watch the West Indian players practising. We were enjoying a close-up look at some of the best cricketers in the world when Lex Muller, a Dutch reporter and friend, rang to tell me that Dennis Bergkamp was about to arrive at Highbury to sign for Arsenal. I said to the boy, 'Change of plan. We're off to Highbury to see Dennis Bergkamp sign for the Gunners.' He didn't appear to be excited about it.

When we arrived outside Highbury, a small knot of people were standing outside the entrance. Most of them were ticket spivs, but four were Dutch journalists. One, Lex, asked the uniformed attendant outside the marble halls, 'Can we come in to wait?'

'No you can't sir,' said the attendant.

'In Holland they let in the Press,' said Lex.

'Well sir, this isn't Holland.'

I said to Lex, 'Are we sure that Bergkamp is here?'

'Someone told us that he was going to be, but we haven't seen him,' said Lex.

At the time Arsenal did not have a press officer, so I dialled the number of the secretary of Ken Friar, the managing director, and asked if Ken could ring me. She wasn't able to confirm that Bergkamp was inside the building. 'I know nothing about it,' she said.

By this time lunchtime had passed and my work experience lad was restless. 'I'm hungry,' he said. I gave him £10 and told him to go to the café on the main road and order sandwiches and drinks for both of us.

While he was away there was a flurry of activity as a large car drew up and out came Bergkamp and his agent. They rushed into the hall without speaking. Eventually Ken Friar rang me and said, 'As soon as there is something to report, we can let you and your colleagues in.'

Halfway through the afternoon the sun came out and my lad said, 'How much longer? I've got to be back home for tea.'

I told him it could be hours, or minutes. 'Hanging around is a key part of the job. You've got to be specially trained to doorstep people.' I persuaded him to stay while mentally marking him down as someone who would never make the grade as a reporter.

Three hours later, my mobile rang and Ken Friar said a press conference had been arranged. 'Come on in,' he said.

Bergkamp appeared to be a very modest, quietly spoken, intelligent, almost shy man. I'd told my assistant to think up a suitable question to ask him, but he failed to come up with one. Bruce Rioch, the manager, said the fee would be £7.5 million and that it would be worth every penny. He was quite right because Dennis Nichols Maria Bergkamp, who was twenty-six, proved to be one of the greatest players to have represented the club. His father, a plumber, named him after Denis Law. Denis was a lively, interesting man whereas Bergkamp was introspective, even boring. But once he got on the pitch, he was a classical ball player who played like a conductor of a band. In 1998 he was voted 'Footballer of the Year' by the journalists, and the PFA members gave their award to him as well.

When he retired in 2006, the FWA decided to invite him and his wife to their Ladies' Night at the Savoy in January, a prestige event that has featured the greatest names in the game. Officers of the FWA committee emailed his agent on countless occasions, but over the weeks we realised that Bergkamp, the shy boy of Amsterdam, wasn't interested. Bergkamp suffered from aviophobia, a fear of flying, caused when he heard that a number of Surinamese-Dutch players died in a plane crash. He wasn't on the flight, but he was with the Dutch international squad in the 1994 World Cup in the USA when my good friend Lex, impatient about the way the aircraft still hadn't taken off, made an injudicious remark about a possible bomb on board. Air marshals who were on the plane jumped on him. He was arrested and later found guilty of breaching the regulations. It was a very sad and unfortunate episode, because Lex lost his job.

Another fifteen-year-old potential journalist on one of my trips was Tom, a public schoolboy who wanted to become a political writer but was also interested in football. I brought him along to the West Ham training ground at Chadwell Heath one Friday morning. There were twenty journalists and radio men waiting to speak to Harry Redknapp. Harry is one of the most eloquent speakers because he is a natural and always comes up with a good line. He provides the writers with a story from the outset and he rarely has to answer tricky questions. Tom was sitting back at the rear and he shouted, 'Harry, who are you going to buy next and how much?'

Harry laughed at his cheek. 'Who are you working for?' said Harry. 'You'll go far in this game.'

One of the most amusing incidents of a bomb scare stopping a sporting event was the England *v.* Poland European Championship Under-21 match on 8 October 1996 at Molineux. On the way to Wolverhampton, I called in at St Andrew's, Birmingham City's unappetising ground, to report on a private meeting of Football League chairmen who were unhappy about the way the League Management Board was running the game. These rogue meetings were common in football at the time. There was always a number of chairmen willing to plot the overthrow of the democratically elected leaders. This meeting was taking place at a club owned by David Sullivan, a man who made his money from pornography. It was raining when the chairmen arrived, most of them driving very expensive cars with personalised plates. The only one who came in a taxi was Jonathan Hayward, the then-chairman of Wolverhampton Wanderers and the son of Jack 'Union Jack' Hayward, the Liberal philanthropist.

After sitting in his car for an hour, Jonathan's taxi driver went up to the entrance of the new stand and asked the person in charge, 'Can I use the toilet?'

At that moment Karren Brady, the managing director of Birmingham City, arrived. 'This is private property,' she said. 'The press are not allowed in here.'

The poor man had to return to his vehicle. The only press people in the vicinity were myself and Tim Abrahams of Sky, who was accompanied by a cameraman and a young lad on work experience.

The only time I had dealings with Ms Brady was when I wrote on behalf of the FWA to ask her if the club could improve its antiquated press facilities. She wrote back: 'We can't afford it, but if the *Daily Mail* could sponsor a new press box we would welcome that.' I had to admire her cheek.

Patrick Murphy of the BBC later fell and injured himself going up to the radio boxes. He sued Birmingham City and eventually won a four-figure sum in compensation. Birmingham's press facilities rivalled those of Portsmouth FC – also among the worst in the land – but in 2008 they made some improvements.

The meeting of rebel chairmen dragged on all afternoon. Tim, realising that it might not yield much footage, asked his cameraman to film the chairmen as they trooped out clutching their briefcases. 'What has been decided?' said Tim.

'No comment,' said the first chairman. Football chairmen have yet to learn from politicians that a quick soundbite can do a lot for their public esteem. Saying 'no comment' never does anyone any good – unless you're covering something up.

'Why don't you ask them if this is the end of the Football League as we know it?' I said to Tim. TV interviewers can ask daft questions because the interviewee is being filmed and cannot react too aggressively. The poor print journalist who tries an awkward question can find himself being abused. Tim's trainee must have learned very little, except that most chairmen were rude and uncommunicative.

I departed for Molineux and when I arrived an hour later there were hundreds of people milling around in the street close to the statue of Billy Wright. The statue is one of the finest of its type, almost as good as the ones of Sir Bobby Robson and Sir Alf Ramsey, who are kept fifty yards away in Portman Road because Sir Alf didn't get on with Sir Bobby. The worst statue was the one of Ted Bates, the lovely man who played in every position at Southampton FC including in goal, as well as managing and serving as President. He was there for almost the whole of his working life. I had some good times with Ted and his enthusiasm was unbounded. There were some strong-minded players under him and he managed to calm them down and get the best out of them. When Ted's statue appeared, the Saints fans were shocked. It was awful. They insisted on one that actually looked like Ted and with a lot of good people chipping in, a new statue is now in place outside the St Mary's Stadium.

An hour before the Under-21 game, only the press were allowed in at Molineux. Louise Hennessy, the Wolves press officer, one of the first to be appointed, announced that a search of the ground at 6.20 p.m., ten minutes before the turnstiles were supposed to open, had revealed a suspicious-looking package in a bin in a toilet in the lower tier of the John Ireland Stand. 'The police are calling up one of their specialist firearms unit and if they can deal with it, they will,' she said. 'If not, a bomb disposal unit from Hereford will be called in. They might fly in by helicopter and land on the pitch.' She added that the mystery object was wrapped in foil.

The spectators were kept out in the road, but the bar in the press room was open and two stewards served hot soup, tea, coffee, and alcoholic drinks without charge. The thirty Polish journalists, an abnormally high turnout for an Under-21 match, were delighted and set about ordering double whiskies and double gins. They were less pleased to learn that smoking was banned. Smoking is still big in Poland.

Ms Hennessy returned to say that the police wouldn't let the public in until the 'object' had been either blown up or cleared. The match was to be shown live on Sky and the harassed commentators were trying to say something that hadn't already been mentioned. In the press room, the Poles ordered more drinks and their voices became louder and louder.

The chief superintendent of the police came in to say the package was under the stand where the Royal Marines band were going to sit. 'We can't take any risks,' he said. 'The Marines have been involved in a number of incidents involving devices, some of which have gone off. The one in Hyde Park was particularly damaging with many servicemen killed.' The journalists filed the news. By now it had become a potential front page story.

Enter Ms Hennessy again. 'The experts say their investigation was inconclusive,' she said. 'We are now waiting for the Army experts and they are expected at 9 p.m.' The Poles did not mind. More drinks all round!

'What are the players doing?' she was asked.

'The England players are playing head tennis and the Poles are lying on the floor,' she said.

'Not paralytic?' said one writer.

The hazy TV screen came to life. The Sky interviewer asked a Polish FA official, 'Will your players start the game so late?'

'No,' the official said. 'We are not combat-ready and we want a postponement for twenty-four hours.'

Outside in the streets, the crowd was thinning. Rain was tumbling down and police officers were unable to give any guidance about when the game might start, if at all. The noise level in the press room was rising fast. Two of the Poles lit up cigarettes.

Someone announced that the Army had arrived, but not by helicopter. 'I wonder what they are earning,' said a journalist. 'Nothing like what these footballers are being paid. And they could be blown up.'

Ms Hennessy came through the door. 'It's been blown up by a controlled explosion,' she said.

'What was it?' I asked.

'It appears to be a sandwich,' she said.

Everyone roared with laughter. 'What kind of sandwich?'

'I don't know,' she said.

Several English journalists, not having had as much alcohol as the Poles, agreed it must have been a cheese one, so they filed that piece of vital information: a cheese sandwich stops play at Molineux.

Graham Kelly, the FA secretary, appeared on TV to say it proved the value of security checks before big matches. The turnstiles were opened and 3,183 of the 6,000-odd people that had bought tickets in advance were let in, many of them youngsters on reduced rates. The game kicked off at 10.20 p.m. and finished and ten minutes before midnight with a 0-0 draw. It was the latest a football match had ever ended in Britain and it must have been one of the dullest.

Just after midnight, the sixty media people covering the non-event poured back into the press room and the first person to arrive at the bar was a tall, red-faced Pole. 'A double gin please,' he said.

'Sorry,' said the steward, 'you've drunk us out of booze. There's none left.' It was noticeable that when the press conferences began, the questions from the Poles were delivered with a slur. One of them kept interrupting when the English contingent tried to ask questions. The next day, the story made just eight paragraphs in the *Daily Mail*.

On another occasion I was covering a Northern Ireland v. England game at Windsor Park and the police warned us to make sure we were ready to leave in the media coach, right behind the England coach. Anyone late would be left behind. There had been a rumour that a bomb might be detonated and I've never seen so many writers rush through their articles and get back in the coach well before the departure time. Everyone was laughing and joking about it, but the jollity stopped when there was a loud explosion, not very far away. The coaches sped off with a massive number of escorts. We were all very relieved, as were the players, and when we arrived at the airport and were able to fly off on time. That was a real scare, unlike the one at Molineux.

CHAPTER TWENTY-FOUR

The Nasties

Most of the sportsmen I have worked with are good people who love their sport, but there are some nasties in the ranks. The nastiest was Ken Bates. When he was forced to end his twenty-two-year reign at Chelsea in March 2004, ushered out by Roman Abramovich, most of the critics were kind to him. 'I'll miss the old boy,' said one. 'In his farewell speech he was more dignified and restrained than many thought possible.' His good friend Lord Attenborough, the club's Vice President, was in tears.

Dickie Attenborough might well have been in tears, but Bates has to be the most disliked man in football. He had few friends, but many enemies. Perhaps the reason why he wasn't exposed was his readiness to threaten with writs whenever anything was published or said that he didn't like. My former *Daily Mail* colleague Harry Harris had numerous litigations with him; Bates won damages in one case and was able to buy a car from the money. On one occasion, Bates stuck a notice – 'The Harry Harris Room' – on the door of the toilet next to the press room and said a payment from another winning case was used to sponsor the loo. Well, I suppose he did have a sense of humour. Newspapers usually backed off after being served writs. His business background was once written about in *Private Eye* but there were no follow-ups.

Bates was born in Ealing in 1931 and his mother died shortly afterwards. His father disappeared, leaving his grandparents to bring him up in a council house. He knew how to handle money and made himself rich through haulage, quarrying, ready-mix concrete, and dairy farming. He paid £1 for the near-bankrupt Chelsea FC in 1982 and spent a lot of time rubbishing the previous chairman, Viscount Chelsea, a decent man, and another predecessor, Brian Mears, who was even more honourable, as well as various other people, including one or two property magnates who wanted to buy what Bates called 'the most valuable property in West London'.

Stamford Bridge wasn't a nice place. 'The Shed' was a crumbling terraced stand filled with hate, spewed up from the standing 'supporters', and there was no money to spend. Bates launched the 'Save the Bridge Fund' with supporters being asked to help pay the costs of running the club. Banks were wary about the fund and wanted two respectable journalists to sign the cheques as a form of guarantee. I was one and the other Bryon Butler. We had to go to the club regularly to sign the cheques and if Bates ever thanked us, it must have escaped our notice. He didn't go in for the normal courtesies of life. He preferred sarcastic 'humour' and coarse language. The 'F' word proliferated.

In those days, members of the press were accommodated in a soulless, draughty area high under the roof of the West Stand. Most days it was cold, often it was freezing, and the view was awful. And after the end of a match, we had to traipse over debris down to the pitch and over to the East Stand on the other side to interview the managers and players. All of us stood in what appeared to be a wind tunnel outside the dressing room, waiting for mundane quotes. Not many players wanted to talk. They were worried about catching pneumonia. It was like being in a spy film set in 1950s East Germany. Stewards were everywhere, always trying to move us on. No wonder that Chelsea was hardly ever praised. Talkative, popular players like Peter Osgood, John Hollins, and Charlie Cooke gave interviews, but it was hard work.

As a former chairman of the Football Writers' Association and its longest-serving committee man, I often raised the subject of the club's abject facilities with Bates. 'You live in f****** pig sties – you like it,' he would say.

He admitted that he told lies if it suited him. He courted younger journalists, inviting them out for expensive meals. Once he invited ten of us to the '192' restaurant near the Royal Albert Hall and in the general chitchat, I raised the subject of his press facilities and several colleagues joined in. Suzannah, his wife, looked distressed.

'You f****** people, all you do is moan, after what I've done for you,' said Bates.

I went to the toilet; I had heard it all before. A minute later, he followed me into the toilet and carried on with the assault.

'Well, you deserve what you get,' I said. 'With a few exceptions, you treat them like dirt. What do you expect?'

When he returned, he helped Suzannah up and they walked out without paying. I had known Suzannah when she was a freelance journalist and she is a nice lady. We asked for ten separate bills for £45, our share of the bill, paid up, and later included them on our expenses sheet by writing 'for entertaining Ken Bates'. If the Inland Revenue had checked on it, they would have discovered that that the rotund Bates had eaten ten dinners on the same night.

Under Ruud Gullit – who soon fell out with Bates and later, with Gianluca Vialli – Chelsea won their first trophy after twenty-six years, winning the FA Cup. My *Daily Mail* colleague Dave Shopland, an award-winning sports photographer, had the idea of publishing a coffee table book about Gullit's year in 1997 titled *Chelsea Azzurri* to reflect the Italian influence. One of my publishers, HarperCollins, was keen. Tom Whiting, the commissioning editor, obtained the backing of the club. Originally priced at £14.99, we agreed on a lower figure for Chelsea fans buying it from the club shop. So Chelsea were going to make money out of it. The print run was 30,000 and it seemed there were no obstacles in the way. Shopland was a lifelong Chelsea supporter and had had his wedding reception at Stamford Bridge. When the book came out, he was very proud of it. One of the pictures featured Ruth Harding, the widow of the late Matthew Harding who fell out with Bates about the control of the club. Harding became a bitter enemy of Bates, but I found him to be a very engaging man and had several meetings with him. He was a jolly man, the opposite to Bates.

Before he fulfilled his ambition of taking over the club, he died in a helicopter crash on the way back from a night game in 1996. By this time, my professional relationship with Bates had deteriorated. 'You're on the side of that f****** Harding,' he said. 'I heard you went round to see him at his office.'

I tried to explain that my job was to talk as many people as possible, not to listen to just one side to any argument. Christmas was approaching and the promotional people at HarperCollins were optimistic about a successful selling campaign, with reprints lined up. Instead, I had a call from Michael Doggart, the publishing director, saying, 'Bates wants £50,000 for the copyright of the club's logo. If he doesn't get it, he will issue a writ.'

Angry and upset, I rang Bates immediately. 'The club told us that they didn't object,' I said. 'Your commercial manager agreed to sell it in the shop. What's going on?'

'Nothing to do with me,' he said. 'He made the decision and I can't do anything about it.' Of course that was nonsense. He controlled everything at the club.

With the matter unresolved, HarperCollins gave the order to pulp the edition of 30,000 copies. A possible £350,000 evaporated. Many ordinary publications have been published about Chelsea FC over the years and this would have been one of the few with style and class. Looking back, you think about Bates and what he has done, about his bad manners, his boorishness, and the tattiness of his Chelsea Village, and you realise that these words – style and class – were rarely associated with him. He was a bully and was despised by so many. It was astonishing that the Premiership was dominated by him in the early years. And it was incomprehensible that the FA should have asked him to handle the negotiations over the building of the new Wembley Stadium in 1997. He was forced out four years later.

One of the last occasions when I saw him was at Bryon Butler's funeral in Guildford. At the service in the crematorium, he and Suzannah sat at the rear and were ignored by almost everyone. He came up to me to shake hands. As a courtesy to Bryon's memory, I shook his hand but I didn't say anything, and neither did he. Bates couldn't be blamed for the hooliganism associated with Chelsea during his reign, but he was partly responsible for building up bad feeling among fans.

I attended many outbreaks of fighting throughout Europe, not all involving Chelsea's louts, and I should have qualified for a campaign medal after being at Feyenoord *v.* Spurs in 1974, Luxembourg *v.* England when the Regent Street of the principality was almost sacked by English marauders, England *v.* Scotland in 1977, Salonika, Turin, Basle, Bruges, and Zaragoza, and at many other distressing scenes of violence home and away.

The most intimidating incident, for me, was after the European Cup Winners' cup tie when Club Brugge beat Chelsea 1-0 in the sanded, muddy, and uneven Olympiastadion. Altogether, 840 people were deported by Belgian police after English police spotters passed on crucial information about the activities of the Chelsea Headhunters, Combat 18, and other groups. I spoke to Police Commissioner Roger de Bree and he said, 'We were confronted by one of the top five hooligan clubs in Europe. These people made it clear both verbally and physically that they would force their way in. This was not possible, the ground was already full. It may be a tradition in

England to go in without tickets but not in Belgium.' I wasn't at Heysel, but that was the main reason why so many people died ten years earlier.

Before the match, I met Tony Banks, the Labour politician who became Sports Minister, and I asked him what he was going to do about these Chelsea fans. He gave a long, rambling oration containing nothing new. David Mellor, the disgraced Conservative minister and a Chelsea supporter, wrote to the Belgians complaining about the excessive use of water cannons and riot squads. That week, Bruce Grobbelaar faced charges of match fixing and Eric Cantona was sentenced to two weeks in jail for attacking a spectator at Crystal Palace. I was in court when the lady magistrate, a school teacher, announced the lenient sentence, but soon afterwards, Cantona's penalty of two weeks in prison was changed to 120 hours of community service. Letting famous footballers off and being defended by ministers of the realm was almost inciting supporters to do their worst. If their heroes were excused, why shouldn't they carry on wrecking European cities?

Long after the match at Bruges, when most of the hooligans had gone off in their charter airplanes and ferries, I was in the hotel and about to go to sleep at 3 a.m. when there was loud knocking on the door of the room next door. 'It's the Metropolitan Police,' said a voice. The occupant opened the door and was rushed by two masked men who departed with his valuables before running off down the corridor. They could have knocked at my door.

Before the second leg, which Chelsea won 2-0, Chelsea captain Dennis Wise was sentenced to three months in jail for attacking a taxi driver before his punishment was commuted. Mr Banks filed a report on the Bruges incidents and instead of exposing the Chelsea fans, he defended them.

There was more. A month earlier I had been at the Romareda Stadium in Zaragoza when the home side scored the second goal in a 3-0 win in the ECWC semi-final first-leg tie against Chelsea and almost immediately, a throng of Chelsea thugs starting ripping up plastic seats on my right and hurling them towards innocent Spaniards: men, women, and young children. Police dived in with batons flailing at the heads of the Chelsea headbangers. So who was at fault? The Spanish police or the Chelsea fans? When the Bruges and Zaragoza fans attended the games at Stamford, not one was arrested. With minor exceptions, there are no instances of European fans causing problems at matches in England.

The biggest crook in football was, inevitably, Robert Maxwell. I have written about him earlier but I have to mention another story about him. In the week before Christmas 1984, the Southend players were told that they wouldn't be paid their wages. Even the manager, Bobby Moore, wouldn't be paid. It was a depressing tale, but riding in to save the players and their families were Ken Bates and his mate Bob Maxwell. They said they were loaning the club £70,000 and Moore told a gathering, 'No words can express how we feel about these friends of ours have done.'

Maxwell, the game's greatest self-propagandist, said, 'We have done this because it is Christmas. It is our way of wishing fans everywhere a happy Christmas.'

I was present at the 'ceremony' and it was a crude PR stunt, not a genuine act of philanthropy. Naturally the 'loan' failed to solve Southend's financial problems, only defer them. Their benefactors' money was not really at risk.

Moore was a fine, much-revered man, and I knew him from the days when he first played for West Ham. When he was at Roots Hall, his career was sadly foundering and his admirers couldn't understand why he was working at that level when the England World Cup captain should have managed a top club. In some ways, he was like David Beckham, handsome, clean living (except for his drinking), totally dedicated to his job, and happily married – until Tina divorced him and he found new happiness with his second wife Stephanie. He was a qualified coach, commanded the utmost respect from the other players, and had been taught by Ron Greenwood, the game's most cerebral teacher. Perhaps he was too nice. You rarely heard him swear or shout. There are plenty of villains in football and sometimes you have to be hard, almost ruthless, to handle them.

In the early 1960s, I worked in the Manchester office of the *Daily Sketch* and often encountered another Bob, Bob Lord, the chairman of Burnley. I had an advantage over my colleagues in the *Daily Mail* office in Deansgate, because they had been banned by Lord from attending home matches at Turf Moor. They wore a tie that had the motif BBB – 'Banned By Bob'. He was pleased to talk to me as the sole representative of Lord Rothermere's Associated Newspapers. It was difficult to have a proper conversation with him as he was partially deaf and wore a hearing aid. His favourite phrase was, 'I believe in calling a spade a bloody spade.' He was just as rude as Bates, although his language was a little better. He owned a butcher's business and after Burnley became League champions in 1959/60, he 'wrote' a book – he was possibly the first chairman to do so. Soon he held high positions in the League Management Committee, football's ruling cabinet, and the FA, which was a damning indictment of the standards applied by those organisations. Butchers and candlemakers ran football before the money men, who knew little about the game, took over in the 1970s. Now the plutocrats have taken charge and they know even less. At UEFA, Michel Platini, a great French footballer, is the President. At FIFA, Franz Beckenbauer, one of Germany's all-time greats, has a top job. You need footballers with brains to run football, not billion-pound footballing ignoramuses.

I met some directors of visiting clubs who joked about 'Bob Lord's turnstile', indicating that the takings from one particular turnstile was given to the chairman to look after and spend for himself. If the money had been declared, it would have been subject to the entertainment tax imposed by the Labour Government. John Cobbold, the chairman of Ipswich, called Lord 'Bollock Chops' after his sideburns. At the time, Ipswich had a population of 119,000 inhabitants against Burnley's 91,000, and these clubs were rivals. You wonder whether they will ever rise to the top again. Lord was constantly quoted – the ban was lifted at the end of the season – and once upset the Ipswich directors with his anti-Jewish comments concerning a Leeds director. Cobbold was so angry that he sent a letter of complaint to the FA and the man who opened the letter at the FA offices was Lord, who was on the disciplinary committee. Lord tossed it into a bin.

Cobbold told me, 'He is a butcher and not a particularly good one, I hate racists and snobs and I won't have them in our boardroom. I would prefer a dustman to a snob.' Not surprisingly, Lord never went to Portman Road again.

Louis Edwards, a chairman of Manchester United, was also in the meat trade and he, too, had a poor knowledge of the game. I was sitting in the press box at Norwich's Carrow Road once and Edwards was sitting a yard in front. He said to a colleague, 'Who is that number seven?'

'That's your superstar, Steve Coppell,' said the man.

His chairmanship was tainted by controversy and the same thing happened with his son Martin, who was also chairman of the club. Doug Ellis, the longtime chairman of Aston Villa, had a questionable reputation, but I got to know him in the World Cup in Italy in 1990 and took a liking to him. Audrey joined me in Rome in the final fortnight of the tournament and strolling down a road near our £300-a-night Aldrovandi Hotel on the Via Veneto – I was on expenses at the time and my total expenditure for the five weeks came to £5,701 – I noticed that Doug and several friends were sitting outside a restaurant. I introduced myself and he invited us to join them. Graham Taylor was Villa's manager and everyone knew that he was going to succeed Bobby Robson – one talkative manager taking over from another. After a bottle or two, Doug promised he would invite me to his hotel the next day for an off-the-record chat. I turned up on time and found him sprawled out on a sunbed next to the swimming pool. He was very communicative and the talk went well. Yes, he said, Taylor would be the England manager, and only the final terms had to be agreed. Suddenly I noticed that something was poking out from his rather floppy, old-fashioned swimming costume – his left testicle. He was talking non-stop and it was impossible to interrupt him and warn him that he might be committing an offence. Half an hour later, I left and his testicle was still on show. After his eightieth birthday, he turned up at a reserve game wearing an old pair of slippers. Before then, he was known as 'Deadly Doug' for sacking so many managers. And like Lord, he wrote a book. Both were flops.

Monty Fresco, the famed Jewish sports photographer who worked with me on the *Sketch* and the *Mail* for many years, once came out with a classic remark about the subject of expenses. Early on in the 1982 World Cup, he fell down a cameraman's viewing area constructed around the back of a goal at the Bilboa ground, and cut his leg. He was taken to hospital and the wound needed forty-four stitches, so he was detained for several days. Some of his colleagues called to see him and when they walked into his room the first question he asked was, 'Have they signed my expenses for the Argentinian trip?'

His *Mail* compatriot laughed, 'No, they're going through it with a red pen.'

Longevity has been a hallmark of the ruling classes in professional football up until recently. As members of the ninety-strong FA Council died, those at the back had to move forward. They dreaded having to sit at the front, on what was known as 'Death Row'. But Doug proved to be the great survivor. Then the FA and the FL brought in an age limit of seventy and Adam Crozier, who was hired as the FA's chief executive from Saatchi and Saatchi, sacked a considerable number of staff over the age of forty, including some of the most efficient and experienced people. He boasted that the average age was now down to thirty-five. Within a short space of time, the FA ran up large debts and its power was largely usurped by the Premiership chairmen. For a while the organisation became almost a joke, a target of the nation's cartoonists. When an independent chairman, Lord Triesman, was appointed, things improved, but he was forced to resign after he became the subject of a *News of the World* exposé. Put in charge of the Royal Mail, Crozier became one of the highest paid people in the public sector. In 2007/08 he was reputedly paid £3.04 million, 180 times the wage of a typical postman. His pension was worth £1.2 million. These obscene figures were in the class of the £60,000-a-week Premiership footballers. He once told me he played a reasonable standard of football in his native Scotland. Not many think he has been a success in any field. In his reign at the Royal Mail, 2,500 post offices were closed, and more face extinction.

When Alan Sugar was chairman of Tottenham Hotspur between 1991 and 2001, during which he spent much of his time rowing with Terry Venables in a series of court actions, he had a reputation of being a real nasty. But I got to know him well because he was right on a number of issues, including the 'bung' culture that still exists. 'Half of them are a bunch of crooks,' he told me, referring to the other managers and chairmen.

In the early months of the Sugar-Venables crisis, I spent some time outside Sugar's house in Chigwell where he lives. That was before I started a long association with his PR, Nick Hewer. Nick has appeared on *The Apprentice*, Sugar's TV programme, and is still marking his card for him. 'He's not cuddly,' said Nick. 'I've seen him being charming but he can tear into you if you've made a mistake.'

Sugar played a big part in Sky's offer for the TV rights of Premiership football and helped convinced the clubs to accept it, saving Rupert Murdoch's business when it got into difficulties. After he sold his shares in Spurs, he described his time at White Hart Lane as 'a waste of time'.

You couldn't dislike Terry Venables. In his playing days, he was nicknamed Sergeant Bilko and perhaps that summed him up. Unlike Sugar, he wasn't a good businessman and lost the battle against Sugar and the inspectors of the Department of Trade and Industry and was forced to pay £500,000 of the costs. In his autobiography, he claimed that he might have been one Hermann Goering's victims in the Blitz in 1943 because his mother Myrtle left the family house twenty-four hours before a bomb dropped on it. So there you are; Terry and I were both lucky. Later, Sugar took an exception to something Venables wrote in his book and to avoid a costly libel action the book was pulped.

I know the feeling.

CHAPTER TWENTY-FIVE

Audrey Meets Pope John Paul II

The forty-nine days I spent in Italy for Italia '90, including the final nine days when Audrey joined me, was one of the best times of our lives and it was crowned by our meeting Pope John Paul II, probably the most popular and most loved of the 265 popes. Audrey came from a Catholic family and I was baptised in the Church of England, but I often accompanied her on visits to Catholic churches all over the world. 'We must try to get an audience with the Pope,' she said.

My World Cup was over and I booked out of my luxurious five-star hotel on the Via Veneto and we checked in at the £90-a-night Nuova Nord Hotel near the main railway station as tourists. An Italian journalist told me how to apply for tickets for an audience and we sped off in a bus to the Vatican to see one of the Pope's administrators. We were ushered in to see a rather formal priest sitting at an antique desk and when I showed my *Daily Mail* pass he said, 'A letter will be delivered to your hotel next morning with all the details. Good day.'

The handwritten letter duly arrived and we bussed to the Vatican on a sultry, hot day and arrived fifteen minutes before the 11 a.m. start. The vast hall was filled with 7,000 worshippers and we sat four rows from the front, right in front of where Pope John Paul was about to speak.

In the Pope's obituary it was said that he spoke ten languages, but in his blessings, delivered for an hour and a half, he went through a list of more than fifty nationalities who were present, and he spoke in each national language. It was an incredible performance for a man of seventy.

Karol Józef Wojtyła was born in Poland in 1920. He lost his mother when he was nine and his father at twenty-one, and was lucky to survive the Uprisings in 1944 when the Germans massacred thousands of his fellow Poles. He was called up for national service but refused to hold a gun. He volunteered for the most menial jobs and saved the lives of many people. When the Germans fled, one of his tasks was to cut away the frozen excreta in the drains below the streets. For a while, he played as a goalkeeper. He was the first non-Italian pope for almost 500 years and was the most travelled, visiting 117 countries and travelling 725,000 miles. As a man who believed in keeping himself fit, he was able to recover from a near-mortal shooting in 1981, and he survived another assassination attempt a year later.

When the last blessing was delivered, Audrey said to me, 'I'm going to get to the front and speak to him.' And she did, leaving me trailing in her wake. The Pope had a kindly face with a faint smile and I had the impression that he personified love and goodness. If he had been put in charge of the stewards at Lord's, Wembley Stadium, or any other great sporting stadia, swearing, sledging, and bad behaviour of any description would have soon disappeared.

He spoke to a number of others before Audrey finally stood in front of him. She smiled and said, 'Good afternoon Father.'

He smiled and shook her hand. 'Where do you come from?' he said.

'Bromley,' said Audrey. 'A big town south of central London.' It was unlikely that he had heard of London's second largest borough.

With dozens of others wanting to meet him, there was no chance for him to say more except, 'Bless you child.'

When Pope John Paul visited England in 1982, Audrey went to his service at the old Wembley Stadium without me. She was lucky to sit within forty yards of him. I went to Lord's instead. My good friend Gill and I were lucky to see Pope John Paul's successor, Benedict XVI, at the Vatican in October 2007. I was on a Forty Club cricket tour and we stayed at the Hotel Cicerone within walking distance of St Peter's Square. The square was filling up when we arrived, an hour and a half before the Pope was supposed to come out at midday. We stood in the rear, facing the area where the Pope normally speaks, a long way away. We were thinking of leaving after standing for more than an hour in a crowd of 30,000 in an 80°F heat when a window on a balcony on our right, no more than forty yards away, was flung open and a microphone was lowered from above. Soon afterwards, the Pope appeared and this old man with a strong voice proceeded to speak in a number of languages. The only word we could catch in English was 'infirmities'. Our Forty Club colleagues were mainly over fifty, with some in their sixties and two in their early seventies, and that word certainly applied to some of them. Many of them were still playing with injuries, but their love of cricket overcame any concerns about health.

It was an uproariously funny, and most enjoyable, tour. A few months later I met Flavio Briatore, the Formula One magnate and a director of QPR, at a gale-ridden match at Blackpool's Bloomfield ground and told him about it.

'Cricket?' he said. 'What is it? I didn't know we had a national team.'

I explained that Simone Gambino, the very personable Presidente della Federazione Cricket Italiana, had formed a league, mainly of immigrants, and that it was now competing in the ICC Associate Members' competition. 'You should sponsor it,' I said. He feigned ignorance.

Our tour took in Stresa on Lake Maggiore, Milan, Siena, Florence, Grosseto, and Rome, but we started by walking out after the first act of the opera *Teneke* at La Scala, Maria Callas' old stomping ground, in protest at being stuck in the sixth-floor galleria with a great view of the chandelier but not of the stage. We paid £85 each, but a travel agent, doubling as a ticket tout, only gave us tickets worth €24. We had to put up with it. La Scala is renowned for its hissing audiences if performances fall below normal standards – and those who stayed on to the end did indeed hear the odd hiss. As we sat outside the square across from the magnificent illuminated Milan Cathedral, supping our litre glasses of beer (costing £14) and mugs of hot chocolate (priced at £5), we were rudely disturbed by the sound of whistles and klaxons. More than 300 cyclists were circling around the square, stopping the traffic. 'That's their weekly demo,' said the Chilean waitress. One of the party suggested that we demonstrate against the ticket arrangements at La Scala.

Earlier in the evening, we had eaten an early supper at an unusual upmarket place called Café Verdi, next to the opera house. As we were having our pasta and pot of tea on the first floor, I looked over the balcony to see a host of books and memorabilia about past heroes, not just opera stars but Hollywood stars as well. The biggest section was devoted to Audrey Hepburn, who had married an Italian doctor and lived in Rome for ten years. Stephanie, my cleaning lady and friend, looked at my holiday photographs a few days later and said, 'She just looks like your Audrey!'

The opening game was against Euratom CC at Cuvio and the buildings looked like the North Korean and Iranian nuclear installations. But hidden by the beautiful trees and under the mountains, there was a scenic little ground with a pitch of rolled mud beneath an astroturf covering. Organiser Dai Kerry, a jolly, Pavarotti-sized Welshman, said, 'It might be a bit slow.'

What an understatement! Barry Peay, one of our better batsmen, said, 'The only way to play on that is to use a croquet stick!'

The home side, mainly from Sri Lanka, had worked through the night and after eight overs ECC were 10-7. One, the tiniest and closest to the ground, failed to get down to block another grubber and was bowled. Hearing my remark 'It's unfair on these midgets, we should give them another chance,' he stopped and returned to the wicket.

'Can I bat again?' he asked.

''Fraid not,' said the umpire.

At Lodi, south of Milan, we played at another beautiful ground eighty metres from a Friesian herd, accompanied by hundreds of horse flies, which were resting in the stables in the 85°F midday heat. The one loo in the mini-pavilion had fractured, but fortunately there were plenty of trees, behind which we could relieve ourselves. That team had five Italians, which is almost up to Premiership standards.

Two days later we were taken to one of Italy's finest polo grounds, where Prince Charles often played. The players of Valdarno CC, all Punjabis, laid out an artificial covering in the middle. The watching polo horses took a keen interest as Valdarno collapsed to 23-7 with our sixty-six-year-old 'fast' bowler taking 6-26. Simone Cipolli, the club's President, invited us to a celebratory dinner in Bucine and when we arrived we were surprised to see a marquee in the car park. It was filled with tables and benches, as if for school dinners. The other fifty-odd seats were filled by Italians in jeans and sweatshirts. We were dressed in smart-casual garb and they looked like pop fans or political agitators. The newly elected mayor, wearing a chef's white apron and a sweatshirt with a slogan on it, yelled for silence and a young, dark-haired lady who turned out to be Ms Malalai Joya, the Afghan politician, got up and called on our Brit and Dutch colleagues to support the campaign to end the fighting in Afghanistan and withdraw all foreign troops. We were aghast; our Dutch umpire Duco Ohm, who is six-foot-one, marched up to the five-foot-one Ms Joya and told her she was wrong to intervene in what should have been a private cricket function. A rent-a-mob had hijacked the meal, but it was good fun, almost like a Dario Fo farce.

In this latest visit to Italy, I experienced a host of coincidences. Before we left home, I saw my dentist Leslie Howe in Wimpole Street about my implants – yes, I now have ten – and when he opened his computer to show the latest inserts waiting for a bridge to be fitted, I said, 'It looks like the bridgehead at Anzio in the Second World War.' I forgot about this until my son Gavin sent me an email from India, where he was directing the India v. Australia ODI series, saying he was reading a book called *Anzio*. When I returned home from Rome, I was twirling through the channels on TV and a film came on: *Anzio*.

Another extraordinary coincidence concerned Ron Noades, the former Crystal Palace chairman, and his wife Novella, whom I knew well. Ron had an advantage over other chairmen and players because he qualified as a referee and a coach. He knew the game better than most of his competitors and was the first person to call for playoffs in the Football League. He was financially astute, and although he wasn't popular among his supporters, without him Palace would have gone under.

My knee was sore during that tour and when I learned that the coach taking the team to one match couldn't get down the road to the changing rooms I faced the prospect of carrying my cricket bag for 600 metres. Joyce Jarvis, one of the wives, volunteered to carry it. Rather embarrassed, I said, 'Don't be silly. I'll soldier on.'

Joyce, a class golfer, said, 'I always carry my clubs and this will be the same weight.' She picked it and strode off, shaming the younger male players.

The next morning, we were talking about a golf club in Croydon owned by Noades where Joyce had just played. Two days later, back at Bromley, a friend rang up and said he had just played on that course and met Ron Noades. I hadn't brought Noades up in the conversation and I hadn't seen him for years, nor his wife.

On the final day in Rome, we went to the Forum. Trying to be funny, I said to some of the wives, 'Where is Frankie Howerd?' Two days later I opened the TV section of the *Mail* and saw a radio programme being featured... about Howerd.

The tour guide, a thirty-five-year-old Italian who knew English history as well as Italian history, had heard of Howerd, and I asked him how many places he had visited in England.

'Many places,' he said, 'but my favourite is Shanklin where the poet John Keats lived. He died in Rome you know.'

I told him I had worked in Shanklin for the local newspaper and covered a number of events about Keats. In her brief stay in Rome in 1990, Audrey visited dozens of art galleries, churches, palaces, and monuments, and also the house where Keats and Shelley had lived. The guide, whom I suspected was gay, told Gill and me how many gladiators had died in the Colosseo in its first year: 15,000. For some reason I spoke about the Charge of the Light Brigade. 'Ah,' he said, 'Lord Raglan.'

I didn't think any more about it until the day after England lost 2-1 in Russia in the European Championship qualifying group. I read Jeff Powell's article, which started with a reference to Lord Raglan and the Charge of the Light Brigade.

The most startling coincidence concerned Julius Caesar. After the visit to the Forum, the coach stopped and the guide said, 'Look on the left, you see the spot where Julius Caesar was assassinated by Brutus.'

Three days later I went to the Forty Club dinner at the Savoy and the comedian Bob 'The Cat' Bevan was finishing his final story. It was about... Julius Caesar. 'Old Julius used to brag a bit,' said Bob. 'He claimed he slaughtered 50,000 Gauls on his last invasion to France but Brutus said, "I counted 25,000, not 50,000. He always exaggerates." Julius Caesar countered, saying, "In European games it counts double."' The audience erupted in laughter and President Charles Fry, grandson of C. B. Fry, patted him on the back and forgave him for exceeding his fifteen-minute limit.

I went up to Bob and said, 'We were at the place where Julius Caesar was stabbed only a few days ago.'

He was most impressed. 'Must be telepathy,' he said.

CHAPTER TWENTY-SIX

The Heart Aches Begin!

Most journalists have trouble sleeping after big games. We are like sportsmen – we play the game through in our minds. Phrases appear and you wonder whether you should have used them. In the middle of the night on 12 August 1997, I felt other concerns – pain around the heart and down my left arm. My fingertips were tingling. Indigestion, I thought, caused by rushing through meals on working days. Working for a national newspaper doesn't allow leisurely lunchtimes, except for those in top positions who need to entertain their friends. I was taking an occasional Rennie. I looked at my watch, the one the *Daily Mail* had presented to me in 1995 'after thirty-five years from the Chairman and Directors of Associated Newspapers' and I had to turn on the light because the face wasn't illuminated. I should have been given a watch after twenty-five years, but it was overlooked; getting one after thirty-five years was slightly odd. I told them that I would go for forty years, taking me up to the end of 2000, and wait for one of the nine-carat-gold watches. But someone couldn't wait. Ah well!

The time was 3.58 a.m.; 4 a.m. is the danger time for people suffering heart attacks. On average, around 100,000 people die every year with heart attacks, so it is still the commonest way of dying. Still believing that I had digestion, I staggered down to the kitchen and took several Rennies and a couple of aspirins. I was sweating profusely and the chest pains intensified. I went back upstairs and sat up in our very large kingsize bed taking in deep breaths and holding them for several seconds. Apparently that helps. Audrey woke with a start. 'What's happening?' she said.

She was a great diarist and she wrote later, 'Brian was awake and I told him to go back to bed but he said "chest pains". Immediately I rushed up and changed and took the car out of the garage. He was by the door in his dressing gown and slippers. I drove him to the Bromley Hospital, less than half a mile away, going through two red lights and breaking the speed limit. The hospital reception was manned by one woman and Brian went up to her pointing to his chest. Straight away a young doctor and a nurse named Gill rushed up and helped him on to a trolley and whipped him into the resuscitation room. He was the only patient, fortunately, and they got working on him, giving him an ECG, oxygen, and an injection to disperse the blood clot. It took an hour and I was massaging his feet. It was very hot and I was longing to sit down. They were sticking needles into his arm and trying to bring his pulse rate down. It had reached 150 and bells were ringing! By 6 a.m. he was back in the coronary unit and later he came round. What a relief! I went home at 7 a.m. to have a cup of tea and lie down.'

I remember that nurse Gill. Before I went under, she asked me what I did for a job and I said, 'Writing about sport for the *Daily Mail*.' She told me she was a fan of Crystal Palace and I said, 'I'll be reporting their match on Saturday.'

She laughed. 'I don't think so!'

I spent a week in the hospital – it was later demolished and replaced with a block of flats! – but I found for a while that I was tetchy and unlike my old self. When you have a heart attack it changes your emotions. They come bubbling up to the surface and you find yourself crying over nothing. I can imagine mothers feel that way after undergoing difficult births. I couldn't recollect this, but years later I read Audrey's diary entry for 18 August, the day I came out of hospital: 'Brian is irritable and refuses to open the windows at night. Says he needs support from the family. I'm furious, after all I've had to go through. I'm shattered, tired, and upset. It was very tense and I am very hurt. He actually shouts out and starts to cry. I can't believe it.'

I can't remember if I apologised at the time but I should have done. I ought be ashamed because Audrey's mother Lucy Regina, aged eighty-nine, only had a few days to live. She was staying at St Raphael's Christian Home nearby and Audrey nursed fed, and bathed her every day. She made etchings of her mother and drew her in her sketchpads. Some of the sketches were the best she ever drew. There were disputes among the remaining sisters about the funeral arrangements and Audrey was the one who took the brunt.

Her brother Pat was staying with us and sometimes he is not the easiest of guests. A few years later, he volunteered to change the tap washers in the kitchen and proceeded to unscrew a tap without turning off the water supply. Water shot into the air and he said, 'Put a towel on it, that'll stop it.' I tried to stifle the geyser, only to scald my hands. The kitchen was flooded before we finally halted the flow. I asked him to refrain from interfering with the taps again but a few minutes later, water was dripping through the kitchen ceiling. I raced upstairs; he had tried to unscrew another tap with the same result. The bathroom floor was filling with water, but we managed to prevent a bigger disaster.

'I'm banning you from any more plumbing,' I told him. He is a ballroom dancer and I advised him to concentrate on that, and not do any more 'jobs' in our house. His latest dancing partner is a former Hollywood starlet.

In the week after my heart attack, one member of the family rang to say that another sister living in California had been rushed to hospital. Louise was about to fly back to New York. Meanwhile, Audrey was being prescribed a high dosage of steroids to counter her liver disease. She was exhausted. She was ferrying people around, including me, and it was a particularly hot period of the year. Ten days after my heart attack, she took me to King's College Hospital, Denmark Hill, for an angioplasty. My consultant, Dr Ray Wainwright, who had a wonderful bedside manner, explained that I would have two stents inserted to keep the affected artery open. Audrey wrote later in the diary, 'He told me that the artery was ninety-five per cent blocked. A couple more hours and it would have been fatal! I was shocked that Brian could have gone first. He was always so fit and healthy.'

When I first met Ray, he asked me, 'Do you drink and smoke and the usual things the journalists do?'

'I don't smoke, never drank alcohol and I've played sport all my life,' I said. 'I'm only a few pounds heavier than when I was in my teenage days and I could still get in my wedding suit, if I had to.'

'It must have been stress,' he said.

'Well,' I replied. 'I'm not normally a stressful person but recently a rather excitable Scots sports editor has taken over and I'm not blaming him but I think the situation contributed!'

I was next for the angioplasty procedure, but a middle-aged woman from Sussex came back from the treatment room and said to me, 'The thingy they stick you into your main artery has broken down so you are being sent home.'

A nurse arrived to confirm that news. 'You'll be done at the London Bridge Hospital on the twenty-sixth,' she said.

Meanwhile a hurricane of telephone calls, letters, emails, flowers, and visitors hit 84 Widmore Road. It lifted my spirits immensely and I was eternally grateful to so many good people, although it did add to Audrey's increasing stress. I loved the letter from Ian Wooldridge, who wrote, 'Now look here. I don't want you skiving about in there when you could be attacking Ken Bates, insulting Michael Atherton, or getting the *Mail* banned from Arsenal. You know perfectly well that our staff is now down to three and I deem it most inconsiderate of you to take such unilateral action without written permission. In short, get out of there as soon as possible and take a terrific rest. I guess these things are sent to give us a little warning to ease up occasionally.'

Another good friend, ITV's Brian Moore, rang and told me he had undergone the same procedure. Robin Wainwright, the heart consultant, explained that if I followed a proper non-fat diet and kept up the exercising, I would have a long life. Brian, sadly, didn't enjoy that long a life. He went into the former Farnborough Hospital near to his house to have minor surgery, and collapsed and died a few days later.

The London Bridge Hospital is nicely positioned on the Thames but it is a very cramped building. When I was escorted to the private patients' floor I was shown to a small room and another patient was sitting on a bed. I thought it was single occupancy. 'Don't worry,' the middle-aged man said. 'I'll be out of there before early afternoon but I don't know whether they will put someone else in as well.' There was a lot of noise outside and I looked out of the door. Several white-robed Arabs were smoking outside and using their mobiles. 'They never stop,' the man said. 'Bit unusual for a hospital but I suppose money talks.'

After being taken on a trolley to the heart unit I was able to watch the procedure from a screen next to my bed. There was no pain as the plastic inserter went into the main artery towards the heart. I could see these arteries and veins waving away like an exotic plant close to the sea floor. The explanation of the absence of pain is that inside the body most veins are pointing inward. Only the ones pointing outward to the skin cause pain. The two small metal stents were placed and it all worked perfectly. But when I got back to my room, I suddenly fainted. Ray said it was due to the effects of the drugs. 'Nothing to worry about.' I said 'It was probably caused by the smoking outside.' He said that the heart is like a muscle; when it is damaged, it fails to regenerate. But a slightly damaged one can function almost normally. He advised me not to get worked up about anything, particularly at the wheel of a car. Instead of giving the 'V' sign when someone cuts me up at a roundabout, I now smile.

It was the end of August 1997. My heart attack could easily have been more damaging; if England had held on at Trent Bridge and drawn the match I wouldn't have gone home. I might have just thought it was indigestion and having no one to help me I could have stayed in bed. I might have died. There wouldn't have been an Audrey to save me. While it was all happening, Princess Diana died in Paris and the whole nation was plunged into grief. We needed a holiday.

When I had my hip operation in 1995, Butch Stewart, who owns the upmarket Caribbean holiday company Sandals as well as Air Jamaica, was seeking publicity in the UK by sponsoring the West Indies cricket. He offered Audrey and me a couple of weeks' holiday at Negril, in Jamaica. My recuperation was aided by Espe, the Sandals trainer who worked on my leg so well that when I returned I was running between the wickets almost as fast as Alec Stewart. She was also an international football referee. It was a fantastic holiday but at the end it was rather scary when a hurricane arrived. But it wasn't a potentially threatening one; it faded fast and didn't do much damage. Two years on, we were both exhausted. I contacted Elaine Vaughan, the UK manager of Sandals, and asked if we could pay for a two-week holiday in Antigua. She offered a deal, $200 per couple per day for full board, and we were delighted.

The complex was on a beautiful bay and we walked a mile every day to the English-style red telephone box to ring St Raphael's to check on Lucy Regina's state of health. It meant collecting a lot of coins to pay for the calls. Lucy was still holding on. She had a very strong heart. We were upgraded to a honeymoon suite and it was much better honeymoon than the one we had had flying about Crete, Rhodes, and Athens in 1965. By the end of the holiday, the whole of Antigua was covered with ash from the volcano near Montserrat. It was as though we were in the Swiss Alps going skiing.

We returned home on 16 September. I started work again on 22 September and Lucy died on 24 September. These had been tumultuous times for our family.

Most people I met back at work asked the same question: 'How did you have a heart attack when you look after yourself and don't drink or smoke?' I told my Mike Atherton story as a part-explanation.

On the Sunday of the Trent Bridge Test, I was increasingly annoyed by the way the England batsmen batted spinelessly in the fifth Test. There were eight hours left to play on a near-flawless pitch and a couple of them needed to do a Peter May and Colin Cowdrey. Only Graham Thorpe stayed on, scoring eighty-two, but he batted selfishly, often giving the strike to the tail-enders instead of assuming the responsibility himself. I noticed that Atherton was sitting on the balcony playing with a yo-yo and occasionally laughing. What he should have done was to send out a message to Thorpe telling him to take the strike and shield the non-strikers. But he never did it. Eight wickets down, Thorpe took a single off the first ball of an over bowled by Glenn

McGrath, leaving Dean Headley to face the next five deliveries. Headley didn't survive and Devon Malcolm lasted two balls. England were bowled out for 186 with seven balls left from the extra half hour.

In the many years that I covered Test cricket I always rang the sports editor at the tea interval to discuss what was going to be on the back page. I usually did the news story and it needed to be straight and to the point. If it was a bad day for news, the story might be buried on a page inside. This time I spoke to Bryan Cooney, the fifty-two-year-old Scots journalist who was the thirteenth sports editor I'd worked under in my time with the Associated Newspapers. He might have brought bad luck for me, I don't know, but he certainly caused a lot of unnecessary hassle for everyone in the department. I had known him well when he worked for *The Sun* and *The Star* – in competition with me. I also played football against him and he wasn't a good player. Mouthy, and not up to standard. He was dismissed by those two red top papers in questionable circumstances and when he was appointed sports editor of the *Mail*, the rest of us were astounded. He told me afterwards, 'They want me to get stuck into these characters who spend all their time in clubs, sipping champers with their feet on the table.' I didn't know who he was talking about. There were fifty-eight journalists working in the department and within three years, twenty-nine of them, mostly top men, had left. I could have been the thirtieth, but I resisted. Some of the newcomers were talented journalists, mainly fellow Scots, and he called them 'Cooney's loonies', which might explain his reprehensible tactics. He had a sharp sense of humour, knew a good story when he saw it, and had bundles of enthusiasm. But he couldn't be trusted. A MORI survey of trust in the professions in 2006 said that journalists were bottom of the table with only twenty per cent of the public believing they were trustworthy. The next class was politicians (twenty-two per cent). Top of the table were doctors (ninety-six per cent). I have to say nearly all the sports writers I have worked with were trustworthy individuals. In Cooney's three and a half years in charge, the *Mail* was bombarded by letters from angry people threatening to sue after they had become victims of his more vigorous style of reporting; some did take out writs.

As the Ashes urn was about to be retained by the Australians for the fifth successive competition. I rang Cooney and told him what I intended to write about the final day's play. I explained that Atherton should have taken firm charge and not sat back playing with a yo-yo. He ought to have passed a message to Thorpe about his niggardly behaviour. Cooney didn't argue about it. He knew little about cricket but now and again he would come up with a good idea, or an occasional daft one.

Ken Mahood, the admirable sports cartoonist of the *Mail*, produced a massive card for all the members of staff to sign and send to me after my heart attack. Cooney wrote, 'We're filling these damned cracks in the pitch, so all will be tickety-boo for your return. Kindest regards, Bryan.' That was rather funny, but there was a point to it. Earlier I wrote a story about a Test pitch cracking up and he said, 'I don't want any rubbish about cracks. It's about people, not cracks in pitches.' I had to explain that the state of the pitch can sometimes affect results and as experts, it is our duty to spell that out. Obviously I would prefer to write about people, but sometimes you have to make an exception.

He showed kindness when he came to see me in hospital the day after my heart attack. He arrived at 5 p.m., a key time for a sports editors, who would normally be at the wheel running the ship in the early evening. I was very impressed by that. But I had been less impressed at 7.15 p.m. on Sunday in Nottingham when he said, 'Right, this is what we have put on your story. The main headline is "Dead Duck" and under that is, "Michael Atherton – you are charged with impersonating an England cricket captain." OK?'

I said, 'It's not OK. I never wrote that. If you want to keep that, take my name off it. What you have written is insulting, unfair, and almost libellous.' He slammed the phone down.

My copy had been put over some time ago and it had been changed to 'Mike Atherton sat on the Trent Bridge pavilion balcony playing with a piece of string (he should have checked that it was a yo-yo, not a piece of string!) and laughing and joking as England's batsmen crashed to a 264 run defeat which keeps the Ashes in Australian hands. England's defiant skipper said last night that he intends to stay in the job for the final Test at the Oval but with pressure on him to quit growing stronger by the day, he gave a hint that he may not be in charge in the West Indies this winter. Atherton, who was dismissed for eight to bring his aggregate to 241, said, "I will sit down after this series ends and ruminate over it. I have always said I will know when it is time to go." England were bowled out for 186 after being set 451 to win and the innings lasted a miserable 48.5 overs on a pitch which everyone agreed was by far the best of the series for batting. There appeared no direction from the captain up on the bridge as several batsmen got themselves out playing over aggressive shots in a situation where England's only chance of survival was to take the game to the final day. There also appeared to be no instructions given to Surrey's left-hander Graham Thorpe about protecting the tail-enders by retaining the strike.'

My piece contained nothing about a dead duck and nothing about charging him as an impersonator. I drove home that night and the next morning I looked at the back page. It was very unsettling but I didn't get too upset because everyone knew that Cooney behaved like that and I wouldn't have written the headlines.

After a quick breakfast, I drove to Chelmsford to interview Nasser Hussain, the favourite to succeed Atherton as England captain. Nasser, whom I respect immensely because of his honesty and frankness, came out with some strong comments about English cricketers. They are too soft and they crumble against pressure, he said. Along with my news story, Hussain's interview filled two pages under the headline, 'Too lovey-dovey to mix it with the hard Aussies'. On top there was a strap saying, 'The best pages in the Fleet Street business bring you another brilliant exclusive and this one comes from English cricket's inner sanctum.' It was an outstanding piece of journalism: the best of Cooney, not the worst. Around this time I was producing a crop of scoops, yet Cooney was trying to kick me out, as I shall explain.

Later the following night I had my heart attack and was in intensive care. When the phone at home rang at 9.30 a.m., Audrey answered. 'This is David Graveney,' a voice said. 'Is Brian there?'

She said, 'No, he's in hospital recovering from a heart attack.'

The chairman of selectors muttered an apology and passed on his best wishes. He wanted to have a go at me about the Atherton 'story'. I met him many times afterwards and he never mentioned it again. Poorly paid, David Graveney did a fine job on behalf of English cricket and it was harsh that after ten years that he was sacked. Most of the problems England faced after losing the Ashes in 2006 were caused by Duncan Fletcher, the coach. As he showed in his autobiography, he was a difficult man who bore grudges, unlike Graveney.

It is ironic that Mike Atherton now holds the best job in English cricket: cricket correspondent for *The Times*. When he played, he was uncooperative with the press and lacked grace. English cricket might have taken a better turn if he had been more helpful and put over a better image. I think he realised that he might have got it wrong, but over the years he has developed into a very fine writer, although his opinions tend to veer from one side of the spectrum to the other. Well read and extremely intelligent, he has enhanced cricket writing. He is not impersonating anyone.

Cooney was an inveterate writer of memoranda. One said, 'Time keeping, again, is becoming a minor problem, with some people straggling in nearer to lunchtime than breakfast time. May I remind you that you should begin your day in the office at 10.30?' He wrote to a sub editor who altered a writer's copy, 'If you can hear a swishing noise it is the sound of the guillotine above your head.' He abhorred clichés and mistakes. In another message to the staff, he wrote, 'There is a proliferation of impatiens on my patio at home – but it does not match the proliferation of clichés in the *Daily Mail* these past couple of weeks. You are reminded again that clichés are anathema to the style and culture of our newspaper.' In another message, he said, 'A plague of grammatical errors continues to blight the pages of Sportsmail. Two paragraphs in the copy of Alan Fraser and Ian Gibb made me cringe while lying in my sick bed. Those subs responsible should also be cringing – it may be a case of picking up my sick bed and walking toward Derry Street.' He waged a losing battle against excessive claims on expenses. Near the end of his disruptive reign he warned, 'We are currently running at a high budget deficit, seventy-five per cent of which is due to increasing staff expenses. You do not need to be a mathematician to realise the consequences of such fiscal inefficiency. Please amend you forthcoming expenses or I will obliged to do it for you.'

The staff was being thinned out and I wondered whether I would be the next to be offered a deal. It was coming up to the first anniversary of my heart attack and I was covering the England *v.* South Africa Test match at Headingley. I had just done an interesting graphic about the speed of the world's fastest bowlers – which upset Fred Trueman – and I noticed that my usual byline was missing. I had Fred down at 85 mph and when I saw him, he said, 'Your bloody paper ought to be its facts right! 85 mph I tell you! That were my warming-up ball.'

'You're right Fred. I don't know who wrote that garbage,' I said.

'You tell them, I were 90 mph *plus* most of the time.'

At 9 p.m. the man on the desk called to say, 'Bryan wants you to be in the office tomorrow doing football – and to do the Arsenal press conference at Sopwell House.'

I realised the dirty tricks had started. To be taken off a Test match and sent 220 miles south in your car to cover an event that a freelancer could have done was unprofessional and costly. 'Who's doing my job at Headingley?' I asked him.

'Peter Ferguson,' he said.

Fergie was one of the most popular football journalists in the North and was well respected, but he was not a cricket expert. But I had to follow orders, and when I arrived at Sopwell House my colleague Martin Lipton, who had joined the *Mail* from the Press Association, was there. I asked him who was supposed to cover the event.

'I don't know,' he said. 'Both of us I suppose.'

The next day, I looked at the sports section and there were just six paragraphs about Arsenal. That evening I said to the news editor, 'I am going back north because I put myself down for the Sheffield United *v.* Swindon game on Saturday before returning to Headingley to do the Sunday play.'

'We want you to go to a game at Palace,' he said.

'Don't give me that,' I said. 'You can't keep moving me up and down the country running up unnecessary expenses. I'm now at Leeds and I intend to go to Bramall Lane as laid down in the original list of matches.'

So I duly covered the Sheffield United match, and upset new manager Steve Bruce after the match by asking him, 'Do you have a full coaching badge?'

He bridled. 'Well, I'm doing it now,' he said.

Bruce turned out to be a good manager and he later passed the necessary examinations. But even now, young managers are still being given managerial jobs in Premiership clubs without having the proper qualifications. Paul Ince is a prime example, and he didn't last long at Blackburn.

The next day, I was at the dank Headingley press box and I asked Fergie if he was supposed to be doing the news story on the back page. He said he thought he would be, but that we should check. I rang the desk and the sports news editor said, 'Fergie is doing it and Cooney wants you to do a feature on Micky Stewart and Alec.'

I said, 'Micky has gone home and I can't do the feature. Is this place being run by madmen? Don't answer that: we all know!'

At 8.30 a.m. the next day I rang Cooney and said, 'Why are you doing this to me?' He failed to come up with a valid reason. I thought about speaking to Paul Dacre, the *Mail*'s long-serving, highly distinguished and admired editor. I knew him from the days when he was a news reporter and I knew he had high regard for my work. I decided to hold back on the idea of talking to him for a while. If you are tripped up from behind, the best way to treat the assailant is to come up with a powerful answer, i.e. an exclusive that demanded proper exposure. I knew I had to find a different story to the one that would come out of the press conference, so I sat outside and listened to the crowd. Yorkshire crowds often dislike players from southern counties and if someone like Keith Fletcher dropped a chance, as he once did at Headingley, he would be heartily barracked. This time they were booing Ian Salisbury, the Surrey leg spinner who failed to take a wicket at the cost of 125 runs in his two Tests. The other journalists wouldn't have heard it because the air-conditioned press box is enclosed with no windows.

Later I went up to David Graveney and I said, 'What did you think of the way Ian Salisbury was treated by the Yorkshire crowd?'

I was surprised by his response. 'Well, he didn't bowl very well and if that happens, you can expect criticism,' he said.

I rang the desk and said, 'I've got a nice little scoop about Salisbury being booed as England are on the way to victory and I'm just about to put it over.'

The next day, the Salisbury story didn't appear. I realised that I had to come up with a better, more stunning exclusive. After the game I was talking to my friend Qamar Ahmed about the umpiring. The fifty-eight-year-old Javed Akhtar was being condemned for making six mistakes in the Test and Ahmed said, 'Do you know how much he was paid?'

I knew that Peter Willey, the other umpire, was paid £2,500 plus a small sum for every appearance.

'Nothing like that,' he said. 'He got 13,000 rupees, which works out as £31.60. It's slave labour.'

I rang Cooney with the news and to be fair, he stuck the story on the back page the next day with a large, blue 'exclusive' on it. An ICC spokesman confirmed the story, saying that umpires are paid in their own countries. 'It still comes up to a rather large amount in their own money,' he explained. Later the system was changed, with the Elite Panel taking over. Inexperienced umpires like Akhtar were left out. I was elated. I had proved my point, or so I thought.

On 13 August, the heart attack's first anniversary, Bob Driscoll rang me and said, 'Bryan wants to put your mind at rest and have a chat.'

'My mind is at rest,' I said. 'If he treats me as he should, there is no problem. He's just been making things difficult for me for no apparent reason.'

He invited me to meet him at the bar at the Royal Garden Hotel, across the road from the *Mail* offices. The sun was shining, English cricket was on the way back, and I believed I had just proved that I was one of the best news gatherers in the department. Driscoll started talking about a deal. 'We can give you a contract to work for three days a week and do a match,' he said. 'What do you think about that?'

'Not very much,' I replied. I told him several times that I intended to finish after forty years with Associated Newspapers and then write books. Not many journalists survive that time, and I am proud of my record. 'If anyone tries to kick me out, I'll be first in to see the editor,' I said.

A week later, they had another try. Cammie Stewart, the deputy, asked me to have a drink at The Greyhound and said Cooney was coming as well. Cooney didn't stay long, merely saying that he would give me a weekly column and the odd match. I said, 'I don't know why you are so desperate to get me off the payroll. I am not in the highest bracket of wage earners. In terms of words and scoops per month you've got a bargain with me.' The talks lasted two hours and I left telling them to lay off and behave themselves.

I never had a big shouting match with Cooney, but his unsubtle tactics were a form of attempted 'mental disintegration', to use cricketer Steve Waugh's favourite phrase. It brought back to me something Norman Giller of the *Daily Express* had said. He had known John Macadam and said, 'The then sports editor Harold Hardman drove John to drink after demoting him from sports columnist to a dogsbody job.'

Rod Gilchrist, the assistant editor of the *Mail on Sunday*, is a good friend from our footballing days and I rang him for advice. 'Sit tight,' he said. So I did. I went the full course and Cooney was the first to go. He departed on 2 November 2000 and made a pretty abject speech in front of a very happy throng who clapped gleefully because we wouldn't see him again – he was going to live in Scotland.

While all these unpleasant things were going on, Audrey was back in hospital for the seventh time in our thirty-five years of marriage, and we knew that she wouldn't last long.

Before Cooney left the staff, he started giving my stories to other reporters and putting their names on them. On one occasion, when I reported on a West Ham, he put John Edwards' name on it. John has worked for many years in the North West; I'm not sure if he had ever visited Upton Park. I reported on the sacking of Bruce Rioch and his assistant Stewart Houston at QPR and interviewed both men, whom I knew from my early days. Someone started 'my' report, 'Regrets, joy and bitter recriminations swept through the streets yesterday as the wheels of the managerial tumbril rattled and clattered through the streets of West London.' It didn't look like my style of writing! I met Bruce and Stewart at a match the following Saturday and they both said they knew it wasn't my work. My match reports would be cut to only a few words and they changed my matches to insignificant ones at the last minute.

One of the oddest stories about Cooney's erratic behaviour happened on 16 May 2000, the day of the funeral of an old friend, Chris Lander of the *Daily Mirror*, at Wells Cathedral. Six of us were intent on going and the Mail sports secretary hired a Mercedes-Benz van to take us. However, Cooney decided to drive the van to Membury, leaving us to drive ourselves to the motorway service station. In a stream of mobile phone calls, he changed the rendezvous to Chieveley and then to Reading, by which time Nigel Clarke, who lives near me in Chislehurst, had picked me up and we had already passed Reading. We had to drive sixteen miles back to the motorway service station where Cooney was waiting. Nigel left his car in the coach park, but when he returned, a traffic warden had stuck a £60 penalty notice on the windscreen. There was no map in the van and we had to ask an AA man for directions. In the confusion, we travelled fifty miles further than we should have done. At one point, we were about to run out of petrol and had to turn off from the M5. We filled up and started driving again, but there was a peculiar noise and the van stopped. There was no petrol cap on, so we searched the garage courtyard and the fifty yards of verge and roadway from the petrol station without any success. Everyone was standing by the vehicle wondering what we should do when Mike Dickson shouted, 'It's on the roof!' Our four-hour journey ended ten minutes before the start of the service, which was brilliantly conducted by Andrew Wingfield Digby, the priest sacked by Ray Illingworth as the England cricket team's spiritual adviser. The reception was held at the rugby club in Bath, but Cooney decided not to go and went home. Nigel had to drive us all back to London. We hadn't eaten properly for seven hours.

Cooney appeared to have an obsession about ducks, particularly Donald Duck. I reported on what was called 'the greatest ODI of all time' – the semi-final of the 1999 World Cup, when Australia beat South Africa at Edgbaston on run rate to reach the final with the teams tied on 213. The Proteas should have won but for the extraordinary behaviour of Man of the Match Lance Klusener. With three balls remaining, the South Africans needed just a single. Instead, he lashed out wildly and hit the ball towards Mark Waugh at mid on and started running down the pitch like a madman. There was no chance of a run. A startled Allan Donald, who was backing up too far, hesitated, dropped his bat, and was run out by half the length of the pitch for a duck. The guilty party was Klusener, not Donald, as I told Cooney on the phone. Martin Lipton was also at the match, as part of the *Mail* team, and Cooney obviously gave him different instructions. The headline of the back-page story was 'Donald ducks out' and the blame was put entirely on Donald. Millions of viewers watched it and they knew it was Klusener's fault. But Cooney knew better.

Earlier in the week, I was in the office when I saw a tall young man go into Cooney's office, which was next to my desk. I said to one of the secretaries, 'Who's that? Another signing?'

'I think he's a freelance,' she said.

Two days before the final, I was invited to the World Cup dinner at the Guildhall. The City of London had been blocked off because of a demonstration by anarchists, so I didn't go. I had not realised we had so many anarchists in the country. Earlier I was leaving a press conference at Lord's and another contact put me onto a scoop about Wasim Akram responding to rumours about match fixing, but the story had failed to appear. Another snub followed. The *Mail*'s allocation of tickets for the final was three and mine hadn't arrived. I asked the sports news editor about it and he said, 'You don't seem to have one.' Asked why, he said, 'He's given yours to John Greechan.'

John was one of Cooney's recruits from Scotland, a fine writer specialising in football. 'He doesn't know anything about cricket,' I said.

'Well, he's doing the colour piece,' he replied.

'That's great,' I said. 'We're not going to have a news man to do the back page story.' Reminding myself that with my cardiovascular history I needed to keep calm, I said, 'In that case I'll take the day off and play cricket.'

At 9.10 a.m. on Sunday I was at home when the phone rang and Alan Thompson, the nice Scotsman who often worked on the desk, said, 'You're supposed to be in the office.'

'No one told me,' I said. So I had to cancel my cricketing match at Crockham Hill in Kent and drove into the office. Cooney always insisted on everyone wearing a tie and jacket but on Sundays the dress code was relaxed, so I wore an open necked shirt.

At 11.20 a.m. I was watching the TV coverage from Lord's after a half-hour delay through rain and Alan said, 'There's a change of plan. Can you go to Lord's?'

'What's happened now?' I said.

'Ian Wooldridge was going to be there but he can't,' he said.

Well, this was no way to treat someone, but I ploughed on. I rang the mobile of one of the girls at MCC and asked if I could have a press ticket at the Grace Gates because I couldn't retrieve Ian's ticket. She rang back to say another would be on the side gate for me behind the Tavern. One of the sub editors was wearing a tie and I asked for a loan of it to enable me to conform to the MCC regulations.

'There'll be a fee,' he said.

'I'll put it on Cooney's expenses,' I said.

I rushed off in a taxi and 200 metres from Lord's the road was blocked by thousands of Pakistanis, most of whom were in a belligerent mood having been excluded from Lord's. I struggled through the throng and managed to get within a few yards of the gate. The young lady was waving my ticket to attract my attention. Unfortunately, dozens of angry Pakistanis were trying to snatch the ticket off her and police officers were trying to hold them back. I could have been stabbed or even lynched, but well done to the constabulary: they managed to clear a small space and I was able to squeeze myself through the gate without being injured. Several years ago I had been present when Prince Philip opened the gate and there is a plaque there to commemorate the occasion. I thought to myself: he doesn't have this trouble getting in.

High above Lord's, in the Media Centre, otherwise known as the Lord's UFO, my colleagues were ribbing me. 'You've missed three wickets already and the game is almost over,' said one.

'I fear it was a Cooney looney day,' I said.

The Pakistanis decided to bat when they should have fielded and they were bowled out for a miserable 132 with Shane Warne taking 4-33. When the nervous-looking Pakistanis warmed up before going on to the field, I noticed that some of them, particularly Shoaib Akhtar, were sweating profusely. Shoaib bowled four overs and conceded thirty-seven runs and it ended at 4.35, with Australia embarrassingly winning by eight wickets. The Jockey Club should have performed tests to find out why the Pakistanis performed so badly. Was it fixed? Later stories appeared about the behaviour of one or two of their players. They hadn't gone to bed as early as expected. Mushtaq Mohammad, the Pakistani coach and a longtime friend, said, 'I am in a state of shock. Our performance was disgraceful.'

But the news story was about the hero of the day, Warne. In his many after-match interviews, he spoke about retiring, but one of my Australian colleagues told me, 'Don't take any notice of that. He's talking that way to push up the ante and make more money from his other ventures.'

I wrote the back page lead and the headline was 'Shane's Warning'. The last paragraph was the key one. I wrote, 'He is thirty on 13 September and it seems inconceivable that he will quit just yet.'

The next morning I told the sports news editor that I had a good follow-up – Warne is carrying on. I was asked to write 1,000 words. Cooney was keen on 1,000 word epics. The following morning, I picked up the papers from the door, turned to the *Mail*, and a whole page was devoted to 'World Cup: The Post Mortem'. The headline was, 'A snap of those magic fingers and the fans rise again to Queenie'. There was a picture byline of one Grant Robins. The 1,000-odd words, 750 of them mine, were there. At the end there was the line, 'Additional reporting by Brian Scovell.' Who is 'Queenie'? We will never know. Who was Grant Robins? The first six paragraphs – about an incident involving Warne in South Africa years previously – was written by young Grant and the rest was mine. No one asked me about this mutilation of my story. When I arrived at Northcliffe House, Cooney was in his office. Calmly, I took the page about Warne and put it on his desk, saying, 'Why has this happened?'

He leaned forward and held his head. 'I'm not well,' he said, reaching for his tablets. For some time, he claimed he had a heart problem and that day he went off home.

He cited health reasons for his departure and he was paid up to go. 'I've worked at the Associated coalface for six years, two and a half years in Scotland, and I am getting out before silicosis claims my lungs,' he said. 'I believe that now the *Mail* has the finest sports section in Fleet Street. My contemporaries may argue about that, but my belief is honed because you can feel their envy in the air.' Right to the end he got things wrong. Fleet Street had been vacated by the newspapers years earlier and as for his grammar, well I ask you! He won the Sports Feature Writer of the Year Award in Scotland in 2002 and still works for a newspaper up there.

In February 2000, I booked a three-week cricket tour in Australia – I told friends it was done to get as far away as possible from Cooney. I made the mistake of walking round the 5.7 kilometres of the Melbourne Grand Prix course without wearing a hat in a temperature of 106°F. That night we had dinner at a posh restaurant and one of our players, Gordon Potter, formerly of Sussex and a colleague of Ted Dexter, walked straight into a glass door and was laid out. He eventually went to hospital. The manager put a notice up, saying, 'This is a glass door. Please don't walk into it.' An hour later, another player, the bespectacled Steve Coltman, a former colonel in the Army who was short-sighted, walked into the same door and suffered less damage. I made a point of avoiding the door but in the middle of the night, in my sea-facing room at the Manley Pacific Hotel in Manley, I was woken by a terrible pain in the head. I rang Audrey in Bromley and started speaking a load of gibberish. 'You must see a doctor,' she said. 'You might have a slight stroke.'

I had noticed that there was a private surgery just thirty metres away and I called in to see a doctor named Meredith Rower. She gave me an instant brain scan and she said, 'It's all clear. You've had a mild TIA, a slight stroke, but it shouldn't cause any trouble.'

For several days I wasn't able to speak properly and no one other than Ron Hart, the man organising the tour, knew I had problems. I said to Ron later, 'They probably didn't notice because I usually talk rubbish.' Again, I was lucky.

CHAPTER TWENTY-SEVEN

Waiting for Lara

In 1994, Brian Lara was voted Trinidad's Sportsman of the Year. I should have been voted Most Patient Journalist of the Year. I must have set a record of sitting around waiting for the greatest cricketer of the generation to turn up. But it was great fun and it was probably my most enjoyable year in journalism. Not many people have the chance to spend half the year watching a superstar at close quarters. After he scored the Test world record of 375 at St John's Recreation Ground, Antigua, on 18 April, I was approached about writing his autobiography and I was really excited by the prospect. Warwickshire signed him before it happened and the publishing company Transworld won the race to buy the rights to his book. He was twenty-four, yet few said it was too early for him to put his name to a book. Everyone interested in cricket wanted to know about him. Unlike a host of sportsmen who had books to their name, – including Andy Murray, Ashley Cole, Wayne Rooney, and Monty Panesar – he had already reached the pinnacle and had set world records. He had a great story, and I was going to help him tell it.

My agent, Jane Bradish-Ellames, arranged a meeting with him and his agents Jonathan Barnett and David Manasseh at a house not far from Lord's, but it soon ran into problems. Jane emerged from another room where Barnett and Manasseh were talking with Lara and said to me, 'He doesn't want you to do it. He thinks it should be done by a younger man.'

I told her, 'Tell him that I probably know more about West Indian cricket than almost any cricket writer in England, without being boastful. I wrote Learie Constantine's column for some years and I know that Brian knew all about him and his records. Learie was one of the all-time-great all-rounders. I also wrote a book for Gary Sobers in 1988, and Gary is Brian's hero. I wrote Clyde Walcott's book and I've been reporting West Indies cricket since I wrote a book about the West Indies tour of 1963. I've been to the Caribbean on fifteen occasions and I know many of the West Indian Test players and some of them are good friends. Tell him he won't find anyone better to do it.'

Jane went back into the room and five minutes later she returned and said, 'You're the man. He's ready to start.' Lara came in wearing a broad smile and after the introductions we talked about the details of how I should tackle the newspaper column and the book. He appeared to be polite and attentive.

With most of my books I insisted on a fifty-fifty split, but this time it was different – we were dealing with a real superstar and I accepted a much smaller percentage. Transworld offered an advance of £60,000 with handsome royalties. In cricketing terms, it was a reasonable deal, but it was tiny set against the sums paid to footballers. He didn't come up with ideas about a title, but I suggested one that suited his style of batting: *Beating the Field*. I said to him, 'That's what you do, beat the field. And no batsman is better than you at finding the boundary. It's ideal.' He agreed and so did the publishers.

He arrived for his first press conference at Edgbaston's ground on 23 April an hour late and Jonathan Barnett explained that it wasn't his fault. 'We had to stop off for an interview on Pebble Mill,' he said.

Lara handled himself well. Clearly he was well educated and well brought up. 'One of the reasons why I chose Warwickshire was because I will be living near Dwight,' he said, pointing to his best friend sitting nearby. Yorke was playing for the Aston Villa reserves at the time and had a reputation for being a playboy.

Dermot Reeve, the animated Warwickshire captain, presented him a Warwickshire cap and said, 'He is the first to be capped by Warwickshire before he actually plays.' There were plenty of laughs.

His agents told me afterwards that he would receive around £250,000 for his summer's work. The *Mail* were paying £40,000 for twenty columns and that included a weekly coaching strip. Manasseh said, 'He insisted on the coaching strip because he wants to put something back in the game.' My opinion of the world record holder zoomed upwards. This is a real man, I thought.

Warwickshire's pay cheque for the four and a half months came to £45,000 and the other cheques came from commercial deals. Barnett said, 'He's a great guy, a well-mannered, young, confident man of steel.'

A week later I called to see him in his large and luxurious rented flat in an exclusive block near the ground, and early in the proceedings I asked him how he had first picked up a bat. 'Rudolph, one of my older brothers [he has seven brothers in a family of eleven], gave me a hand-carved bat when I was three and I started hitting marbles in the porch of our bungalow,' he said. 'As I grew a bit older, there were a lot of pot plants dotted around and I put them in fielding positions. When I hit the marble, the idea was to miss them.' I have seen almost all of the great batsmen since Bradman and none of them avoided fielders as well as Lara. He angled his bat to find the gaps and rarely played the ball straight to a fielder. If he did, it was a misjudgment.

He hadn't slept on his first night because the club had put him into a pokey flat with a broken window. 'I tried to sleep on a settee,' he said.

His agents soon upgraded him to the other flat but they should have signed a valet to look after him because the flat looked as though it had been burgled when I arrived. Hundreds of letters and packages, many unopened, were strewn around the carpet and on the furniture. 'I haven't had time to sort things out,' he explained. Later Warwickshire sent a secretary to deal with his mail, which is reminiscent of Denis Compton when he became England's first cricketing superstar.

As I walked through the lounge, I saw what appeared to be a body under a huge sofa. 'There's a body under there!' I shouted.

'That's Russell Latapy, my friend,' he said. 'He must have had a late night!' Latapy was a revered footballer in Trinidad who played for his country, as well as Hibernian and Porto.

Lara's mobile was ringing constantly. One caller rang about his new BMW. 'Sorry about that,' he said. 'I'll have to collect it and I should be back at midday.'

He came back an hour late and made some coffee. After a few questions and some brief, guarded answers, he said, 'I have to do a few things. Can you come back at five?'

You can't argue with a genius so I went for a walk round Edgbaston's leafy suburbs. Right on five, I knocked and was relieved to find that he was there. We sat opposite each other in the opulent chairs and the conversation about his early life was going well until he said, 'Can you come back at eleven?'

'You mean tomorrow?' I said.

'No, tonight,' he said.

'Well,' I said, 'I don't know about you but I usually go to bed around eleven.'

We arranged to meet at nine in the morning; it turned out to be another disrupted day. One of the players told me, 'He likes a night out but he's not an excessive drinker.'

His debut day for the Bears was a let-down. Thirty-two male journalists and one female writer were in the press box, including Ian Wooldridge, and Glamorgan won the toss and batted through the day scoring a laboured 291-6. Lara wore two sweaters and spent much of his time blowing on his hands to keep warm. He fielded at first slip. Ian noticed that he was practising his golf swing and said, 'He's right-handed!' Ian proceeded to write an article about Lara's ambidexterity.

At his best, Lara's handicap came down to low single figures and Manasseh, who often partnered him, said, 'He's got a beautiful swing and if he took it up seriously, he could have been a star.'

I had a chat with Bob Woolmer and he told me, 'He's a natural. He puts bat to ball and doesn't use his pads like some players. He leaves room for the shot and with his high backlift is looking to dictate, looking to score off every ball with power and accuracy. I couldn't see a weakness, except his running between the wickets. His hand-eye coordination is exceptional and he plays the ball very late, the hallmark of a great player. Bowlers can't give him width because he dispatches the ball to the boundary.'

The next day, Lara lived up to his billing by scoring 147 off 160 balls with twenty-three fours and two sixes and when I interviewed him for his first column he revealed that he talked to himself at the crease. 'I kept telling myself, "Don't let this one get you out,"' he said, 'and when I was getting over-excited I would say, "Cool down."'

He told me he had fallen asleep in front of the TV the night before. When he woke up as dawn broke, he was still lying on the settee. He had an irregular pattern of sleep, interrupted by frequent visits to clubs, where he loved listening to music and 'chilling out' – the favourite occupation of the typical West Indian. Lara wasn't a big gambler, but Manasseh put money on him reaching a century and collected a goodly sum at the odds of 9-2. Most days at that time he was sleeping in the treatment room, often under the treatment table.

Because of football commitments, I missed his next county game at Leicester when he scored 106 and 120 not out, scoring fifty-two per cent of his side's runs on an up and down pitch at Grace Road. Could he last the pace? And what about me? Could I last the pace?

Another time, I actually got to him early when he had a day off. I phoned my story over and was relaxing in the pool of a five-star hotel in Birmingham when the sports editor rang my mobile to say he didn't like the theme. 'Can you come up with a better line?' he said. 'You've got half an hour.'

It was 7.35 p.m. I dialled Lara's number and surprisingly he answered. I explained my predicament and asked where he was. 'I'm about to tee off at the fourth hole at the South Herts Golf Club,' he said.

'Well, I'll make it quick,' I said.

I asked him one question – I can't recall what it was about – and he spoke for no more than a minute. 'Is that all right?' he said.

'Fine,' I said, 'and thanks.' I ad-libbed 500 words and it went in.

One of his perks was free air miles from British West Indies Airways, the Caribbean airline that went out of business in January 2007. I was visiting Barbados and Trinidad that year to research my biography of him, *Brian Lara – Cricket's Troubled Genius*, and I flew one of the last flights. There were only sixty-seven passengers in a 380-seat Airbus. In 1994 he flew back home three times in the first two months, a sure sign of homesickness. On 23 May I was on my way to cover the final day of Warwickshire's match against Somerset at Taunton and with a lot of rain there was little prospect of a result, or of another Lara century to add to his fourth in succession. Following his example, I arrived late and bumped into my *Mail* photographer Ted Blackbrow.

'Did you see him making a call on his mobile when the Somerset innings started?' he said.

'I've only just arrived,' I said. 'I did a Lara and was late.'

Ted showed me some pictures of Lara talking on the phone while Mushtaq Ahmed was about to take strike. 'That's one for the back page,' I said. Ian Botham and Allan Lamb had brought out a mobile phone during games in the past but no one had published a picture of them in action. To see the world record holder doing that was, well, historic.

When I arrived in the ramshackle press box, I didn't mention the incident and no one talked about it. So I thought it might be a scoop. With the game about to die, Dermot Reeve did a deal with Andy Hayhurst, the Somerset captain, and Warwickshire were set to score 321, initially for ninety-five overs. It looked a friendly declaration but with further rain, the odds were still on a draw. The light was poor and when Lara came in he started hitting out as though he was back at Queen's Park CC on a balmy Trinidadian day. Graham Rose bowled two beamers at Lara, which angered him, and in trying to avoid the second one, which he just managed to do, he ricked his neck and needed prolonged treatment. I tried to speak to him at tea but the dressing room attendant said he was in the treatment room. I told the man, 'I need to speak to him urgently when he is out and I'll be waiting at the rear door to see him.'

Lara's incredible innings roared on with fours and sixes raining into and over the spectators and his fifth hundred, off seventy-two balls, equalled the record of the peerless Sir Everton Weekes. Tiredness eventually got him bowled by Mushtaq for 136 and I raced around to the pavilion and spoke to the attendant again. 'It's very, very important,' I said. 'Let me know when he has changed.'

'I'll tell him,' he said.

Twenty minutes later, with the match won, there was no sign of Lara. I knocked on the door again. 'Oh,' said the attendant. 'He's driven off!'

I needed him to talk about the mobile affair in private and I shot over to the car park thinking he had given me the slip again. But there he was, about to get into his soft-top BMW. Fortunately a large contingent of boys were trying for his autograph. He rarely spurned autograph hunters.

I approached him and said, 'Can I sit in your car for a few minutes?'

He looked up. 'I'm sorry, I've got to get back to Edgbaston for treatment on my neck.'

Half a dozen journalists were bearing down on him, so I decided not to mention the mobile incident. He told the journalists he was doubtful for the next match and they were satisfied with the story and went off.

'Just one thing,' I said to him, 'What about your phone call out there?'

He smiled bashfully. 'Yes, I shouldn't have done it and I have apologised to the umpires. So much has been happening to me, so many people are calling me that I took it out with me. It is extraordinary what has happened since I arrived. I suppose the man above is really behind me.'

Ray Julian, the senior umpire, told me later, 'We had a quiet word with him. He is a lovely man, so friendly and he always had time for me. Once I gave him out lbw on ninety-five and he used to joke about it. Another time he tried to chat up my daughter and I asked him to sign a card and he wrote, "For your lovely daughter". He's a real gentleman. He is almost in the same class as Don Bradman.' The story appeared on the back page, as I hoped, but they failed to display the mobile story properly, burying it in the main piece. The picture of him holding his phone up to his ear, to answer a joking call from Dermot Reeve, was also badly displayed. Oh well!

Now we were at Lord's taking on Middlesex. Another hundred would equal the record of six successive centuries set by Bradman, Mike Procter, and C. B. Fry but the weather was vile. After the first day was rained off, he reached twenty-six when he nicked a catch to wicketkeeper Keith Brown down the legside and walked before the umpire's decision. 'Win some and lose some,' he said, like a gambler.

On the Monday I was there again when he struck the second highest shot directed at the Lord's pavilion. It hit the guttering on the roof of the South Turret and a few feet higher it would have equalled the only occasion when the ball went over the pavilion. Albert Trott was the man who did it, in 1899. Lara told me he wasn't really a six hitter. 'I haven't got that power,' he said. 'This one wasn't hit very hard and it was just timing.'

In the days of Don Bradman, rich people jumped into taxis to go to Lord's to watch him. When Lara was scoring 140 in 147 balls on the final day, I was half expecting a similar invasion. But a few MCC members turned up, that's all. With the game teetering towards a draw, Dermot Reeve asked him to bowl. Lara told me he wanted to improve his leg spin bowling but Reeve set an attacking field to get the Middlesex batsman to open up. Not surprisingly, Lara went into a sulk. He bowled a couple of overs, mainly full tosses, and went off to the pavilion complaining about his knee. It was the start of the falling out between the superstar and the innovative captain.

I thought the sports editor should have ordered me to stay with Lara with these hundreds pouring out but on 6 June I was sitting in the Trent Bridge press box waiting for the fall of the last New Zealand wicket against England when Jack Bannister, the former Warwickshire bowler and a well-respected journalist, told me, 'Lara is going like a bomb at Edgbaston. He's hurtling on towards 200 and apparently Phil Bainbridge, Durham's captain, isn't prepared to do a deal with Reeve over a declaration so he has a good chance for the world record of 499. I'm going over there to see him.' I rang the desk and they agreed to let me go. It turned out to be one of the greatest days in the history of cricket and I was privileged to see him take his unbeaten 111 on the start of the day to 501. Fifty years earlier, to the day, bombs had been raining down on the Normany beaches. Now runs were coming like a torrent and the scorers had difficulty taking it all down. His monumental innings passed twenty milestones and broke many records. Days later, they were still unearthing more.

He had more than a dozen bats littered around the dressing room and chose a fairly new Gray-Nicolls scoop bat weighing two pounds seven ounces with a blue handle and sponge under the grip – not the one he used for his 375. It was like a wand. Every time it waved something good and exciting happened. You sensed that he would beat Hanif Mohammad's record of 499. Luck went his way. He was 'bowled' for twelve by a no ball from Andy Cummins, dropped by keeper Chris Scott at eighteen, and better catchers than the Bajan Cummins and substitute Mike Burns should have caught skiers on 238 and 413 respectively. Bainbridge was injured but still on the field. David Graveney, also injured, was sitting in the away dressing room and said, 'The more runs he scores, the more ice I'm going to put on my leg!'

The west boundary was no more than sixty yards – similar to today's Twenty20 contests – and Bainsbridge's phalanx of fielders stationed on it were left helpless. Keith Piper ensured that the record was reached. His maiden century of 116 in a stand of 322 taking the final total to 810-4 was vital, but he also acted as counsellor, coming up to him and saying, 'Please, please, don't get out!'

Lara didn't know that the 136th over of the innings would be the last, with his total on 497. Incredibly, he blocked the first three deliveries from John Morris, essentially only a net bowler. Was he going to leave it to the last ball to crown himself, a great show of bravado? Morris slipped in a bouncer with his fourth delivery and it hit him on the helmet. 'I've found his weakness,' Morris said to his colleagues.

Piper checked with umpire Peter Wight about how many overs were left. 'This is the final one,' said Wight, 'the rulebook says 5.30 is time.'

Piper went up to his partner and said, 'There are only two balls left.'

'You sure?' said Lara.

'Yes, I've just checked,' he said.

Morris came in to bowl and as the ball left his hand, Lara jumped out of his crease with his bat held high, swung it through the line and drove through extra cover for his 62nd four. It wasn't the most elegant shot of his innings but it was probably his hardest.

He told me later he wanted to get on his knees to kiss the pitch – as he had done forty-nine days earlier for his 375 – but there was no chance of that happening. Within seconds, he was engulfed by hundreds of cricket lovers. Bradman was the only other Test batsman who had held both the Test and first-class top scores and the comparisons between the two were soon brought up; Jack Bannister was one of the first. But for some strange reason, the debate never really started. The former Test stars and experts had all accepted the argument that Bradman towered over the rest of the field and no one could be challenged. I started my biography of Lara thirteen years later by questioning whether Bradman could match the West Indian's feats against faster bowlers and superior fielders to the cricketers he opposed in the 1930s. Bradman was the star of a team that was the best in the world, whereas Lara played in a struggling team that was no longer feared. I still believe Lara won more matches himself than Bradman. The difference between the men was that Bradman kept accumulating runs whatever, only just failing to attain his objective of an average of 100, whereas Lara sometimes lost interest in meaningless matches and would get out. He didn't prize his wicket like Bradman did. But when he had to, he would bat on and on, like he did when he played 'pass' cricket in Mitchell Road where he grew up. If you missed the ball, the batsman was out. Young Lara rarely missed it.

The Warwickshire players formed a guard of honour as he came into the dressing room. As he slumped down in a chair, they soaked him with champagne. He had a glass of it, although champagne is not his favoured drink. I spoke with Manasseh about how to handle my interview with him. We agreed that the photographers and the TV and radio people should go first with a press conference in the dining room next door to the dressing rooms. After all that was done, including several essential one-on-one radio and TV interviews, I sat down with him and went through everything, making sure that my quotes were better than any others. I thought he would be exhausted and reluctant to say much, but the adrenalin was still pumping and we talked for twenty minutes. I wrote a story made almost entirely of quotes for the back page and a full-page story appeared inside, headlined, 'I'm not invincible – It doesn't make me a great player, there is still so much to achieve'. I asked him what he ate for lunch. Most people in the middle of big innings drink large quantities but ignore food. 'Some mashed potatoes and a blackcurrant juice,' he said. That must have been another record!

It was past 8 p.m. when he left with Keith Piper to travel to London for the semi-final of the Benson & Hedges Cup at the Oval the next day. 'I was so tired that I asked Keith to drive,' he said. 'I could have fallen asleep if I'd driven.'

Bannister was making the same journey and he heard Lara on BBC Radio Five saying, 'As a twenty-four-year-old, I've got plenty of time to learn and get better.'

Jack said later, 'He was so tired that he forgot that he'd had his twenty-fifth birthday thirty-five days before!' Piper couldn't find the right route and it was 2 a.m. when they arrived at the Tower Hotel next to Tower Bridge. They were given a waking call at 8 a.m. and were too late for practice. He complained of a headache and hoped that

Warwickshire would win the toss and bat but Adam Hollioake won and his Surrey side scored 267-7 on a hot, polluted day. After an hour, he asked to come off to rest but was refused. Near the end of the innings he was finally allowed to depart and tried to sleep. He couldn't and Woolmer said, 'You've got to get back out there otherwise you won't be allowed to bat very long.' So he went back on. It was no way to treat a world record holder! Showing immense character, he scored a match-winning seventy off seventy-three balls after coming in at 120-4.

Afterwards Manasseh told me Lara had booked a first-class flight to Port of Spain and dozens of journalists from radio, TV, and the newspapers wanted to go with him. We agreed that the *Mail* couldn't make it an exclusive and I said, 'We should let them visit his mother and spend a few hours and after that, there will be no more access.' All the parties agreed.

The *Mail* booked three economy seats for myself, Ted Blackbrow, and Anne Barraclough, a features writer. We were right next to the business section and as the time for departure grew closer there was no sign of Lara and his agent. Five minutes from the scheduled take-off, neither man had appeared. I said, 'They've given them the bum's rush! The others will be livid.' The curtains were drawn, the captain made his announcements, and the engines started. I said to Ted, 'It looks as though we are going to have a brief holiday instead of working.'

When the seatbelts sign was switched on, I asked the chief steward if our star passenger had turned up. 'They just managed to do it,' he said. 'By a couple of minutes.'

I asked Lara later how it happened. 'I had to do some shopping at Selfridge's and the traffic to Heathrow was very heavy,' he said. 'But we made it.'

Anne interviewed him on the aircraft and it turned out to be a brilliant article. She asked him about drugs and he admitted that if he hadn't been brought up the right way he might well have gone down the path of so many young people in Trinidad, an island with one of the highest murder rates in the world. After his 375, the Government honoured his achievements with a medal and the naming of a road: the Brian Lara Promenade. In 2006, someone was murdered in that road.

Only one journalist ignored our agreement that Lara wouldn't be pestered after the first day's access and she was a lady working for an evening newspaper. One of the places Lara took us to was his school, Fatima College, and the 900 pupils gathered in the playground to pose for Ted Blackbrow. Ted was taking the photos from the first floor and suddenly noticed the woman in the middle of the throng close to Lara. He shouted, 'If you don't scarper, I'll fill you in!' She took the advice.

Lara was mobbed by boys thrusting bits of paper torn off their exercise books in front of him and some even used banknotes to get his autograph. He signed literally hundreds.

I flew back on the same plane as Lara and the other media people went two days earlier. Lara was always involved in dramas and this was another. Just before flying off, someone rang to say there was a bomb in the aircraft and everyone had to disembark. There were no sniffer dogs at the airport and it took three hours to complete a search before the all-clear was given. The holdup meant that the pilot was running out of time and it was decided to abandon the stop in Barbados and go straight to Heathrow. There were 126 London-bound passengers at the airport at Barbados and they were left stranded. There was uproar and later they had to be compensated. Lara had to attend a match at Sir Paul Getty's ground in Wormsley, off the M40, on the day he travelled and one newspaper claimed that the 126 angry holidaymakers were sacrificed for the sake of a friendly cricket match, just to please the Getty family.

The Getty ground is one of the most beautiful in the world and has one of the best squares. Getty, an American oil billionaire and philanthropist, bought the huge estate and turned one part of his 3,000 acres into a cricket ground. He loved cricket, although he never played the game at a good level himself, and he was the biggest contributor to the building of one of the stands at Lord's. He died in 2003 and stipulated that his fortune should go to his second son Mark in 2010. Mark owned *Wisden Cricketers' Almanac* and Getty Images, the biggest company in the UK selling photographs to newspapers and other outlets

The most exhilarating and most pleasurable day's cricket of my whole life took place at the County Ground at Northampton on 23 June and it was billed – initially by me when I wrote Lara's old column – 'the Battle of the Greatest Batsman [Lara] against the world's Greatest Bowler [Curtly Ambrose]'. Lara wasn't happy about it. 'It's put extra pressure on me,' he said. He had played against the fearsome Ambrose on nine previous occasions without losing his wicket and Curtly was ready to take him out.

I arranged to see Lara at 9.30 a.m. but it was 10.40 a.m. when he turned up, looking harassed. 'I got lost in the one-way system,' he said. Sir Richard Hadlee was waiting in the car park with half a dozen bats that he wanted signed, so it was a few minutes before I had a chance to say what I needed to say. 'Can I pop round at lunch to see you, or when you are out?' I said.

It was only then that he knew Warwickshire were batting first and that he was first wicket down. 'OK,' he said.

Later I spoke to Bob Woolmer and he said, 'We were panicking a bit to see that he hadn't turned up on time. Fortunately Andy Moles and Roger Twose put on seventy-one for the first wicket.'

When Lara came in, the reasonably sized audience must have been startled to see that he was not wearing a helmet. Was he mad? Curtly was furious, like a bull in the Plazo de Toros. Lara tried to explain it away, saying afterwards, 'The one I was carrying in my hand was slightly suspect and I asked the twelfth man to bring another one.'

His first ball came from medium-paced Tony Penberthy, not Ambrose, and hit him on the pad. Everyone on the Northampton side went up appealing for lbw but he was reprieved, claiming later that it was pitched outside the line of the leg stump. Lara used his brain to give the strike to his partner and when he had to face the intimidating Ambrose he took evasive action against short-pitched deliveries. Anything straight at him, he jumped back in line to play the ball down. Early on he took his eye off a bouncer and the ball hit him on the back of his helmet, cracking it. The advice of the experts is to tell batsmen in these circumstances to switch to another new helmet, but few do. He had a bump on his head and complained about a headache. Several times he was in danger of another crusting – the cricketers' word to describe being hit in the helmet – but his sense of anticipation kept him on his feet. Ambrose bowled several spells and each time Lara had to face few deliveries. When Kevin Curran dropped him on 170, Ambrose shouted, 'These guys don't catch anything!'

I was hoping he might reach 200 and get out before the close to enable me to write my piece and on 197 he hooked yet another short ball from Ambrose and it flew high towards Mal Loye at fine leg. Loye jumped up and brought off a superb catch. Lara faced forty-five balls from Ambrose, whose figures were 1-37 off twenty-five overs when the wicket fell. Almost half of Warwickshire's total of 463 came from Lara's bat and his eighth century in eleven innings equalled Bradman's record in 1938/39. I made the contest even: two great champions slugging themselves into exhaustion with the honours shared.

I stationed myself upstairs outside the dressing room after he was out and half an hour later he showed up. 'I can't speak,' he said. 'My head is throbbing. I've got to lie down.' I might have reminded him about his responsibilities but I didn't. I felt sorry for him.

The next day, he was complaining about his knee and when umpire Allan Jones turned down an lbw against Rob Bailey, who is now an umpire himself, he made a remark intimating that Jones had made a mistake. According to Reeve, Lara used the 'F' word and Jones said, 'There was nothing wrong with my eyesight yesterday when I gave you not out first ball. You concentrate on your fielding and I'll do the umpiring.'

There followed another exchange, with Reeve who saying, 'Brian, you are turning into a prima donna.' Lara responded with several more 'F' words. In mid-afternoon, he walked off, saying he was not match fit. He came back to bat in the second innings and miscuing a sweep, the ball hit him in the face close to an eye. The row between the big star and the captain was now irretrievable and it soured his year of triumph.

My favourite story about that mad, frantic summer, and the most repeated, was the one about his unexpected disappearance on 30 June. I was supposed to be meeting him at Edgbaston at 9.30 a.m. Fifteen minutes late, he turned up wearing a black sports shirt and dark flannels. A photographer was there waiting to take pictures for his coaching strip.

'Is it all right to wear this?' Lara asked me.

No, it's got to be done in your cricket gear,' I said.

He excused himself and said he had to see Bob Woolmer. Ten minutes later I was standing outside the dressing rooms and the photographer shouted, 'I've just seen him drive off!'

I sped off to Woolmer's office. 'Where is he?' I asked.

'He's driving to Heathrow and is flying off to Port of Spain,' said Bob. 'He brought in a certificate from a gynaecologist, I ask you, saying his knee ligaments have been slightly damaged and advising him against playing in this match.'

I tried to ring Lara's mobile phone without success. The previous night I had managed to reach him; wanting a punchy column, I asked him, 'Who is the most hostile batsman you've faced?' I was thinking of Wasim Akram because Akram was going to play against him for Lancashire in the four-day game about to start. Right on cue, he said, 'Wasim Akram. He's got a quick arm, he's quick, bowls both sides of the wickets, swings it both way, varies his pace and bowls several types of bouncer.'

That was enough for 500 words, but what about the coaching strip? The young Warwickshire wicketkeeper Keith Piper was in earshot, standing on the ground in front of the pavilion, and I thought he might be the man to pose for the Lara pictures. Behind a helmet, he might look like the hero. He was the same height, build, and colour, and I asked him if he could pad up and play a few square cuts for the strip. 'I don't know about that,' he said. I offered him £25. 'OK,' he said.

The photographer took some striking pictures but when they arrived at the *Mail's* picture desk, the man in charge rang my mobile and said, 'Are you sure that was Lara?' I had to confess and the strip was ditched. But the column about Wasim appeared. Good, lively stuff. Five days later, he was back in England and I succeeded in getting through to his mobile. He never mentioned his holiday and didn't apologise. I thought it was wise to let it go.

The next time I met him he was dressed in a bowler and a city suit posing for pictures in front of Tower Bridge. He was advertising Mercury Asset Management, one of Britain's biggest investment companies. According to Barnett, he was to be paid £130,000, for wearing a cap with 'MAM' on it and making personal appearances around the world. Good money, I thought. There was a throng of journalists and photographers and most of them worked for financial newspapers. A tall, pushy lady from the *Financial Times* kept pressing him about the money and he referred the matter to his agents. She insisted that it was worth £500,000 and some of the other newspapers used the same figure. Everyone trusts the *Financial Times*, or should do.

As a PR exercise it was a success, particularly with the unusual pictures on most front pages. The next day, shareholders were ringing up complaining and asking why their company was paying out so much money for so little. An MAM executive had to write to all the newspapers saying, 'While you gave magnificent exposure to the story, the figure of £500,000 is completely wrong. We are actually paying £100,000 for the period of July this year to September 1996.'

It was supposed to be a day off for him, but an hour later he drove his sponsored Peugeot up to the Honourable Artillery Company's cricket ground – the world's most unusual ground, as it is surrounded by huge office blocks in the middle of the City – to give support to a charitable function. He was refused admission on the grounds that he wasn't a member. Someone had to explain that this small man was the star of the show and had to be let in.

Russell Latapy was there and he told me he was catching a flight to Porto at 2 p.m. 'Well, it's almost midday and if you don't leave now you'll struggle to get to Heathrow,' I said to both men. They laughed and continued talking to some City people, not driving off until 12.30 p.m. 'You'll never make it,' I shouted.

They didn't and Latapy was heavily fined by Bobby Robson, the manager of Porto at the time. Bob is a keen cricket fan and later he told me, 'I'd love to watch this little fella. I think he's similar to Latapy and Yorke. Their timekeeping is dodgy!'

As the cricket season was ending I still had 10,000 words to write to complete his autobiography. Manasseh promised he would arrange eight days for me to meet him after his final match. I checked with him near the date and he said, 'He's gone off somewhere. You wouldn't be able to contact him.' Later I discovered he spent those eight days entertaining a young lady in a five-star hotel in London. I didn't complain. I finished the manuscript myself and the book came out on time. I was happy that I was able to complete our mission. Over the years, I rarely met him, but in 2006 I started my own book about him. I interviewed more than seventy people who either loved him or couldn't stand him. There were no middle-of-the-roaders. I wanted to produce a balanced work about a troubled genius and didn't bother to contact him. It would have been very difficult to reach him and with his record of keeping appointments, the book would never come out. Towards the end, his literary agent David Godwin wrote to Tempus, my publisher, warning that my unauthorised book could face legal restraints. Rob Sharman, the editorial director at Tempus, wrote back assuring Mr Godwin that he had no cause to worry because 'Mr Scovell is a huge admirer of Mr Lara and not only represents him as the greatest batsman of his generation but begins the book with a compelling argument that he may even shade Sir Don Bradman as the best of all time.' There was no response from Mr Godwin. I heard from a writer on Mr Godwin's books that Lara was engaged in writing his own book and that it would come out later in the year. It has yet to appear.

Mine was published in May 2007 and it was reasonably well received. I did several TV interviews, including one with David Gower during the Old Trafford Test in a tea interval, and sixteen radio interviews around the country. I had plenty of fun at eighteen signing sessions at county and Test match grounds, and several in Waterstone's stores. At a Twenty20 thrash at Hove, a young man came up to me and said, 'Are you Brian Lara?' I was very flattered.

I learned that Lara was due to open a part of the MCC Museum devoted to his cricketing life and was surprised that I didn't receive the usual invitation to these functions. I rang the PR department at Lord's and was told the event was oversubscribed. Nonsense. No one would turn away someone representing the *Mail*, especially someone who has written about the MCC since 1960. So I rang the museum curator, whom I had met previously – his predecessor Stephen Green had worked there for more than thirty years and I knew him well as a fellow Isle of Wighter. He was somewhat evasive. 'I wrote Lara's book and I have just brought out my own work about him,' I said. 'Surely I should be there.'

He said, somewhat strangely, 'It wouldn't be appropriate for you for to be there.' Alarm bells rang in my head. Was I about to be sued?

Meanwhile an old MCC friend, John Williams, formerly President of Wimbledon CC, invited me to come along as a guest. When we turned up, on 15 May, the Long Room was full and I kept looking out for Lara but couldn't spot him.

Jonathan Crystal, a lawyer who was fired from the Tottenham Hotspur board by Alan Sugar, appeared. I said, 'What are you up to? You're not a cricket man?' He muttered a few words and walked off. I sensed that he might be representing Lara.

I bumped into Sir Tim Rice, former MCC President and the Shane Warne of his Heartbreaks CC and I told him about my concerns. 'You'll love appearing in the High Court!' he said with a laugh.

Eventually Lara emerged from a back room. Dressed in a smart suit and tie, he addressed the 200-odd attendees with substance and some wit. They were captivated by him. Then he left and half an hour later and John and I went to the first floor of the museum to look at the Lara exhibits. The place was soon to close and I started going down the marble steps to the ground floor. Coming up the other way was Lara. He saw me and smiled. I smiled back and started to put my right hand out to shake his hand. As he drew close, he turned his head upwards to the balcony above and said, 'So good to see you!'

I turned to see who was on the balcony... no one. By the time I looked back, he had run up the steps. It was a classic bum's rush! Later in the summer there was no lawyer's letter, but why should there have been? I had been honest about him in my book.

Over the years I wrote articles in *The Cricketer* but when it became *The Wisden Cricketer* I was ditched. I wasn't too concerned. I still have good relations with the new administration, and that includes Stephen Fay, a man of my age who has come late into cricket writing after a career writing about politics and finance. He wrote the review of my book and it filled a page in *The Wisden Cricketer*. The heading was, 'No need to gild the lily,' a cliché that no self-respecting writer would use. His verdict was highly destructive. 'It is not a considered life,' he wrote. 'It is a hurried piece of work and like many biographies of this kind, it is repetitive, poorly edited and there is no index. Fans will enjoy reliving Lara's triumphs and researchers will find this a useful first draft of one of cricket's greatest enigmas. But I cannot help feeling that Scovell, like other writers who dabble in this trade, would do much better if they halved their output and doubled their fees. Much less could be so much more.' His phrase 'dabbling in this trade' made me sound like a courtesan! Up to then I had never had a cross word with Fay, who worked with *The Sunday Times* and *The Independent on Sunday* and briefly edited *The Wisden Cricketer*.

A lawyer friend of mine thought his last paragraph was defamatory but I didn't want to waste money on lawyers. Instead I sent him an email, saying, 'You obviously got out the wrong side of the bed when you wrote that and you come over as an old sourpuss.'

He emailed back saying that he was told a long time ago that a bad review should be ignored and signed his email, 'old sourpuss'. Well, he was right on the second bit! Over the years I have been involved in several literary spats and they are hugely enjoyable. This one was near the top of the table.

I asked several friends to write to John Stern, the editor, to set the record straight. I rang John and he agreed to use one letter, plus a small one by me.

I said, 'Two short letters won't add up to Fay's whole page. What about a few more?'

He was firm. 'I can't fill the letters page with your book!' he said.

So my school friend Jed Steele wrote a letter and 104 fulsome words appeared. My letter was cut down to sixty-three words.

I had lost contact with Jed until a signing session in Canterbury, when two men of my age started talking. One said, 'I played against you at Chestfield some time ago. You know who is this is?'

I looked at the other man and without thinking said, 'No, who is he?'

'I'm Jed,' he said.

I signed Jed up immediately to write his letter and we have revived our friendship, thanks to Brian Lara.

Fay might have had the advantage over me because he went to university and gained a bachelor's and a master's, but I really don't think it was an advantage to go to a university. Starting work at fifteen brought me into contact with real people who learned from their experiences. I did not pick up knowledge from blinkered tutors in universities who don't have that experience of the outside world. Fay wrote six books to my twenty-five and none of his were bestsellers. Ten of mine were, and eight were serialised. So there! Perhaps his had indexes and his words were better edited than mine?

A few weeks later I met Tim Rice again and told him about my little fracas with Fay. 'All my shows were rubbished by the critics and they all made large amounts of money,' he said.

'I still haven't been paid by my latest publisher and I am certainly not making large amounts of dosh!' I said. Tim is universally popular; a thoroughly good man to know.

CHAPTER TWENTY-EIGHT

You Think It's the End...
But It Isn't

Things were hotting up in 2000, my last year with the *Daily Mail* before I 'retired'. I started freelancing for various newspapers. On 11 August, the temperature reached a new height in London of 37.8°C, two of my implants fell out, my 'frozen' shoulder prevented me throwing the ball straight into the keeper's gloves, and Audrey went to New York to try to sell some of her etchings. Every spring she entered some of her works to be considered for the Royal Summer Exhibition in Piccadilly, which is open to all classes of artists. It was a major operation to convey them to the Royal Academy because it is almost impossible to park in the area. Her carrier (i.e. me) had to be dextrous in driving down the narrow street at the back. I then had to take them to the counter without causing too much distress to other exhibitors, many of whom showed signs of neurotic panic. Each year it was the same. In the days leading up to the acceptance day, she would scour the mail to discover whether her works were hung, on reserve, or rejected. More than 15,000 works were entered each year and only around 1,300 were accepted. She had her work exhibited on eleven occasions, but there were as many rejections. It was like being an author; it is down to someone's whim. Mainly through her own efforts, and the advice of her academician friend Tony Eyton and the well-known artist Tony Farrell, hard work and perseverance enabled her to become an extremely talented etcher and drawer in pastels. One of her models at the life class at the Royal College of Art was Quentin Crisp, who entertained the artists with his whimsical humour. I attended many of Audrey's exhibitions and although I have little knowledge of art, I relished meeting people from a different culture, in many ways the opposite to the world of sport.

Late in October we went to Southampton on a double mission, firstly for me to inspect the press facilities in the new St Mary's Friends Provident Stadium next to the River Itchen, with which I helped as an unofficial consultant, and secondly to find the fifty etchings Audrey sold to P&O for the newly launched *Aurora*. There were no problems locating the impressive new press box, the successor to the fire-prone original at The Dell. The journalists used to pack into the tiny press box at the back of the wooden stand and it had only one central exit. If someone dropped a smouldering butt, the place could have gone up in flames. Luckily it didn't. This one was comparatively spacious, except that the double seats were cramped because the safety experts wanted extra width in the stairwells. By Premiership standards, it was a pass mark.

When we boarded the gigantic liner, no one knew where Audrey's etchings were placed, so we walked around three of the floors, looking into hundreds of cabins. 'We'll be here all day,' she said. So after a fruitless search, we went to collect our new Honda SE Executive car from a nearby garage. I learned it had been built as an export vehicle, with the driver's controls on the left.

The salesman explained that there had been a rush of buyers. 'If we give you £500 off, can you take it?' he said.

'Well, all right,' I said.

Then he said, 'You better fill up. There's a shortage of petrol down here.' A few miles up the road, at Fawley, they refine oil to turn it into petrol and diesel. What were they up to?

While Audrey was away in New York, I reported on my last Test match in England and it took me back to the first Test I attended in 1953 at the Oval. On that final day, Denis Compton struck the winning four against the Australians and 30,000 people were there. Most of them invaded the pitch to celebrate, including me. Now the Oval was full, with a joyous crowd of 18,500 to see England bowl out the West Indies for 215, the first time the ground was packed on a last day for forty-seven years. It was England's first Test series win over the former world champions for thirty-one years. Like a true champion, Lara topscored with forty-seven before he was harshly given out lbw. He went without demur because he was brought up to accept the umpire's decision. Not many do that. One Sky commentator, Nasser Hussain, recorded two ducks in that match with scowls, and another, Mike Atherton, gave a rueful smile when he was awarded the Man of the Match for his eighty-three and 108. These two have emerged as outstanding professionals in their new careers; they are worthy heirs to the great Richie Benaud. Two great fast bowlers, Courtney Walsh and Curtly Ambrose, also retired on that day and were given a guard of honour. Fortunately for me, there was none of that. John Arlott rose from his seat at Lord's on the last time, saying, '...and now over to Christopher Martin-Jenkins.' I didn't know who was taking over my role, but it turned out to be Chris Foy, an upstanding young man who has done a fine job.

Later I asked Bryan Cooney about my retirement party. Cooney would leave the *Mail* before me, but he stayed long enough to attend my first farewell. He told me the budget was overstretched. I suggested it should be at the Lord's Media Centre, which hosts dinners and parties. He said £2,000 would have to be the limit. I said, 'Well, we'll have to invite at least fifty people.' The next day he came back and said, 'You'll have to reduce it to twenty-five.' So I abandoned that idea and went to see Guy Zitter, the managing director, who is a very zestful and humorous man. Once I was in hospital and the office sent a card to me. He signed it, saying, 'Get back to work you slacker!' He was agreeable to holding a party on the fourth floor at Northcliffe House on 24 November and around 100 friends and colleagues attended a very enjoyable evening, only diminished by Bryan's somewhat freakish speech. Well, he wasn't a cricket lover. My cricketing hero Ted Dexter sent his apologies and enclosed a poem, which I forgot to read. Audrey was desperately ill but no one knew that she only had a month to live. She was still very beautiful, almost regal. She told me my speech was too long and she was right. Not many of the sub editors, the real workers, were available, so I said to Cooney we should have a gathering at Scribes, the club that Terry Venables once owned, which is beneath Barker's, the jazzy food store that is next to Northcliffe House. Reluctantly he OK'd it, and his assistant Graham Hunter made an adequate speech for a Scot who didn't love cricket. Two farewells proved to be too much for Cooney's budget and when the evening wound up, Graham handed me the drinks bill and asked me to pay it. I did; it took all but £5 of the collection, which I was going to use to buy a laptop. I still have the fiver in case of a very rainy day.

Cooney left his post on 3 November, so I beat him by seven weeks. He was replaced by Colin Gibson, who worked with me some years before at the *Mail* and we knew the job was in good hands because he played cricket. In quick succession, he became Head of Communications at the FA, at the ECB, and now the ICC. Years ago I was tapped by the FA and the TCCB (now the ECB) regarding the post. I told them that I was not interested. 'You finish up as a punchbag between two warring factions,' I said. Tim Jotischky became the new sports editor, and he, too, is a cricket man; he went on the Mihir Bose Fleet Street tour of India with us. Tim is a wicketkeeper and it was refreshing to work under someone who understood the greatest game of all.

Audrey contracted chronic active hepatitis in 1982 while staying on holiday with Dr John Shepherd and his family in Tampa, Florida. John thought the illness came from eating seafood. Her immune system took a pounding and she also had a thyroid that didn't function too well, but she hardly ever talked about any of it. She never complained, although some days she would say she was tired. She was a patient in a number of hospitals on countless occasions and each time she emerged smiling and laughing. I was immensely proud that she had the strong will to lead a full and enjoyable life, running a home and bringing up a family while working as an extremely productive artist. In the week of Christmas 2008 I was watching a TV documentary about a woman in her forties who suffered from the same illness. She was filmed over several weeks and seemed to spend most of her time whingeing and moaning, screaming at her family and lying down asking others to look after her. I shed a few tears because I realised that Audrey suffered the same pain and distress but the difference was that she loved other people and life and her illness wasn't going to dominate her life. My chest swelled with pride. How lucky I had been, having such a wonderful lover, friend, and inspiration.

On 30 October 2000, fifty-four days before she died, she woke up and said, 'I've got a stabbing pain in the liver.' Neither of us mentioned cancer, but I suspected that she now had cancer in that vulnerable organ. Her stomach was alarmingly swollen.

Some years previously, a female locum doctor had examined her when it was not much bigger than normal and told her, 'You are pregnant.'

She had roared with laughter. 'I'm close to fifty and I had a hysterectomy at least eight years ago'.

The family doctor recommended an instant admittance for her at the University College Hospital. A succession of consultants had worked on her case since 1982 and the latest one was Professor Roger Williams, famous for treating George Best. A week later she had a second liver biopsy and we went to see Dr Williams to get his verdict.

He is a wonderful, caring man and he kept looking at her file and holding up X-rays, but he didn't come up with a verdict. 'They've left the latest report upstairs and I'll get it read over to me,' he said. He rang someone and was waiting for some minutes for an answer. He seemed reluctant to give us the damning news. Eventually he put the phone down, looked up and said, 'It doesn't look too clever, I'm afraid.'

'Is there a tumour?' I said.

'Yes, a large one,'

'Is it malignant?'

He hesitated. 'Well, all I can say is that sometimes in a few cases the patient can get through it.' He was giving us a glimmer of hope. A very slim chance of a miracle. Audrey smiled and thanked him. It was such a jolt and she looked unnerved and slightly wan. I drove her home, hardly knowing what to say. I had to speak at the Cricket Society the next day and she told me to carry on with it. I did, but my mind was wandering.

Two days later, Mr Williams' secretary rang and asked her to come in for a few days to have a course of chemotherapy. Back in room 147, Audrey looked shattered after her first session with chemo. By coincidence, the name of the doctor in charge of it was a Dr Plowman. That was the name of my mother's mother. He apologised. 'I am afraid we've had to give her a harsh dose,' he said.

Two days later I helped Audrey home and she vowed that she wouldn't have any more. 'It's far worse than the original problem,' she said.

Tony Farrell came in to see her and she was wearing the Indian turban presented to her in Bombay in 1989. She said to Tony, 'I've lost all my hair.' Tony was dismayed. She removed the turban, showing a full head of hair. 'I'm only joking,' she said.

In early December she looked a little stronger and was sipping chicken soup. Then her condition suddenly deteriorated. John Bromley, our friend from years back, was in hospital suffering from cancer and wasn't expected to survive. The wife of the cricketer John Barclay, another good man, died the same day. On 11 December, another locum prescribed a stronger painkiller, Temazepam BP. Audrey was back at Cromwell Hospital and within two days she was in a coma and never came out of it. A doctor explained that she shouldn't have had that drug. 'The liver can't pass it through and it goes through the whole body, and the brain,' he said. Audrey couldn't speak any more.

I woke on the morning of 18 December dreaming that she had died. Our friend John Shepherd called and knowing that her sisters wanted a second opinion, he gave us the name of another consultant. As Catholics, her sisters were praying for a miracle. The other consultant came in later in the day. After a brief examination, he emerged to say, 'I'm sorry. There is nothing we can do.' On the same day, Father John, a priest from Brompton Oratory, came in and administered the last rites. Audrey's convulsions were getting longer and obviously more painful and I prayed for an early release for her.

She was still fighting; her eyes were flickering. I prayed that she could hold on to Christmas Day before going, because she was such a special and stand-out lady and she deserved that. They gave us a booklet entitled 'When Someone with Cancer is Dying'.

On the night of 23 December a young blond doctor from Brisbane named Luke Bennett came in and asked if we would agree to giving her a larger dose of morphine. We didn't hesitate. 'Anything to relieve her pain,' we said.

Luke told me he played some cricket. 'That's all right,' I said. 'Cricketers are good people!'

We played Kate Bush's 'Don't Give Up' and she must have heard it, but it was too late. On Christmas Eve she was still hanging on and we all spent another fitful night. I was doing the 4 a.m. to 8 a.m. shift and then Gavin would take over from me. For some reason, I decided to stay in the empty room next door and watch the highlights of the Premier League matches instead of going back to the hotel. I don't know how long it lasted, but I fell asleep and was suddenly woken by the raucous voice of my friend John Motson shouting, 'Ipswich have scored!'

Ipswich has been my favourite club since I first went there in 1960. I helped design the press facilities in 1982/83 and 2000 and I looked on them as a club of gentlemen. The only other major club that can claim that is Arsenal. Sir Samuel Hill-Wood, the chairman of Arsenal before the Second World War and the grandfather of present chairman Peter Hill-Wood, was the man who advised Captain John Murray, the father of the Cobbold brothers, to take over Ipswich. And he did. Today the club is run by Marcus Evans, a businessman who is not a football man. He bought a controlling share as an investment to make money. Known as 'Howard Hughes' to some Ipswich fans – because they've never seen him – he watched the club sink into the relegation zone in the Championship under the intimidatory managerial style of Roy Keane.

I thought to myself, Motty has given me a wake-up call. It was another sign. I had to go back to room 147. I said to Gavin, 'Can I have a few quiet minutes alone with her?' He went next door to lie down and I held her hand and without any cue, I started talking about her great love for so many people, including us, her laughter, her jokes, her compassion, her inspiration... I thanked her and kissed her on the lips. I finished by saying, 'You will be swept to the highest peaks of heaven by a tide of love.'

I knew she heard it. Hearing is one the last of the senses to go. A single tear trickled down her cheek and her heaving body fell still. I felt her pulse. It had stopped. One of her jobs at ITN was to time pieces for the news. She had timed this one perfectly, with the assistance of Motty. I looked at my watch: the time was three minutes past nine. I called Gavin in and before I could ring Louise she was already walking into the room. 'I had a premonition that she had died,' she said. None of us cried. We felt relieved; her agony was over. It seemed odd, but we felt like celebrating, not mourning. She had crammed so much love, so much goodness, into her life that we were buoyed up into an almost intoxicating state. We called for a nurse and she commiserated as she had to do, but she soon caught the gist of it. 'I didn't really know her but she struck me as a lovely lady,' she said. She asked us if we wanted to stay on for Christmas lunch. I said we would have to think about that and let her know later.

Within minutes, as though Audrey had passed on the message, the phone rang and it was John Shepherd. He expressed his sorrow and said, 'Why don't you come round for lunch? The family are here, it will be a good day.' He was right. Before setting off to his house in Dulwich, we went to the 11 a.m. mass at Brompton Oratory and

Audrey's name was read out. We had plenty of laughs and reminiscences with the Shepherds. It seemed almost physic that he had been with Audrey at the start of her health problems in Tampa and that now we were together again, of all days.

Back at home, the family were gathering, including Thelma, her eldest sister from California, and her brother Pat. On the next day, I took them to the morgue in Beckenham. I thought, 'So young, and so beautiful.' One of the first of the many wreaths came from David Sheepshanks and Ipswich FC – a huge one in the club's blue and white colours.

More than 300 people turned up for the memorial at Brompton Oratory on Monday 22 January and as we crossed the road a van was coming towards us and its registration was 'AUD'. She was at work, giving us moral support. We invited Sir Trevor McDonald to read my address. He arrived early and he read it a number of times before saying, 'Can I make a little addition?'

My last paragraph was, 'We felt no despair or agony but almost a feeling of joyousness and celebration. Her next task, spreading happiness, has already started in another place.' He suggested 'a better place' at the end.

'You're right, I said. 'I always get upset when the sub editors alter my copy but that's one change I would welcome.'

A few days later, Trevor – a passionate cricket fan who was a good friend of Lord Constantine – wrote to me saying, 'Audrey's memorial service was one of the most moving experiences of my life. I thought the choir was extraordinarily brilliant and no one who was there could have been untouched by the dignified splendour of it all. As you said, Audrey would have been proud. Once again, thank you for the honour you did me of allowing me to be a part of a service remembering Audrey.'

Speaking to him later I learned yet another coincidence. Trevor attributed his job at ITN to Learie Constantine, whom he had first met at the Trinidad and Tobago Independence Conference at Marlborough House in the early 1960s. 'I was totally at sea and Learie saved my bacon,' he said. 'It is perhaps not too much to say that he is principally responsible for the fact that I managed to make something of this profession.'

We had hundreds of letters of condolence and I answered every one in person. The one I cherished most was the one written by Gavin. He said, 'What a magnificent service! Mum is so proud of all we have done in her honour. The darkness of the last three months finally gave way to hope. So many golden tributes for a golden girl! These coincidences occur to remind us that in heaven the garden is very rosy. We may have trouble in trying to comprehend what has happened but the truth is Mum is now on a higher plane of existence. She was indeed called early to perform greater tasks that everyday existence warranted. Pray to St Jude for the promise of hope – hope that is held out for all those who believe. Keep in constant touch. Soon we will be on the beach talking cricket. Chin up mate, aim high. Your loving son.'

Bryon Butler also wrote beautifully and I cherished his letter as well. He wrote, 'Sorrow may be indefinable but everytime I think of Audrey I hear the tinkle in her laughter, the warmth in her voice, the enchanting way in which she added to any company and, above all, remember her compassion and the love she had for her family and for life itself. She leaves beautiful memories – and, in that very real sense, she hasn't left us and never will.' He was right!

I have to be honest: not every day was easy. When you lose someone you love so dearly, your emotions come to the surface and the smallest word out of place can cause upset. This soon happened and I suddenly flipped – I started shouting and screaming and crying. It was my repressed feelings letting rip and I felt ashamed of my behaviour. It was something new, something to worry about. The children were with me in my bedroom, along with Audrey's sister Thelma, trying to calm me down. I told them of my experience as a teenage reporter when I interviewed a man in his eighties after his wife had died. A few days later, I rang the funeral director and asked about the week's deaths. He said that the same man had died of a broken heart. I said, 'That could happen to me. There's is plenty of evidence to show that people can die from a broken heart.'

They told me not to worry. I accepted that – you can live on with a broken heart – but I knew that Norma, the wife of Learie Constantine, died for that reason. Learie died in 1971 and Norma went a few weeks later. Their marriage was one of the happiest and most rewarding I'd known. They married in 1927 and Norma, a much-loved and respected lady, devoted herself to looking after this extraordinary, pioneering man, the first man of African descent to be made a life peer. They would have been very proud of Barack Obama. When my father was in his eighties and he lived in a rather magnificent nursing home overlooking the English Channel, he often spoke about committing suicide. 'There's nothing left for me,' he would say. 'I'm going to do myself in.' He never did, basically because he had a good sense of humour and loved joshing with the female staff. A broken heart is one thing, but ending your life is, in my view, a crime against humanity. I never once thought of it. You have been given the greatest gift of all, the emergence into the world as a child, and you should live that life until you die by natural causes. Live life to the full, right to the end, like my good friend Bobby Robson, who beat four bouts of cancer in the final seventeen years of his life before he was bowled out by the fifth.

In 2005 there was another instance of a loving couple who died in a short space of time, Jim and Audrey Callaghan. When I was young, I attended one of Jim's political meetings and he was a powerful and convincing orator. He was born in Portsmouth and was known as 'Sunny Jim' because of his optimism. He was generally regarded as one of the best Labour Prime Ministers. He was in charge of the party between 1976 and 1980, when he resigned after losing the election to Margaret Thatcher. When he returned from a world summit in Guadeloupe, he was interviewed and said, 'I don't think that other people in the world would share the view that there is mounting chaos.' A tabloid newspaper editor stuck a headline on a story – 'Crisis, what crisis?' – and Callaghan was ridiculed and thrown out of office. Margaret Thatcher took over, cleared up the litter, and changed Britain.

Callaghan left office with an untainted reputation but there was one odd peccadillo on his CV: he was the only premier to have tattoos on his arms. According to Lieutenant Commander Lawrence Phillips of Northwood, 'He enlisted in the Royal Navy in 1943 and, in time-honoured fashion, got himself tattooed. He was commissioned the following year and the tattoos remained a lifelong embarrassment. He never wore short-sleeved shirts in public. I wonder what those tattoos depicted?'

The Callaghans were married for sixty-seven years and Audrey Callaghan died from Alzheimer's at their home in East Sussex where Jim looked after her. Jim died eleven days later, a day before his ninety-third birthday. That was a true love story. Was the tattoo about Audrey and his love for her? Or his pending naval career? Most years half a million people die, but hardly any couples die at the same time unless they commit suicide. So one or the other may be heartbroken and face a miserable life. But you don't need to be heartbroken. I decided to keep busy and follow Audrey's example of cramming every minute of the day by doing something worthwhile, which she relished. I once read an interview with Mikhael Gorbachev after his beloved wife Raisa died of cancer in 1999. 'I was so shattered in those first days of grief,' he said. 'I told myself, "I don't want to live." I crumpled.' But he threw himself into several charitable campaigns and now has a meaningful life. But he still pines for his wife. There is no closure for this kind of person. I know.

Any feeling of anger I had was directed at the company in Bristol who kept writing threatening letters to me claiming that I hadn't paid Audrey's medical bills. I explained I had been a member of BUPA for twenty-five years and all her expenses, which were considerable, were covered by the family policy. Around that time, the *Daily Mail* had transferred the policy to another company, which caused the misunderstanding. The debt-collecting company's last letter said they were calling in bailiffs but after taking up the matter with Cromwell Hospital and BUPA, I was assured that there were no outstanding payments to be made. The Bristol company never apologised. These people are sharks!

Gavin helped remove my lingering fears about a possible early demise by fixing me up with a trip to New Zealand early in February when he was working for Sky New Zealand and covering the Test series against Pakistan. I reported some cricket there for the *Mail* and *Telegraph* and it was a stimulating time. On the way out, I had a stopover in California, staying with Thelma and her husband Stan. I was reading a book about Queen Victoria on the flight over and I was startled by the way she handled her misfortunes when her husband Prince Albert died of the age of forty-two in 1861. Their marriage was a true love match and she never remarried. For three years she became a recluse, mainly living in Osborne House on the Isle of Wight. This tiny lady, just under five feet in height and, according to recent reports, wearing bloomers with a fifty-inch waist, almost ruled a third of the world from the Island. Before Marconi came along, there was no direct dial or email, only letters transported in ships. She laid out her husband's night clothing on a bed and had two large portraits of him put up next to her after he died. I have two small pictures of Audrey next to my portable TV set in my bedroom but I didn't lay out her nightdress on the bed. I wasn't going that far! As I was reading the book, I looked up and saw a stewardess approaching who looked just like Audrey. She had a broad smile and I took that as a message – don't copy Queen Victoria, be happy!

One of Audrey's favourite places in the USA was Laguna Beach, near San Diego. Most of the beaches in California, like the one featured in *Baywatch*, are flat and dull, but Laguna Beach, with its imposing cliffs, has style. I revisited it and sat in the sun trying to write the words I wanted on her gravestone. It took some time. How can you sum up someone's life in a few words? Eventually I came up with this: 'She brought beauty, laughter, and love to the world.' With most things I write I go back to it thinking I ought to improve the quality, but those nine words were, in my view, faultless, the best I have ever written. They summed up Audrey

I visit her grave every fortnight or so to clean the marble. The cemetery is next to a field and on the far side there is a stable. Horses often come up to the fence, which is only a few yards from the family grave. Her parents were buried there and when she visited it, she always brought lumps of sugar to give to the horses. There is a bench close by and it is beautifully restful to sit there under the trees listening to the silence and reflecting on my good fortune. Louise did an excellent job designing the gravestone, which features irises from one of Audrey's etchings. Years later, the black marble edifice is now crazily tilting like a oil tanker caught up in a storm. The reason for that is the cemetery is on clay. In the heat of the summer, everything starts moving. Audrey would see the joke. 'Those O'Sullivans!' she would have said.

Gavin met me in Auckland at the start of my trip to New Zealand and told me that someone had been murdered at the back of his sixteen-storey block of flats at the harbour. That was a rarity. New Zealand is still the most orderly, best-conducted country in the world. When I stepped out of the lift and went into his tasty flat, I marvelled at the view. 'What's that liner?' I said, pointing to a very large vessel 200 metres to the left.

'That's the *Aurora*,' he said. 'It's St Valentine's Day today and Mummy's etchings are welcoming you!' A few days later, there was another 'Aud' event. When I woke up, I noticed the picture of her holding a huge bouquet of flowers was missing from a shelf. I opened the door and there it was: at least four yards away, facing up. The window was barely open. It couldn't have blown there.

In one of the ODI matches, played at Christchurch, there was a controversy as Craig McMillan reached a century by scoring twenty-four off the last over bowled by Saqlain Mushtaq. Two of the deliveries were no balls and both went for sixes. Someone suggested that if it had happened on a racecourse there would have been a stewards' inquiry. In another match I had a scoop about Shoaib Akhtar being reported for throwing. Shoaib was the first man past the 100 mph mark, but he has a different personality to Brett Lee, the second fastest bowler. Lee is one of the good guys.

Back home, life was speeding on – cricket games, meetings, dinners, and no time to mope. Late in April I started visiting Bryon Butler in the Mount Inverna Hospital in Guildford. At the age of sixty-one he contracted cancer and beat off three tumours in the next five years. He was my best man and when I spoke at his memorial service at St Bride's Church, I said, 'One of his proudest achievements was that he never lost a hair on his head despite being constantly pumped with chemotherapy. He was the bravest man I ever met. He fought and overcome cancer but the fourth tumour, in the back, got him with a googly which crept up on him unexpectedly.' Bryon loved football, but he loved cricket even more. He was never more happy than when wheeling away with his slow off break bowling in village cricket matches.

On 21 April I was woken by the telephone and I picked up the receiver and said 'Hello Barbara.'

His wife Barbara was on the line and she said, 'How do you know it was me?'

'I've just dreamt that he's died.'

'Good gracious. He died at eight minutes past one.'

An hour later I was walking to my newsagent and I was thinking about what Audrey would she say when he arrived at heaven. He loved her and he called her 'Big Aud'. There was a long line of slow-moving cars going the opposite way and I caught a glimpse of the registration of a car. The letters were 'AUD'. I rang Barbara back and said, 'He's arrived safely!'

I have to say that I don't spend most of my time looking at car registrations, otherwise I would have been killed in a car crash by now. No, I really think I have extrasensory powers, a present from Audrey. The only car plates I spot are connected to Audrey.

In May I attended the annual dinner of the Football Writers' Association, my thirty-eighth, at the Royal Lancaster Hotel. The Footballer of the Year was Teddy Sheringham. Before he received his trophy, the FWA chairman Paul McCarthy started talking about someone who had done so much for the game, and went on to praise this mystery man. I wondered who he was talking about. He hadn't mentioned the name. After several minutes, I realised he was talking about me. I was going to be given the FWA Life Member award, an inscribed paperweight. Suddenly, all round the room, everyone stood up clapping. The attendance, I learned later, was 720. I had to walk between the tables and saw so many faces I knew. The noise welled up, almost to a roar. Paul bent over from his position on the top table and presented the award to me and I felt overwhelmed by emotion. I should have asked him to give me the mike. I hadn't thought about making a speech but now I should have taken the opportunity to dedicate the award to Audrey and all the wives. The wives of sports writers have a tough time. Their husbands are away for most of the year and their careers can last many years. But the moment passed. It was too late. As I walked back to my seat I felt light-headed. It was the nicest thing I've experienced in my career. The Cricket Writers Club gave me a similar award some years earlier, giving me life membership, and I think I am the only person to receive both. Sheringham was cheered when he made his speech and someone on my table said, 'He didn't get a bigger reception than you! In fact, much shorter.'

In October I had more confirmation that Audrey is still in my corner. I was on a Forty Club cricket tour to Malaysia and much of the time it rained. We were about to depart for a game in Penang when the clouds opened and within minutes roads were filled several feet high with rainwater. Back at our huge, spread-out hotel, I was walking to the dining room when I noticed a statue hidden behind some bushes. I went up to it and it was a shrine devoted to a Buddhist named Datur Kong. The inscription said, 'Souls are not necessarily in the netherworld. They are around us.' True – I had been thinking about Audrey.

I went on football trips to Moscow and Milan with Ipswich FC in the autumn (at half-time at the San Siro, the AC Milan staff served ice cream in the directors' room) and ended the year in Barbados with the Coziers and their friends. There were more parties, more laughs, and more connections.

John Bromley held on until February 2002. He was down to five stone at the end. He died in the same hospital, Cromwell. He was a most gregarious and happy man and he was a massive loss to humanity. Another casualty was Brian Moore, who died six months earlier. He was a similar type of person – upbeat and enthusiastic and he never said a nasty word about anyone. He was one of the finest football commentators in English football and I remember him telling me when he retired that he would live to ninety 'because I've been on a strict diet for years'. Sadly he died at home at the age of sixty-nine after returning from a minor operation in hospital.

In March I went on my third cricketing tour of South Africa. I told Ron Hart, the organiser, 'I'm only here for the tea at the Mount Nelson Hotel.' There is no hotel in the world that can equal their tea!

One of the highlights was a visit to Robben Island off Cape Town where Nelson Mandela was imprisoned for twenty-seven years. The wind speed on the catamaran was 50 mph and it was a very bumpy ride. One of the guides, who claimed he had been imprisoned there as well, took an anti-British stance while taking us round and I said to him, 'Have you heard of Harold Macmillan, the former British Prime Minister?'

'No,' he said.

'Well, Macmillan started things going with his 'wind of change in Africa' speech in 1960. Before he retired, his Government granted independence to Malawi, Nigeria, and Ghana.'

'Oh,' he said, but I knew he wasn't interested. Most South Africans never leave Africa and the same applies to the citizens of the USA. If they did, they would be better, more rounded people.

What do you do when you are put next to a twenty-five stone man in an aircraft? It happened to me on my fourth tour to South Africa on 6 February 2005. When I approached my seat this man had pulled up the arm rest on his left and occupied almost half of my eighteen-inch wide seat. The 'pitch' forward to the seat in front measured twenty-eight inches, which meant that this aircraft would be bottom of the league in terms of comfort. I got up and went to see the nearest steward and explained my predicament. He said, 'We can't do anything about it. The plane is full and you will have to return to your seat.' I knew he wasn't telling the truth because one of our party had a seat in business class and there were odd seats free. The flight was about to depart and I had to go back and squeeze my thirteen stones and my artificial right hip hard against this gargantuan-sized man, who I later learned was an Afrikaaner. Almost half of my body was sticking out into the aisle and when refreshments were served, my friend on the right couldn't lower his table because his chest was pressing hard against the back of the seat in front. So he held the tray by his left arm at eye level as he ate. I looked at the stewardess with an exasperated look but she failed to respond.

'There must be a spare seat available?' I asked her.

'Speak to the chief steward,' she said.

'I have,' I said. 'I've already spoken to him and he was rather unhelpful.'

I had just read a book about William Wilberforce, the man who ended slavery in Britain and it caused me to imagine how slaves were packed into ships and transported to the Caribbean islands. During the night, when my hip was aching and my other arthritic leg was being kicked and trod on, I got up and sat at a jump seat at the rear. These seats are reserved for staff and another steward approached and told me to return to my seat immediately. Again, I went through the story but he said, 'If you remain here, you will be reported for breaking air regulations and could face prosecution.'

'Be reasonable,' I said. 'The other staff who are off duty have retired upstairs. No one needs this seat.' He went off.

Later another man arrived and told me, 'You can stay for a few minutes but if you ignore our warning, you will face charges.'

I remained where I was. When I left the plane, I told the chief steward I would report the matter in London and he said, 'And we will be filing our report as well!'

My bad experience certainly didn't ruin the trip and I soon had two wonderful 'Aud' coincidences. I bought a ticket for the Audrey Tatou film *A Very Long Engagement* and the girl who handed it to me had 'Audrey' written on her blouse. Then I bumped into Tom and Meg Clarke. Tom was the finest sports editor I have worked for and he had great affection for Audrey. Every time she was in hospital, he would write an encouraging letter and send flowers when she returned home.

Before the flight back from Johannesburg, I asked one of the ground staff for a seat with leg room and nominated a seat. Yes, I had studied the chart and knew what I was doing. But she said that seat was 'inoperable'. I asked why.

'It's inoperable,' she said.

I was given another, but when I boarded the plane I found I was in a bulkhead seat. They reserve those rows for young mothers with babies! There was a minimum amount of space in front and when I sat down, I had to spread my stiff right leg in front of the Danish woman on my right. 'This is not right,' she said. 'You should be given a proper seat for someone who is disabled.'

I called up a steward and explained the problem. 'I am sorry you must stay in this seat, there are no others free,' she said.

It seemed like a plot of SAA's. Despite my protestations, they failed to find a solution and I spent another thirteen hours in acute discomfort. Just before the pilot took off, he finished his introductory remarks by saying , 'If you have a problem, let me know.' So I wrote a note to him headed 'SOS'.

I wrote, 'I am trapped here and would appreciate your help in moving me to a seat where I can sit which can accommodate a stiff leg.' Two hours later, not having heard from him, I asked Sanjav, the steward, and he said, 'He doesn't want to respond.'

I must have been public enemy number one on that flight! Walking round the plane, I discovered the 'inoperable' seat I had requested was now filled by an able-bodied member of the SAA staff.

There is no law about obese people filling other peoples' seats in the UK, but there is in the USA. Over a certain weight, the person has to buy two tickets. I wrote to SAA head office in London and said I wanted to be upgraded in a future trip to South Africa and they wrote the usual fobbing-off letter. I wrote several letters without any response, so I enlisted the help of a good lawyer and friend David Roodyn, a Fulham fan, and he helped put pressure on them. A woman from Skitty, Wales, once won £13,000 damages from Virgin after a similar experience sitting next to a oversized person, but I didn't want that, only upgrades. SAA's lawyers were called in and kept rejecting me – running up big bills – but after two years of heated correspondence on my side, SAA climbed down and offered me two upgrades. You need extreme persistence to win a case against major airlines and my advice is to stick at them, don't give up.

A very peculiar thing happened after I had returned. I was half awake when I heard a whooshing noise from the bathroom next to my bedroom. I turned the light on and went to look and saw Audrey's red dressing gown crumpled on the floor. After she died, I left her three dressing rooms hanging from the door between the two rooms. I have two dressing gowns, a heavy one for the winter and a light one for the summer. Both were placed on top of hers and they were untouched. Her other two dressing gowns were there under mine. How did the red one fall while the others, on top and below hers, were still there? I thought about it. Red... was it a signal to stop? Over the years, several members of her family had been in dispute over the distribution of the money made from her parents' old house in Bradford on Avon and it still lingered on after Audrey died. Perhaps she was telling me to tell the others to end the saga. So I wrote letters to all of them appealing for common sense and an end to this aggravating problem. Two days later, there was another rustling noise at 4 a.m. and her black silk dressing gown started sliding down the door to the ground, followed by her red and white one, and, finally, the red one. My two dressing gowns stayed where they were. I rushed over and took a picture of the ones on the floor and I still have a copy of it. She might have approved of my action because I heard no more about the family dispute. It was over. But perhaps it was merely her saying, 'Throw them all away!'

On 19 March – after Audrey died I invariably recorded any connections in my diary – I went to cover the Norwich *v.* Gillingham game and arrived early enough to call in at the cathedral, which in my view is the airiest and most pleasant of all the thirty-nine cathedrals in England. As I went through a side door, I heard the sound of a choral service and a roughly dressed, middle-aged man approached me and asked for money. I shook my head and he said, '**** off.'

I was shocked. You don't expect behaviour like that in a cathedral. I moved past him and sat in one of the pews. Suddenly I felt as though I'd just had a shower and a feeling of calmness spread downward through my body. It was soothing and looking around the building, I thought about our two visits to the Taj Mahal in Agra, which had a tremendous effect on both of us. The Taj Mahal was built in the sixteenth century in memory of Mumtaz Mahal, the wife of Emperor Shah Jahan, who died at a young age after having eleven children. The author Rupinder Khullar wrote, 'Distraught with grief, the Emperor sought consolation in expressing his love and admiration for his wife in a monument the world would never forget. It took twenty-two years and the labour of 20,000 skilled workmen.' I would have loved to do something similar, but Lord Rothermere failed to pay me the riches I needed. Instead, the Royal Parks department allowed me to sponsor a sweet chestnut tree in front of the gates of

Kensington Palace, where the Princess of Wales lived and close to the Royal College of Art where Audrey worked as a mature student in her later years. My tree, planted in 2002 in a row of six, had a troubled history. The trees were prospering with the exception of mine and in 2007 it began to fail in the drought of that summer. It has been replaced. When I arrived back from Norwich in the early hours, I listened to a message left by Louise. She said she'd had a wonderful dream about Audrey, who had told us she was in good spirits and had asked us not to grieve like the emperor who built the Taj Mahal. Those were her words. Enjoy your lives, she said.

I think Audrey was looking after me because two weeks later I was skipping down the fourteen stairs to the hall of my house when I lost my footing and fell through the air. When you face a possibly damaging accident, your senses slow down. Anyone who has been in a car accident will know that feeling. Now I was thinking I might have dislocated my artificial hip, but I prayed quickly to St Audrey and as my backside hit the ground, my right leg crashed into a chest of drawers. There was no feeling of pain and I staggered to my feet. I was fine!

I experienced a similar scare on 24 August 2007. I was about to catch a train to meet someone at the Oval when I tripped as I raced down the concrete steps at Bromley South Station. A woman's dress was touching the steps in front of me and I tried to avoid it, fearing that if I trod on it, her dress might be stripped off. As I took off, I bounced off a step halfway down the twelve remaining steps, like the bombs in *The Dam Busters*, and landed on my left shoulder on the platform. Several young ladies rushed up to help me but I got up and said I wasn't hurt. 'You could have finished up in hospital,' said one. I was wearing an old Jaeger jacket with thick shoulder pads, purchased by Audrey, which may have helped.

I knew it was my day because I went to Waterstone's in Piccadilly later and signed some copies of my Brian Lara book. On the same table there was a book about 'guardian angels'. Actually I have two – the one above, Audrey, and my niece Brenda, who lives in Newport on the Isle of Wight. After she and I attended the funeral of my *Isle of Wight Chronicle* friend Lew Grant, we were unable to locate the street where the hotel was staging the reception. We were totally lost and the people we asked were overseas students and couldn't help. Suddenly a car with 'AUD' came around the road and Brenda, who might have been sceptical about my claims, said, 'Well, that's the proof. Let's try this way.' So we did and we got there on time. Following the incident at Waterstone's, I went back to Bromley and visited their store to sign some more copies. I asked the young man behind the counter where he lived. He named the block of flats opposite my house.

With all these 'messages' and connections I was beginning to think I should write a feature about it. Late in October I went on another Forty Club tour to Alfaz, near Benidorm, and most of the time the ground was underwater. On 22 October, I joined the party on an excursion to the Benidorm Palace, which staged nightly shows. Audrey didn't like Bernidorm and the only time we went there – we were taking our own car – she said, 'This is so awful, let's drive on.' And we did. I wasn't overexcited by attending the performance and when we arrived, ten minutes late, the lights had been dimmed. We were shown to our seats, in bays of six of both sexes, and I realised I was the only person next to an empty seat. I remembered what Audrey had said and as I said it a spotlight focused on the fire curtain carrying just one word: 'Dolly'. Audrey's nickname, used only by us, was 'Dollies', short for 'Dolly-Wallies'. The music started up and it was Stevie Wonder's 'I Just Called to Say I Love You'. It shook me, but I was soon smiling as I told the ladies about it. They thought it was very significant, but the men started talking about cricket.

Christmas was coming up and I realised I should go ahead on this article for the *Mail*. I contacted Charlotte Kemp of the features department and she was keen. I sent in my 2,000 words and the features editor liked it, too. The festivities came and went but on 4 January, Sarah Newton rang to say it would be in the paper the next day. When I came down to collect the newspapers the next morning I looked at the oriental lilies in a vase on the hall, next to a picture of Audrey and me in our poshest attire, and saw that all four stems had collapsed, like cranes at a dock when a ship is launched and everyone is celebrating. She liked it, I thought. I opened the *Mail* and was overjoyed. 1,473 words and a photograph taken at our wedding filled a whole page. It was beautiful picture and a happy story. A lot of people congratulated me and some said I had been courageous to write it. John Barnwell, the former Arsenal, Nottingham Forest, and Sheffield United footballer and the chief executive of the League Managers' Association before he contacted cancer and retired, said, 'When I read it, I felt I was proud to know someone who was brave enough to write it.' Others suspected that I was another David Icke, the Coventry City and Hereford goalkeeper who became a sportscaster and then an evangelist on the Isle of Wight.

Scores of people, mostly women, wrote in to 'Femail' and some managed to reach me at my address. One letter stood out. It was written by a lady named Gill who lives three miles away in Chislehurst. Her husband died at the age of fifty-seven in 1997 of cancer and she wrote, 'Please don't feel you have to answer this, but in your darkest moments you can always call me, or meet for a chat, I'll understand. I've been there.' I rang immediately and told her I was off to Sri Lanka to play cricket and report the Sri Lanka *v.* Australia series, but promised that I would ring her on my return. One of the Sri Lanka hotels, the Culture Club, was some distance from the Dambulla Test ground and when I was not reporting on the match I spent time relaxing, reading, and talking, mainly to John Dyson, the Australian who was coaching the Sri Lankan cricketers. The Culture Club's desserts were up to the same standard as the ones at the Mount Nelson Hotel, and the man in charge kept chatting me up every night. One night he said to me, 'Excuse me sir, I wonder if I could come to your room tonight?' I had to say I had an engagement and for the rest of the stay I avoided him. I had to miss out on the desserts in the final days. What a catastrophe!

On St Valentine's Day a couple of the team players and I went for a walk around the lake and there were two trees where you could climb up to a reasonable height to look at the birds. I was the first to reach the top and I turned to see that someone had carved a large 'A' in a heart, similar in style to the one I wrote on Audrey's 1995 card. That was uplifting.

During the flight home, I noticed that the aircraft appeared to be going back to where it had come from: the mountains that had initially appeared on the left now appeared on the right. The pilot announced that there was an emergency and we were going to land in Dubai. I looked at the indicator above. We were flying close to Baghdad. Later we learned that a man had suffered a heart attack and needed treatment. Crisis over! But the day after I returned, a taxi driver was stabbed four houses from my property in a disagreement over drugs. In 2008 nine people were charged with various offences after a knife and machete fight 450 metres from my house, in the Bird in the Hand pub. You're not safe anywhere these days!

I rang Gill and said I would be coming to see her for tea. I parked my car in one of the nicest areas of Chislehurst and knocked at the door of her pretty cottage. She opened the door and laughed. 'I was expecting a bowed, old man,' she said.

'I was expecting an old woman in her dotage,' I replied and laughed, too.

She took out her best china cups and it was one of the nicest cups of tea I've had, even better than the ones I had in Sri Lanka, one of the world's largest producers of tea, where the women who pick the leaves earn around £1 a day. Gill told me she had five sisters and three of them were artists. I said, 'Audrey had seven and she was an artist.'

I told her Audrey's date of birth and she said she was born six days earlier in the same year. But the most amazing aspect of our budding friendship was that she lived 300 metres from Audrey's grave. I said to her, 'I think Audrey has arranged this. If I hadn't written that article you wouldn't have known about me.' She agreed.

She is a vivacious and very attractive blonde who gets on with everyone and we have been on some marvellous holidays and trips together. We have brought great happiness into our lives. We always talk about our spouses because we still love them. But we now have a new love as well. We think this period of our lives, the last lap, is the best, and I can't thank her enough for writing that beautiful handwritten letter. I said to her once, 'When you lose a loved one who has lost a third of his or her life, God offers you something back.' I think that is true and we are benefitting from it.

Life is good. In recent years we have celebrated Christmas with our great friend Barbara Hillier and her children Alastair, Melanie, and Patrick in Dulwich, and we always toast Audrey. We play all sorts of games and in 2009 it was about writing words and putting the paper into a pot with the contestants having to describe them by mime while others guess the words. One of Barbara's was 'Roman Holiday'. The night before, I had watched Audrey Hepburn and Gregory Peck in the 1953 black and white film *Roman Holiday* – a wonderful comedy that shows just how charismatic Audrey Hepburn was; it still captivates millions of people around the world. She played a royal princess, just like Lady Diana Spencer, and Peck was an American journalist. I think my Audrey played some part in this affair!

In her final years, Audrey often wore a bright red, chequered woollen scarf, and after she died, I wore it too. Early in January 2009 I was wearing the scarf when I travelled to Manchester's Malmaison Hotel to meet officials from Lancashire CCC in my role as chairman of the facilities committee of the Cricket Writers' Club. Their architects were planning a major redevelopment of Old Trafford. I had bought two single advance tickets at a much reduced cost, but as I was about to board the train at Euston a ticket collector said, 'You ticket is dated 24 January, not today. You can't use it.' He advised me to go to the ticket office and pay an excess of £28. I had to do it, almost missing the train, and faced the same prospect on the return journey, having to pay another £28, which wouldn't please the treasurer of the CWC. After our successful meeting, I walked to the nearby Piccadilly Station and explained my problem to a very friendly, middle-aged lady clerk – who looked very much like Gill.

'Oh, what lovely scarf!' she said.

'My late wife always wore it,' I said.

She smiled and wrote on the ticket, 'Dated in error, no extra charge.'

Audrey's influence still reigns over my life and I hope that will continue forever. Sometime, we will be united again. Does that really happen? No one knows for sure, but if you passionately believe in something, it will happen.

On the eve of the final Test, which England won to regain the Ashes in 2009, I had half a dozen incredible 'messages' that strengthened my belief that she is waiting for me. One was part of an advertisement on a hoarding that I saw while driving past the Horniman Museum in Dulwich on the way to the Oval. It read, 'Audi – two services free.' I laughed. They were trying to plug their Audi cars. Several hundred yards ahead, a tune came on the radio, 'When Will I See You Again?' I thought to myself, 'Not too soon because I've got such a lot to finish... but I'll definitely be there, don't worry!'